Flagging Standards

D1590374

Flagging Standards

Globalization and Environmental, Safety, and Labor Regulations at Sea

Elizabeth R. DeSombre

The MIT Press
Cambridge, Massachusetts
London, England

© 2006 Massachusetts Institute of Technology

All rights reserved. No part of this book may be reproduced in any form by any electronic or mechanical means (including photocopying, recording, or information storage and retrieval) without permission in writing from the publisher.

MIT Press books may be purchased at special quantity discounts for business or sales promotional use. For information, please e-mail special_sales@mitpress.mit.edu or write to Special Sales Department, The MIT Press, 55 Hayward Street, Cambridge, MA 02142-1315.

This book was set in Sabon on 3B2 by Asco Typesetters, Hong Kong.
Printed and bound in the United States of America on recycled paper.

Library of Congress Cataloging-in-Publication Data

DeSombre, Elizabeth R.
Flagging standards : globalization and environmental, safety and labor regulations at sea / Elizabeth R. DeSombre.
p. cm.
Includes bibliographical references and index.
Contents: Introduction: international standards at sea—Globalization, competition and convergence: racing to the middle?—Exclusion as incentive: the power of clubs—Ships and states: the evolution of flags of convenience—Port-state control—The International Transport Workers Federation and labor standards—Regional fishery management organizations and trade restrictions—Industry self-governance—Ships, states, and sovereignty.
ISBN-10: 0-262-04234-7 ISBN-13: 978-0-262-04234-5 (alk. paper)
ISBN-10: 0-262-54190-4 ISBN-13: 978-0-262-54190-9 (pbk : alk. paper)
1. Shipping—Government policy. 2. Shipping—Standards. 3. Globalization.
4. Competition. I. Title.

HE581.D47 2006
343.09′65—dc22 2006044862

10 9 8 7 6 5 4 3 2 1

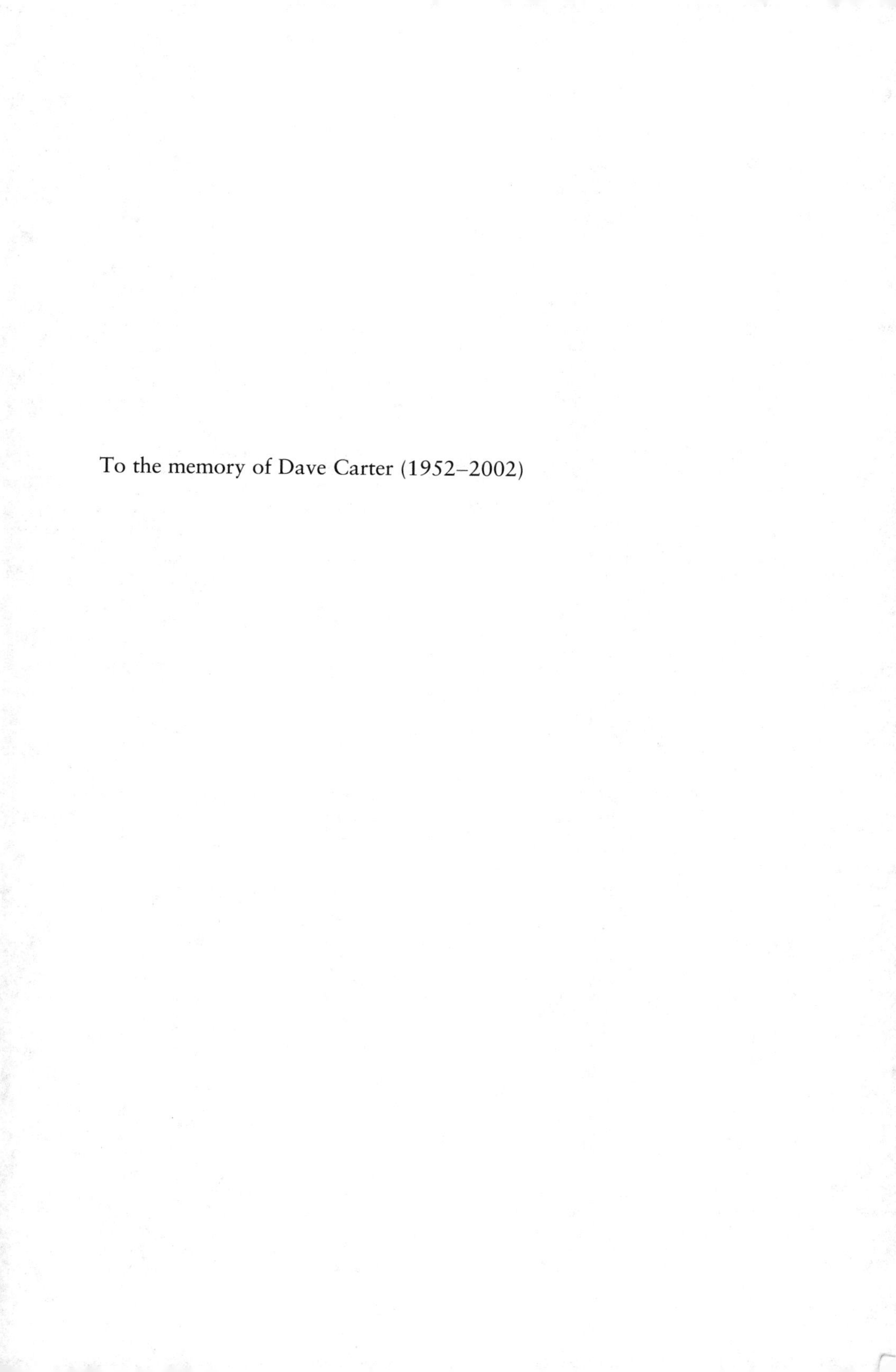

To the memory of Dave Carter (1952–2002)

Contents

Acknowledgments ix

1 Introduction: International Standards at Sea 1

2 Globalization, Competition, and Convergence: Racing to the Middle? 11

3 Exclusion as Incentive: The Power of Clubs 55

4 Ships and States: The Evolution of Flags of Convenience 69

5 Port State Control 87

6 The International Transport Workers Federation and Labor Standards 135

7 Regional Fisheries Management Organizations and Trade Restrictions 151

8 Industry Self-Governance 181

9 Ships, States, and Sovereignty 199

Appendixes 231

References 275

Index 299

Acknowledgments

One of my favorite things about my career is that my teaching and research constantly inform each other. This project began, in part, when a set of students in the introductory environmental studies course at Colby College, where I used to teach, were undertaking a project to examine the aftereffects of an oil spill in Portland Harbor. They were puzzled, though: "What was a Liberian oil tanker doing in Maine?" As I explained the open registry system to them, I began to consider all the times the issue of flags of convenience had come up in other research projects I'd done: the transfer of U.S. fishing vessels to foreign flags after the United States passed dolphin-protection legislation in the 1980s (an element in my first MIT Press book); the difficulties faced by various regional fisheries management organizations—pretty much all the ones I'd looked at—in dealing with the ships of nonmember states (most of which fly flags of convenience) fishing in their regulatory areas; the efforts to regulate whaling historically. In turn, the research I was doing for this project began to show up in my teaching on international environmental law and environmental policy. I have been fortunate to teach at two fantastic liberal arts colleges in my career thus far, Colby and Wellesley, that allow this interaction between teaching and research.

I am grateful to both Colby and Wellesley for the variety of support they gave to this project and to my professional development more broadly. Both institutions provide superb scholarly support. This support includes fantastic reference librarians; thanks in particular to Toni Katz at Colby and to Betty Febo at Wellesley. I benefited from research assistance from some of the best students one could have the privilege of teaching: Kate Litle, Katie Wasik, and Carolyn Szum at Colby and Jessica Bernfeld, Anne LaRue, and Catrina Huynh at Wellesley. Jess's contributions are especially important. During the course of this project she moved from student to colleague, undertaking a senior thesis on second registries and eventually a master's degree at the Seafarers International Research Centre in Cardiff. Both Colby and Wellesley also provided financial resources for research travel for this project. In addition, I appreciate the dedication of Camilla Chandler Frost (Wellesley College class of 1947) to issues of the environment, and am grateful to her for the donation to Wellesley that created the chair I now hold there and its associated research funding. At Wellesley I also want to thank the wonderful people at Information Services (and Flick Coleman, in Chemistry) for helping to solve many graphing crises. Thanks are due as well to the University of Florida Department of Political Science, which gave me office space and a great collegial atmosphere during two different periods in residence there.

Earlier versions of work from this broader project have appeared elsewhere. Much of the empirical discussion in chapter 7 can be found in "Fishing under Flags of Convenience: Using Market Power to Increase Participation in International Regulation," *Global Environmental Politics* 5(4). Some early analysis of port state control can be found in "Globalization and Environmental Protection on the High Seas," in Peter Dauvergne, ed., *International Handbook of Environmental Politics* (Cheltenham: Edward Elgar, 2005).

The research in this book would not have been possible without access to information in the often-secretive world of international shipping and ocean regulation. I appreciate assistance with this access from those in the International Labour Organisation, the International Maritime Organization, the International Transport Workers Federation, the Seafarers International Research Centre, Lloyd's Register, and A. Bilbrough and Co.

The small cadre of young scholars in all parts of the globe currently working on issues relating to open registry ships and the efforts to hold these ships to high standards have been truly generous in sharing their work and responding to mine. These include Nathan Lillie, Paul Bennett, Lisa Fallon, and Nik Winchester. Most of these scholars have their own books forthcoming on some of the issues addressed here, which should be read by anyone interested in issues of global maritime regulation.

Enormous thanks for comments on the entire manuscript are due to Ken Conca, Peter Haas, and three anonymous reviewers for MIT Press in what has been the most useful peer-review process I have ever experienced. (Thanks to Clay Morgan as well, acquisitions editor extraordinaire at MIT Press, and to Kate Blakinger, acquisitions assistant.) Additional valuable feedback on aspects of the project has come from Daniel Drezner and the participants in the Program on International Politics, Economics, and Security speaker series at the University of Chicago, Aida Hozic, and Craig Murphy. Feedback and support on all of my academic endeavors have come from Audie Klotz, Ron Mitchell, Wil Burns, and Mia Bloom. Sammy Barkin, who may have read drafts of this manuscript even more often than I have, deserves the greatest gratitude possible for theoretical, empirical, and grammatical assistance as well as moral support throughout the project. Lynda Warwick and Jen Stiles (and Molly), as well as Sophie, are responsible for providing perspective, encouragement, distraction and, sometimes, really yummy cake.

Those who know me know that my academic work is a major focus of my life. Fewer know that another is folk music, which was the original source of my interest in politics three decades ago. Singing, playing, and listening to music is what makes everything else meaningful for me. The musician who most inspires me is Tracy Grammer. This book is dedicated to the memory of my favorite songwriter, Dave Carter, who left too soon and is greatly missed.

1

Introduction: International Standards at Sea

On November 11, 2002, the oil tanker *Prestige*, flying the flag of the Bahamas, under the command of a Greek captain with a crew of Filipinos and Romanians, chartered by a Liberian-registered company based in Switzerland, and probably owned by Russian nationals, ran into a storm as it carried its load of 77,000 tons of heavy fuel oil from Latvia to Singapore. Two days later the captain sent out a distress call, indicating that the hull had been breached and the ship was leaking oil, and asking to be towed into a Spanish port to offload its oil and avoid catastrophic environmental damage. Spanish authorities, fearing damage to local waters, refused (as did those from Portugal), and when the ship drifted shoreward anyway, towed it out to sea where it eventually broke in two and sank in 2 miles of water 150 miles off the coast of Spain, discharging much of its oil into the water.[1] It caused precisely the catastrophic environmental damage the captain had hoped to avoid.

The tanker was operating legally, but only just. At twenty-six years old, it was older than most currently operating oil tankers.[2] It had only a single hull, making an oil spill more likely if an accident occurred. But international laws requiring double hulled tankers initially applied only to newly built tankers,[3] and the provisions of a 2001 amendment to the

1. "The Politics of an Oil Spill," *The Economist*, November 21, 2002, 46–47; David Ljunggren, "Ban Ships with Flags of Convenience—Canada," *Reuters News Service*, November 21, 2002; Melissa Rossi and Christian Caryl, "Just Missing the Boat," *Newsweek*, December 2, 2002, 7.

2. Miguel Vida, "Stricken Tanker Towed Away from Spanish Coast," *Reuters News Service*, November 18, 2002; Lloyd's Register Fairplay, *World Fleet Statistics 2002* (London: Lloyd's Register, 2002), 13.

3. 1992 Amendments to the International Convention for the Prevention of Pollution from ships (1973/1978).

International Convention for the Prevention of Pollution from Ships requiring double hulls on all tankers were not due to take effect until 2015.[4] In fact, under the earlier law, a tanker that did not otherwise meet the new regulations would have to be retired before age thirty, which would have taken the *Prestige* out of commission in a mere three years.[5] European Union law, passed in the wake of a similar oil spill three years prior, added provisions for banning ships from EU ports if they had been repeatedly detained for environmental or safety violations or if they flew the flag of a state whose vessels are known to be at high risk for causing environmental damage.[6] But though it might have, this particular vessel did not appear on that list. For a variety of reasons—including the age and condition of the vessel and the international nature of the crew—the ship could not have been legally registered in the United States or most European states. Its owners would not have wanted to register it there anyway; the environmental, safety, and labor laws they would have had to follow would have been too strict, and the fees and taxes too high.

The *Prestige* serves as an excellent example of the globalized state of maritime shipping and the consequences thereof. In addition to its polyglot crew and tangled web of ownership and registration, it was classified by a U.S. classification society, the American Bureau of Shipping, which certified that the ship had at least the minimally required equipment. Its protection and indemnity insurance was provided by British-based London Steamship Owners Mutual Insurance. It had been inspected, though not since 1999, under the European port-state inspection system, which required that 25 percent of all ships that enter Euro-

4. 2001 Amendments to the International Convention for the Prevention of Pollution from Ships (1973/1978).

5. 1992 Amendments to the International Convention for the Prevention of Pollution from ships (1973/1978). EU Law in 2001 had also adopted the 2015 deadline for ships, whether flagged in MARPOL signatory states or not, to have double hulls in order to traverse European waters, and with the earlier U.S. Oil Pollution Act (1990) the U.S. banned the use of single-hulled tankers but included a variety of grandfathering provisions until 2015. U.S. Congress, 101st Session, "Oil Pollution Act of 1990," 101 P.L. 380; 104 Stat. 484, Title IV, Subtitle A, Section 4115.

6. European Parliament and European Council, Directive 95/21/EC, December 19, 2001.

pean ports be inspected for safety and environmental problems. It had been registered in five different states since it was built.

And its journey was international as well. As such it is representative of much of the way global commerce is conducted. Ninety-five percent of goods traded internationally as measured by weight, and two-thirds as measured by value, are transported on the oceans by ships.[7] Most of these ships fly flags of convenience. An estimated 64 percent of the world's merchant-fleet tonnage is registered in flag-of-convenience states, including 68.7 percent of bulk carrier and 64.3 percent of container-ship tonnage.[8] States compete for ship registrations by intentionally keeping taxes and fees low and by having lax, or poorly enforced, environmental, safety, and labor standards; shipowners respond by flying these convenient flags in an effort to compete internationally through lower operating costs.

This ability to choose a level of international regulation by choosing where to register a ship introduces considerable difficulties for those trying to protect the marine environment and ensure the well-being of those who work or travel on ships. It also engages important theoretical questions about the role of international regulation in a globalized economy, the role of the state and the impact on sovereignty under these conditions, and the extent to which international competition increases the incentive for keeping regulatory standards low. What does the extent and pattern of foreign flag registry (and degree of regulation adopted by individual ships) tell us about when we should expect regulatory races to the bottom or upward harmonization? What does the process of responding to lowered standards on ocean vessels suggest about the role of the state—or of nonstate actors—in responding to the regulatory problems created by a system that allows states, or individual businesses, to opt out of global regulatory structures? The *Prestige*, whether simply the unlucky victim of a bad storm or a ship ill-equipped to avoid environmental disaster, is representative of the collision between globalization and international regulatory standards. Examining efforts to respond to this collision may help it have a more buoyant future than did this particular ship.

7. Philip E. Steinberg, *The Social Construction of the Ocean* (Cambridge: Cambridge University Press, 2001), 14.

8. Institute of Shipping Economics and Logistics, *ISL Shipping Statistics Yearbook 2004* (Bremen: ISL, 2004), v.

Flagging Standards?

This book examines the relationship between globalization and environmental, safety, and labor standards in the context of the shipping industry. There are nearly as many definitions of globalization as there are scholars who write about it, but the most important aspect of globalization for the purposes of this study is the reduction of barriers (be they political or technical) to international economic activity. Goods move long distances, are assembled in one location from parts made in other locations, and may be used somewhere else altogether. Freer international trade, the reduced relative cost of transportation, and increasing economic integration make possible this global movement of goods, much of which happens on the oceans on ships.

The shipping industry is among the most globalized of industries. By its very nature international shipping necessarily involves crossing between jurisdictions and traveling long distances in nonterritorial spaces. Shipowners can choose where to register their vessels and thereby choose the international and domestic regulations within which they operate. The labor market for ship workers is as global as any; shipowners can hire workers from anywhere in the world and there is often little connection between the nationality of a shipowner, the country of origin of those who work on the ship, and where the ship travels.

The underlying mechanism for the potential lowering of standards in the shipping industry is the system of open registration, a phenomenon that began in the first half of the twentieth century but gained popularity after World War II and increased in importance beginning in the 1960s. Open registries, also known as flags of convenience (FOCs), are generally characterized as ship registries that do not require citizenship of shipowners or operators, levy no or minimal taxes, allow ships to be worked by nonnationals, and have neither the will nor the capability to impose domestic or international regulations on registered ships.[9] Because these registries do not have nationality requirements for shipowners, they have created a globalized system in which shipowners have the ability to

9. Frank L. Wiswall, Jr., "Flags of Convenience," in William A. Lovett, ed., *United States Shipping Policies and the World Market* (Westport: Quorum Books, 1996), 116; Jim Morris, "Lost at Sea: 'Flags of Convenience' Give Owners a Paper Refuge," *Houston Chronicle*, August 22, 1996, 15.

choose where to register their vessels based on cost and convenience. The possibility of a race to the regulatory bottom, or the existence of regulatory havens, is realistic in a circumstance such as this when individual economic actors are not required (legally or practically) to undertake their activity in their home states. When they have the ability to choose where to operate, the locations in which they might operate (and that can thus earn revenue from their operations) may choose to compete to attract them. This process sets the stage for competition in regulatory laxity.

This system does allow low-quality ships to choose a ship registry in order to avoid internationally accepted regulation, and does allow for a collective level of regulation on ships lower than would be required in the home states of most shipowners. But it is balanced by a set of processes put into place by self-interested actors (including states and nonstate entities) that attempt to hold ships and states to higher standards. This ongoing opposition underlies the efforts of economic actors to traverse the tensions inherent in globalization. The processes that succeed or fail in lowering costs or raising standards in this issue are instructive for addressing these conflicts in other areas of the globalized economy.

Book Overview

The book as a whole seeks to evaluate and explain decisions by states and shipowners about what environmental, safety, and labor standards to adopt as they attempt to balance the economic advantages of low standards and the increasing international political advantages of raising those standards. It examines the strategies used by those who seek to raise standards on ships in the context of determining the broader implications of these decisions for efforts responding to potential downward pressure on international regulation under conditions of globalization.

Chapter 2 examines the relationship between globalization and standards generally in order to frame the broader debate into which the experience of shipping fits. It concludes that rather than leading to either upward harmonization or a regulatory race to the bottom, globalization of ship registration has lead to what might be termed a "race to the middle." Truly open registries start with low standards that then are pushed upward through pressure from a variety of sources. At the same time, the creation by traditional maritime states of international or second registries lowers to some extent the standards on ships that register in these locations, leading to a set of middle-range standards in most major ship registries. In addition to adopting moderate levels of international regulation, open registries specialize in the types of standards they adopt, creating regulatory niches that shipowners make use of when deciding where to register their vessels.

The incentive structure provided by international economic competition underlies the development of successful strategies to raise the standards upheld by open registry states and the ships that fly their flags. Chapter 3 examines the challenges faced in international cooperation and the advantages of free riding made possible in an era of global competition and cooperation. The difficulties facing collective action come from the inability to exclude those who do not participate in cooperation from the benefits of that cooperation, giving them little incentive to cooperate in its provision. Additionally, many international problems, especially pertaining to the environment, are rival (also referred to as subtractable), meaning that those who continue to access a resource outside of a cooperative agreement can diminish the ability of the cooperating group to protect it. One important way around these problems is to attempt to change the issue structure: to create cooperation on issues that are both nonrival and excludable. While the nature of a problem itself may not be amenable to change, it may be possible to set up the cooperative process by which it is addressed so that those who do not cooperate are excluded from the benefits of cooperation. This process involves cooperation as a club good, and has led to great success in the area of shipping standards. If those who adopt low standards as a strategy of competition under globalization are excluded from the benefits of globalization itself, they lose the incentive to avoid at least some international regulation.

Chapter 4 begins the empirical consideration of shipping registration and standards, by laying out the history of the globalized shipping industry and the growth of flags of convenience. The rest of the book examines the specific strategies followed by states, nongovernmental actors, and international organizations that have brought about the level of environmental, safety, and labor standards eventually adopted by flag states or by individual vessels. First is the attempt to improve the physical condition of ships as they enter port, and to require improvement in substandard ships before they are allowed to leave. Second, once in port, ships face the possibility that dockworkers or others will refuse to unload or service them if labor standards are not sufficiently protected on board. Finally, goods from ships, once unloaded, may not be allowed to enter the market of states to which they have been shipped, if the shipowners cannot demonstrate that they have been obtained within the required regulatory standards. In addition, once all these strategies of exclusion are in place, industry organizations create their own collective processes in efforts to help members better compete within these port, ship-worker, and market strategies designed to exclude substandard ships.

Chapter 5 examines this first stage: the state-based port state control, a system of international agreements under which states agree to inspect a certain percentage of ships that enter their ports and detain those in egregiously poor condition until they are no longer a threat to safety or environment at sea. This system induces flag states to increase their standards, and ships to flag in states that meet a certain level of quality, by focusing inspections on ships from those flags that have had the greatest percentage of detentions in previous years. Shipowners do not want their ships to be singled out for inspection, and flag states, eager to attract ship registrations, seek to reassure potential registrants that they will not be negatively impacted by the reputation of the flag state. As a result, a number of ship registries have persuaded the states in which they operate to ratify international agreements and to create their own inspection systems and rules to increase the standards to which ships are held.

Chapter 6 examines the second stage: the work of the International Transport Workers Federation (ITF), an international labor union that attempts to prevent ships from registering in open registries by conducting labor actions against flag-of-convenience vessels. The ITF offers individual flag-of-convenience registered ships the opportunity to agree to a set of international labor standards and thereby gain ITF certification; if these vessels refuse, the organizers can call for a dockworker boycott of the ship in a given port. A large percentage of open registry ships have negotiated these agreements with the union in order to avoid such a labor action, and some businesses that hire ships to transport goods have begun to use only ships that have ITF agreements. Labor standards on ships worldwide have increased as a result of these efforts.

The final stage is even more intrusive: it involves efforts to prevent the goods on the ships themselves from finding a market inside the state to which they have been brought. International fisheries are one resource that suffers when open registry states choose to remain apart from regional fisheries management agreements in order to attract ship registrations. Chapter 7 looks at the actions undertaken by international organizations and states in an effort to respond to open registry vessels that fish outside of such international agreements. International organizations have begun to require member states to restrict trade in regulated fish to ships from states that have accepted, or otherwise agreed to abide by, the relevant fishery conservation measures. While many of these measures are fairly recent, they have encouraged some flag states to join international agreements or to cease registering fishing vessels.

Chapter 8 examines industry-based organizations that have taken on clublike characteristics in response to state, international organization, and labor union strategies of exclusion. For centuries ships have been inspected by classification societies that determined whether they were built to the correct specifications, and have obtained protection and indemnity insurance for assistance in case of disaster. These services, obtained by shipowners themselves, have now come to be used in the process of ship registration and port state control. The port state control inspections process discriminates based on the detention record of a ship's classification society, which has given societies an incentive to choose the ships they will classify in order to improve their records and become competitive to shipowners choosing a society. Protection and Indemnity clubs self-insure, and therefore gain from limiting their membership to ships unlikely to experience disasters. Other industry organizations for those who own, operate, or hire the services of ships have also begun to discriminate in membership to form clubs of higher-standard ships, used to help those ships avoid exclusion from ports, services, or markets.

The most successful efforts to raise the standards upheld by open registry states and the ships registered there collectively point to the advantages of exclusion as a strategy for regulatory cooperation. Ships register in open registries because of the cost advantages such registries provide, and registries compete to offer low-cost (and low-standard) options for registration. When ships can no longer sell the fish caught outside of fisheries agreements, find that the goods they transport rot on the docks because workers at port refuse to unload them, or are subject to increased scrutiny from port state control because of the policies of their flag states, the advantages of registering in these states decreases. What these strategies have in common is that they create a "club" of ships that can gain access to a set of advantages (markets for fish, labor services at ports, preferential treatment in port-state inspections), based on their willingness to adopt a set of standards. Ships that do not adopt such standards, or that register in flag states that do not adopt them, are excluded from the benefit. This processes makes registering a ship in a truly low-standard registry (or operating a substandard ship) less cost-effective than it would otherwise have been.

The strategies that have successfully worked to raise environmental, safety, and labor standards on ships also suggest that in a number of instances it is not only states that play the centrally important role in raising international standards. International organizations can be instrumental in providing the context in which states operate such clubs. Additionally, nonstate actors like labor unions can raise standards without the cooperation of states. And others affected by ships that operate outside the international regulatory framework, like the fishers who lose when flag-of-convenience fishing vessels undermine fishery conservation, can play important roles in persuading states or international organizations to take action.

Finally, chapter 9 explores the connection between state sovereignty and globalization in the consideration of how states respond to increasing economic integration and trade. Contrary to what many argue, globalization—and the use of offshore locations for economic activity—does not inherently signal a fundamental shift in sovereignty and diminution of state control. To some extent the presence of flags of convenience and other forms of offshore activity can be seen as a voluntary abdication by states of responsibilities in exchange for the systemic advantages these opportunities present. It is because of these competing advantages of high standards and low costs that such offshore opportunities are created. But the acquiescence of states in "offshore" economic activity suggests that states have the ability to diminish its importance if they so choose; the nonstate actors involved in pushing for increased standards may therefore tip the balance in persuading states to race to the regulatory middle.

There are impacts on the environmental conditions affecting the ocean, on the safety of those who work or travel on ships, and on labor conditions in the shipping industry, from the globalized nature of shipping. Globalization *has* led to a downward trend in standards. But globalization has created many opportunities to raise these standards as well. Ultimately the conditions on ships and in the oceans result from a constant interaction between those who benefit from lower standards and those who prefer higher ones.

2

Globalization, Competition, and Convergence: Racing to the Middle?

As a report from the Australian Parliament noted, "it is a world of too many ships that are over aged and under maintained chasing too little freight for too little return."[1] Most of these ships engaged in interstate commercial activity are now registered in what are called flags of convenience (FOCs) or open registries.[2] This trend challenges the ability or willingness of states to regulate activity undertaken by their nationals in a way that is comparable to, but temporally precedes, the globalization of the late twentieth and early twenty-first centuries. In this context, ships compete for business by keeping their costs as low as possible. Ship registries compete for ship registrations with policies that promise low costs, by keeping taxes, fees, and regulatory requirements low. This situation mirrors broader trends in globalization.

Those concerned about globalization generally have long been concerned that international competition will lead to a convergence of environmental and labor standards internationally, and that such a convergence will be downward. This could happen individually—states could competitively lower standards in an effort to lure industry and thus gain economic advantage. Or it could happen collectively, as international standards mandate a least-common-denominator level of regulation. U.S. Representative David Bonior (D-Mich.), for example, suggested that the World Trade Organization "threatens to undo internationally everything we have achieved nationally—every environmental

1. The Parliament of the Commonwealth of Australia, *Ships of Shame: Inquiry into Ship Safety*, Report from the House of Representatives Standing Committee on Transport, Communications, and Infrastructure (Canberra: Australian Government Publishing Service, December 1992), x.

2. Institute of Shipping Economics and Logistics, *ISL Shipping Statistics Yearbook 2004* (Bremen: ISL: 2004), v.

protection, every consumer safeguard, every labor victory."[3] In a world of freer trade, as Miles Kahler points out, more and more state policies have come to be seen as "disguised protectionism" or "non-tariff barriers," and concern has arisen about demands that they be removed to support trade without obstacles.[4] A more nuanced variation of this concern is that, rather than forcing standards downward, globalization will cause them to fail to rise when they otherwise should; the economic disadvantages in a globalized world to being the first state to increase environmental regulation will prevent states from doing so. Lyuba Zarsky refers to this process as being "stuck in the mud."[5]

Others, however, argue that a globalized world leads to upward harmonization and increased levels of regulation. David Vogel points to the "California effect" by which economically important states with high product standards can provide the context to move standards generally upward, because their trading partners need to adopt higher standards for their markets.[6] Certainly the incentive exists for states that have already passed domestic regulations to push for international acceptance of these standards to avoid competitive disadvantages for their industries.[7] In addition, multinational corporations, operating simultaneously in many states, face several incentives to raise standards across their areas of operation. If regulated strictly in one state they may prefer to hold all operations to that higher standard so as to avoid working with different procedures in different locations. They may hold the actual goods produced to similar standards regardless of production location,

3. David Bonior, "Defending Democracy in the New Global Economy," Statement to an AFL-CIO Conference on Workers' Rights, Trade Develoment, and the WTO, Seattle, Wash., December 1999; quoted in David Wheeler, "Beyond Pollution Havens," *Global Environmental Politics* 2/2 (2002): 1–10 (quote on 2).

4. Miles Kahler, "Modeling Races to the Bottom," paper presented at the 1998 Meeting of the American Political Science Association, Boston, September 1998.

5. Lyuba Zarsky, "Stuck in the Mud? Nation States, Globalization, and the Environment," in Kevin Gallagher and Jacob Werksman, eds., *The Earthscan Reader of International Trade and Sustainable Development* (London: Earthscan, 2002), 19–44.

6. David Vogel, *Trading Up: Consumer and Environmental Regulation in a Global Economy* (Cambridge: Harvard University Press, 1995), 6.

7. Elizabeth R. DeSombre, *Domestic Sources of International Environmental Policy: Industry, Environmentalists, and U.S. Power* (Cambridge: MIT Press, 2000).

because in a globalized world the products could thus be sold in states with the strictest requirements. Or they may bend to political pressure and promise that goods produced elsewhere will not be made with lower standards than those in their home state.[8] High regulations in one location may also demonstrate to other states that such regulation is possible, or to domestic constituents that they can demand it.[9]

It is instead possible that harmonization would not happen in either direction, but rather that "regulatory havens," areas with particularly low standards in one or more types of regulation, could persist alongside high-regulation states. At any given point of time, in almost any sector, there are states that have stricter regulations than others. Perhaps this distinction could simply persist over time, with some states prioritizing environmental and labor protection and others prioritizing the additional income from keeping standards low. Gareth Porter, for instance, sees rapidly industrializing states "stuck at the bottom" in terms of regulatory stringency, without necessarily pulling higher-standard states downward.[10]

Shipping is a particularly relevant issue within which to examine these competing hypotheses about the effects of globalization. This industry demonstrates the very real threat of lowered standards in response to globalization and freer trade. If regulatory havens or races to the bottom are to be encountered anywhere, they would likely be found in shipping. Ship registration is an often-overlooked method of "moving" industries to a location with lower environmental and labor standards. The shipping industry is among the most global of international industries, and this globalization began earlier and has gone deeper than in most other traditional industries.[11]

8. For a broader discussion of the role of MNCs in upward harmonization, see Ronie Garcia-Johnson, *Exporting Environmentalism* (Cambridge: MIT Press, 2000).

9. Otto Pohl, "European Environmental Rules Propel Change in U.S.," *New York Times*, July 6, 2004, F4.

10. Gareth Porter, "Trade Competition and Pollution Standards: 'Race to the Bottom' or 'Stuck at the Bottom'"? *Journal of Environment and Development* 8/2 (June 1999): 133–151.

11. Michael Bloor, Michelle Thomas, and Tony Lane, "Health Risks in the Global Shipping Industry: An Overview," *Health, Risk & Society* 2/3 (2000), 329–340.

Moreover, running an open registry presents a potentially easier form of encouraging industrial movement than do standard pollution havens. From the perspective of ships, registration in an open registry does not require physically relocating an industry; it simply means changing the flag flown and the port listed on the stern. Fees are sent to an office and inspectors, if any are required, generally go to where the ship is. Many ships registered in such localities never even visit their flag states. As Dale Murphy characterizes it, shipping is an industry marked by low asset specificity and is thus a likely candidate for a race to the bottom.[12]

From the perspective of a state that runs an open registry and attracts ship registrations by keeping environmental standards low, it bears no more of the environmental cost of the lowered standards than does any other state. In fact, if the ships it registers never visit its ports or pass through its national waters it may bear less of the environmental damage than do other states.[13] At minimum, the environmental situation is one of a common-pool resource, in which the state of registration bears all the advantages[14] and only a small portion of the costs. In a standard pollution-haven situation the state that draws environmentally detrimental industries itself suffers the primary effects of the pollutants. A similar argument can be made about safety and labor standards. But because one of the policies most open registries follow is not requiring that shipowners or crew be nationals of the registry state (unlike traditional registries), eschewing international labor standards will have no disproportionate effect on the registry state, since most employed on the vessel will have no link to the registry state.

Ships have been willing to take advantage of the demonstrated willingness of some states to lower standards to attract ship registrations, resulting in at least initial lowering of environmental, safety, and labor standards for some industrial activities. Competitive pressure internationally, from free trade and the generally increasing globalization of production, has led to incentives to decrease standards. Moreover, this

12. Dale D. Murphy, *The Structure of Regulatory Competition: Corporations and Public Politics in a Global Economy* (Oxford: Oxford University Press, 2004).

13. Recent trends for landlocked states, such as Bolivia, to create ship registries, demonstrate this phenomenon particularly forcefully.

14. These advantages can be large. See chapter 4.

global race to the bottom is not a new phenomenon; it began early in the twentieth century. Substandard shipping itself confers a competitive advantage. Even apart from wages and labor standards, an OECD report found that lack of compliance by ships with international safety and environmental regulations conferred economic benefits on shipowners. The study concluded that nonobservance of these standards distorts competition in the shipping industry.[15] Another OECD study found that owners of substandard ships manage to externalize the costs associated with these ships, and rarely suffer serious economic loss from the problems that arise from lack of adherence to collective standards.[16] The ease of movement of ship registration, in conjunction with these competitiveness effects, should provide the ideal conditions for downward harmonization.

But the result is neither a worldwide race to the regulatory bottom nor even a stable set of regulatory havens. Many states newly offering ship registration intentionally offer low standards to attract ships to the registry, and ship registrations have indeed increased at these locations. At any given point in time, some states or even individual ships have lower standards and others higher ones pertaining to environmental, safety, and labor issues on the high seas. But the regulatory environment does not remain stable. Once a registry enters the world market with low levels of regulation, a variety of actors begin efforts to increase the standards followed by the ships in those registries. The registries with the lowest standards generally give in to the pressures to increase the environmental, safety, and labor regulations that registered ships must uphold. As standards increase in these registries, new entrants to the global ship-registration market appear, offering lower standards than the prevailing ones, but they are eventually subject to the same pressures and change their behavior as well.

There is thus a kind of harmonization upward that occurs across some states, over time. But it does not fulfill quite the optimistic projections of

15. Organisation for Economic Cooperation and Development, *Competitive Advantages Obtained by Some Shipowners as a Result of Non-Observance of Applicable International Rules and Standards* (Paris: OECD, 1996).

16. SSY Consltancy and Research, Ltd. (for the OECD Maritime Transport Committee), *The Cost to Users of Substandard Shipping* (Paris: OECD Directorate for Science, Technology, and Industry, January 2001). The report notes that much of the cost is borne by the insurance industry.

some scholars. What we get instead is a race to the regulatory middle. Standards increase upward until they reach an equilibrium where the FOC states require more environmental, safety, and labor protections then they initially did, but fewer than adopted by most of the advanced industrial states.

At the same time, these traditional maritime registries, with the highest standards, join the race to the middle as well. Because they are concerned about losing ship registration to FOC registries, they respond by opening international registries, which allow nationally registered ships operating internationally to be held to some different standards than under the traditional registry, and by encouraging "second registries," operating in oversees territories of the home state, which can also have a different set of requirements and fees. The development of these registries is discussed further in chapter 4.

The phenomenon of FOC ship registration thus suggests that regulatory havens will exist, and will draw industry actors. But ship registration suggests that regulatory havens not only will not lead inexorably to races to the bottom; they can, in some circumstances, help motivate pressure to harmonize regulations upward, though perhaps at a lower level than would have been the case without the havens in the first place. Understanding the regulatory pattern required by registry states and adoption of standards by individual ships can therefore provide useful information for those engaged in a broader investigation of regulatory havens and races to the bottom. Previous research on these topics may in turn help to explain the particular patterns of harmonization and havens experienced in international regulation pertaining to ships.

Competitiveness Effects of Regulation

The logic for a "race to the regulatory bottom" is sound: in a world of mobile capital and free trade, and with the assumption that there is a cost to regulation, producers will choose to produce in an area that will cost them less. H. Jeffrey Leonard points out that there is more to the question of location of industry than naturally existing comparative advantage and that, in particular, "artificial factor endowments [such as low levels of regulation] created by governments have become at least as important as natural factor endowments" for states that want to attract industries.[17] If there are costs to industries that have to follow higher levels of regulation than their competitors operating elsewhere, those that have to take on higher levels of regulation will be disadvantaged competitively, unless those costs are canceled out by some countervailing factor. Examination of this question has for the most part been carried out separately in the realm of environmental and labor regulations.

On the environmental end, there are those who posit beneficial economic effects to environmental regulations, perhaps even for the industry itself.[18] It is plausible that innovation undertaken to comply with increased levels of environmental regulation could lead to decreased production costs due to some previously unforeseen technological or production innovation,[19] though economic theory suggests that if such an outcome were universal or even common, industries would invest in innovation of this sort without the regulatory requirement to do so. Some empirical studies suggest that savings due to increased efficiency in production may not offset the costs of the technology that creates the efficiency.[20] Others suggest that whether or not there are economic benefits to environmental regulations, there are at least no major costs. Assertions, for instance, that U.S. economic slowdown in the 1970s and 1980s could be attributed to increasingly stringent environmental regulations are not empirically supported.[21] In a larger, comparative study,

17. H. Jeffrey Leonard, *Pollution and the Struggle for World Product: Multinational Corporations, Environment, and International Comparative Advantage* (Cambridge: Cambridge University Press, 1988), 6.

18. Michael E. Porter, "America's Green Strategy," *Scientific American*, April 1991, 168; Michael E. Porter, *The Competitive Advantage of Nations* (London: Macmillan Press, 1990), 647–649.

19. OECD, *Environmental Policy and Technical Change* (Paris: Organisation for Economic Cooperation and Development, 1985).

20. Anthony J. Barbera and Virginia D. McConnell, "The Impact of Environmental Regulations on Industry Productivity: Direct and Indirect Effects," *Journal of Environmental Economics and Management* 18 (1990): 60.

21. Edward P. Denison, *Accounting for Slower Economic Growth: The United States in the 1970s* (Washington, D.C.: Brookings Institution, 1979); J. R. Norsworthy, Michael J. Harper, and Kent Kunze, "The Slowdown in Productivity Growth: Analysis of Some Contributing Factors," *Brookings Papers on Economic Activity* 2 (1979): 387–421; Paul R. Portnoy, "The Macroeconomic Impacts of Federal Environmental Regulation," in Henry M. Peskin, Paul R.

James Tobey found no relationship between relative stringency of environmental regulations across countries and net exports.[22]

Most of these studies purporting to find no serious costs to environmental regulations focus on the level of the economy as a whole. Decisions about industrial location, however, are much more likely to take into consideration localized costs to particular firms. For these groups the evidence suggests that there are indeed costs to environmental regulations, or at least a reasonable perception or anticipation of costs. Environmental regulations can have an impact on costliness of producing for a domestic market or for export.[23] An early study by Anthony Barbera and Virginia McConnell showed that in five U.S. industries in the 1970s, pollution regulation reduced productivity.[24] A study by the consulting firm Arthur Anderson reported that regulatory costs collectively in 1977 for forty-eight companies studied (constituting 8 percent of sales in major sectors of the U.S. economy) amounted to just over $2.6 billion, of which 77 percent could be attributed to costs that came from regulations from the Environmental Protection Agency.[25] The Council on En-

---

Portnoy, and Allan V. Kneese, *Environmental Regulation and the U.S. Economy* (Baltimore: Johns Hopkins University Press, 1981), 25–54. Gray, however, argues that 30 percent of productivity decline may be attributed to environmental, health, and safety regulations; see Wayne B. Gray, "The Cost of Regulation: OSHA, EPA, and the Productivity Slowdown," *American Economic Review* 77 (1987): 998–1006.

22. James A. Tobey, "The Effects of Domestic Environmental Policies on Patterns of World Trade: An Empirical Test," *Kyklos* 43 (1990): 191–209.

23. Adam B. Jaffe, Steven R. Peterson, Paul R. Portnoy, and Robert N. Stavins, "Environmental Regulations and International Competitiveness: What Does the Evidence Tell Us?", unpublished draft, December 21, 1993, 5, 14; James Tobey, "The Impact of Domestic Environmental Policies on International Trade," in OECD, *Environmental Policies and Industrial Competitiveness* (Paris: OECD, 1993), 48.

24. Anthony J. Barbera and Virginia D. McConnell, "The Impact of Environmental Regulations on Industry Productivity: Direct and Indirect Effects," *Journal of Environmental Economics and Management* 18: 62; the decline was due both to the direct costs of pollution-abatement technology and to the indirect effects on output.

25. In 1977 $US. Arthur Anderson and Company, *Cost of Regulation, Study for the Business Roundtable* (New York: Arthur Anderson and Company, March 1979), iii. The largest of the EPA-derived costs was $765 million for incremental capital costs (p. v). The regulations examined were those from the Environmental

vironmental Quality estimated the cost of pollution control on U.S. industries in that year at $12.8 billion.[26] A comparable study by Robert Litan and William D. Nordhaus had more modestly estimated the cost at between $13.4 and $37.9 million, but suggested that even that cost accounted for between .7 and 2.0 percent of GNP.[27] More generally, Gary Yohe modeled the relationship between pollution controls and production and found that the stronger the regulation, the more of an impact it had on production costs.[28] Richard B. Stewart examined a range of existing studies on the competitiveness effects of environmental regulations, and found that these regulations do negatively affect productivity.[29] Related evidence suggests that a large number of manufacturing and utility plants that closed in the United States in the 1970s indicated that the difficulty of meeting air-pollution requirements was a factor in their decisions to close.[30]

These costs, moreover, have been found to influence the international competitiveness of the regulated industries. Joseph Kalt found that the higher the cost of domestic environmental regulation, the worse the export performance of the U.S. industries subject to them.[31] A more recent study by the U.S. Environmental Protection Agency predicted that the balance of trade in industries most regulated by the 1990 Clean Air Act

---

Protection Agency, Equal Employment Opportunty Agency, Occupational Safety and Health Administration, Department of Energy, Employee Retirement Income Security Act, and Federal Trade Commission. The study also implies that the costs of these regulations account for up to 3 percent of GNP.

26. Cited in Anderson, 20.

27. Robert E. Litan and Wiliam D. Nordhaus, *Reforming Federal Regulation* (New Haven: Yale University Press, 1983), 22, 24.

28. Gary W. Yohe, "The Backward Incidence of Pollution Control—Some Comparative Statics in General Equilibrium," *Journal of Environmental Economics and Management* 6: 197.

29. Stewart, 2084. The studies he examined were of U.S. regulations.

30. Ingo Walter, "Environmentally Induced Industrial Relocation to Developing Countries," in Seymour J. Rubin and Thomas R. Graham, eds., *Environment and Trade* (Montclair, N.J.: Allanheld, Osmun Publishers, 1982), 67–101.

31. Joseph P. Kalt, "The Impact of Domestic Environmental Regulatory Policies on U.S. International Competitiveness," in A. Michael Spence and Heather A. Hazard, eds., *International Competitiveness* (Cambridge, Mass.: Ballinger, 1988). He did, however, find that "economic regulation appears to be even more costly than environmental regulation" (p. 256).

Amendments would decline.[32] Leonard and Duerksen pointed out that with respect to U.S., Japanese, and European companies operating in their home states in the era when new environmental regulations were increasing, "every estimate showed the costs of complying with these new regulations skyrocketing." They also argued that, competitively, specific regulations and the social reactions in support of them could make it impossible for certain industries to operate cost-effectively within Europe, Japan, and the United States.[33]

Discussions of the competitiveness effects of labor standards are more than a century old. Concern expressed by industries that domestic labor regulations would lead to competitive disadvantage is what led to the founding of the International Labour Organisation (ILO) in 1919.[34] Despite historical concern, however, as Steve Charnovitz argues, "there is little literature on the impact of differing labor standards on trade."[35]

It is generally agreed that "employment standards usually impose costs on employers that they cannot fully shift onto employees."[36] The most obvious of these involve regulations—such as a minimum wage law—that increase the amount of wages paid to low-skill workers. These types of regulatory costs differ from the types of costs attributed to environmental regulation, to the extent that labor costs in terms of wages are necessary inputs into a production process, while frequently environmen-

32. Carl A. Pasurka Jr. and Deborah Vaughn Nestor, "Environmental Protection Agency: Trade Effects of the 1990 Clean Air Act Amendments," unpublished study, 1992. The industries in question were chemical manufacturing, automobile manufacturing, and iron and steel manufacturing; Dale W. Jorgenson and Peter J. Wilcoxen, "Impact of Environmental Legislation on U.S. Economic Growth, Investment, and Capital Costs," in Donna L. Bodsky, ed., *U.S. Environmental Policy and Economic Growth: How Do We Fare?* (Washington, D.C.: American Council for Capital Formation, 1992), 1–39.

33. H. Jeffrey Leonard and Christopher Duerksen, "Environmental Regulations and the Location of Industry: An International Perspective," *Columbia Journal of World Business* (summer 1980): 54, 64.

34. Bernard M. Hoekman and Michael M. Kostecki, *The Political Economy of the World Trading System: From GATT to WTO* (Oxford: Oxford University Press, 1995), 263.

35. Steve Charnovitz, "Environmental and Labour Standards in Trade," in *The World Economy* 15 (1992): 342.

36. Ronald G. Ehrenberg, *Labor Markets and Integrating National Economies* (Washington, D.C.: Brookings Institution, 1994), 39.

tal damage is an externality. The higher the wage level of an area, the costlier it is to an industry (by definition) to hire workers. Because increased wages raise the costs of goods, those who produce them with higher wages will "be placed at a competitive disadvantage if foreign producers are not subject to similar standards."[37] In this form, labor is one of the most costly aspects of many industries, though its costliness varies widely across industries depending on the capital-versus-labor intensity of the industry.

Often overlooked, however, are other types of labor regulations that are more likely to follow the environmental model. Rules about the health and safety of workers, or those limiting hours or ages or mandating certain benefits, can form an important component of the cost of doing business. Litan and Nordhaus's estimate for the annual costs of health and safety regulations to U.S. industry in 1977 was between $7.4 and $17.1 billion.[38] Rodriguez and Samy find that rate of unionization and level of protection against occupational injuries "support the general view that low labor standards can improve export performance."[39] J. S. Mah found that acceptance by states of ILO core labor standards including freedom of association, collective bargaining, and discrimination correlated with a decrease in export performance.[40] Vivek H. Dehejia and Yiagadeesen Samy expanded on Mah's study, controlling for more aspects of natural comparative advantage and adding factors to ensure the fulfillment, in addition to ratification, of ILO labor obligations. They too found that lower labor standards correlate with improved export performance.[41]

The initial (and unsuccessful) post–World War II efforts to create an International Trade Organization recognized the competitiveness impacts

37. Ehrenberg, 40.

38. Litan and Nordhaus, 22.

39. Gabriel Rodriguez and Yiagadeesen Samy, "Analysing the Effects of Labour Standards on US Export Performance: A Time Series Approach with Structural Change," *Applied Economics* 35/9 (June 15, 2003): 1043–1051.

40. J. S. Mah, "Core Labour Standards and Export Performance in Developing Countries," *The World Economy* 20/6 (1997): 773–785.

41. Vivek H. Dehejia and Yiagadeesen Samy, "Trade and Labour Standards: Theory and New Empirical Evidence," *Journal of International Trade & Economic Development* 13/2 (2004): 179–198.

of labor standards, incorporating an article that states that "the members recognize that unfair labor conditions . . . create difficulties for international trade and, accordingly, each member shall take whatever action may be appropriate and feasible to eliminate such conditions within its territory."[42]

Will States Choose Low Regulatory Levels?

In the early years of industrial environmental regulation, even the United Nations advocated the selective use by states of lower levels of regulation as an aspect of competitive advantage. UNIDO listed "permissive environmental legislation" as one of the policy options developing states could pursue to increase their mineral processing industries, suggesting that governments consider lax environmental standards as they would consider any other industrial subsidy "and use [that approach] to the extent that the benefits exceed the social costs" by more than other types of subsidies.[43] Leonard and Duerksen quote a Jamaican official as representative of developing-country approaches to attracting industry: "We will do just about anything to assist a new industry in establishing itself—that's how badly we need them."[44] To what extent have states followed this strategy of creating or maintaining low environmental or labor standards in an effort to entice industrial relocation?

Examining this question is harder than it might seem.[45] There are a variety of reasons apart from attracting industry that regulatory levels may be kept low. In general, developing states have lower levels of environmental and labor protection than industrialized states, and wage rates

42. International Trade Organization (1948), Article II (Chapter 7); as cited in Drusilla K. Brown, Alan V. Deardorff, and Robert M. Stern, "International Labor Standards and Trade: A Theoretical Analysis," in Jagdish Bhagwati and Robert E. Hudec, eds., *Fair Trade and Harmonization*, vol. 1 (Cambridge: MIT Press, 1996), 232.

43. UNIDO, *Mineral Processing in Developing Countries* (New York: United Nations, 1980), 94.

44. Leonard and Duerksen, 54.

45. See Smita B. Brunnermeier and Arik Levinson, "Examining the Evidence on Environmental Regulations and Industry Location," *Journal of Environment and Development* 13/4 (March 2004): 6–41.

are lower as well. Simply measuring regulatory levels will not indicate whether these levels were adopted for competitiveness reasons, without the careful interviewing that Leonard did to attempt to understand regulatory strategy; this method would be nearly impossible in a large-scale study. Even then, government officials may be less than forthcoming about the reasons they adopted a policy, or may have received pressure from a number of groups in favor of the policy for different reasons,[46] so ascertaining the true cause of a policy may still be difficult.

Though some, such as Daniel Drezner, see races to the bottom as explicitly structural theories,[47] domestic politics can also play a role in the levels of regulations states choose to adopt. Most who observe potential races to the bottom attribute suboptimal collective government behavior to lack of information or to influence over the government by a strong interest group. Scott Basinger and Mark Hallerberg argue that it is frequently domestic politics (both the transaction costs of legislating and the constituency costs of the policy change) that prevent races to the bottom from happening.[48]

But with environmental issues, particularly those pertaining to ships, the opposition to keeping environmental standards low is unlikely. The underrepresentation of environmental interests within political systems is likely, given that the costs to environmental regulation are generally borne by concentrated, well-organized interests, and the benefits accrue to diffuse and poorly organized actors.[49] And since environmental regulations also benefit politically disenfranchised future generations, the likelihood that such interests will not be as well represented politically as those of industry actors increases. On ships in particular, many of the potential impacts of low standards will not be borne by the state whose standards are low.

46. See DeSombre, *Domestic Sources*.

47. Daniel W. Drezner, *All Politics is Global: Explaining International Regulatory Regimes* (Princeton: Princeton University Press, 2007).

48. Scott J. Basinger and Mark Hallerberg, "Remodeling the Competition for Capital: How Domestic Politics Erases the Race to the Bottom," *American Political Science Review* 98/2 (May 2004): 261–276.

49. David Vogel, "Representing Diffuse Interests in Environmental Policymaking," in R. Kent Weaver and Bert A. Rockman, eds., *Do Institutions Matter? Government Capabilities in the United States and Abroad* (Washington, D.C.: Brookings Institution, 1993), 237–271.

Low levels of environmental regulation need not be a conscious social or economic decision, however, on the part of a state. That levels of environmental regulation increase, and degrees of pollution intensity decrease, with increased levels of economic wealth within a state has become nearly a truism.[50] That production has simultaneously shifted to developing countries, while perhaps a legitimate cost-saving choice on the part of industry actors, need not suggest that the states in question intentionally kept their environmental standards low for this purpose. As David Wheeler points out, we would have to see developing-country growth in pollution-intensive industries outstripping growth in other sectors to be persuaded that keeping regulations low is an intentional bid by such states to attract industry.[51] The same can be said for labor standards or wage rates; the mere presence of low wages does not indicate an intentional plan to lure industry on that basis.

On the whole the evidence for the existence of individual states lowering environmental or labor standards to attract industry is mixed. John Douglas Wilson suggests that in terms of state intention there is "little evidence of any such 'race'" to the bottom in environmental regulatory standards.[52] Individual examples, however, suggest otherwise. Leonard's study of four states—Ireland, Spain, Mexico, and Romania—showed that in the 1970s all took steps to attract industry with low standards.[53] Ireland, for example, attempted to lure chemical manufacturers to the state, with internal policies of "less stringent pollution controls than in Europe or the United States."[54]

Dangers exist to states that choose to lower (or maintain low) environmental standards to attract industry. They bear almost entirely (depending on the type of environmental regulation in question) the environmental externalities of their actions. In fact, the most common

50. See David Wheeler, "Beyond Pollution Havens," *Global Environmental Politics* 2/2 (May 2002): 3–5.

51. Wheeler, "Beyond Pollution Havens," 5.

52. John Douglas Wilson, "Capital Mobility and Environmental Standards: Is there a Theoretical Basis for a Race to the Bottom?", in Jagdish Bhagwati and Robert E. Hudec, eds., *Fair Trade and Harmonization*, vol. 1 (Cambridge: MIT Press, 1996), 393–427.

53. Leonard, 7.

54. From an interview with James Shine, chief planning office, Waterford County, Dungarvan, Ireland (1980); quoted in Leonard, 127.

model suggesting that races to the bottom are unlikely allows for regulatory jurisdictions large enough that environmental externalities are eliminated.[55]

The states that Leonard examined that took some activity to lower standards in an effort to lure industries all eventually reversed or moderated their laxity.[56] There are those, such as the World Bank, who predict that individual states will necessarily follow a domestic process akin to what Leonard found internationally, beginning with pollution-intensive industry and then cleaning up as rising income allows it and public demand for environmental protection increases.[57] It is clear that maintaining low environmental standards is not inevitable regulatory behavior on the part of states. It is less clear, however, that the evidence convincingly contradicts the advantages or existence of such strategies.

Analysis of this question with respect to labor standards is problematic as well. Economic theory predicts that some states *should* lower their standards in order to be able to better compete in an international market. As Brian Langille put it, "if competition in supply of widgets is socially desirable, why not in the production of labour regulation?"[58] Again, however, it is extremely difficult to examine whether they do so intentionally.

The relationship between globalization and wage rates is complicated. On the one hand, labor markets are the most national of markets: labor is the factor of production that states most consistently control. In other words, the fact that most people cannot simply move to another state in

55. Kahler, 6; Charles Tiebout, "A Pure Theory of Local Expenditures," *Journal of Political Economy* 64 (1956): 416–424.

56. Leonard, 7.

57. World Bank, *World Development Report 1992: Development and the Environment* (New York: Oxford University Press, 1992), 25–43; Gene M. Grossman and Alan B. Krueger, "Economic Growth and the Environment," *Quarterly Journal of Economics* 110/2 (May 1995): 353–377. Note that there is a difference between the analytic studies that show a relationship between per capita level of income and level of pollution and those who use this relationship to advocate a focus on raising income levels as a means to decrease pollution levels.

58. Brian A. Langille, "International Labour Standards and Economic Interdependence," in Werner Sengenberger and Duncan Campbell, eds., *International Labour Standards and Economic Interdependence* (Geneva: International Institute for Labour Studies, 1994), 334.

order to take a job suggests that the policies that states make should have a strong impact on wage rates and other labor standards in a given country. But apart from setting certain minimum standards, the wages that are actually paid in a particular location by a given industry are determined by the market (along with local social norms). While there may be a governmentally set minimum wage, a company that sets up operation in a location will have to take or exceed the prevailing wage or it will not attract qualified workers.

The willingness of states to set up Export Processing Zones, in which labor and other standards are lowered and trade barriers removed with the guarantee that industries export most or all of the products made in these locations, suggests that many states willingly relax domestic rules in order to lure internationally competing business. While in some locations labor standards in these zones are as high as in the surrounding, more highly regulated state, most include restriction of unions, low wages, long hours, and few benefits.[59]

Even within the shipping industry itself there is some discussion of state-based competition in labor laxity as a competitive strategy. A study of the demographics of seafarers from the most prominent "labor-supply" states to the global shipping industry explores the strategic decisions facing the Philippines and China (the first and fourth largest suppliers of seafarers), including the possibility that they will compete by "depressing each other's wages and standards."[60]

Even comparing regulatory levels, apart from ascertaining intention, can be difficult. In the case of environmental standards there are so many different types of regulations that could be relevant that it is hard to characterize an overall regulatory level. Different states choose to mitigate or prevent potential environmental problems in such different ways that determining the relative laxity of existing regulations can be hopelessly complex. Likewise, there is no clear hierarchy of what constitutes

59. International Labour Organisation, *World Employment 1995* (Geneva: ILO, 1995), 73; Organisation for Economic Cooperation and Development, *Trade and Labor Standards* (Paris: OECD, 1995), 39, 60; Ethan Kapstein, "Racing to the Bottom? Regulating International Labor Standards," *Politik und Gesellschaft* 2 (1997): 155–160.

60. Minghua Zhao and Maragtas S. V. Amante, "Chinese and Filipino Seafarers: A Race to the Top or the Bottom?", *Modern Asian Studies* 39/3 (2005): 536.

high labor standards: whether, for example, a state that mandates extensive worker protection but has a low minimum wage is more or less protective of labor rights than a high-wage state with few safety or job-protection rules. Those who examine the question of regulatory level have thus generally used proxy measures for state policy, such as average wage or some measure of pollution generation itself, rather than actual regulation. While this approach has some advantages over simply examining regulations, in that it investigates state behavior rather than stated intentions, it is nevertheless an imperfect measure. For instance, if a state has a high level of output of pollution, that could be because it has a few industries that pollute intensively, or it could be because a large number of industrial actors each pollute to a small degree. If average wages are high, how are they distributed across society? How does wage level compare to the cost of living?

Even examining regulations themselves, particularly when they are international, can be a problematic measure, since doing so does not measure implementation or enforcement of these international agreements or domestic laws. Certainly some of the concern—generated, for example, in the context of the North American Free Trade Agreement—is that states that have regulations on the books will not enforce them, sometimes as an intentional way of gaining economic advantage.

Any effort to compare regulatory levels will have to lay out explicitly what it is comparing. This difficulty of comparison also suggests that individual businesses deciding where to locate may examine the suite of regulations to look for laxity in the specific ones that concern them. A simple analysis of low versus high regulatory levels, or conflation of industry (or even individual businesses), may not be sufficient for predictions of industrial location.

Will Industries Move to Take Advantage of Lower Standards?

It does not matter if there is a theoretical advantage to lowering regulatory standards if empirically industries do not move to localities with lower regulations. It is important to note, however, that this stage of the investigation does not rest on the assumption that low standards have been intentionally created; evidence that industries tend to concentrate in areas with the lowest standards could be sufficient to suggest the relevance of a "haven" model even without evidence of state intention in creating low standards. There are certainly a number of factors that could influence whether industry actors will move to an area of low regulation, including wage rates as well as labor and environmental standards.

Some argue that empirically the evidence is in, and that "the literature as whole presents fairly compelling evidence across a broad range of industries, time-periods, and econometric specifications, that regulations do not matter to site choice."[61] Ingo Walter, despite noting the contribution of environmental costs to plant closing in the United States, concludes that the bulk of the evidence "does not suggest massive environment-induced locational shifting thus far."[62] Peter Thompson and Laura Strohm, after evaluating the evidence from three different types of studies to explore the pollution-haven hypothesis, conclude that the evidence "shows no sign that dirty industries are migrating in the face of increasing environmental regulations and liberal trade."[63]

Evidence exists, however, of some degree of movement of industries. Walter, despite the broad conclusion of minimal shifting, does point to smelters, refineries, and asbestos plants that were constructed outside of the United States due to weaker environmental controls elsewhere. Likewise, in Europe, chemical and petroleum plants originally planned for high-regulation states were resited in areas of lower regulation.[64] The earliest evidence for industry movement to avoid environmental regulations came in the 1970s in Japan. The Ministry of International Trade and Industry (MITI) created a fund to help establish petrochemical facilities outside of Japan. One of the reasons given for this action was the difficulty of dealing with the levels of pollution created by such plants. Importantly, the pollution level itself was a less important concern on the part of the government than the domestic protest that came because

61. Arik Levinson, "Environmental Regulations and Industry Location: International and Domestic Evidence," in Jagdish Bhagwati and Robert E. Hudec, *Fair Trade and Harmonization: Prerequisites for Free Trade? Vol. I: Economic Analysis*, 450.

62. Walter, 89.

63. Peter Thompson and Laura A. Strohm, "Trade and Environmental Quality: A Review of the Evidence," *Journal of Environment and Development* 5/4 (December 1996): 384.

64. Walter, 89.

of it.[65] Japan encouraged the relocation of facilities for aluminum refining, oil storage, and metals manufacturing.[66] Japan reduced domestic aluminum-production capacity by half in the 1970s through shifting production to New Zealand, Indonesia, the Philippines, and Venezuela, as well as to Canada and the United States.[67] More recently a U.S. General Accounting Office study of wood furniture manufacturers in the Los Angeles area found that between 1 and 3 percent of the firms (consisting disproportionately of large firms) relocated to Mexico between 1988 and 1990. Of these, 78 percent indicated that air-pollution standards played a major role in their decision. An even greater percentage—83 percent—attributed their moves to the high costs of wages and worker's compensation insurance in the United States.[68]

It is remarkably difficult empirically, however, to examine the hypothesis that industry location is influenced by regulatory level. Even examining whether investment is highest in states with the lowest regulatory burdens is potentially problematic. While evidence that industrial output is highest in regions with the lowest level of environmental regulation would support the pollution-haven hypothesis, a lack of relationship does not refute it, since factories may choose to locate in some of these areas (explicitly because of their low standards) but not others (possibly because of other disadvantages), and thus a pattern could be difficult to discern. Almost all of the studies purporting to examine this hypothesis have thus used some type of proxy measurement to do so.

One of the ways many have examined this question is by simply comparing the level of pollution with the level of economic development. The idea is that if poor states are producing more pollution than rich states, they are necessarily producing more pollution per amount of generated wealth. This relationship could mean that these states have attracted

65. Derek Hall, "Environmental Change, Protest, and Havens of Environmental Degradation: Evidence from Asia," *Global Environmental Politics* 2/2 (May 2002): 22.

66. Hall, 23.

67. Walter, 93–95.

68. U.S. General Accounting Office, *U.S.-Mexico Trade: Some U.S. Wood Furniture Firms Relocated from Los Angeles Area to Mexico*, Report to the Chairman, Committee on Energy and Commerce, House of Representatives GAO/NSIAD-91-191, April 1991.

more heavily polluted industry; at a minimum they could choose to lower the level of pollution if they wanted to, and the fact that they have not done so implies a policy choice. Lucas, Wheeler, and Hettige, for instance, find that the intensity of toxic pollution is higher in low-income countries than elsewhere.[69]

A related way to attempt to ascertain whether industries move is to examine the balance of trade in industrial states. The idea here is that if these states import more than they export from heavily polluting industries, then polluting industries have located in places away from where their goods are being sold. Martin Jänicke, Manfred Binder, and Harald Mönch argue that by this measurement there is no evidence of relocation of dirty industries to developing countries, since wealthy (and highly regulated) states remain net exporters of fertilizer, pulp and paper, steel, lead, and zinc.[70]

Another proxy variable used to explore the pollution-haven hypothesis is level of foreign direct investment (FDI) compared with levels of environmental regulation. Here the logic is that if environmental regulation decreases the value of outputs, those with money to invest will do so in a place where they will get the greatest return from their investments. For industry, Yuqing Xing and Charles D. Kolstad suggest, "locating its production capacity oversees is basically foreign direct investment." If states with the lowest level of environmental protection have the highest level of investment, that would tend to support the pollution-haven hypothesis. Xing and Kolstad find among the strongest empirical evidence for the existence of pollution havens using this approach. They examine high- and low-polluting industries and compare FDI in these industries in high- and low-standard states. Their study finds that FDI in pollution-intensive industries depends on the strictiness of environmental regulations (with greater investment in lax regulatory areas); moreover, the same does not hold true for low-polluting industries, for which there is

69. Robert E. B. Lucas, David Wheeler, and Hemamala Hettige, "Economic Development, Environmental Regulation, and the International Migration of Toxic Pollution: 1960–1988," in Patrick Low, ed., *International Trade and the Environment* (Washington, D.C.: World Bank, 1992), 89–103.

70. Martin Jänicke, Manfred Binder, and Harald Mönch, "Dirty Industries: Patterns of Change in Industrial Countries," *Environmental and Resource Economics* 9 (1997): 467–491.

no relationship between FDI and regulatory strictness.[71] Even a lack of relationship using this measure, however, would not doom the hypothesis. Xing and Kolstad themselves point out one of the potential problems with this measure: a state could specialize in polluting industries without doing so through foreign direct investment. In addition, the multiplicity of factors that likely go into a decision on where to invest, impossible to hold constant in a study of real-world investment decisions, suggest that the possible impact of pollution havens does not depend on such a relationship. Again, what is important for support of the hypothesis is not that all investment happen in areas with low levels of regulation, but that some does.

An additional problem with studies attempting to examine the potential migration of industries due to environmental conditions is in determining what constitutes a "dirty industry." As Jennifer Clapp points out, the regulations and industries examined in the pollution-haven discussion are heavily biased toward manufacturing;[72] even the term chosen suggests a focus on pollution rather than resource use or other environmental hazards. Clapp's concern is that the efforts to explore the issue leave out consideration of such things as the hazardous-waste industry and overlook the extent to which toxic materials are transported to developing countries, with lower regulatory standards or capabilities, for processing or disposal. Even when studies do include these factors, they aggregate them, without acknowledging the possibility (or empirical evidence) that manufacturers who deal with particularly hazardous substances may be more likely than the norm to relocate their firms for environmental reasons.[73] The increased complexity of environmental regulations in an era more recent than that examined in most pollution-haven studies may suggest the need for a more nuanced discussion of the conditions under which industries might move. Clapp suggests, for example, that pollution-haven studies as currently designed would likely miss the incentive of industries that make use of toxic substances to

71. Yuqing Xing and Charles D. Kolstad, "Do Lax Environmental Regulations Attract Foreign Investment?", *University of California Santa Barbara Department of Economics Working Papers* 5-95 (revised August 2000).

72. Jennifer Clapp, "What the Pollution Havens Debate Overlooks," *Global Environmental Politics* 2/2 (May 2002), 11–19.

73. Leonard, 232.

relocate once the ban on hazardous-waste trade between developed and developing states under the Basel Convention on the Transboundary Movement of Hazardous Wastes and Their Disposal enters into force.[74]

Clapp points out that ignoring resource extraction in these examinations also excludes sources of serious pollution that come from the process of extraction; she in turn ignores the environmental problem that overextraction of the resources themselves (even without explicit externalities) can represent. In any case, there are clearly many under-examined aspects of the relationship between environmental regulation and industry location.

The costs of environmental regulations per se may not be the only factor that impacts choice of location for industry; in some cases environmental regulations may simply make it impossible (or extremely difficult) for manufacturers to build new plants or expand old ones.[75] Other evidence suggests as well that industries that move for environmental reasons do so less to avoid costly regulations than to avoid the delays those regulations impose on approval of new facilities.[76]

But there are reasons that, even if competitive lowering (or avoidance of) environmental standards existed, firms might not move to take advantage of them. One would be if the firm has already adapted to the regulatory costs. Thompson and Strohm suggest that the low relative cost of environmental regulations (due largely to incomplete regulatory internalization of environmental costs) accounts for the limited empirical support for the pollution-haven hypothesis despite its strong theoretical basis.[77] Jänicke et al. agree, and also suggest that the willingness of advanced industrialized states to abandon environmental regulation when it threatens to impact competitiveness is a contributing factor.[78] Particularly in the case of environmental controls that require investing in equipment or altering production processes, there is little to be gained from going back to a form of production that does not control pollution. When the cost of relocating and the other disadvantages (such as a

74. Clapp, 15–16.

75. Leonard, 65.

76. Walter, 92.

77. Thompson and Strohm, 384.

78. Jänicke et al., 473.

lower-quality labor force) that may accompany a move to a pollution haven are factored in, there may be little incentive for an industry to take advantage of low regulations in a new location. There also may be additional costs—a less skilled labor force, for instance, or increased transportation costs—that are not offset by the economic saving from avoiding environmental regulation. As Drezner points out, those who anticipate regulatory races to the bottom do not expect labor productivity to make a difference in the location choices of industry.[79] This may be an unrealistic assumption; in many instances labor (and hence productivity) may be the largest input cost to an industry. Most of these fall under the *ceteris paribus* exception however; all else equal, we should still expect firms to choose to locate in areas with less costly regulation levels.

And evidence, both anecdotal and statistical, does suggests that industries sometimes will move to take advantage of low environmental regulations. An examination of level of environmental regulation and industry-location choices in OECD states does find a relationship between environmental regulations and level and patterns of exports.[80] Studies most likely to find a relationship are those that examine the most polluting industries, though frequently this is still examined using air-pollution data only.[81] As Wheeler points out, even those who do not find support for the pollution-haven hypothesis should exercise caution, because "there is no theoretical reason why industries with exceptionally high pollution control costs should ignore regulatory concerns."[82] The jury appears to be out on the extent to which pollution havens will come to exist and to draw industry to them.

Even studies that suggest that businesses will not move to take advantage of low environmental costs argue that labor costs are sufficient to determine industry location.[83] A study of overseas investment decisions by West German firms in the 1970s found that 25 percent of firms made

79. Drezner, *All Politics Is Global.*

80. Cees van Beers and J. C. J. M. van der Bergh, "An Empirical Multi-Country Analysis of the Impact of Environmental Regulations on Foreign Trade Flows," *Kyklos* 50/1 (1999): 29–46.

81. See Leonard.

82. Wheeler, "Beyond Pollution Havens," 6.

83. Gene M. Grossman and Alan B. Krueger, "Environmental Impacts of the North American Free Trade Agreement," in P. Garber, ed., *The Mexico-U.S.*

overseas investment decisions based on wages (and an additional 20 percent mentioned production costs as a basis for locational decisions without specifying what contributed to those costs). Moreover, the modal answer given by these firms about how important labor costs were to locational decisions was "very important."[84]

Labor standards, more difficult to measure than wage rates and less likely at first glance to have an impact on industry location, can be shown to have some impact as well. Dani Rodrick found that the number of statutory hours in a normal work week correlated positively with an increase in textile and clothing exports (as a measure of labor-intensive industry), indicating that states with longer working hours were more likely to have an industry for which labor is a major input.[85] Cees van Beers, however, found no significant relationship between stringency of labor standards and labor intensity of exports, contrary to expectation.[86]

Interestingly, even industries relating to ships are used as examples of the movement of operations based on the costliness of labor and of environmental regulations in developed countries. Shipbreaking (the taking apart of ships once they are no longer in service) had been done primarily at the major European and American shipyards until the 1970s, at which points "labor costs and environmental regulations drove most of the businesses" first to the rapidly industrializing countries in Asia and then to India, Bangladesh, and Pakistan, where most of it is currently done.[87]

Free Trade Agreement (Cambridge: MIT Press), 13–56; David Vogel, *Trading Up*, 257.

84. Gabriele Knögden, "Environment and Industrial Siting: Preliminary Results of an Empirical Survey of Investment by West German Industry in Developing Countries," in *Zeitschrift für Umweltpolitik* (December 1979): 416, 418.

85. Dani Rodrick, "Labour Standards in International Trade: Do They Matter and What Do We Do About Them?", *Oversees Development Council* (1996), 20.

86. The predicted relationship was there, but not at the level of statistical significance. See Cees van Beers, "Labour Standards and Trade flows of OECD Countries," *The World Economy* 21/1: 68.

87. William Langewiesche, *The Outlaw Sea: A World of Freedom, Chaos, and Crime* (New York: North Point Press, 2004), 203.

Racing to the Bottom?

An additional distinction should be made, however, in order to examine both the theory and existing empirical studies on regulatory behavior and globalization. There is a conceptual and practical difference between the emergence of pollution havens and a true "race to the bottom." So-called pollution havens, or other pockets of low levels of domestic and international regulation, are at worst indications that a race may be in progress, and at best suggestions that the race has not been won. According to the strongest form of the theory, regulations should equalize at the lowest level of regulation across states, rather than allowing the competitive advantage of lower regulations to exist in localized areas. Is there evidence that such a race could or does exist? Or can individual areas of lower levels of regulation persist despite higher standards elsewhere? Diagnosing what encourages or prevents such potential races from being completed is essential in determining what the theory leaves out.

The theory for a regulatory race to the bottom is strong. If we expect globalization assisted by free trade to result in harmonization of national policies, logic would suggest that the harmonization should be downward rather than up. States that do not participate in weakening or leaving weak their domestic standards will see their economic competitiveness erode.[88] The race to the bottom that would arise from the existence of a pollution haven can be modeled in game-theoretic terms as a classic prisoner's dilemma. A state in isolation can choose trade-offs between the costs (in human impacts) of pollution and the costs of pollution control, arriving at an optimal level of regulation. In a two-state model in which states can set their environmental regulatory levels, firms will relocate if their costs saved under a lower regulatory system are greater than the costs of moving. A state will lower its regulatory standards if its benefits from a firm's relocation exceed its cost from environmental damage. The prisoner's dilemma comes in as states decide whether to lower standards in an effort to attract industry. Each would do so in order to attempt to lure industry away from the other, with the result that both would lower standards and neither would gain

88. Miles Kahler, 3.

the increased revenue, because firms, if they did relocate, would do so roughly evenly.[89] The same story can be told of labor regulations.[90]

It is true that environmental damage will rarely impact only those in the state where it is created, but that only makes the model above (and the race to the bottom it implies) more convincing, because states would thus only bear some of the costs of keeping environmental standards low, with other environmental costs felt elsewhere. Likewise, that human—and other—costs of pollution are rarely fully accounted for suggests even greater discounting of environmental effects and a likely choice of competitive lowering of environmental standards. Muthukumara Mani and David Wheeler find evidence for transitory pollution havens, but argue that they are self-limiting and thus do not create a race to the bottom.[91] Instead, the economic growth that pollution havens would theoretically foster appears to happen, and brings with it a societal demand and capability to address environmental problems.

At its extreme, this process leads to what Vogel calls the "California effect," whereby states that adopt higher levels of regulation will lead others to do so as well. The analogy here is to a U.S. domestic process in which California was allowed to choose stricter air-pollution standards than other states under the U.S. Clean Air Act. In later revisions of the legislation other states were permitted to choose between national standards and (higher) California standards, and many chose the higher standards; over time, the federal standards have moved upward to reflect the regulatory choices of these states.[92] On the international level Vogel's "California effect," however, is likely to be found in regulations that pertain to products rather than processes,[93] for reasons that relate to the

89. Richard L. Revesz, "Rehabilitating Interstate Competition: Rethinking the 'Race-to-the-Bottom' Rationale for Federal Environmental Regulation," *New York University Law Review* 67 (December 1992): 1229–1233. See also Peter P. Swire, "The Race to Laxity and the Race to Undesirability: Explaining Failures in Competition among Jurisdictions in Environmental Law," *Yale Law and Policy Review* 14 (1966): 88–89.

90. Langille, 329–338.

91. Muthukumara Mani and David Wheeler, "In Search of Pollution Havens? Dirty Industry in the World Economy, 1960 to 1995," *Journal of Environment and Development* 7/3 (September 1998): 215–247.

92. Vogel, *Trading Up*, 259–260.

93. Swire also makes this observation, 83.

structure of the international trading system under the GATT/WTO. Since most environmental regulations considered in discussions of pollution havens and races to the bottom relate to the production process (either as pollution byproducts or as unsustainable use of resources), that may limit the applicability of Vogel's model.

The race-to-the-bottom logic holds for labor issues as well. As Bruce Elmslie and William Milberg point out, "free international competition puts pressure on nations to bid down their social standards towards the level of the lowest standard country."[94] Paul Pierson and Stephan Leibfried suggest in the European context that without Europe-wide labor standards, firms in low-regulation areas could out-compete those with higher labor regulations, and that "these actions could fuel a downward spiral in social provision, eventually producing rudimentary, lowest-common-denominator social policies."[95]

Studies of labor standards in a domestic federal context provide additional evidence of the potential for different regulatory standards to lead to downward harmonization. In the United States up through the early twentieth century, individual states were responsible for laws (or lack thereof) regulating child labor. States with the strictest prohibitions on child labor found both that they lost industry to those with weaker rules, and also that the children themselves were brought from areas with high standards to those without. Ultimately child labor standards in the states became more uniform at a lower level, until federal legislation in 1906 began the process of restricting child labor.[96]

Interestingly, though, economic theory also suggests that the reverse may be true with some aspects of labor standards: low wage areas may not create a race to the bottom and instead may work to raise wage rates eventually. To the extent that states with low wages attract industry, there may be an upward pressure on wages once the industry is established in a given location. Increased competition for workers in an

94. Bruce Elmslie and William Milberg, "Free Trade and Social Dumping: Lessons from the Regulation of U.S. Interstate Commerce," *Challenge*, May/June 1996, 46.

95. Paul Pierson and Stephan Leibfried, "Multitiered Institutions and the Making of Social Policy," in Leibfried and Pierson, eds., *European Social Policy: Between Fragmentation and Integration* (Washington, D.C.: Brookings Institution, 1995), 27.

96. Elmslie and Milberg, 49–50.

expanding industry can drive wages up in the short run, and increased development in an area that results from industrial location can drive them up in the longer run. The garment industry illustrates this process, by which manufacturers move to locations to take advantage of low rates, and then move again once competition drives wages up.[97] The existence of different levels of labor standards—and, most obviously, wage rates—across states is thus clear.[98] What these differing levels mean about the evolution of standards in the longer run is less clear.

Finally, one important countervailing pressure to domestic decisions to lower standards may come from international regulatory cooperation. Katharina Holzinger and Christoph Knill suggest that instead of considering races to the bottom or harmonization upward as the two possible outcomes of competition under globalization, they should be seen as acting simultaneously in countervailing ways.[99] This perspective suggests that the incentives for races to the bottom may be operational, but may bring forth efforts at international cooperation by those determined to thwart such races. As the experience of shipping standards demonstrates, cooperative efforts to increase standards may indeed be motivated by the pressures on standards to race downward.

Standards of Major Ship Registries

It is already clear that ships are "moving" their registration to open registries. As discussed further in chapter 4, more than half of large commercial ships are currently flagged in open registry states, with a dramatic increase in the past several decades. Are these open registries providing the opportunity for ships to take on lower standards than registration in their "home" state would? Open registries certainly appear to use lax standards in their advertising, to lure ship registrations. Many

97. Ashoka Mody and David Wheeler, *Automation and World Competition: New Technologies, Industrial Location, and Trade* (New York: St. Martin's, 1990).

98. See, for example, Edward E. Leamer, "Wage Effects of a U.S.-Mexican Free Trade Agreement," in Peter M. Garber, ed., *The Mexico-U.S. Free Trade Agreement* (Cambridge: MIT Press, 1993), 63–71.

99. Katharina Holzinger and Christoph Knill, "Competition and Cooperation in Environmental Policy: Individual and Interaction Effects," *Journal of Public Policy* 24/1 (2004): 25–47.

registries not only advertise on the Internet but some even allow registration online.[100] Ship-registration sites make oblique comments about lax environmental standards ("shipowners can transfer foreign-registered vessels under twelve years old to the Bahamian flag without a survey"[101]) and labor standards ("liberal labor laws concerning Panama flag vessels are also an important consideration"[102]). Open registries generally promise low registration fees, tonnage taxes, and inspection fees, as well as no nationality requirements for owners or ship workers. What is the relationship between the standards offered by individual FOC states and global shipping standards? What happens to these standards over time?

One way to evaluate the question of what standards flag states are requiring of the ships they register is to look at which international agreements they have signed and ratified pertaining to environmental, safety, and labor protections on ships. These international agreements become domestic law in the states that ratify them, and it seems fair to assume that if states take the trouble to sign and ratify an international agreement it represents at least the minimum level of regulation that the state hopes to uphold. There are important advantages to comparing standards across states in this manner. Given the difficulty, discussed above, of comparing domestic regulations that take widely varying approaches, looking at international agreements compares acceptance across states of the same set of regulations. In addition, for states that are competing on the international market to attract ship registration, adoption or avoidance of international regulations is an obvious means of signaling level of regulation in a way that is publicly available. It is also important for understanding the politics of efforts to raise standards on ships, since nongovernmental organizations and some international agreements concerned about shipping standards use participation in

100. See, for example, Corporate and Maritime Administrator for the Republic of the Marshall Islands, "Vessel Registration and Mortgage Procedures—Register IRI," http://www.register-iri.com/content.cfm?catid=28.

101. Bahamas Investment Authority, "The Bahamas' Shipping Registry," http://www.interknowledge.com/bahamas/investment/shipng01.htm (as accessed: 8 February 2001). Recently registries have become more careful about not clearly advertising that they will not hold ships to international environmental standards.

102. Intertrust, "Ship Registration in Panama," http://www.intertrustpanama.com/panama/ship.html.

international agreements as one way to single out ships for additional scrutiny.

There are obvious problems with relying on ratification of international agreements as a measure of environmental, safety, and labor standards on ships, however. First, there are a few states that traditionally avoid participation in multilateral agreements despite relatively high standards in the regulated areas. In most cases, though, states that meet the level of regulation offered in an international agreement are likely to sign and ratify such an agreement. States that are generally reluctant (such as the United States), or are prevented from signing most international agreements (Taiwan), can be identified as outliers.

This approach likewise for initial analysis counts all treaties as equal, by simply comparing numbers of treaties accepted in a given issue area. Clearly this is unfair: some are more substantive or stringent than others, or deal with a more important aspect of the regulated area. (Compare ILO Convention 147 on minimum standards on a wide range of issues for merchant shipping to Convention 69 on "Certification of Ship's Cooks.") This is especially problematic with some international agreements (most prevalent under the ILO) that aggregate or replace previous agreements.[103] As needed individually, it can be observed whether states under consideration have ratified those agreements considered most important.

It is also worth noting that looking to treaty ratification (or even other domestic laws) to determine standards on ships assumes that states will in fact uphold, and require their ships to uphold, the standards they have officially adopted. While that is unlikely to be completely true, it is still likely that a state's willingness to take on international regulations does signal something about the level of environmental, safety, and labor standards it will require of ships in its registry. As such, this is a good initial proxy to get at the variations in standards across states. As avail-

103. Even more problematic are situations where one agreement replaces an earlier one, and the earlier one is no longer open for signature. In those cases, the old treaty must still be counted because some states may be party to it and not to the new one. But it does mean that states that gain a new interest in shipping do not have the full slate of ship treaties available to sign. The high numbers of labor treaties, where this issue is most prevalant, however, suggest that this problem should not make an enormous difference and that useful information can still be gained by looking at the percentages of treaties that states have ratified.

able, additional rankings of states on shipping-related standards are used. The most important of these is the *Flag State Audit*, by Nik Winchester and Tony Alderton, of the Seafarers International Research Centre (SIRC) in Cardiff, referred to here as the SIRC study.[104] They evaluate labor standards and practices of thirty-eight open registry states and include an A to E ranking of the standards adopted and welfare and labor rights of these registries. It is particularly useful to have this study as a point of comparison, since there are reasons to have less confidence in the representative nature of participation in ship labor agreements than in either the safety or environment agreements;[105] the SIRC data can therefore increase confidence in the assessment of an open registry as having high or low labor standards.

For the purposes of this study, the environmental regulations considered are twenty-four international agreements pertaining specifically to environmental protection from ships. These agreements are all under the auspices of the International Maritime Organization. The labor regulations initially considered are forty-seven agreements negotiated under the auspices of the International Labour Organisation (ILO). These include all agreements that specify that they pertain to ships or seafarers. The safety regulations considered are nineteen international agreements that focus on safety on ships, all but one under the IMO (the remaining one is an ILO agreement). See appendix B for a list of all international regulations included in this analysis.

Examining the international regulations adopted by the ships with the largest registries (as measured by registered gross tonnage (GT)), several things become immediately apparent (see table 2.1). The first is that there is no clear harmonization. Flag states have adopted different levels of registration, with some accepting a high number of regulations across the board (the Norwegian International Registry has accepted 91.6 percent of environmental, 94.7 percent of safety, and 68 percent of labor

104. Nik Winchester and Tony Alderton, *Flag State Audit 2003* (Cardiff: Seafarers International Research Centre, 2003).

105. The large number of potential agreements, some of which replace earlier ones, and some of which date back to before the time when many registries were operational, as well as a lower degree of international institutional mechanisms to determine whether states that agree to these standards uphold them, suggest that the international labor measurement is somewhat weaker than the environment and safety measures.

Table 2.1
Percentage of international agreements adopted by major open registries

State	GT2004	Environmental (percentage)	Safety (percentage)	Labor (percentage)
Panama	131,451,672	54.17	42.11	51.06
Liberia	53,898,761	70.83	57.89	29.79
Bahamas	35,388,244	66.67	52.63	12.77
Marshall Islands	22,494,505	66.67	57.89	0.00
Malta	22,352,570	62.50	57.89	29.79
Cyprus	21,283,373	58.33	73.68	19.15
NIS (Norway)	15,416,521	91.67	94.74	68.09
UK second registries	15,110,431	79.17	84.21	46.81
GIS (Germany)	8,246,428	88.00	84.21	46.81
DIS (Denmark)	7,284,769	92.00	84.21	42.55
Antigua and Barbuda	6,914,568	54.17	36.84	8.51
St. Vincent and Grenadines	6,324,289	50.00	52.63	14.89
French Antarctic Territory	3,524,865	75.00	84.21	63.83
CSR (Spain)	1,823,323	100.00	78.95	76.60
Cambodia	1,821,464	37.50	36.84	6.38
Vanuatu	1,756,498	83.33	52.63	0.00
Belize	1,687,460	37.50	31.58	44.68
Netherlands Antilles	1,661,631	75.00	78.95	59.57
MAR (Portugal)	1,143,306	62.50	63.16	38.30
Honduras	784,125	20.83	36.84	8.51
Luxembourg	689,658	33.33	47.37	42.55
Barbados	580,262	62.50	52.63	17.02
Myanmar	444,330	8.33	31.58	6.38
Comoros	388,519	33.33	31.58	6.38
Mongolia	359,901	25.00	15.79	6.38
Bolivia	302,971	25.00	36.84	6.38
Lebanon	184,055	33.33	42.11	23.40
Sri Lanka	156,608	50.00	47.37	17.02

Table 2.1
(continued)

State	GT2004	Environ-mental (percentage)	Safety (per-centage)	Labor (per-centage)
Jamaica	131,215	58.33	36.84	14.89
Tonga	109,074	75.00	68.42	0.00
Mauritius	79,000	62.50	47.37	17.02
São Tomé and Príncipe	57,809	25.00	36.84	6.38
Equatorial Guinea	27,933	37.50	42.11	10.64
Cook Islands (NZ)	26,108	58.33	68.42	31.91

Source: IMO, "Status of Conventions: Complete List," http://www.imo.org; ILO, "ILOlex: Database of International Standards," http://www.ilo.org/ilolex/english/convdisp2.htm. Lloyd's Register Fairplay, *World Fleet Statistics* 2004 (London: Lloyd's Register Fairplay, 2005).

agreements pertaining to ships) and some a much lower level of international regulation (Mongolia has adopted 25 percent of environmental, 15.8 percent of safety, and 6.4 percent of labor agreements).

Second, there is reasonable variation in which types of regulations states have adopted. Liberia, for instance, has adopted average-level environmental regulations (66.7 percent, which is the mean for the top twenty-five registries[106]), somewhat lower-than-average safety regulations (52.6 percent, with the top-twenty-five mean at 68.2 percent), and significantly lower-than-average labor regulations (12.8 percent, with a mean for the top twenty-five registries of 30.7 percent).

Third, the newest ship registries have lower standards, as indicated by adoption of international agreements, than the more established registries. For these purposes, states are counted as functional registries in the first year in which they have registered ten or more ships greater than 100 GT. Figure 2.1 shows the standards adopted by the thirteen newest registries, listed from most recent. The first thing to note is that the overall level of adoption of international standards is lower in this

106. Omitting Hong Kong, because of its change in sovereignty and the resulting changes in its regulatory oversight.

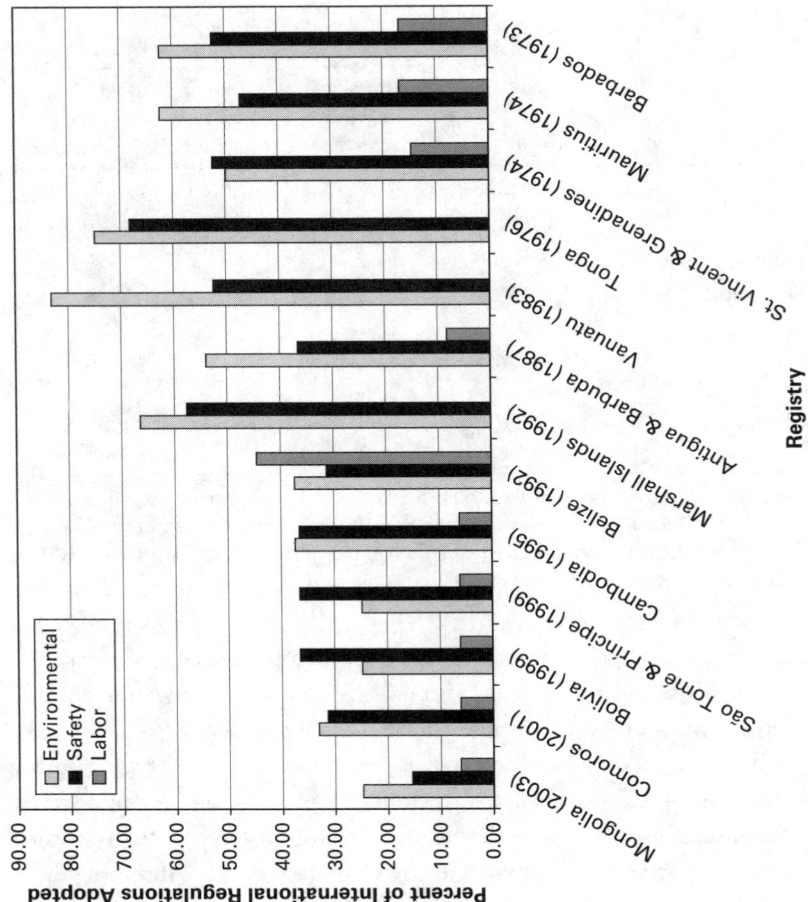

Figure 2.1
International regulations adopted by new registries

group than among the more established registries. Even more important, however, is that the older of the new registries have generally adopted more shipping regulations than the newest. The newest registries begin with particularly low standards and raise them over time.

At the same time, the standards required by ships registered in the major maritime states have been allowed to decline as well, though to a lesser extent. The increasing phenomenon of second and international registries, created by or in some way affiliated with traditional maritime states, accounts for a relaxing of some of the shipping standards previously upheld by major maritime states. Denmark, Germany, Norway, Portugal, and Spain have created international registries. These are open registries, in that they allow registration from any state, but they are targeted at, and generally composed of, ships whose beneficial ownership is in these states. Because these registries are located in the states in question, ships in the international registries are held to the same international agreements that the states have adopted. Two important constraints are relaxed, though: taxes and fees for registration are generally lower, and crewing restrictions are relaxed, allowing shipowners to hire crews from a wide variety of nationalities, at lower pay rates, and often with less experience.

A similar phenomenon is the opening of "second registries" in offshore territories. The UK, France, the Netherlands, and Belgium[107] all have a variety of second registries in their territories.[108] These function similarly to international registries but with more independence from the home state; while offshore territories generally adopt the same international agreements as their parent state, they do not always do so, including in the realm of shipping.[109] These, too, are general open registries, but also tend to register ships with beneficial ownership in the home state. They relax crewing requirements as well. The result is standards on the whole

107. Luxembourg serves as a nontraditional second registry for Belgium.

108. The differentiation between international and second registries is less clear than may be assumed. This list is based on Jessica S. Bernfeld, *Changing Tides: The Effects of Globalization on the Shipping Industries of Traditional Maritime States*, Wellesley College Honors Thesis, Wellesley, Mass., 2004, 21–45.

109. See, for example, Jean-Yves Hamon and Jean-Claude Dubois, "L'Avenire de la Flotte de Commerce Française," Affaire No. 1999-0217-01 (Paris: Conseil Général des Ponts et Chaussées et Inspection Général des Services des Affaires Maritimes, 1999), Annexe 5.

that are somewhat lower than in international registries and standard closed registries. That is particularly apparent when comparing SIRC's ranking of welfare provision and rights protection; in all cases where the home state and its second or international registry is examined, the home state has a better record on shipping labor protections than the international or second registry.[110]

These results can be characterized as a "race to the middle" in terms of level of standards adopted globally. Traditional maritime states begin with high standards and relax them a bit (through establishing international or second registries) in order to keep ships of their nationals from "flagging out." Most new states enter the market to offer ship registrations with quite low standards and they are persuaded, by a variety of mechanisms examined in this book, to raise them at least somewhat. They rarely do so to the level of the traditional maritime states, ending up instead somewhere in the regulatory middle.

Regulatory Niches

Even more interesting is that these standards do not end up in the same regulatory middle—instead, ship registries seem to specialize within a range of midlevel regulatory options. How can the various regulatory niches of the open registries be characterized? It has already been suggested that states that newly offer ship registration do so with generally low standards on environmental, safety, and labor issues. But what of longtime registries? How can their level and type of standards be characterized, and what is the relationship between these standards and the number and type of ships that choose to register there? It is worth examining the strategies of several specific states or groups of states. This section only considers states that have been functional registries[111] since 1995 or earlier. It also evaluates only the regulatory records of the open registries (as opposed to the national registries) because it is only they who can "compete" for additional ship registrations.[112]

110. Winchester and Alderton, 23.

111. With the same definition as above: more than 10 ships of 100 GT registered.

112. The standards adopted by closed (national) registries are important, but since they cannot be used strategically, it does not make sense to consider these states as carving out regulatory niches.

The High End

As suggested above, the international and second registries with a connection to Norway, Germany, Denmark, Spain, Portugal, France, the Netherlands, New Zealand, and the United Kingdom (and, to a lesser extent, Luxembourg, which acts as a second registry for Belgium) are on the higher end of international standards. Though they have a poorer record on labor than do the home registries from these states, their efforts to attract registrations do not come primarily from lowered standards. Together these registries account for about 9 percent of all registered tonnage.[113]

The Low End

Honduras, one of the first open registries, beginning before World War II, is currently placing itself on the low end of international regulations across the board. It adopted 20.8 percent of environmental, 8.5 percent of labor, and 36.8 percent of safety international agreements pertaining to ships. In addition, SIRC ranks it as "poor" (the second to lowest ranking) in all of the categories the study examines. As of 2004 it was the sixty-third largest ship registry, accounting for .12 percent of registered tonnage. Though this may seem like a small number, it represents 1,094 ships larger than 100 GT.[114] Unlike many open registries that attract large numbers of ships from specific countries, there are no states that account for more than 10 percent of the beneficial ownership of Honduran-registered vessels.[115] Honduras thus seems to serve as the classic flag of convenience for shipowners that want consistently low standards. There is some evidence that the Honduran registry is making an effort to improve its record,[116] but it remains to be seen how serious this effort is.

113. Calculated from data in Lloyd's Register Fairplay, *World Fleet Statistics 2004*.

114. Calculated from data in Lloyd's Register Fairplay, *World Fleet Statistics 2004*.

115. Winchester and Alderton, 190. "Beneficial Ownership," as measured by Lloyd's Register, counts ships that are beneficially owned and/or controlled in foreign countries.

116. Winchester and Alderton, 188.

Low Labor

For the purposes of this study, ship registries are considered to have low labor standards if they have adopted fewer than 20 percent of the relevant ship labor agreements, and are also rated "poor" or "very poor" on ship-related welfare and rights provision by SIRC. This double bar to being designated a "low-labor" registry requires that states both have avoided international obligations on ship labor and have a poor record of protecting the rights of ship workers in domestic practice. Not counting Honduras (which is considered low in all categories as discussed above), eight open registries meet this standard: Antigua and Barbuda, the Bahamas, Barbados, Cambodia, the Marshall Islands, St. Vincent and the Grenadines, Cyprus, and Vanuatu.[117]

There is evidence that ship registration takes note of these regulatory choices. Passenger and cruise ships, the most labor-intensive of shipping operations, are overwhelming registered in states identified here in the "low-labor" niche. The largest registry for cruise ships by far is the Bahamas, which has adopted only 12.8 percent of relevant ILO labor agreements and is ranked by SIRC as "poor" on labor and welfare rights. Approximately 40 percent of both cruise and passenger ships worldwide are registered in the Bahamas,[118] with additional tonnage registered in the low-labor states of the Marshall Islands, Cyprus, and Saint Vincent and the Grenadines.

High Environment

States are assigned to this category if they have adopted more than 70 percent of the relevant ship-related international environmental agreements. The only two truly open registries that meet this standard are Liberia and Vanuatu. Note as well that Vanuatu was listed as having

117. Tonga could technically fit either on this list or—after a very recent spate of ratification of environmental agreements—onto the "high environment, low labor" list, but Tonga closed its registry in 2002 after several Tongan ships were found with links to terrorists or carrying weapons. Ships already in the registry have up to 5 years to find a new registry, and the registered tonnage has begun to decrease dramatically. See "Tonga Pulls the Plug on Tarnished Register," *Lloyd's List*, April 16, 2002, 1. In addition, Jamaica, Myanmar, and Sri Lanka are not ranked by SIRC and are therefore excluded from this list.

118. Institute of Shipping Economics and Logistics, *ISL Shipping Statistics Yearbook 2004* (Bremen: ISL, 2004), 94, 100.

particularly low labor standards; it might be reasonable to speak of a specific "high-environment, low-labor" niche to which Vanuatu belongs. Liberia accounts for 8.51 percent of registered tonnage, and Vanuatu for .28 percent.[119]

High Safety

States are considered as having a high safety ranking if they have adopted more than 70 percent of the relevant ship-related international safety agreements. The only truly open registry that fits in this category is Cyprus, which, notably, is also in the low-labor category as well. Cyprus could thus be more accurately characterized as occupying a "high-safety, low-labor" niche. Cyprus accounts for 3.36 percent of registered tonnage.[120]

The True Middle

While all open registries not listed in other categories here have neither especially high nor low levels of regulations on these three issues, Panama represents an almost quintessential race to the middle. It has adopted just about half of all agreements examined here (54 percent of environmental, 51 percent of labor, and 42.1 percent of safety agreements). It is characterized by SIRC as having "moderate performance" in its use of flag-state authority.[121] Panama is the largest ship registry in the world, accounting for 20.8 percent of registered tonnage.[122]

Note that that there is no "high-labor" category for open registries, though of course the states listed as "the high end" obviously have reasonably high labor standards, along with moderately high environmental and safety records. These international and second registries are ranked lower on welfare and labor rights pertaining to ships by SIRC, however,

119. Calculated from data in Lloyd's Register Fairplay, *World Fleet Statistics 2004*.

120. Calculated from data in Lloyd's Register Fairplay, *World Fleet Statistics 2004*.

121. Winchester and Alderton, 23. The SIRC study does rank it as "poor" in welfare and rights provisions and protection, however.

122. Calculated from data in Lloyd's Register Fairplay, *World Fleet Statistics 2004*.

than their national registries are. The open registry with the highest adoption of international labor standards is the Spanish second registry in the Canary Islands (77.6 percent), ranked by SIRC as "moderate" on welfare/rights. Second is the Norwegian International Register (68 percent), but since it is ranked by SIRC as "poor" on welfare/rights, it seems unrealistic to characterize it as a true high-labor-standards registry. More importantly, though, while there are registries that have low or middling standards in two of the three categories that choose a high level of regulation in the third, that phenomenon does not happen with labor standards. If registries are choosing to single themselves out for those ships that want high standards in one category but not others, it is not high labor standards in which they choose to specialize.

The bulk of this book examines the process by which ship registries arrive at the standards they have adopted, and in particular the efforts by others to persuade them to raise those standards. It is that pressure upward, combined with the downward pressure exerted by cost in an era of global competition, that leads to the general regulatory middle in which ship registration falls.

Conclusions

Theory and research on the relationship between globalization and standards suggest several things of relevance to understanding ship registration and regulation. First, if there is to be movement of industries, it is likely to happen with those with particularly high environmental or labor costs from regulation, rather than all industries. With labor the most expensive operational cost in shipping,[123] it is no surprise that "movement" of ship registration should be as prominent as it has become.

The observation that industries will move when environmental regulations in industrialized states make it simply impossible to operate also applies: in some cases older ships that are not physically constructed in ways that meet newer environmental standards would not be able to register in traditional maritime states, at least not without expensive retrofitting. If their owners want to operate them, registering abroad may be the

123. Martin Stopford, *Maritime Economics*, 2nd ed. (London: Routledge, 1997), 160.

only option. This observation also has implications for efforts to eliminate substandard ships: if there will always be states willing to register these vessels, then efforts to make them uneconomical will have to target the locations to which they travel, rather than those at which they register. And since the effects of any accidents will more likely be experienced at their destinations rather than their point of registration, this may be politically possible.

One of the dangers of using low environmental standards to attract or maintain industry is that the environmental externalities of industrial activity will accrue primarily to the state that has done so. This is, in fact, one of the reasons given for eventual upward pressure on environmental standards, as those who experience the environmental effects put pressure on a government to decrease pollution.[124] But in the case of ships, this logic does not hold, since ships need not even call at ports in the states in which they are registered (and, in the case of landlocked open registries like Bolivia, they cannot). The globalization of labor on ships, likewise, suggests that nationals of registry states are not any more likely to be employed on these ships, and thus will not be particularly impacted by low labor standards.

As such, ship registration should be a more likely opportunity for states wishing to maintain low standards to attract business than would be the case for other types of industry. Conversely, it should be harder to persuade registry states to increase standards, since their domestic populations, which never feel the effects of low regulations, are unlikely to demand it. If standards are to be improved, domestic pressure will not be the primary impetus. This issue area is thus simultaneously an easy and hard case for examining the relationship between globalization and standards.

Evidence that industries might not move if they have already adapted to regulatory costs, or that demands across different markets would influence harmonization in an upward direction, suggests different incentives for different ships. Those that have already adopted costly equipment standards (like double hulls or segregated ballast tanks for oil

124. World Bank, *World Development Report 1992: Development and the Environment* (New York: Oxford University Press, 1992), 38–43; Jordi Roca, "Do Individual Preferences Explain the Environmental Kuznets Curve?", *Ecological Economics* 45/1 (April 2003): 3–10.

tankers) required in traditional maritime states may indeed lose incentives to register elsewhere based simply on those types of environmental regulations. (In fact, they may join the call for higher standards elsewhere as a strategy to drive competitors out of business.) But much of the costliness of shipping comes from the types of standards—such as the labor costs and non-equipment-based environmental and safety standards—that will continue to be costly once adopted and that ships could avoid by moving to a location without these requirements. The general observation that industrialized states are willing to scale back regulations when they threaten to impact competitiveness nicely explains the development of second and international registries by traditional maritime states when their ships began flagging out to truly open registries.

Overall, the broad evidence that different levels of regulation and widely divergent wage rates can persist across states despite high degrees of globalization accurately reflects the situation in global shipping.

In turn, decisions by shipowners about where to register (locate) their vessels may resolve some of the disagreements about regulatory havens and races to the bottom. First, to the extent that the cost or difficulty of moving a business to an area of low regulation makes a difference in the decision of industry actors about where to locate, the ease and costlessness of ship registration should suggest that it is an easy case for industry relocation for standards. Indeed, the fact that most large commercial ships are now registered in open registries, with lower standards in aggregate, suggests that industrial relocation will happen. If races to the regulatory bottom were going to happen anywhere, this is where we should expect them. But while there are opportunities for ships to choose lower standards, no actual race to the bottom ensues.

Moreover, to the extent that the "race" to the middle in shipping can fit Zarsky's "stuck-in-the-mud" characterization, the causal relationship is the reverse of what she predicts. Zarsky argues that globalization, as an exogenous process, prevents states from increasing standards they otherwise might, because of the costliness—in a competitive global economy—of being the first state to improve environmental protection.[125] In the case of shipping, states had much more agency in creating

125. Zarsky, 24.

globalization in the first place, precisely as a way to avoid increasing domestic standards. As discussed in chapter 4, the United States allowed, and even encouraged, the creation of the Panamanian open registry (and others that followed) as a way to protect shipping costs from rising domestic standards.

Nevertheless, the correlate to Zarsky's argument is that standards will only rise in conjunction; no state is willing to do so alone. As the next chapters illustrate, states do not make individual decisions to increase environmental, safety, and labor standards to which ships under their flags are held. Instead they do so collectively, through international collective action both to establish the higher standards and to enforce them.

But the shipping case also challenges the argument that standards are stuck (either "in the mud" or "at the bottom").[126] They do increase over time, to at least a middle regulatory range. The observation from the literature that even initially low (or, more tellingly, lowered) standards tend to be raised over time is reflected in even this preliminary overview of ship regulation, in a way that may allow an in-depth analysis of shipping standards to comment more broadly on globalization/regulation debates. The low standards that continually exist are there because new entrants to the ship-registration market offer low-standard ship registry when previous low-standard states raise theirs, not because states with low standards are unable to raise them.

It is important, but not sufficient, to observe that these standards can be raised over time; we need to understand the mechanisms by which this happens. Is it, as sometimes implicitly suggested, a simple evolution? Does the domestic population, when faced with higher income alongside environmental degradation, begin to demand higher standards? Does the labor force, better trained, begin to demand higher wages or better labor protections? Do pressures from outside the state—other states, international organizations, or international nongovernmental organizations—pressure governments to raise their standards? How? Simply noting that there is a tendency for states (especially developing states) to increase labor and environmental standards over time, or with increased income, does not itself specify the process by which that transpires. Vogel and Kagan observe that we should only expect upward harmonization when

126. Zarsky or Gareth Porter's characterizations, respectively.

states with high standards have market power.[127] Close attention to this process in the shipping industry may thus contribute insights to other areas where similar tensions exist. If races to the bottom do not transpire, understanding what prevents or reverses them is important.

The observation of regulatory niches in the shipping industry may also be an insight that can be usefully examined in other issue areas. To what extent are these niches happenstance versus intentional efforts to court ship registrations of a particular type, and do they succeed for the states that follow these strategies? If regulatory specialization, especially among states that have not adopted especially high standards, is an intentional strategy in shipping, it suggests important lessons about how regulatory havens can persist and can avoid becoming races to the bottom.

127. David Vogel and Robert A. Kagan, eds., *Dynamics of Regulatory Change: How Globalization Affects National Regulatory Policies* (Berkeley: University of California Press, 2004), 23.

3

Exclusion as Incentive: The Power of Clubs

As the following chapters demonstrate, the low standards with which most new open ship registries begin, and that individual shipowners prefer, can be moved upward significantly. This is not an automatic process, but rather one that requires concerted collective action to challenge the economic incentives faced by almost all involved in the industry to keep costs as low as possible. Examining what types of actions have succeeded, or failed, in moving standards upward is important to understanding the shipping industry and the international regulation of the ocean. It can also shed light on efforts to raise international standards under globalization more generally, suggesting broader conclusions about which actors, in which ways, will have both the incentives and the abilities to increase the level of regulation followed in an anarchic system. The innovation of the collective action undertaken to raise environmental, safety, and labor standards on ships is that it involves changing the issue structure of the problems faced. Cooperation that would have been about a common-pool resource or a public good becomes a club good instead, in which actors can be excluded from benefits if they do not participate in increasing standards.

Much of the difficulty inducing states to create, implement, or enforce international regulation comes in cases where states can receive much of the benefit from actions taken by others without having to uphold an agreement themselves. If by free riding they can receive the advantages without the cost, there is an incentive to remain apart from cooperation. States that remain outside of the set of international agreements to prevent climate change, for instance, would benefit from the effect on the global climate system that comes from the actions of others, without having to undertake costly economic changes themselves. A related difficulty comes from the benefit that states can gain by *not* adhering to an international standard. States may avoid adopting international labor agreements mandating higher wages or better benefits, or may prefer not to accept mandated technological requirements to prevent pollution. If they can avoid the costs associated with implementing high standards, they would often prefer to do so, especially when engaged in economic competition with those who do adopt these standards.

Both of these problems can be seen in the case of flag-of-convenience shipping. To the extent that open registry states may suffer from oil pollution in the ocean or depleted fishery resources, the negative utility from these problems is shared by all actors, while the positive utility of undertaking actions that contribute to these problems goes entirely to the FOC state.[1] To the extent these states are even affected by the issues at hand,[2] they may be able to benefit from the collective action taken by others without having to protect these resources themselves. Similarly, if they avoid taking on internationally mandated equipment to decrease the likelihood of oil pollution or International Labour Organisation standards that raise the wages or labor protections of ship workers, they save money in a global shipping industry that runs on thin profit margins.

To understand the types of strategies we should expect to be successful at raising standards on ships, it helps to begin with an examination of the structure of various types of goods. It is useful to think of two different characteristics of goods (or issues) that each have two ideal-type states. The first is whether the good is excludable: can actors be kept from access to it? The second is whether something is rival (also referred to as subtractable): can it be used up, or its use diminished by the use of others? These characteristics are illustrated in figure 3.1. Private goods are those that are both rival and excludable. Because they are things that are clearly able to be owned by a given actor who can keep others from using them, they tend not to be discussed in the context of international relations. A state's own sovereign territory can be considered to

1. This is Hardin's classic "tragedy of the commons" formulation. Garrett Hardin, "The Tragedy of the Commons," *Science* 162 (December 13, 1968): 1243–1248.

2. Recent landlocked open registry states, Bolivia and Mongolia, are less affected than others by the threat of oil pollution and depleted fisheries, and thus even less likely to be harmed by their own low-standard activity than others are.

		Excludable	
		Y	**N**
Rival	**Y**	**Private goods** (ex: a sandwich)	**Common-pool resources** (ex: a fishery, a commons)
	N	**Club goods** (ex: toll highway)	**Public goods** (ex: public radio)

Figure 3.1
Types of goods

be a private good, and in some ways its control over the actions of its nationals traditionally fits within this category. Globalization, however, challenges a state's control over the behavior of its citizens, creating a set of international problems with different types of characteristics.

The examination of international cooperation, particularly relating to environmental protection, focuses primarily on common-pool resources or public goods, with the important distinction involving whether the issue in question is rival. J. Samuel Barkin and George E. Shambaugh argue that most international environmental issues can best be characterized as common-pool resources. Most environmental resources—the atmosphere, the oceans—are not realistically excludable. They are also rival, in that a lack of cooperation allows for the diminishment of the resource.[3] This dynamic is especially easy to understand in the ocean environment. Unregulated access to ocean resources (be they fisheries or deep seabed minerals) can lead to their depletion; the quality of the ocean ecosystem diminishes when not protected from pollution.

3. J. Samuel Barkin and George E. Shambaugh, eds., *Anarchy and the Environment: The International Relations of Common Pool Resources* (Albany: SUNY Press, 1999).

Take the protection of fish stocks, for example. With respect to excludability, it is nearly impossible in a practical sense for fishers to be excluded from physical access to fish in the open ocean. That means that even if many states join together to create fishery conservation agreements that restrict their fishing behavior, those who are not members cannot be prevented from access to the resource. This lack of excludability is true both legally, since states cannot be forced to join international agreements, and practically, since areas in the open ocean cannot be fenced off. Likewise, the resource is rival: every fish that is taken by someone leaves one fewer in the ocean (and, in the longer run, one fewer to reproduce, so many fewer in the future).

The combination of rivalness and nonexcludability creates a situation in which it is difficult to prevent the resource from being depleted. States are reluctant to create or join strong cooperative agreements to protect the fish stock, since they know that it is difficult to prevent access by others (or even illegal access by those in the agreement) to the resource. More importantly, anyone who does access the stock outside of the regulatory restrictions is not simply avoiding participation in a cooperative outcome, but is in fact undermining the ability of others to protect it, since the resource is rival. A strong and fully enforced agreement to restrict fishing by the members of a fishery conservation organization may fail to protect a resource if a major actor outside of the agreement fishes without regard to the restrictions.

International cooperative agreements are difficult under many circumstances. In most cases the best option for a state would be free riding—not cooperating (e.g., fishing as much as it can), while others cooperate (e.g., restrict their fishing). But the fact that all states have that preference structure makes cooperation difficult, since all would prefer to free ride while others cooperate. In the case of a rival resource, this potential for free riding is particularly damaging, since actors who want to protect the resource know that their protection of it can fail entirely with sufficient free riding. If they are not persuaded that such free riding can be avoided they may not be willing to cooperate themselves, since to do so would be doubly problematic: they would forgo the advantages of unrestricted fishing in the present *and* fail to protect the fishery for the future. If cooperation is likely to fail, it would be better at least to get some access to the resource before it does. Counterintuitively this incentive structure might account for the weakness of most fishery conservation agreements: states are unwilling to restrict their own behavior when they are not certain that the regime can sufficiently restrict the behavior of others.

This dynamic also has implications for the negotiations to address these types of problems, since the states that rely less on the resource and can thus afford to hold out on agreeing to a cooperative solution are in a better bargaining position and thus likely to gain more (relatively) in a cooperative agreement. This gain is possible because the state that needs the resource more cannot afford to let it be depleted and must concede in order to gain agreement on a cooperative solution.[4] Weak agreements result.

Other international issues that are less subject to rivalness but are still not excludable are properly described as public goods. These include financial and monetary stability, and collective security. They experience the free-rider problem as well in the provision of the good itself. Since it would always be better, if possible, to leave the provision of a good to others if you are still free to take advantage of it once it is provided, public goods are underprovided. The lack of rivalness in these issues, however, makes the problems caused by free riders potentially less dire. Once a public good is provided it does not become less useful if additional actors use it. The benefit one state receives from a stable monetary system does not decrease its advantage to others; it may even increase the economic gains to all. If there is a set of actors that is willing and able to provide a public good for the advantages they can receive from doing so,[5] they may do so even if there are large numbers of free riders.

4. J. Samuel Barkin, "Time-Horizons and Multilateral Enforcement in International Cooperation," *International Studies Quarterly* 48/2 (June 2004): 363–382. See also J. Samuel Barkin and Elizabeth R. DeSombre, "Unilateralism and Multilateralism in International Fisheries Management," *Global Governance* 6 (2000): 339–360.

5. See, for example, Mancur Olson, *The Logic of Collective Action: Public Goods and the Theory of Groups* (Cambridge: Harvard University Press, 1965); Stephen Krasner, "State Power and the Structure of International Trade," *World Politics* 28/3 (April 1976): 317–347; Robert Gilpin, *U.S. Power and the Multinational Corporation* (New York: Basic Books, 1975); Robert Gilpin, *War and Change in World Politics* (Cambridge: Cambridge University Press, 1982); Robert O. Keohane, *After Hegemony: Cooperation and Discord in the World Political Economy* (Princeton: Princeton University Press, 1984); Duncan Snidal, "The Limits of Hegemonic Stability Theory," *International Organization* 39/4 (autumn 1985): 579–614.

In some instances of international regulation, however, the benefits created are excludable, and can be kept from those who do not participate. This type of issue generates added incentives for states to adopt the international standards in question. It creates what is sometimes known as a club good, because the benefits of membership belong to those in the "club" and not to others.[6] Some refer to this type of good as a toll good.[7] Free-trade agreements, in which trade barriers are reduced but only for those who participate in the cooperative agreement, are the quintessential example of agreements that accomplish their goals in part through the creation of a set of advantages that accrue to members and that are not available to those who do not join the agreement. Collective defense—as distinct from collective security—is another example.

Club goods are less frequently discussed in international relations than are public goods or common-pool resources, but certainly play an important role in international cooperation. The main advantage that club goods have over public goods or common-pool resources for the creation of cooperative agreements is the element of exclusion. It is the possibility of free riding—actors gaining the benefits of an agreement without fully participating—that is seen as the main cause of the underprovision of collective goods.[8] Club goods, by allowing those who do not cooperate to be kept from the benefits of the cooperative arrangement, increase the likelihood that those who would benefit from access to the advantages of the club can be persuaded to join the cooperative effort.

There are some issues that have characteristics of club goods on their own. In other cases, however, it may be possible to create elements of a club good within an international agreement or other action. Free trade, for example, does not exist without states cooperatively removing trade barriers; generally it is applied as a club such that the barriers are removed only with respect to other states that agree to do the same. The type of good provided, then, is an essential element of the cooperation itself. Any time you can exclude actors from some benefit they desire if they do not undertake the action you want, you are creating club aspects

6. J. M. Buchanan, "An Economic Theory of Clubs," *Economica* 32 (1965): 1–14.

7. Elinor Ostrom, Roy Gardner, and James Walker, *Rules, Games, and Common-Pool Resources* (Ann Arbor: University of Michigan Press, 1994), 7.

8. See, for example, Keohane, *After Hegemony*.

to a good. A collective-defense pact in which all members of the group agree to come to the aid of others if they are in danger (but not to the aid of those not in the pact) is a club.

In some ways the creation of a club can have a similar effect to side payments, where actors are granted additional benefits if they take certain actions. But in its purest form a club good is nonrival; in other words, club goods are not diminished by the number of actors that partake of the club, which is not the case with side payments. It is for this reason that international fisheries organizations themselves do not create club goods; the rival nature of a fishery (in that the fish caught by one is no longer available to be caught by another) means that what these organizations explicitly regulate is a common-pool resource. Side payments to actors to persuade them to refrain from fishing[9] become increasingly expensive as more actors are brought in to the agreement. Such an arrangement is also subject to moral hazard, as those that might have been willing to restrict their fishing behavior without side payments discover that they can refuse to do so as a bargaining strategy unless offered such payments.

Access to markets, however, has a nonrival aspect and thus has the characteristics of a club. Because actors benefit from the access to the club itself, they do not have to "paid" as such to be brought in; the membership in the club is itself the reward. And increasing the number of actors does not necessarily increase the cost. In fact, it can have the opposite effect: if some actors are excluded from the market, those who do participate may be able to sell more fish and may be able to sell at a higher price. When states agree to only import fish from other states that have accepted provisions of international fisheries agreements, they create a club, and those in the club profit.

Clubs are rarely free. The creation of some type of exclusion mechanism where it does not naturally exist is likely to have some degree of cost. A toll highway works by restricting access and setting up a process for collecting the toll; neither aspect exists naturally and both entail a cost to create. Free-trade agreements require the ability to distinguish where goods are coming from in order to determine the level of protection applied to them, and a process for implementing restrictions or

9. Even apart from the fact that such an agreement would be difficult to enforce.

tariffs on those that are not a part of the agreement. The cost of these mechanisms will presumably be less than the benefit that accrues to members; otherwise the good is unlikely to be provided.[10] The ability to create a club, therefore, can depend on the costliness of the method of exclusion, and the benefits of the ability to exclude to those who bear that cost.

Clubs can also be created by different types of actors: states, international organizations, nonstate actors, or some combination thereof. Which actors participate in the creation and enforcement of a club will have an impact on the type of mechanisms of exclusion that are possible. There are many strategies, such as those that pertain to what can cross borders or not, that are available only to states. In addition, enforcement powers are likely to be greater on the part of states, which can bring their resources and authority to bear in ensuring that a club remains closed to outsiders. Nevertheless, sufficiently motivated nonstate actors should be able to create clubs or processes with clublike exclusion mechanisms that pertain to their interests and abilities. It could be argued that labeling—such as the "dolphin-safe tuna" label and associated consumer pressure to purchase only tuna caught in ways that do not harm dolphins—can be seen as a club created and enforced primarily by nonstate actors. Because these actors do not have the same types of resources or control over territory (or official governmental operations) that states do, the point of access will likely be different. We should expect clubs created by nonstate actors to have their primary effect on nonstate actors.

A club is most likely to be created in the enforcement stage, but the types of rules chosen (or other characteristics of the issue area) can influence the ease of creating a club through enforcement mechanisms. Ronald Mitchell, for example, argues that for the purpose of preventing intentional oil pollution from tankers (which discharged oily waste in the water they took on as ballast), discharge standards were almost impossible to enforce because it was hard to trace an oil slick to the ship that generated it, and each ship had the ability to discharge oil on each trip it made. Equipment standards, on the other hand, proved relatively easy to enforce in this case, because it was easy to determine whether ships were constructed with the necessary pollution-prevention equipment,

10. R. Cornes and T. Sander, *The Theory of Externalities, Public Goods and Club Goods* (Cambridge: Cambridge University Press, 1996), 349.

and their opportunities to pollute were virtually eliminated if they had the required equipment.[11] Determining what labor standards a state (or more importantly, an economic entity within a state) is applying requires more intrusive, and constant, monitoring; there are no obvious ways to ensure that these standards are being followed. We may, therefore, expect certain kinds of clubs to be easier to enforce than others.

The creation of a club to enforce collective standards is a logical response to race-to-the-bottom regulatory incentives. Those that are concerned about the impacts of globalization on sovereignty point to the potential for globalization to undermine the ability of states to make regulatory decisions within their jurisdictions. If citizens find ways to avoid income taxes by sheltering their income in secret offshore bank accounts, or engage in activities via the Internet that are prohibited within the state they live in, states are seen to have lost some degree of control. It is in the absence of this type of control that a potential race to the regulatory bottom (or at least the creation of regulatory havens) can happen. As long as states do not have the ability to control the behavior of their citizens, others are free to compete to offer them options to escape the regulatory environment their states wish to impose. That this competition would be in laxity is understandable: it is only because citizens seek to avoid the regulatory stringency of their own states that they go looking elsewhere. This structure does not ensure that an actual race to the bottom will happen, but it does suggest that the incentive exists for some jurisdictions to enter the "regulatory" market at the low end.

Sovereignty is in a way the power of exclusion, and the globalization of economic activity has removed this power of exclusion. In doing so, it has transformed issues about either private or club goods into those that instead become public goods or common-pool resources. Some of this transformation is physical: the human ability to degrade the environment has increased dramatically through advancing technology, and issues that once would have been local now become global in ways that change the issue structure because the harms and the advantages of an activity no longer accrue to the same actor.[12] These are assisted by the

11. Ronald B. Mitchell, *Intentional Oil Pollution at Sea* (Cambridge: MIT Press, 1994).

12. It is also the case that activities that appeared to be local, such as cutting down a tree, are now known to have impacts at a much greater geographic distance.

increase in international transport and economic interchange, and the ability of actors to escape domestic regulatory control. The creation of club goods is a way to attempt to bring exclusion back into the regulatory process.

As the rest of this book demonstrates, in the efforts to respond to low shipping standards the actions that have enjoyed the most success at gaining adherence to international standards have done so by creating the elements of some kind of club. Equipment standards created under International Maritime Organization agreements that require that ships be constructed in certain ways set the stage for the creation of a club. But it is through port state control agreements—like the various memoranda of understanding (MOUs)—that the club is implemented, as discussed in chapter 5. States agree not to admit ships without certain equipment into their ports, or to detain ships until they meet the prevailing requirements.

Labor unions can form clubs. As discussed in chapter 6, the International Transport Workers Federation (ITF), a global labor union, organizes dockworkers and others who service ships in important ports. They can create a sufficiently influential club that ships can be excluded from important services if they do not adopt prevailing standards. If time (or perishable merchandise) is lost due to the unwillingness of ITF members to service a ship, the advantages to shipowners of lower labor standards diminishes. If the price of access to dockworkers is upholding certain labor protections, a reasonable number of open registry vessels have concluded that admission to the club is worth the cost. The advantage to the club is augmented when those who choose to ship cargo demand that the ships they use participate in this club.

The success of economic sanctions at gaining adherence to fishery agreements discussed in chapter 7 likewise comes from the creation of a trading club. Those that want to sell fish to anyone within a set of fishery agreements, which often includes the large American or Japanese markets, must live up to certain fishery agreements or regulations in order to be able to do so. This requirement has caused some open registry states to join fishery conservation agreements and other owners of individual fishing vessels to lose their incentive to flag in states that do not take on the regulations. In the trading club created around fishing regulations it is most frequently the state rather than the individual vessel that is held to the standard. It is therefore more difficult for individual vessels to gain admission to the club if they are flagged in open registry states, especially those that have been identified as operating outside the regulatory system.

And though industry actors, such as shipowners and those who use ships to transport their goods, are generally the ultimate target of existing clubs, they too create some clublike organizations to attempt to help them better face the types of clubs others create. There are now large numbers of industry-based inspection processes that ships choose to undergo in an effort to enable them to better face the more official and exclusionary inspection processes that they will face externally. And the creation of these processes itself discriminates so that membership in an industry organization (be it the classification society that classes the ship, or the organization of shipowners that negotiates on behalf of its members) confers benefits via its good reputation. These arrangements are examined in chapter 8.

The evidence shows that clubs can indeed be hard to enforce, especially by nonstate actors. Part of what is remarkable about the degree of success of the ITF campaign is that many of the standards that organization attempts to enforce are in fact quite difficult to maintain as club goods. Determining whether ships pay a sufficient wage for reasonable working hours to crew members requires intrusive documentation and interviewing. To be willing to do so implies a particularly strong interest in the outcome. In this case the ITF is more likely to be willing to undertake the effort because its members directly benefit from the raising of labor standards on ships. Moreover, the shipowners agree to contribute money to ITF programs in order to obtain membership in this club, and this funding goes to support the ITF's efforts to operate the club. Some developing countries initially suspicious of the ITF came to understand that it could protect their role as labor suppliers to the global shipping market by excluding new entrants (especially from East Europe) to the shipping labor pool.[13]

Exclusion of fish from a market also requires a willingness to undertake fairly intrusive action, since it would not be apparent from the shipment

13. Nathan Lillie, "Global Collective Bargaining on Flag of Convenience Shipping," *British Journal of Industrial Relations* 42/1 (March 2004): 58.

of fish itself whether it had been caught in compliance with fishery regulations. It is precisely for this reason that these types of sanctions have been frequently found to be in violation of international trade law, as discussed further in chapter 7.

Perhaps the most effective efforts at exclusion are now being practiced by one of the most influential clubs on the international scene: the European Union. The European Commission warned Cyprus and Malta that their shipping policies could have an impact on the willingness of the EU to accept their membership, after which the two states radically upgraded their shipping standards. Moreover, joining the EU required that these two states (as well as any other future entrants) meet EU maritime safety standards.[14] For a number of states, EU membership is a sufficient advantage in other ways that they are willing to increase environment, safety, and labor requirements across a number of issues to be able to join. And although there is little to guarantee that Cypriot- or Maltese-registered ships would not reflag elsewhere, the general efforts to raise standards are limiting the number of opportunities to fly a true flag of convenience. Other potential EU entrants have recently raised their shipping standards. For example, in 2005 Turkey adopted ten ship-related ILO labor agreements,[15] as well as other international agreements relating to environment and safety rules.[16]

Other proposed solutions to the problems of open registries and low-standard ships would also have the characteristics of clubs, but those that would be particularly costly to enforce. The possibility of limiting trade to that which can be carried on nationally flagged vessels, discussed further in chapter 9, is introduced periodically in most of the major maritime states, but never makes it particularly far in the political process. While such a measure would be theoretically possible, and would certainly end the incentive for most ships to flag in open registry states, it would be incredibly costly, and thus unlikely to be worth the benefits it would create for the states that have considered adopting it.

14. Janet Porter, "The Sorry State of Cyprus Ships," *Journal of Commerce*, June 11, 1997, 7A.

15. ILO, "ILOlex: Database of International Standards," 2005, http://www.ilo.org/ilolex/english/convdisp2.htm.

16. International Maritime Organization, http://www.imo.org.

The less successful efforts to increase standards or end the open registry system altogether likewise share the characteristic of attempting to create cooperative agreements to provide public goods or common-pool resources, rather than club goods. This is particularly true of the frequently discussed idea of mandating a "genuine link" between ship registries and the ships they register. While a number of international agreements exist requiring just that (as discussed in chapter 4), the ones that have entered into force are weak, and many have not entered into force or do not bind precisely those states that run open registries. Existing international agreements referred to throughout this book that establish environmental, safety, and labor standards for ships address these public goods and common-pool resource issues, but it is precisely those states that offer open registries that do not participate in these agreements.

Experience with shipping standards supports the idea that a club-goods framework can be used by a variety of different actors. States are in many ways the actors that can form the most successful clubs—the impact of port state control comes largely from the fact that it is run by states. But the port state control system shows the weaknesses of state-run clubs as well; even the industrialized states themselves have competing interests (high standards on ships versus low transport costs for the ships that deliver most international trade) that lead to an unwillingness to impose the most stringent standards on ships entering ports.

On issues about which states are not as concerned, nonstate actors have shown an ability to create their own clubs and exclude actors that refuse to participate. The ability of the International Transport Workers Federation to raise wages and other labor standards on ships has come without any major role for states. To the extent that states benefit from allowing access by their nationals to low-cost registries, the increased labor standards and wage rates that result from the ITF actually contravene state interests that might exist in protecting open registries. But because high labor standards benefit the workers who comprise the ITF, they are willing and able to act, even without state support.

More frequently we see an intersection between states and nonstate actors in the creation of club goods. Trade restrictions have been used by some individual states and eventually mandated by international organizations against flag states that continue to remain apart from regional fisheries management organizations. This policy was generally initiated after pressure from domestic fishers in the dominant fishing states. In the United States, the source of many of these restrictions, they were initially imposed only after the U.S. government was sued by non-governmental organizations and legally forced to impose such measures.[17]

Whatever the relevant extent of state or civil-society action in increasing global standards on ships, these standards have generally increased. This process appears to have been accomplished almost entirely through the creation of club goods, as the following chapters demonstrate. Ironically, then, it is through creating mechanisms of exclusion that the ability to include the widest number of actors in international regulatory efforts is most likely to succeed.

17. Elizabeth R. DeSombre, *Domestic Sources of International Environmental Policy: Industry, Environmentalists, and U.S. Power* (Cambridge: MIT Press, 2000), 179–226.

4

Ships and States: The Evolution of Flags of Convenience

To understand the process of responding to the growth in flags of convenience, it is necessary to understand the context of ship registration by states and the way this process has been transformed to allow for open registration of ships. As far back as the early 1800s (and in many instances earlier),[1] ships have had nationality. The idea of ships as legal "residents" of states was first reflected in numerous bilateral treaties on friendship, commerce, and navigation in which parties indicated their willingness to recognize the nationality of each other's ships.

This practice was followed within decades by a general acceptance of the idea that states could determine the rules for awarding nationality to a ship with the expectation that others would recognize the nationality that had been granted.[2] The U.S. Attorney General in 1854 noted that "the Law of Nations and common sense require that every ship shall have a nationality."[3] By 1905, as was made clear in a decision by the Permanent Court of Arbitration at The Hague, the ability of "every sovereign to decide to wh[ich ships] he will accord the rights to fly his flag and . . . to prescribe the rules governing such grants" had passed into customary international law.[4] It has become commonplace in international

1. Rienow argues that there is evidence to suggest that some level of "national" ship registration took place under ancient Roman law, and suggests that the earliest modern forms of recognition of the nationality of at least some ships can be found in peace treaties in the seventeenth century. See Robert Rienow, *The Test of Nationality of a Merchant Vessel* (New York: Columbia University Press, 1937).

2. Boleslaw Adam Boczek, *Flags of Convenience: An International Legal Study*. (Cambridge: Harvard University Press, 1962), 95–96.

3. Quoted in Rienow, 13.

4. "Muscat Dhows Case, Award of the Tribunal," August 8, 1905, *Hague Court Reports*, The Hague, 1916, 96.

agreements regulating ships to indicate that the treaty applies to "all vessels registered in a territory for which this Convention is in force."[5]

There is a logic to nationality for ships: oceangoing ships traverse a global commons, and it would not otherwise be clear who was responsible for them or what rules they were obliged to follow under international law. National registry for ships has been compared to passports for people.[6] Such a system could have been created in a variety of ways, however. For instance, nationality could have followed the captain of the ship, a suggestion congruent with the argument of many anti-FOC activists calling for a "genuine link" between flag state and ship operation. There is also no inherent reason that ships would have to have a nationality at all in order for them to be subject to rules. Port states could simply impose regulations on ships visiting their ports, and those on the high seas would not be required to uphold any externally imposed standards. The initial granting of nationality to ships was almost certainly for the benefit of crew and owners; they gained the protection of powerful states in the anarchy of the high seas in the eighteenth and nineteenth centuries. This idea that states can grant nationality to ships, and that ships must have a national identity, became codified in the Geneva Convention on the High Seas (1958).[7]

A related historical issue was the right or ability of landlocked states to register ships. Some, such as Switzerland, had traditionally chosen to deny to their citizens the right to fly their flags on maritime vessels. The broader logic against the practice was that states without ports could not themselves guarantee a safe place for their ships.[8] The Treaty of Versailles, however, allowed the recognition of flags of landlocked states. Acceptance of this practice was then broadened by a declaration signed at the 1921 Barcelona Conference on Communications and Transit.[9] This set the stage for registration of ships in locations they did not visit.

5. Example taken from International Labor Organization, Convention Concerning Crew Accommodation on Board Ship (Revised 1949), Article 1(1), but prevalent in many others.

6. C. John Colombis, *The International Law of the Sea*, 6th ed. (New York: David McKay, 1967), 295.

7. The Convention on the High Seas (1958), Article 5(1).

8. Colombis, 293–294.

9. Treaty of Versailles (1919), Article 153; Colombis, 294.

For centuries ship registration was nevertheless a reasonably simple process. The owner of a ship registered it in the state in which he (almost inevitably he) lived, and the ship's operations were thus covered by the laws of that state, both domestic and international. But this practice has changed over the last century.

Flags of Convenience

Occasional shipowners have strategically chosen to fly another state's flag for almost as long as there have been shipping records. U.S. merchant vessels flew Portuguese flags during the War of 1812 to avoid difficulties with the British. Slave-trading ships owned by citizens of both the United States and various Latin American countries flagged elsewhere to avoid detection in the nineteenth century when international agreements prohibited the slave trade.[10] Even earlier, British ships flew flags of obscure German principalities during Napoléon's shipping blockade.[11]

Widespread use of such flags, however, came only with the decision by certain states beginning around the 1920s to create open registries, where ships were not required to have onerous ties to a state in order to register. The first state to create such a registry was Panama, followed shortly thereafter by Honduras and later Liberia.[12] These three were the primary FOC states until recently, when they have been joined by such states as Cyprus, Malta, the Marshall Islands, and the Bahamas. Ship registry trends are indicated in figure 4.1. Some of the original open registries are still among the most important, however. Since 1993 more ships have been registered in Panama, as measured both by number of ships and by gross tonnage, than anywhere else in the world.[13] Second in both categories is Liberia.[14]

10. Rodney P. Carlisle, *Sovereignty for Sale: The Origins and Evolution of the Panamanian and Liberian Flags of Convenience* (Annapolis: Naval Institute Press, 1981), viii.

11. Boleslaw Adam Boczek, *Flags of Convenience: An International Legal Study* (Cambridge: Harvard University Press, 1962), 8.

12. Boczek, 9–13.

13. Lloyd's Register, *World Fleet Statistics 2004* (London: Lloyd's Register, 2005), 11–18.

14. "Panama Increases Lead as Merchant Fleet Reaches Record Tonnage," *Lloyd's Register News Release*, n.d., http://www.lr.org.news/pr/41wfs.html.

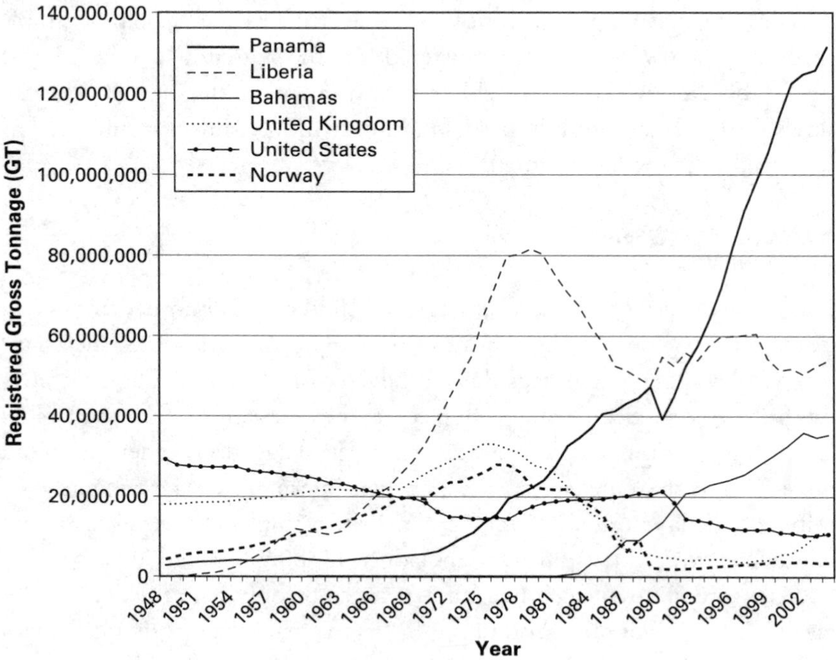

Figure 4.1
Ship registry trends. *Source:* Lloyd's Register Fairplay, *World Fleet Statistics 1948–2004* (London: Lloyd's Register, 1949–2005)

From the beginning, the modern FOC phenomenon was partly driven by the desire of shipowners to avoid the costs and restrictions associated with ships registered in the major maritime states. An officer of the first shipping company to transfer a U.S.-flagged ship to Panamanian registry explained the appeal: "The chief advantage of Panamanian registry is that the owner is relived of the continual ... boiler and hull inspections and the regulations as to crew's quarters and subsistence," pointing out that as long as the ships pay the registry fee and yearly (low) tax, "we are under absolutely no restrictions."[15]

Major maritime states, particularly the United States, are complicit in the formation and growth of open registry shipping. The Honduran registry, for instance, was created to ensure that the U.S.-based United Fruit Company would have reliable and inexpensive ways to transport its

15. W. L. Comyn, of Pacific Freighters; quoted in Carlisle, 10–11.

bananas.[16] The Liberian registry was conceived by businessman and former Secretary of State Edward Stettinius and accepted by the United States as a Cold War necessity; it was seen initially as a fleet of neutral ships the U.S. could call on in the case of Soviet aggression.[17] U.S. officials could, under some circumstances, register ships for the Panamanian registry: under a 1916 treaty between the United States and Panama, the United States was to act in Panama's interests in ports internationally where there was no Panamanian consul. That meant that the United States would sometimes actually perform the actions required for a ship to obtain Panamanian registry.[18] Registration in the current era also does not need to be accomplished in the physical territory of the flag states. The Marshall Islands registry is actually run out of an office in Virginia, and the Panamanian one is located in New York City.[19]

To some extent which states offered the first flags of convenience was simply luck that begat path dependence. Panamanian shipping law, similar to that in other Central American states in the early twentieth century, allowed Panamanian consuls abroad to register ships in Panama, as a way to encourage ship ownership by Panamanian citizens living outside of the country. In 1916 the rule was relaxed to allow ship registration by Panamanian corporations that had foreign ownership; this legal relaxation was not unique to Panama, however. Other characteristics of Panama—its strategic shipping location, the fact that its currency was pegged to the American dollar and that contracts in English were considered to be legally binding, and the presence of a subsidiary of an American shipping company in Panama to help arrange logistical aspects of conducting business—made it potentially attractive as a place for U.S. shipowners to register their vessels. In addition, a history of peaceable relations between Panama and the United States, including the fact that the United States played a role in the creation of the Panamanian state, led people, on the U.S. side of the relationship at least, to see Panama as almost an American offshoot. Of particular importance was that by

16. Boczek, 10; Ronen Palen, *The Offshore World* (Ithaca: Cornell University Press, 2003), 52.

17. Carlisle, 115; Jim Morris, "Lost at Sea: 'Flags of Convenience' Give Owners a Paper Refuge," *Houston Chronicle*, August 22, 1996, 15.

18. Carlisle, 31–32.

19. Morris, 15.

treaty Panama was militarily dependent on the United States for its defense; ships registered in Panama would thus be under U.S. protection.[20]

While Panama had not initially intended to court international ship registrations, once it began to attract them it continued to refine its laws in order to gain the advantages of vessel flagging while attempting to avoid attracting the most disreputable ships to its registry. To increase the benefits to Panama, it included a rule that 10 percent of the crew, to the extent possible, be Panamanian. The registration fee was also increased, if only slightly, to retain its attractiveness to foreign vessels while raising more revenue for the Panamanian state. The revisions to the registration rules in general were the first time a state had knowingly written legislation to attract foreign ship registrations.[21]

The origins of the Liberian flag as an open registry, after World War II, owed even less to design by the Liberian authorities than did Panama's evolution as a registry. The Liberian registry was essentially created by Edward Stettinius, who had been U.S. Secretary of State during the Second World War. Stettinius incorporated a company in 1947, a subsidiary of which (The Liberia Corporation) was set up as a profit-sharing arrangement with the Liberian government, which would receive one-quarter of its revenue. (An additional 10 percent would go to a nonprofit organization promoting social welfare in Liberia.) The remaining profits would return to the company owned by Stettinius. While the original vision called for a variety of revenue-generating enterprises, most of them did not get off the ground and others—such as iron mining—did so only under separate management. It was the ship-registration plan, not even initially a part of Stettinuis's vision, that became the primary result of his efforts. The scheme was thus a combination of a plan for supporting the state of Liberia with an effort to find a cost-effective foreign registry for oil tankers. In the wake of a variety of troubles with the Panamanian registry involving concern from American labor organizations that the registry led to unemployment among U.S. seafarers, European concerns that the flag represented unfair competition, and political turmoil in Panama, tanker owners were ready to take advantage of a different registry.[22]

20. Carlisle, 1–2.
21. Carlisle, 21.
22. Carlisle, 111–114.

The first transfers of U.S. ships to open registries (initially, Panama) came at a time of rising costs and regulation for the U.S. shipping industry. Because the United States was trying to encourage a strong merchant marine, it put into place a number of regulations in the period between 1915 and 1922. One such provision mandated regular inspections of U.S.-registered ships (undertaken by the American Bureau of Shipping) to examine the boilers and hulls. U.S. regulations also increased the costliness of repairs to ships by strengthening and enforcing a tax of 50 percent on work done in foreign shipyards. At the same time, domestic social legislation was increasing the restriction on working hours of U.S. employees, including on ships: the La Follette Seaman's Act of 1915 required that seafarers work shifts no longer than 8 hours, and provided for a day off every week as well as other holidays.[23] All these regulations had the impact of raising the costs of shipping. At roughly the same time Prohibition in the United States was interpreted to mean that alcohol could not be served on board, or transported by, U.S.-flagged ships.

Since all U.S. ships were bound by these provisions, ships were not disadvantaged relative to each other domestically. But this era coincided as well with an increase in global shipping and trade more generally, such that U.S. shippers were competing internationally with others not bound by these rules, and thus at a competitive disadvantage.

The first large-scale transfers of ships from U.S. to Panamanian flag ironically came at the behest of the U.S. Shipping Board, which had been constituted to prevent ships from reflagging outside the United States. The ships in question had such large debts that, between the large number of ocean vessels at the time and the costly labor and safety standards U.S. ships had to live up to, it would be unlikely that the ships could be sold to pay off the debts if they would have to operate within the U.S. system. The Shipping Board agreed that they should be sold to U.S. corporations that would flag them elsewhere, on routes that would not compete with U.S.-flagged ships. Six ships were thus sold to Pacific Freighters, an American corporation, and flagged in Panama to trade a route in the Pacific.[24] The next ships to transfer were two cruise ships, which did so explicitly to be able to serve alcohol on board, which would

23. Carlisle, 3–5.

24. Carlisle, 10–11.

otherwise have been forbidden, since the Eighteenth Amendment to the U.S. Constitution prohibited the consumption or sale of alcohol not only in U.S. territory, but in "all territory subject to [its] jurisdiction."[25] Ruling on the issue of whether this regulation applied to ships, though later overturned, initially found that it did.[26] It is likely, however, that the lower operating costs played a role in the decision to transfer the cruise ships to Panamanian registry as well.

Indeed, the first U.S.-owned ships to transfer to the Panamanian flag took full advantage of the lower regulatory oversight that their new flag afforded them. The very first non-Panamanian-owned ship registered in Panama, the *Belen Quezada*, was acting both illegally—running liquor from Canada to the United States during Prohibition—and with questionable labor standards that led the crew to fear that it would not be paid.[27] More importantly, the set of ships that transferred to the Panamanian flag with not only the blessing but to some extent the mandate of the U.S. Shipping Board hired multinational crews and paid them on the much lower Japanese wage scale. Similarly, the articles of agreement under which several of the ships hired workers did not contain the same labor protections as recently passed U.S. legislation, which many of the crews initially believed they would be working under; some workers had been hired without even knowing the terms.[28]

During the era when the U.S. Shipping Board had to approve transfers of U.S.-flagged vessels to other registries, ships registered in Europe (often owned or partially owned by U.S. corporations) could easily reflag in Panama and many did, foremost among them the European subsidiaries

25. United States, *National Prohibition Act*, ch. 85, 41 Stat. 305 (1919) (repealed 1935).

26. *Cunard Steamship Co. Ltd. et al. v. Mellon, Secretary of the Treasury et al.*, Supreme Court of the United States, 262 U.S. 100; 43 S. Ct. 504, decided April 30, 1923.

27. The broader issue of liquor smuggling aboard Panamanian-flagged vessels brought to a head the relationship between the Panamanian flag and the U.S. government, when the United States attempted to board and seize liquor on Panamanian vessels (most of which were likely indeed smuggling), in contravention of a U.S.-Panama treaty that allowed the U.S. Coast Guard to board Panamanian vessels only within an hour's steaming time of the U.S. border. For more information on this controversy, see Carlisle, 21–31.

28. Carlisle, 6–14.

of Standard Oil of New Jersey (ESSO) and the United Fruit Company operations out of Panama.[29] Shipowners of other nationalities made use of the Panamanian flag in the 1930s; some, like Basques who wanted to avoid the requisitioning of their ships by Nationalist forces during civil war in Spain, did so for political reasons. Others, like some of the main Greek shipping interests, did so for the same cost savings and avoidance of regulations that the first U.S. ships to transfer to Panamanian registry did. Aristotle Onassis transferred all his shipping and whaling ships to Panamanian registry, and Norwegian whaling ships transferred there as well,[30] which thereby allowed them to escape the restrictions of the International Convention for the Regulation of Whaling, to which Panama at that time was not bound.

War only accentuated this trend. During the early part of World War II when the United States wished to maintain official neutrality but nevertheless supply Britain with supplies and fuel, it made use of vessels already registered in Panama for these purposes and also reflagged U.S.-controlled vessels in Panama. By mid-1941 more than 1 million deadweight tons (dwt; a measurement of the amount of oil or other cargo the ship can carry) of shipping operations was flying flags of Panama, Honduras, or Venezuela.[31]

After the war, additional transfers of U.S. ships to foreign flags occurred. In the first half of the twentieth century, the United States had been concerned with maintaining a merchant marine not only for reasons of commerce but also to have access to a fleet "capable of serving as a naval and military auxiliary in time of war or national emergency."[32] When it became clear by the 1950s that there were insufficient incentives for replacing obsolescent ships under U.S. flag, the U.S. government adopted a policy of "trade-out-and-build," by which older ships built for war could be transferred to registry in Liberia, Panama, or Honduras, provided that the owner flagged a new vessel in the United

29. Carlisle, 44–50.

30. J. N. Tønnessen and A. O. Johnsen; *The History of Modern Whaling* (Berkeley: University of California Press, 1982), 534–538; Carlisle, 59–60.

31. H. P. Dewry (Shipping Consultants), Ltd., *The Performance of "Open Registry" Bulk Fleets*, No. 81 in a Series (London: H. P. Dewry (Shipping Consultants), Ltd., March 1980), 3.

32. Merchant Marine Act of 1936, 49 Stat. 1985 (1936), as amended.

States.[33] This policy gave U.S. approval to the general idea of a transfer. The idea behind it—and particularly the choice of foreign flags under which U.S. ships could register—is that the ship is still U.S.-owned and available to the United States to be requisitioned in case of emergency.[34] There is some evidence the acceptance by the United States of U.S.-owned ships registering in open registries was an explicit strategy by the United States to increase the dominance of U.S.-based multinational firms in the global shipping economy, previously dominated by European states and firms,[35] by making shipping less costly.

There are advantages to the states that run open registries and few disadvantages. In Panama, for instance, the fees charged for the registry contribute 5 percent of the national budget.[36] In Liberia, where revenue from the registry accounted for approximately 10 percent of the national budget before the civil war, during the civil war estimates of how much the ship registry contributed to the annual state range from 30 to 90 percent.[37] More recently, information from the Liberian central bank suggests that the registry and its associated activities contribute one-sixth of total revenue.[38] The registry in Cyprus brings $10 million in revenue annually to that government.[39] Running an open registry can bring other types of benefits to a government as well. The Cambodian registry is a source of otherwise-scarce foreign capital.[40]

It is also important to realize that many open registry states do not actually run their own registries—they contract out this job to profes-

33. Boczek, 33.

34. Boczek, 34.

35. Alan W. Cafruny, "The Political Economy of International Shipping: Europe versus America," *International Organization* 39/1: 79–119.

36. Morris, 15.

37. Aviva Freudmann, "Liberia Taps DC Lawyers to Handle Registry," *Journal of Commerce*, December 21, 1998, 2B; Ryan Lizza, "Double Take: Can Charles Taylor's Apologists Explain His Ties to Al Qaeda?", *The New Republic*, November 19, 2001, 21–23.

38. Michael Peel and Toby Shelley, "Liberia Under Pressure to Become More Shipshape," *Lloyd's List*, September 6, 2004, 16.

39. Larry Luxner, "Cyprus Tightens the Screws on Its Ship Registry," *Journal of Commerce—JoC Online*, August 3, 2000 (Lexis/Nexis).

40. "Cambodia—Tribulations Continue for a Poor Performer," *Lloyd's List*, February 10, 2003, 16.

sional ship-registry firms, many of whom also provide services for other offshore businesses. For instance, a firm operating out of Virginia called International Registries currently runs the Marshall Islands registry and until recently ran the registry for Liberia; it provides services not only for vessel registration but also for offshore corporations.[41] The company that currently runs the Vanuatu ship registry, Vanuatu Maritime Services, is part of an American-owned group that specializes in offshore banking and insurance.[42] The registries themselves, often with a connection only in name to the state whose flag they peddle, are in the business to earn money as well. International Registries earns 18 percent of the gross revenue of the registry.[43]

Recent Trends in International Shipping

In some ways it is remarkable the extent to which the fundamental structure of ocean shipping has remained consistent. Despite enormous changes in trade and in the technology of transport over this time period, the oceans have remained the predominant mode of conducting international trade.

The early 1970s nevertheless saw a dramatic change in the scale of international shipping; the size of ships increased as well as their numbers, and the way they were purchased and operated changed. First, a revolution in technology made possible sizes of ships that had previously been unimaginable. Where formerly the largest oil tankers had a capacity of about 28,000 dwt, tankers of 250,000 dwt became common and those up to 330,000 dwt became possible. Likewise, cargo ships went from about 10,000 to 200,000 dwt in a two-decade period, and new container vessels were seven times larger than conventional break-bulk liners.[44] This change can be seen by looking at British-registered shipping in the late 1960s and early 1970s: despite a decreasing number of ships (from

41. International Registries, "Welcome: Maritime and Corporate Administrator for the Republic of the Marshall Islands," http://www.register-iri.com/index.cfm.

42. Keith Hindell, "Hong Kong Owners Are Biggest Users of Vanuatu," *Lloyd's List*, March 29, 1995, 9.

43. Tom Baldwin, "Who's in Charge Here?", *Journal of Commerce*, January 15, 1999, 1B.

44. A. D. Couper, *Voyages of Abuse: Seafarers, Human Rights, and International Shipping* (London: Pluto Press, 1999), 10.

1968 to 1975 the number of ships over 100 GT registered in the UK decreased from 4,020 to 3,662), the overall tonnage registered to the British flag increased during that period from 21.9 to 33.2 million GT.[45] See appendix A for specific trends in registered tonnage across ship registries.

At the same time, the structure of the industry was changing as well. Certainly the post–World War II economic recovery increased the belief that shipping would continue to become ever more profitable. In addition, the abundance of inexpensive oil in the late 1960s increased its demand and the advantage of transporting it across the ocean. The 1967 closure of the Suez Canal increased the demand as well for larger ships that could more economically make the longer trip around Africa to transport oil.

The increase in ship size increased the amount of capital required to purchase a ship. While previously owners would buy a ship with close to 100 percent equity, few owners could afford that kind of investment in the new large ships. Banks increased their financing of such purchases to a point where it was common for shipowners to finance up to 90 percent of the cost of a ship, allowing them to purchase bigger and greater numbers of ships. Ship manufacturers also increased the available credit to encourage purchases, and governments, in an effort to expand their national flags, introduced new tax breaks for those who bought ships. This dramatic change in financing lured many into the shipping industry, often borrowing against expected future income.[46] Initially the investment in a ship proved cost-effective: ships could nearly triple in value in five years.[47] But as global shipping capacity increased, and as many states subsidized their shipbuilding industries, the economics of the industry were bound to change. By the early 1980s there was more shipping capacity than demand for it,[48] and many owners could not afford to pay off the loans with which they had purchased ships. When ships were repossessed there was no economic advantage from scrapping them, so

45. Data from *Lloyd's Shipping Register* from the years in question.

46. Couper, 9–11.

47. Helmut Sohmen, *Profitability in Shipping* (Tübingen: J. C. B. Mohr, 1983).

48. Frank Broeze, "Containerization and the Globalization of Liner Shipping," in D. Starkey and G. Harlaftis, eds., Global markets: *the Internationalization of the Sea Transport Industries since 1850* (St. Johns: International Maritime History Association, 1998), 867–876.

their new owners (be they governments or banks) kept them operational, only adding to the surplus capacity and increasing downward pressure on freight rates. An additional impact of this economic downturn in the industry was the increasing management of ships by third-party ship management companies. As banks repossessed ships owned by those who could no longer afford to pay the mortgages, they needed to hire someone with shipping expertise to run the ships profitably.

As these companies took on management tasks, they determined that economies of scale in such things as crew hiring and management could be achieved through managing large numbers of ships, and sought to expand their role in managing ships. Now most seafarers are hired via ship-management companies rather than directly by shipowners or captains,[49] which adds to both the centralization and globalization of the industry. Some management companies or shipowners intentionally took to registering each of their ships in a different registry,[50] to spread their risk.

During this period, some of the major players that had been traditionally involved in international shipping bowed out. The oil majors, steel corporations, and other industrial actors that used to own their own shipping fleets began to sell them off and instead charter ships owned by independent shipowners.[51] This led to increased competitiveness pressures as individual shipowners began to compete for the business of those who had previously owned their own ships. The main ways to compete were based on low cost or freedom from regulation. In this context the rise of registration in open registries, with lower taxes and fees and fewer regulations pertaining to environment, safety, and labor practices, was the next logical step.

Second Registries

As the growth of registration in open registries came at the expense of national fleets, traditional maritime states looked for a way to stem the

49. Michael Bloor, Michelle Thomas, and Tony Lane, "Health Risks in the Global Shipping Industry: An Overview," *Health, Risk & Society* 2/3 (2000): 331–332.

50. Couper, 15.

51. Couper, 11.

"flagging out" of nationally registered vessels. Previous efforts to prevent nationals from registering ships elsewhere having failed, the traditional maritime states turned instead to creating their own "second" or "international" registries. Since one of the primary reasons ships were flagging out was to cut costs, these states assumed that creating registries where their nationals could register nationally, while avoiding some of the costly regulations they would normally encounter in the national registry, would keep some national control over or access to these ships, particularly in times of emergency.

The first of these international registries began when France bowed to pressure from shipowners for a lower-cost registry, by setting up a registry in 1986 in the Kerguelen Islands, part of France's territorial claim in Antarctica.[52] In doing so, France changed crewing requirements such that only 25 percent of the crew (rather than 100 percent under traditional French registry) would have to be French nationals. By 2004 there were 126 ships totaling more than 3.5 million gross tons registered in the French Antarctic Territory.[53] In 2005 France officially created an international registry (RIF),[54] and it is likely that most of the tonnage registered in the Kerguelen Islands will transfer to RIF. Since the first alternate French registry was created, Norway, Germany, and Denmark have added international registries (referred to as NIS, GIS, and DIS). Portugal began an international ship registry based in Madeira, and Spain opened one in the Canary Islands. The United Kingdom's use of second registries is more complex; it has registries in a variety of territories, but only four states states qualify as Category One "red ensign" registries: Bermuda, the Cayman Islands, Gibraltar, and the Isle of Man.[55] Ships registered in red ensign registries benefit from British naval protection, which was useful for some Kuwaiti owned tankers that reflagged there during the Iran/Iraq war.[56]

52. Richard M. F. Coles, ed., *Ship Registration* (London: LLP, 2002), 26.

53. Lloyd's Register Fairplay, *World Fleet Statistics 2004* (London: Lloyd's Register, 2005).

54. Andrew Spurrier, "How New French Register Became an FOC," *Lloyd's List*, April 22, 2005, 7.

55. David Osler, "Europe: Red Ensign Group Sets Agenda," *Lloyd's List*, June 2, 2000, 3.

56. Coles, 48.

New international registries are considered with some frequency. In 2005 Russia began the process of setting up an international registry to capture back some of the 90 percent of shipping owned by Russian corporations registered in flags of convenience.[57] Other states have either considered the creation of an international registry or felt domestic pressure to do so. Japanese shipowners have called for Japan to reform its ship-registration process to make it more conducive to ship registration by Japanese nationals who currently register their ships elsewhere.[58] The European Union has even considered the possibility of an EU-wide international registry,[59] though the plan has not been implemented.

It is less than obvious how these states gain from having these second registries. Certainly states running international (as opposed to second) registries get a modest financial benefit from registration fees and taxes. States with second registries (where the revenue goes to the territory itself rather than to the home state) trumpet the advantages of being able to call on the ships in these registries in case of national emergency or war,[60] though the evidence of states doing so is nonexistent.

Ships choose this type of registry for the reputational advantages that come with national registries. There is variation in the extent to which these alternative registries are bound by the same international environmental, labor, and safety laws (or domestic rules) as the "parent" state, though many of the territories used are required to abide by the same international agreements as the home state. One important difference, however, is that second registries generally relax nationality requirements for crewing. While they may have a nominal requirement of some number of nationals in officer positions, generally most positions on a ship may be filled by nonnationals who can be paid lower wages, and even the modest nationality requirements may sometimes be waived.

57. Lyuba Pronin, "Moscow Gives Green Light to Ship Register Reforms to Boost Maritime Industry," *Lloyd's List*, June 16, 2005, 3.

58. Sam Chambers, "Flag Failure Costs Tokyo a Yen Fortune," *Lloyd's List*, July 12, 2005, 10.

59. Sean Moloney, "Euros Flag Drive Stepped Up," *Lloyd's List*, February 3, 1994, 12.

60. David Osler, "Registers 'Bring Benefits,'" *Lloyd's List*, November 22, 1996, 3.

Responding to Open Registries

Major maritime states expressed concern about the development of open registries. They and others have attempted several unsuccessful strategies to prevent large numbers of ships from registering in these locations apart from the creation of second registries. The first type of strategy was to prohibit ships from registering in open registry states in the first place. Beginning in the 1920s, the U.S. Shipping Board considered requests from shipowners to move the registry of ships from the United States to elsewhere, and could deny permission to do so if a vessel did not have a legitimate reason for transfer, if the transfer would hurt the U.S. merchant marine, or if the transferred ships would compete with U.S. businesses.[61] On the whole this approach met with little success, since ships seeking registration can obtain it wherever states are willing to allow them to register, and ships that have not yet been registered anywhere would not be faced with the possibility that their transfer could be denied.

The most prominent international effort to circumvent difficulties caused by FOC-registered ships involved the use of international law to mandate a "genuine link" between a ship and the state in which it was registered. The idea was that if ships were required to be connected to the states whose flags they flew, these states would take more responsibility for their conditions and actions. Requiring a genuine link would also decrease the advantages of open registries, since shipowners would have less freedom in choosing their crew, generally needing to crew a ship with nationals from the location in which it was registered. The first effort along these lines came at the suggestion of the International Law Commission in the 1958 Geneva Convention on the High Seas, which includes the requirement that "there must exist a genuine link between the State and the ship,"[62] but does not further define it. In the 1970s the United Nations Conference on Trade and Development discussed what

61. Carlisle, 33.

62. Geneva Convention on the High Seas (1958), Article 5(1); Paul Stephen Dempsey and Lisa L. Helling, "Oil Pollution by Ocean Vessels—An Environmental Tragedy: The Legal Regime of Flags of Convenience, Multilateral Conventions, and Coastal States," *Journal of International Law and Policy* 10 (1980): 59.

the elements of a genuine link should be. It decided that to qualify as having a genuine link, the ship must contribute to the national economy and be reflected in national accounting, must employ nationals on board, and must be owned in a manner beneficial to the state.[63]

Reference to the concept has appeared in a number of treaties since then, including the United Nations Convention on the Law of the Sea,[64] and scholars have argued for decades over what should constitute a genuine link. The first legal definition can be found in the 1986 United Nations Convention on the Conditions for Registration of Ships (UNCCORS). This agreement requires of a registry that "a satisfactory part of its complement consisting of officers and crew of ships flying its flag be nationals or persons domiciled or lawfully in permanent residence in that state."[65] The convention has not yet entered into force, and it is unlikely that it ever will. Not surprisingly, the major open registry states have not ratified this latter agreement, nor have they ratified the Geneva Convention on the High Seas (1958), which includes a modest provision for a genuine link. Also interesting is that even the major maritime states, those that claim they are negatively affected by the open registry system, have not ratified UNCCORS.[66] Major maritime states either concluded

63. United Nations Conference on Trade and Development, Trade and Development Board, "Economic Consequences of the Existence of Lack of a Genuine Link between Vessel and Flag of Registry," TD/B/c.4/168, March 10, 1977, paragraphs 71–76, pp. 20–21.

64. United Nations Convention on the Law of the Sea (1982), U.N.T.S. 31363, Article 91(1). Articles 91 through 94 outline the rights and duties of flag states.

65. United Nations Convention on the Conditions for Registration of Ships (1986), Article 9; alternately, states can follow the provision in Article 8 that requires a certain level of participation by the state or its nationals as shipowners. See also H. Edwin Anderson III, "The Nationality of Ships and Flags of Convenience: Economics, Politics, and Alternatives," *The Maritime Lawyer* 12 (fall 1996): 149–50.

66. The seventeen states that have ratified are Algeria, Bolivia (before it opened its own open registry), Cameroon, Côte D'Ivoire, Egypt, Ghana, Haiti, Hungary, Indonesia, Iraq, Libya, Mexico, Morocco, Oman, Poland, Russia, and Senegal. See International Union for the Conservation of Nature (IUCN), United Nations Environment Program (UNEP), Tufts University's Fletcher School of Law and Diplomacy, British Columbia Ministry of Environment, Lands, & Parks, Antarctic Research Center, American Society of International Law (ASIL), and Center for International Earth Science Information Network (CIESIN), "Environmental Treaties and Resource Indicators (ENTRI) Query Service" (Palisades, N.Y.: CIESIN, Columbia University, n.d.), http://sedac.ciesin.columbia.edu/entri.

that such an agreement would be unworkable without the participation of the major open registry states, or they benefit sufficiently (as discussed further in chapter 9) from the general open registry system that they do not want to work to undermine it entirely.

As Paul Dempsey and Lisa Helling conclude, "in the final analysis, perhaps the concept of the genuine link has only created a furor in academia, without having a significant impact on the course of international law."[67] The effort to hold states to enforcing a genuine link with the ships they flagged was unrealistic as long as these states gained from attracting ship registrations without a real connection to the flag state.

Efforts to stem the process of "flagging out" to open registries has thus generally failed. The percentage of ships registered in flags of convenience has grown dramatically and is continuing to grow. As chapter 2 demonstrates, these open registries at least begin their operations adopting low levels of international environmental, safety, and labor standards. The next four chapters examine the processes followed by states, international organizations, and substate actors that have the effect of raising the standards followed by ships flagged in open registries, at least somewhat, over time.

67. Dempsey and Helling, 61.

5
Port State Control

Port state control is the power of actors from a state to "board, inspect, and where appropriate detain a merchant ship" flying a foreign flag that enters its port.[1] The legal authority to do so can be found in a number of international agreements from the past three decades, many of them under the auspices of the International Maritime Organization. For example, the International Convention for the Prevention of Pollution from Ships (MARPOL) (1973/1978) gives authority to port states, by allowing officials appointed by states to inspect ships in their ports "for the purpose of verifying whether the ship has discharged any harmful substances in violation of the provisions" of the agreement.[2] Moreover, the agreement provides for inspections in port when the port state has received an allegation from another party to the treaty that the ship has discharged harmful substances anywhere.[3]

Port state control has come to be important in determining the standards ships uphold, particularly with respect to environmental and safety regulation. Detaining ships in port is the first line of defense against substandard ships; states use their sovereign authority over their territorial waters to prevent substandard ships from accessing the location to which they intend to transport goods.

Under initial IMO conventions the authority to inspect ships only applies to ships whose flag states have signed a given agreement. These agreements, however, form the basis for broader rights of inspection, extending to the right to inspect any ship in port, as the system is

1. John Hare, "Port State Control: Strong Medicine to Cure a Sick Industry," *Georgia Journal of International and Comparative Law* 26 (summer 1997): 571.

2. MARPOL 1973/1978, Article 6(2).

3. MARPOL 1973/1978, Article 6(5).

currently practiced. MARPOL in 1973 was the first well-specified version of this process. Earlier references to the practice were vague—the International Convention for the Safety of Life at Sea (SOLAS), first negotiated in 1914 in the wake of the Titanic disaster, includes provisions for port-state authority over foreign ships in port, but without specific mechanisms. These provisions were modified over the following years,[4] leading to the current incarnation of Port State Control in the 1974 SOLAS agreement (as amended). Regulation I/19, for instance, indicates that officers of ports may inspect certificates about the safety equipment on board, and may examine a ship if there is doubt that the ship equipment corresponds to the certificate. The International Convention on Standards of Training, Certification and Watchkeeping for Seafarers (STCW) (1978) authorizes port state control officers to ascertain that all seafarers on the vessels required under the agreement to be certified indeed are, and to assess whether the seafarers on board are able to maintain the watchkeeping standards required under the convention, particularly if there is reason to suspect they may not be.[5] Importantly, MARPOL, SOLAS, and STCW all indicate that on the basic obligation to ensure that a ship not leave port until it can "proceed to sea without presenting an unreasonable threat of harm to the environment,"[6] port states need not differentiate between ships registered in states that are signatories to these conventions and those that are not, in terms of the standards the port-state inspectors can hold ships to.[7] Several other agreements—in particular the International Convention on Load Lines (1966) and the International Convention on Tonnage Measurement of Ships (1969)—include some provisions for port states to make sure that ships in ports meet given standards.

The primary locus of authority for the broad jurisdiction of Port State Control, however, comes from the United Nations Convention on the Law of the Sea (UNCLOS) (1982). The UNCLOS provisions build on nascent (but not previously well-developed) aspects of international law

4. Z. Oya Özçcayir, *Port State Control* (London: LLP, 2001), 95.

5. International Convention on Standards of Training, Certification and Watchkeeping for Seafarers (STCW) (1978); Article X and Regulation I/4.

6. MARPOL 1973/1978, Article 5(2).

7. MARPOL 1973/1978, Article 5(4); SOLAS Protocol 1978, Article II(3); STCW 1978, Article X(5); see also Özçcayir, 96.

that see ports as part of the sovereign territory of a state and thus an area to which states have the ability to restrict access. Though there has been some controversy historically about the right of states to control access to their ports, legal decisions suggested that by the second half of the twentieth century this concept was becoming more fully accepted. For instance, the arbitration panel in the dispute between Saudi Arabia and The Arab American Oil Company (Aramco) over whether the government of Saudi Arabia was allowed to give preferential port access to ships flying its own flag ruled that "it is indispensable that every sovereign State has the right to control its ports."[8] Similarly, the International Court of Justice ruled in the case between the United States and Nicaragua that "by virtue of its sovereignty ... the coastal state may regulate access to its ports."[9] This development, combined with a general lack of customary international law supporting a right of access to ports (except in case of distress), can be seen as the basis on which UNCLOS found and developed a broader right of port state control.

UNCLOS lays out the ability of states to "establish particular requirements for the prevention, reduction and control of pollution of the marine environment as a condition for the entry of foreign vessels into their ports," and requires that flag states hold their ships responsible for providing information to port states that require it for these purposes.[10] It also outlines a number of rights a port state has "when a vessel is voluntarily within a port or at an off-shore terminal of a state," which include the right to inspect the vessel to ascertain whether it is abiding by international obligations to prevent or control pollution (as well as pollution-control rules established by the port state for operations within its exclusive economic zone or territorial sea) and to ensure that the vessel is seaworthy. UNCLOS spells out the obligation of a ship in this circumstance to provide information on its "identity and port of registry, its

8. *Saudi Arabia v. Arabian American Oil Company (Aramco) Arbitration* (1963), 27 ILR 117.

9. *Nicaragua v. United States* (1986), ICJ Rep. 14, 111 (June 27).

10. United Nations Convention on the Law of the Sea (1982), Article 211. Similar provisions are established in the same Article to require that those who enter a state's territorial sea or exclusive economic zone live up to standards the coastal state has passed to prevent or mitigate pollution in accordance with internationally accepted rules; states may even adopt standards that are stricter than international rules when ecological conditions warrant.

last and its next port of call and other relevant information required to establish whether a violation has occurred." In addition, port states that have determined that the ships they inspect are in violation of an applicable rule that "threatens damage to the marine environment" have an obligation to prevent the ship from leaving port until the problem has been resolved.[11] The right of port states to impose their own domestic regulations (allowed at least in part under UNCLOS for the protection of ecologically sensitive areas) on visiting ships has generally been interpreted quite conservatively, however.[12]

There are also some provisions for port state control within international labor agreements under the auspices of the International Labour Organisation (ILO), and these actually created the seeds of the current port state control regime. In particular, ILO Convention 147, The Merchant Shipping (Minimum Standards) Convention (1976), allows for port states to inspect the ships of member states when they are in port and the port state has evidence or has received a complaint that the ship is not living up to the standards in the agreement. Such complaints may be lodged by "a member of the crew, a professional body, an association, a trade union or, generally, any person with an interest in the safety of the ship."[13]

The port state, however, has little ability to effect change directly under this agreement; the evidence collected in an inspection is to be sent to the flag state as well as to the ILO. Referrals to flag states of problems with environmental or safety standards have seldom resulted in penalties for the ships or a remedy for their shortcomings. A U.S. government study showed that of 111 referrals the United States made to foreign flag states identifying environmental malfeasance by ships, the flag states took action in only two of them.[14] The only immediate action

11. United Nations Convention on the Law of the Sea (1982), Articles 216, 218, 219, 220.

12. Özçayir; see especially the discussion of the Australian Appeals Court on pp. 86–89.

13. C147 Merchant Shipping (Minimum Standards) Convention (1976), Article 4; quotation comes from Article 4(3).

14. U.S. General Accounting Office, "Marine Pollution: Progress Made to Reduce Marine Pollution by Cruise Ships, but Important Issues Remain," GAO/RCED-00-48 (February 2000); Douglas Franz, "Gaps in Sea Laws Shield Pollution by Cruise Lines," *New York Times*, January 3, 1999, 1, 20.

that may be taken by the port state in these circumstances is that "necessary to rectify any conditions on board which are clearly hazardous to safety and health."[15]

The system of port state control as it is currently practiced is explicitly governed by a group of memoranda of understanding (MOUs), in an attempt to create a system that has a greater effect than simply reporting problem ships to flag states. In response to the implicit control granted to port states under ILO Convention 147, eight European states[16] signed a memorandum of understanding in The Hague in 1978 to create a method for implementing these provisions and others contained in IMO agreements. Before this agreement could become fully operational, however, the Amoco Cadiz oil spill refocused attention away from labor standards and onto environmental and safety issues on ships. The states involved in this process decided to modify and expand this agreement and to focus it on ensuring maritime safety and avoiding pollution.

This broadened agreement, negotiated with the help of both the ILO and the IMO and initially involving fourteen European states, became the Paris MOU of 1982. This and other similar agreements explicitly build on the UNCLOS framework and also incorporate the relevant IMO and ILO agreements (though the labor aspects have been minimized in the process). There are now MOUs covering most regions of the world, including the Viña del Mar (or Latin American) MOU (1992), the Tokyo MOU (1993), the Caribbean MOU (1996), the Mediterranean MOU (1997), the Indian Ocean MOU (1998), and the MOU for the West and Central Africa Region (1999). The most recent MOUs have been those for the Black Sea (2000) and the Persian Gulf (Riyadh MOU, 2004). The United States has its own shipping inspection program, conducted by the U.S. Coast Guard, that shares most of the characteristics of the MOUs.

The MOUs generally make no new laws pertaining to ships; they refer to existing international agreements on labor, safety, and environmental protection that ships must uphold. In particular, the standards in question can be found in the International Convention on Load Lines, SOLAS (and its protocols), MARPOL, STCW, the Convention on the

15. C147, Article 4(1).

16. Belgium, Denmark, France, West Germany, the Netherlands, Norway, Sweden, and the United Kingdom. See Özçcayir, 115.

International Regulations for Preventing Collisions at Sea (COLLREG) (1973), the International Convention on Tonnage Measurement of Ships (1969), and ILO Convention 147, the Merchant Shipping (Minimum Standards) Convention (1976). ILO Convention 147 itself amalgamates standards from eight previous ILO maritime labor conventions, so those standards are included as well.[17]

These MOUs do, however, create a systematized process of enforcing these existing international rules, which thereby brings into being new obligations specifically for the port states that participate. In the existing MOUs the port-state authorities agree to inspect some percentage (for the Latin American agreement it is 15 percent and for Tokyo and Paris (until recently) it has been at least 25 percent) of ships that enter their ports during the course of a year. They agree to use a standard inspection process that, while it allows discretion on exactly how the inspection is done, holds ships to a set list of international obligations. The MOUs also set up a process for sharing information with the other members of the agreement, which requires member states to provide information of a particular sort and in a given format.

When port state control officers (PSCOs) inspect ships, they undertake a number of activities. First, they examine the documents ships must have with them to signify compliance with international agreements and also to indicate that they are registered, classed, and insured. The PSCO then examines the general condition of the ship to make sure that it meets the requirements of the certificates. If no problems are found at this point, and there have been no specific complaints against the ship, the inspection terminates. If, however, the ship is missing some of its required documentation, if the brief visual inspection raises concerns, or if someone has registered a complaint about the ship, it will be subject to a more detailed inspection. In addition, certain types of ships (tankers, passenger ships, and older ships) are subject to an expanded inspection once every year.[18]

17. These are C138: Minimum Age Convention (1973); C58: Minimum Age (Sea) Convention (Revised) (1936); C7: Minimum Age (Sea) Convention (1920); C73: Medical Examination (Seafarers) Convention (1946); C134: Prevention of Accidents (Seafarers) Convention (1970); C92: Accommodation of Crews Convention (Revised) 1949; C68: Food and Catering (Ship's Crew) Convention (1946); and C53: Officers' Competency Certificates Convention (1936).

18. Paris MOU, Paragraph 3.1; Özçcayir, 126–131.

As a result of the inspection process, a ship can be found to be "clean" (to pass with no problems), or it can have some number of recorded deficiencies. If there are enough deficiencies or they are serious enough, the ship can be detained in port until the most egregious ones are corrected. A postreport form indicates what deficiencies exist and what needs to be done to correct them. In the event of "deficiencies which are clearly hazardous to safety, health or the environment, the Authority will . . . ensure that the hazard is removed before the ship is allowed to proceed to sea."[19] The agreements do not define what constitutes such a sufficiently hazardous deficiency, however; such decisions are made by individual MOU member states and the ship inspector. If a ship is detained, the port state must notify the flag state and the ship's classification society. The ship is not allowed to put to sea until the PSCO is satisfied that the deficiencies that led to the detention have been corrected.[20]

One of the most important aspects of this regime is that discrimination in inspection is encouraged: port states determine which ships to inspect based on the record of the individual ship, the type of ship it is, and most importantly, characteristics of the flag state in which it is registered. The goal across an MOU is to increase the odds that a given ship will be inspected in at least one of the ports at which it stops, and to target for inspection those ships that the port states believe are most likely not to meet the required standards. Ships are therefore targeted for inspection if they have not called at any port in the region in the last year, or if they have not been inspected at any in the previous six months. Ships are also likely to be singled out for inspection if they have recently been inspected but found to be deficient. In addition to factors that single out individual ships, certain types of ships are more likely to be inspected: oil and chemical tankers, gas carriers, passenger ships, and bulk carriers are given a higher priority for inspection than are other types of ships. Similarly, older ships are of greater concern.

There are also characteristics on which groups of ships are singled out—these primarily include characteristics of their classification societies or their flag states. In the case of flag states, ships registered in states that are not parties to the international agreements covered by the MOU

19. Paris MOU, Paragraph 3.7.

20. Özçayir, 135.

are more likely to be targeted. This practice provides an ironic twist on the way international law generally operates: through this process ships flagged in states that have not adopted international standards can nevertheless be held to them in the inspection process, even though their flag states do not require that they adopt these standards. The other main impact of the state a ship is registered in is that average detention rates are kept for all ships and are aggregated by flag state. An overall average detention rate (a three-year rolling average) for all inspected ships is calculated, and flag states whose ships exceed the average during that period are then identified as those that should be more frequently inspected. The Paris and Tokyo MOUs also list states on black, gray, and white lists to indicate the overall level of risk by ships that fly that state's flag. (The Paris MOU black list is further disaggregated into levels of risk.) The U.S. Coast Guard PSC inspection process does not use this system, but it maintains a list of states that have a higher-than-average detention rate for the previous three years and thus receive additional attention.[21]

The use of a three-year average has some disadvantages, however. While it ensures that states are not unduly penalized for one bad year, it does mean that it can take several years before a problem registry will be singled out. Conversely, states that attempt to improve their standing will not be able to avoid additional scrutiny for several years after they begin their efforts. The Belize registry, which made an effort at the turn of this century to improve its image, complained that using three-year averages "effectively encourages some flags to specialize in sub-standard shipping,"[22] because it can be too hard for a state to get off the target list and thereby attract reputable ships to its registry. Belize dramatically improved its detention rate under the Paris MOU beginning in 2001 (moving from a detention rate of 24.81 percent in 2000 and a high of 50 percent in 1993 to only 13.39 percent in 2001), but was still under

21. There are other differences in the way the U.S. Coast Guard (USCG) system keeps records that have to be accounted for in comparing across PSC systems. The USCG primarily calculates inspection percentages by ship rather than by inspection. A ship inspected twice in one year is only counted once. Calculations have been done here with additional USGC data to determine overall inspection percentages instead, and USCG inspection results are reported in this recalculated way.

22. Nigel Lowry, "Mare Forum—Belize Protests over Three-Year Black-List Rule," *Lloyd's List*, September 20, 2002, 5.

increased scrutiny because of its earlier detention rate. The following year (2002) its detention rate was 20.35 percent, suggesting that there are good reasons not to reward one good year. (In the years since then its rate has fallen below 10 percent, but is still well above the regional average.)[23]

In the case of the Paris MOU, information on all of the above elements is collected in a centralized computer, which uses a targeting formula to suggest which ships entering a given port should be inspected. Each factor is assigned a certain point value. The "target-factor" calculator considers elements of the ship itself: the type and age of the ship (5 points are added if a ship is a bulk carrier more than twelve years old, a chemical tanker more than ten years old, an oil tanker more than fifteen years old, or a passenger ship of any age; for all other types the ship gets 3 points if it is older than twenty-five years, 2 if it is between twenty-one and twenty-four, and 1 if it is between thirteen and twenty); its history of visiting and being inspected in a port in the region (20 points if it has not been in port in the area in the last twelve months; 10 points if it has not otherwise been inspected in the previous six months); how many times it has been detained in the previous year (15 points for one detention, 30 for two, and 45 for three); and how many deficiencies it had from its inspections in the last year (from each previous inspection no deficiencies results in a subtraction of 15 points, one to five gains 0 points, six to eleven results in 5 points, eleven to twenty adds 10 points, and more than twenty-one deficiencies adds 15 points), as well as whether any of the previous deficiencies remain (one point added for some deficiencies and two deducted if all have been successfully rectified).

The system also assigns points on characteristics of the ship's affiliations: classification society (if the ship is classed by a classification society not recognized by the European Union it gains an extra 5 points; if the classification society has an above-average deficiency ratio the ship gets 1 point), flag state (if the state is on the annual black list the ship receives 20 points if the flag is characterized as "very high risk," 14 points for a state designated "high risk," 8 points for "medium to high risk," 4

23. Detention rates taken from Paris MOU, *Annual Reports* from 1993, 2000, 2001, 2002, 2003, 2004 (Paris: Paris MOU, 1994, 2001, 2002, 2003, 2004, 2005).

points for "medium risk," and an additional point if the flag state has not ratified all the relevant conventions). These are then calculated so that a "target factor" is suggested for each ship entering port.[24] The U.S. Coast Guard inspection process has a similar "boarding priority matrix" that assigns points based on owner, flag, class, inspection history, and type and age of ship.[25]

The Paris MOU states have also agreed to increasingly strict penalties, beyond detention, for ships that have repeatedly been judged problematic. Under rules that took effect in 2003 the organization decided that ships registered in flags classified as "high risk" or "very high risk" on the Paris MOU black list would be banned from calling at ports in member states if they are detained twice in a period of two years, and ships registered in flags considered "medium to high" or "medium" risk on the black list would be banned if detained three times over the course of two years. A shipowner can apply to have the ban lifted by submitting a petition to the state that issued the ban, and presenting a certificate from its flag state that it meets all the requirements of IMO and ILO agreements considered under the port-state inspection regime; its classification society must also indicate that the ship meets its requirements. After such a petition, the ship must undergo and pass an expanded inspection (with the costs borne by the shipowner).[26] The Paris MOU also decided in 2003 to attempt to inspect ships with a target factor of 50 or more once a month.[27]

Individual MOUs may also decide to focus on particular issues or ships in their inspection process. For instance, the Paris MOU decided to target cruise ships for three months in 2003, requiring that the ships perform emergency drills when in port.[28] The Tokyo MOU focused in 2002 on compliance with the International Safety Management (ISM)

24. Paris MOU, "Target Factor Calculator," http://www.parismou.org/.

25. U.S. Coast Guard, "Boarding Priority Matrix," http://www.uscg.mil/hq/g-m/pscweb/matrix.htm.

26. "Two Strikes and You're Out," *Lloyd's List*, May 14, 2003, 1; "New Requirements from 22 July 2003," Paris MOU Press Release, May 13, 2003, http://www.parismou.org/.

27. David Osler, "Slovenia Signs Up to Paris MOU," *Lloyd's List*, May 21, 2003, 5.

28. "Michael Grey, "Inspectors Target Cruiseships," *Lloyd's List*, April 11, 2003, 14.

Code, and on 2003 on safety on bulk carriers.[29] Similarly, the Latin American MOU undertook a concentrated inspection campaign in 2002 on the STCW 95 Convention, in 2003 on the ISM Code, and in 2004 on passenger vessels.[30]

Although the MOU statistics do not obligate any other organization to act, the International Transport Workers Federation (ITF), discussed further in chapter 6, uses target lists from the various MOU inspection processes as one of the factors that determines which flag states it will single out for its labor actions.[31]

The cooperative system for inspections does not, of course, work perfectly. Even in the most established PSC system—the European process under the Paris MOU—national variation continues despite the best efforts at coordinated inspections. It has been suggested that some states fill out paperwork without conducting anything but cursory inspections, and that others scrupulously fulfill their inspection targets by inspecting those with good records. It is even charged that some inspectors in the European system can be bought off.[32]

In 2004 the Paris MOU Committee decided at its annual meeting to remove the requirement that 25 percent of ships be inspected. This change came in part because members were concerned that to meet the inspection quota, port inspectors were focusing on ships that were less likely to have violations, which could be inspected faster. Such an approach would be exactly counter to how the MOU process is supposed to operate.[33]

Port state control has created an incentive for flag states to increase standards. Individual vessels would prefer not to be detained, and flag states do not want to gain a reputation for requiring more than their

29. Tokyo MOU, "Press Release: The Twelfth Meeting of the Port State Control Committee in the Asia-Pacific Region Held in Chile," April 8, 2003, http://www.tokyo-mou.org/psc12prs.pdf.

30. Acuerdo Latino, "Concentrated Inspection Campaigns," http://200.45.69.62/Campanas_concentradas_i_htm, [as accessed: 23 July 2003].

31. David Osler, "Registers Targeted in ITF Campaign," *Lloyd's List*, September 25, 2001, 2.

32. William Langewiesche, *The Outlaw Sea: A World of Freedom, Chaos, and Crime* (New York: North Point Press, 2004), 92–93.

33. Brian Reyes, "Paris MoU Plans Radical Overhaul of Inspections," *Lloyd's List*, May 18, 2004, 1.

fair share of inspections, particularly since their attractiveness as a registry decreases with the inconvenience borne by vessels flying their flag. In the words of Julio Sosa, the Panamanian Maritime Consul in Houston, "No one wants to be in a flag where the coast guard is going to be fingering you all the time."[34] Under a system of port state control, truly substandard ships have fewer options about what ports to enter.[35] As suggested by the comments from the Belize registry, flag states recognize the impact that PSC detention statistics have on their ability to attract a certain type of ship to the registry.

Early PSC Impacts: Liberia

The impact that early versions of port state control had on Liberia is an important early indicator of the potential for success, and the broader impacts, of this mechanism, though the process happened before the MOU process (with its clear record-keeping) was in place. Liberia used to be the standard example of the worst problems of flag-of-convenience shipping. Liberian ships were more prone than average to accidents, and had older equipment that was not especially well maintained. Now Liberian-registered oil tankers are among the safest and least polluting on the oceans, and have better records than some traditional registries. The mechanism of port state control provided the context for increasing standards to be taken on by the Liberian registry, but the primary action came with pressure from the companies that shipped oil on Liberian-flagged tankers.

It was in the context of the nascent port state control regime that Liberian-registered oil tankers sought to take on higher standards than their registry required. This change came in the wake of several major oil-tanker disasters in the late 1960s and early 1970s. American shipowners who registered their vessels in Liberia realized that increased scrutiny of the Liberian registry might result in lost advantages, if this attention resulted in legislation to diminish their ability to flag offshore.

They therefore convinced the Liberian government to ratify the SOLAS convention and persuaded the registry to implement an inspection pro-

34. Morris, 15.
35. Hare, 593.

gram for all Liberian-flagged vessels.[36] Liberia joined most of the major International Maritime Organization agreements relating to oil pollution (including MARPOL, the main agreement to prevent intentional oil pollution at sea, and a variety of agreements on preventing or addressing accidental oil spills) in 1980 or 1981.[37] The state was willing to do so to protect the revenue it gained from the registry (and the registry was willing to do so to protect its revenue as well); shipowners favored this move because the tax and labor advantages of Liberian registry far outweighed any cost of increased safety inspections, and they hoped that an improved safety record would remove international pressure to address FOC issues more intensively. In addition, for some shipowners who already met the proposed safety standards, endorsing such regulations could only help their position both competitively and in terms of public relations.[38]

While port state control, and fear of greater international regulation, provided the context for this change, it is important to note that the action taken was by Liberian-flagged shipowners, convincing the Liberian registry (which has little to do with the actual Liberian state) to create a regulatory framework—a club of shipowners that met higher standards than their competitors. This club was able to benefit from the increased reputation for safety its registry created. Oil tankers that could not meet the higher standards registered elsewhere. The timing of Liberia's niche as a registry with moderately high standards on oil-pollution prevention coincides with a somewhat dramatic decrease in registered tonnage, beginning just after 1980. Likewise, the decrease in Liberia's registered tonnage came at the same time that Panama and other registries grew, as indicated in figure 5.1, suggesting that Liberia's tougher standards fed the growth in other registries.

Port State Control Effects

The Liberia example is suggestive, but before a consistent port state control process was followed and clear records kept it was difficult to

36. Julie A. Perkins, "Ship Registers: An International Update," *The Maritime Lawyer* 22 (winter 1997): 198. Liberia joined the SOLAS Convention in 1977. International Maritime Organization, http://www.imo.org.

37. International Maritime Organization, http://www.imo.org.

38. Rodney Carlisle, *Sovereignty for Sale* (Annapolis: United States Naval Academy Press, 1981), 185–186.

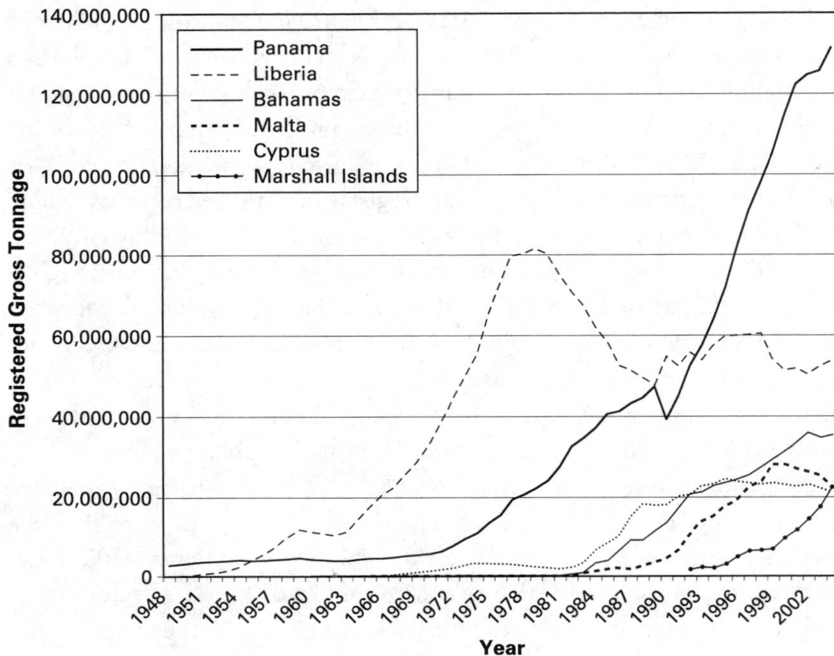

Figure 5.1
Major open registry tonnage 1948–2004. *Source:* Lloyd's Register Fairplay, *World Fleet Statistics 1948–2004* (London: Lloyd's Register, 1949–2005)

examine systematically the impact of a port state control inspection system on flag-state standards. This section evaluates the effects of the formal inspection processes that have taken place. It includes the three major inspection regimes: the Paris MOU process, beginning in 1985; the Tokyo MOU process, beginning in 1994; and the U.S. Coast Guard inspection process, beginning systematically in 1998.[39] Other MOU inspection processes are more recent or in areas without major ship traffic and thus less likely to have had a major impact on ship standards or registration choices. Some manipulation of the data has been necessary to arrive at comparable and meaningful statistics. Each inspection regime keeps an average (called "regional average") of the percentage of ships

39. The Coast Guard system actually began in 1991 but records were not publicized until 1998. Reference is made here to earlier inspection results under the Coast Guard system where relevant.

inspected in that year that are detained.[40] From this can be calculated a "detention ratio"[41]—the detention rate for a given flag state divided by the regional average. In any given year a detention ratio greater than 1 means that ships from that flag state were detained more often than the average for that year under that inspection process. Note that this ratio is different from the process used to single out states for increased scrutiny; all three inspection processes use a three-year rolling average to determine which ships to list on white or black lists. The detention ratio indicates how a flag state is doing in an individual year, compared to all flag states whose ships were inspected.

The MOU data provide additional support for the characterization of the regulatory levels of states in chapter 2. First, second registries tend to have consistently higher detention rates than their "home" states. The comparison of inspection results under the PSC systems for the Netherlands and the Netherlands Antilles is illustrative (see figure 5.2 for a comparison under the Paris MOU). While both have better-than-average inspection records, the detention ratio for ships from the Netherlands is consistently notably lower (an average of .38 across all years for Paris, .27 for Tokyo, and .39 for the U.S. Coast Guard) than for ships from the Netherlands Antilles (with an average of .72 for Paris, .42 for Tokyo, and 1.48 for the U.S. Coast Guard). Similarly, with the exception of Bermuda, the detention ratios for the British second registries are all higher than that of the UK national registry. While the detention ratios for these second registries are occasionally above the regional average, they never are high enough to gain blacklisting (and the extra attention that follows) for these second registries.

40. The U.S. Coast Guard inspection process reports its numbers slightly differently than the MOU process. The MOUs count each arrival of a ship as a separate possible opportunity for inspection. A ship that arrives in a port twelve times will be counted as twelve ships. The Coast Guard counts "distinct vessel arrivals," meaning that a ship that enters a port twelve times is only counted once for the purposes of calculating inspections and detentions. For the purposes of comparison, the Coast Guard data have been disaggregated so that the total number of arrivals is used in calculating detention ratios.

41. Note that the terminology also differs across systems. What the MOUs call a detention *rate* (percentage of inspected ships that are detained), the Coast Guard calls a detention *ratio*. In this book, however, *detention ratio* is used to refer to the detention rate (as the MOUs use the term, and applied to the Coast Guard data) divided by the regional average in a given year.

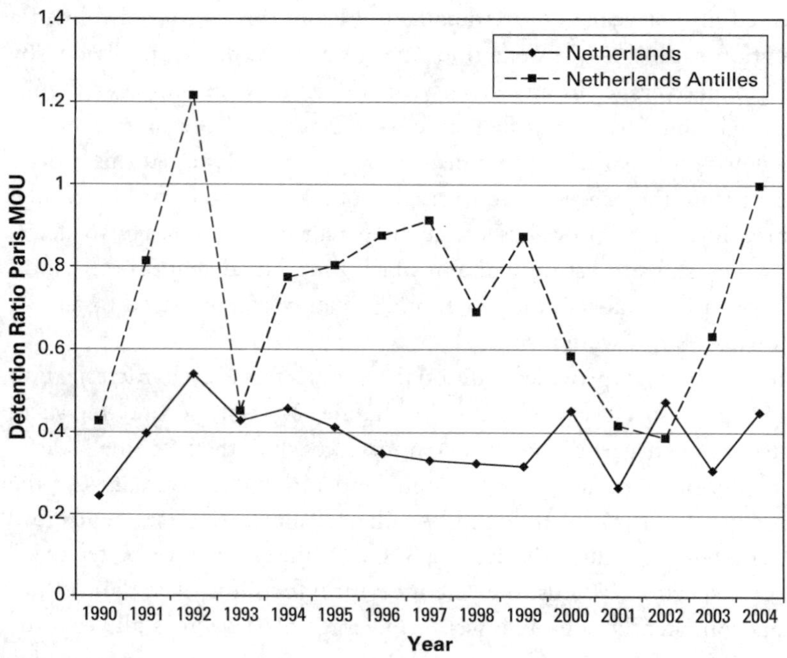

Figure 5.2
Paris MOU detention ratios: Netherlands and Netherlands Antilles calculated from: Paris MOU, *Annual Reports 1985–2004* (The Hague: Paris MOU, 1986–2005)

Second, for environment and safety standards (the primary issues examined under the PSC regimes), there is a strong relationship between the characterization of flag states based on their levels of adoption of international regulations, in chapter 2, and their inspection records. Honduras, singled out as the all-around low-regulation open registry, has above-average detention rates in all years of all three inspection processes examined (see figure 5.11 later in this chapter). Panama, listed as the quintessential middle, has detention ratios close to 1 in all inspections processes (see figure 5.13 later in this chapter). This means that Panama is always right at the margin of being included in target lists for inspections, but not high enough to receive serious scrutiny. While Panama has recently been on the target list for the U.S. Coast Guard, it has been on the White List in 2002 and 2003 for the Tokyo MOU, and is listed at the low end of "Black list—medium risk" under the Paris MOU.

What is more interesting, however, is the extent to which the information about port state control inspections and detentions can explain the process by which states choose the level of regulation to adopt. First and foremost, PSC detention rates provide information about the quality of the standards upheld by ships in a given registry. A registry with a high detention rate has ships that have generally failed inspections. But this detention rate then serves as a piece of information: it indicates to shipowners deciding where to register a ship both what the general quality of oversight from the registry is, and how likely ships registered there are to be singled out for inspection. It thus increases transparency both for shipowners and for port states. And because shipowners do not want to be singled out for inspection, it creates an incentive for flag states, which want to attract and keep ship registrations, to improve their standards. They can do so only by demanding that ships registered under their flags meet the type of standards for which the PSC systems inspect, or by removing ships that do not meet the standards to which they aspire.

Examination of the relationship between registered tonnage in a registry and its PSC record can be illuminating. It can be difficult to ascertain a causal relationship here from the numbers alone, because ships may choose on their own to leave a registry if its detention rates are too high, or a registry may choose to delete substandard ships from its registry to improve its PSC record. Conversely, when a registry adopts more stringent standards, ships that cannot meet them or choose not to may leave to seek lower-standard registries. Nevertheless, the trends in registrations and PSC records, combined with additional evidence provided by statements or actions by states and registries, can provide some evidence of the effectiveness of the PSC system. A number of open-registry states provide clear evidence that they have chosen levels of regulation because of this inspection process. A discussion of some of the most important open registry states and their strategies follows.[42]

Marshall Islands

The Marshall Islands, a true open registry, underwent a dramatic shift in its PSC record fairly early in its history. It began offering ship registrations

42. The registries examined here are those for which there is persuasive evidence that the registry undertook action in response to PSC inspection results; the focus here as well is on particularly influential open registries.

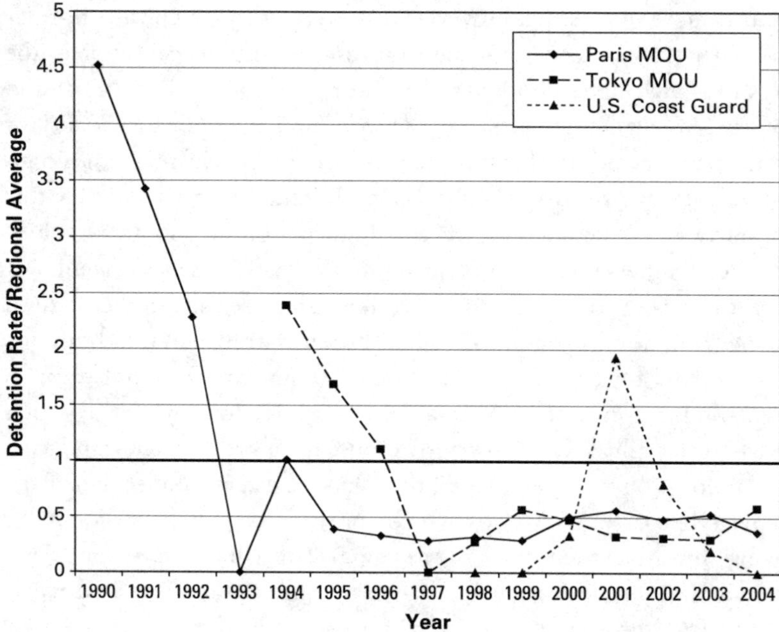

Figure 5.3
Marshall Islands detention ratios calculated from: Paris MOU, *Annual Reports 1985–2004* (The Hague: Paris MOU, 1986–2005); Tokyo MOU, *Annual Reports on Port State Control in the Asia-Pacific Region 1994–2004* (Tokyo: Tokyo MOU, 1995–2005); U.S. Coast Guard, "Port State Control in the United States," *Annual Reports 1998–2004* (Washington, D.C.: U.S. Coast Guard, 1999–2005)

internationally in 1990,[43] and in its first few years was above the regional averages for detentions in the two major inspection regimes (Paris and Tokyo) that existed at that point. The state made the decision, however, to operate as a high-quality registry, and undertook important steps to improve its reputation and inspection rates. Its ship-registration company, International Registries, until recently, also ran the Liberian registry, involved during Liberia's dramatic move from disreputable to above average.[44] The Marshall Islands began using the same registry-based in-

43. Nik Winchester and Tony Alderton, *Flag State Audit 2003* (Cardiff: SIRC, 2003), 307.

44. Liberia left International Registries in 1999 when it accused the registration company of pushing ships toward the registry of the Marshall Islands rather than that of Liberia. See Tom Baldwin, "Who's in Charge Here?", *Journal of Commerce*, January 15, 1999, 1B.

spection process discussed earlier that raised Liberia's reputation. This inspection process examines compliance with all of the major safety and environmental conventions used as the basis for port state control inspections, though going beyond that which would be required for these inspections.[45] International Registries moved in 1992 to require that the classification societies that class its vessels be members of the International Association of Classification Societies (IACS), and undertook a public campaign to persuade insurance underwriters to only insure IACS-classed vessels, or to grant a rate reduction for them.[46] In addition, the International Registries' Maritime Operation Department was certified under ISO 9002 (Quality Management System), making it the first ship registry to receive recognition from the International Organization for Standardization.[47]

In the mid-1990s the Marshall Islands joined most of the main international safety and environmental agreements it had not previously joined. In 1994 it joined the International Convention on Civil Liability for Oil Pollution Damage and its protocol, as well as the United Nations Convention on the Law of the Sea (UNCLOS). In 1995 it ratified a number of recent shipping-related agreements, including the International Convention Relating to Intervention on the High Seas in Cases of Oil Pollution Casualties, the International Convention for the Establishment of an International Fund for Compensation for Oil Pollution Damage and its protocol, the Protocol Relating to Intervention on the High Seas in Cases of Pollution by Substances Other than Oil, the Convention on Limitation of Liability for Maritime Claims, the International Convention for Safe Containers, and also the older International Convention on Standards of Training, Certification, and Watchkeeping for Seafarers (STCW).[48]

45. Doug Woodyard, "IRI Advances on Strength of Safety Inspections," *Lloyd's List*, October 12, 1994, 11.

46. The IACS is a group of high-standard classification societies, discussed further in chapter 8. See Andrew Guest, "Liberia Calls for IACS Backing," *Lloyd's List*, July 6, 1992, 1.

47. Alan Thorpe, "Special Report on Quality Assurance and Management," *Lloyd's List*, July 17, 1995, 7.

48. International Union for the Conservation of Nature (IUCN), United Nations Environment Program (UNEP), Tufts University's Fletcher School of Law and Diplomacy, British Columbia Ministry of Environment, Lands, & Parks,

Nevertheless, while these efforts brought a dramatic reduction in the detention rates in the European and Asian inspection processes, the Marshall Islands had a higher detention rate in the U.S. Coast Guard system, and was added to the list of targeted states in 1996.[49] It also was still targeted by the International Transport Workers Federation (see chapter 6) for labor standards in 1997.[50] Eventually its registry-based inspection process paid off, removing it from the U.S. Coast Guard target list in 1997 and landing on the "white list" in the Paris MOU system.[51] By 2001 the Marshall Islands had been singled out by the U.S. Coast Guard as among the ten registries with the best port state control inspection results, thus decreasing the level of attention ships registered there will receive in future inspections.[52] The president of the company administering the registry touted these accomplishments as a way to encourage other ships to register in the Marshall Islands. Saying that "quality [is] our main driver," Bill Gallagher pointed to "Paris and Tokyo MOU detention statistics and the fact that ours is the only open register to qualify for the US Coastguard Qualships 21 programme."[53] By 2003 the Marshall Islands registry was turning down one-third of the ships that applied to register (and others were asked to leave the registry), on the grounds that they did not meet the high standards of the registry. Gallagher directly linked this strategy to port state control: "quality comes first and any problems we have, such as a port state detention,

---

Antarctic Research Center, American Society of International Law (ASIL), and Center for International Earth Science Information Network (CIESIN), *Environmental Treaties and Resource Indicators (ENTRI) Query Service* (Palisades, N.Y.: CIESIN, Columbia University, n.d.), http://sedac.ciesin.columbia.edu/entri.

49. Joel Glass, "Eleven Registers Added to 1996 USCG Blacklist," *Lloyd's List*, April 16, 1996, 12; U.S. Coast Guard, "Port State Control 1996 Flag List," unpublished document supplied by CDR Lonnie P. Harrison Jr., Commandant, U.S. Coast Guard Headquarters, Washington, D.C.

50. Robert Ward, "ITF Gets Set for Action," *Lloyd's List*, September 19, 1997, 9.

51. Paris MOU, *Annual Report 1997* (Paris: MOU, 1998); U.S. Coast Guard, *1997 Port State Control Report* (Washington, D.C.: U.S. Coast Guard, 1998).

52. Michael Grey, "U.S. Guard Identifies 400-Plus for Qualship 21," *Lloyd's List*, August 28, 2001, 3.

53. "Marshall Islands Wins Stamp of Approval from US Programme," *Lloyd's List*, February 6, 2002, 19.

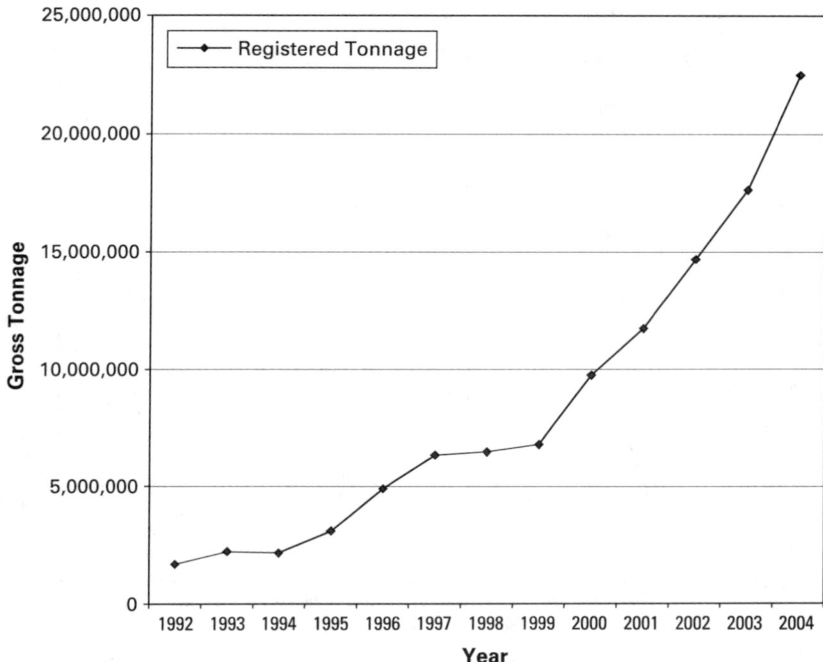

Figure 5.4
Marshall Islands registered tonnage. *Source:* Lloyd's Register Fairplay, *World Fleet Statistics 1992–2004* (London: Lloyd's Register, 1993–2005)

hangs over us like a black cloud."[54] The Marshall Islands also was one of the first registries to agree to IMO-developed voluntary flag-state audits.[55]

This effort paid off, with the Marshall Islands as one of the fastest-growing registries as indicated in figure 5.4, the seventh largest ship registry as of the end of 2004.[56] Most of the ships transferred to its registry came from the United States or from Liberia (often owned by U.S. companies).[57]

54. "Marshall Islands—It's the Applications They Turn Down ...", *Lloyd's List*, February 10, 2003, 16.

55. Hugh O'Mahoney, "Mitropolous Praises State Audit Scheme," *Lloyd's List*, March 30, 2005, 5.

56. Lloyd's Register Fairplay, *World Fleet Statistics* (London: Lloyd's Register Fairplay, 2005), 10.

57. Winchester and Alderton, 311.

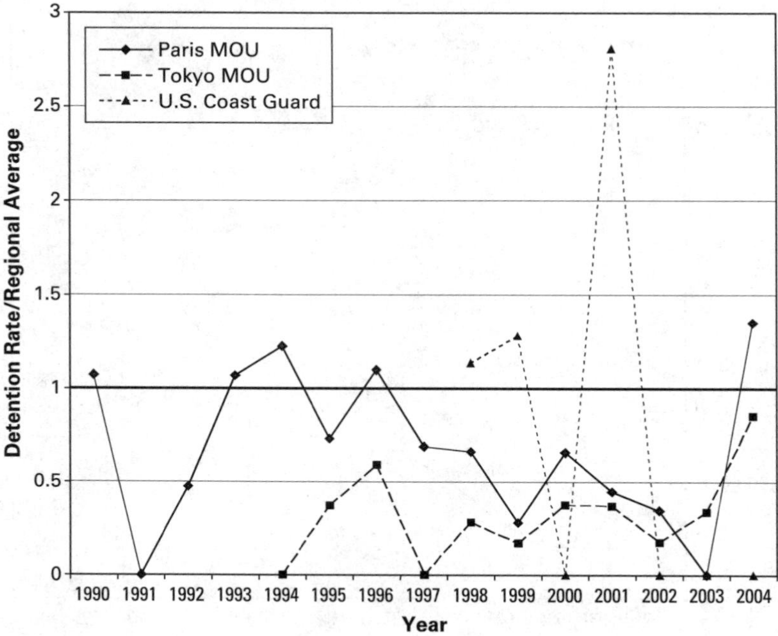

Figure 5.5
Vanuatu MOU detention ratios calculated from: Paris MOU, *Annual Reports 1985–2004* (The Hague: Paris MOU, 1986–2005); Tokyo MOU, *Annual Reports on Port State Control in the Asia-Pacific Region 1994–2004* (Tokyo: Tokyo MOU, 1995–2005); U.S. Coast Guard, "Port State Control in the United States," *Annual Reports 1998–2004* (Washington, D.C.: U.S. Coast Guard, 1999–2005)

Vanuatu

Vanuatu has a similar downward trajectory of detention rates under port state control (see figure 5.5), though with much greater variation. Its operation as an open registry began earlier, in 1981. It quickly gained a reputation as "one of the less responsible registers," with a small registry staff and no surveyors to determine ship quality or compliance.[58]

Its ships were not inspected by any of the main PSC systems until 1990. Early Paris MOU inspections put it just above regional average in several of the first few inspection years, though not sufficient to be on

58. Andrew Guest, "Vanuatu Agrees to New Contract," *Lloyd's List*, March 31, 1993, 12.

black lists. Similarly, it had early Coast Guard detention rates higher than average.[59]

In early 1993 the government of Vanuatu decided change ship-registration companies, to Vanuatu Maritime Services, part of an American-owned offshore banking and insurance group.[60] The new registry indicated that it aimed to increase the extent to which its ships conformed to international standards. One of the first things the new company did was challenge the 1994 Coast Guard targeting of Vanuatu-flagged ships. It successfully appealed the detention of one of the ships that had been listed on the grounds that the deficiency was not sufficiently serious. Once this detention was removed from the calculations, Vanuatu fell below the target level and its ships were no longer slated to be singled out,[61] a status it was able to maintain the following year. The vice president of the registry indicated that Vanuatu made an effort to avoid registering older ships, and was trying to position itself "as a safety-conscious flag."[62] One of the most persuasive pieces of evidence that the Vanuatu registry is serious about its increased standards comes from an undercover investigation in 1998 done by a reporter for the daily shipping newspaper *Lloyd's List.* The reporter pretended to be the owner of a ship in "appalling condition," unable to comply with a number of specific international standards. Of all the flags to which the reporter appealed, the only one to reject the application immediately was Vanuatu.[63]

In 1999 at least partly in a strategy to frame itself as a high-quality registry to lure ships that might want to leave the Liberian flag, the Vanuatu government created a government agency, the Vanuatu Maritime Authority (VMA), that would coordinate safety and environmental

59. U.S. Coast Guard, "Port State Control 1996 Flag List," unpublished document.

60. Keith Hindell, "Hong Kong Owners Are Biggest Users of Vanuatu," *Lloyd's List*, March 29, 1995, 9.

61. Jim Mulrenan, "Vanuatu off USGC Hit List," *Lloyd's List*, August 12, 1994, 10.

62. Robert Ward, "Vanuatu Puts Focus on Safety," *Lloyd's List*, March 27, 1996, 14.

63. David Osler and Nigel Lowry, "Flags Offered for 'Appalling' Ships," *Lloyd's List*, September 10, 1998, 1.

programs relating to ships.[64] The registry appeared on the Paris MOU Grey List beginning in 1999. It also received ISO certification in 2001, and worked to combat fraudulent ship-worker documentation.[65] With the exception of a bad Coast Guard PSC detention rate in 2001 (and some inspection results in 2004 that a registry official characterized as "an anomaly in the continuing downward trend in detentions),"[66] Vanuatu's detention rate has been generally below average in the three major inspection systems in recent times.

This new focus on safety, however, helped create conflicts between the registry and the state, involving complicated domestic politics. Beginning in 1999 the VMA began to audit the activities of the registry. The most telling incident came when a cargo ship carrying athletes traveling to an important national competition was detained for serious safety problems by the new regulatory agency. The cargo ship was owned by the president of the international ship registry, who ordered it to leave, despite the VMA requests.[67] In a bizarre conclusion to this conflict, the chief executive of the registry was indicted at the end of 2002 in the United States for running an unrelated international lottery scam.[68]

Coincidentally or not, Vanuatu's ship registrations began decreasing (see figure 5.6) just as its early port state control inspection results appeared. They continued to decline until a recent upswing at the turn of the century, just following its efforts to reposition itself as a high-quality registry.

Belize

Belize has also exhibited a strong effort to improve its port state control experiences, but with a bit less success than the Marshall Islands and Vanuatu. Belize began operating as an open registry in 1991 (though

64. "Vanuatu Emphasizes Safety in Bid to Be the 'First Alternative,'" *Lloyd's List*, September 6, 1999, 9.

65. "Vanuatu: Active Year Sees Further Reduction in Detentions," *Lloyd's List*, February 6, 2002, 19.

66. "Support Vessels Underpin Vanuatu Growth," *Lloyd's List*, February 7, 2005, 11.

67. "All Is Not Well on the Island of Vanuatu," *Lloyd's List*, June 30, 2001, 4.

68. David Osler, "Vanuatu Registry Chief Bohn Arrested over $100 M Scam," *Lloyd's List*, December 10, 2002, 1.

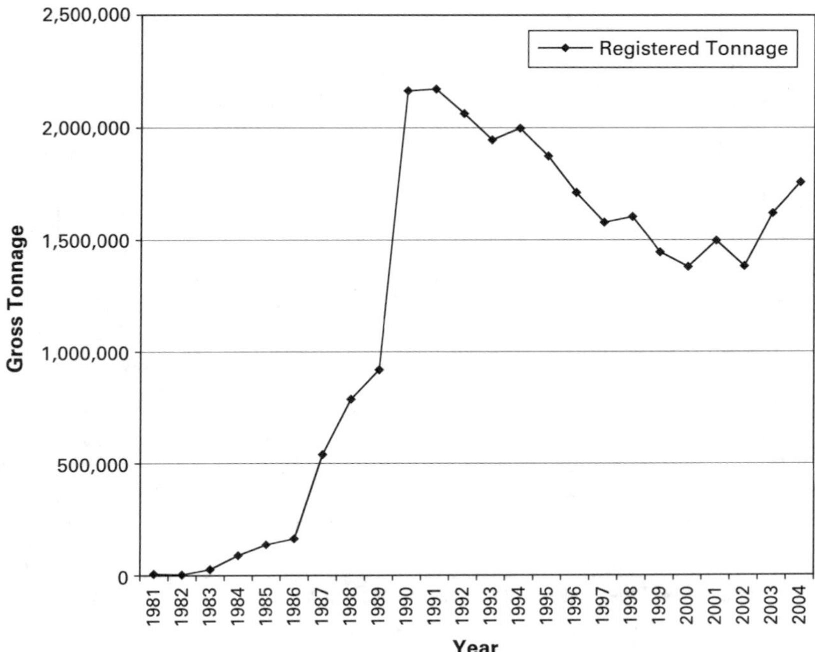

Figure 5.6
Vanuatu registered tonnage. *Source:* Lloyd's Register Fairplay, *World Fleet Statistics 1982–2004* (London: Lloyd's Register, 1983–2005)

some shipowners had flown the Belize flag without authorization beginning in 1989) and quickly attracted ship registrations, including 94 ships (32 above 100 GT, the rest small) in its first year. At that point it had not ratified any major international shipping agreements, and many of its ships transferred from the Honduran registry, another low-standard registry.[69] It immediately found itself an inspection target for all three major inspection regimes. It also was second only to Honduras in percentage of ships lost at sea between 1993 and 1997 as measured by the Institute of London Underwriters.[70] As late as 1998 the general secretary of the

69. Andrew Guest, "Belize Flag Popularity Grows," *Lloyd's List*, March 31, 1993, 12.

70. Institute of London Underwriters, *Casualty Statistics 1998* (London: Institute of London Underwriters, 1999).

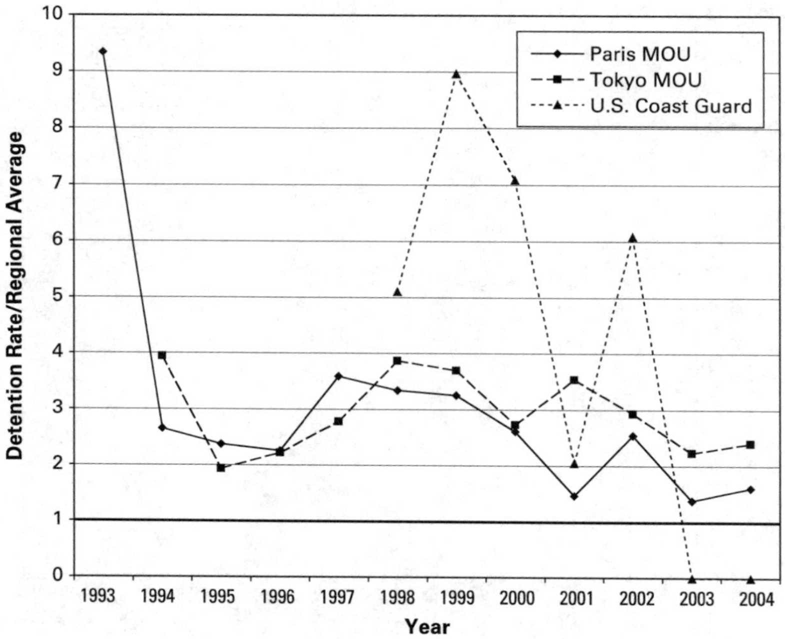

Figure 5.7
Belize MOU detention ratios calculated from: Paris MOU, *Annual Reports 1985–2004* (The Hague: Paris MOU, 1986–2005); Tokyo MOU, *Annual Reports on Port State Control in the Asia-Pacific Region 1994–2004* (Tokyo: Tokyo MOU, 1995–2005); U.S. Coast Guard, "Port State Control in the United States," *Annual Reports 1998–2004* (Washington, D.C.: U.S. Coast Guard, 1999–2005)

International Transport Workers Federation called it "one of the shabbiest, shoddiest and most unscrupulous flags in the world."[71]

In 1996 the former director of the Panamanian registry's marine safety office in New York was appointed to run the Belize registry. At that point Belize conducted no inspections of registered vessels. The new head of the registry acknowledged that "up until now, the register has just been registering vessels" (and not undertaking the "other responsibilities" of ship registry, such as inspection).[72] Despite the addition of inspectors to the registry, however, its detention rates remained high. In 1999, for

71. David Osler, "British Tory Party Has a Stake in Belize Flag," *Lloyd's List*, November 21, 1998.

72. John McLaughlin, "Gonzalez to Head Belize Ship Register," *Lloyd's List*, February 2, 1996, 12.

example, it had the worst detention rate in the Tokyo MOU inspection system.[73] In that same year Belize had the worst U.S. Coast Guard detention rate, with more than half of its vessels detained over the previous three years.[74] Belize, in an effort to improve its standings, cut ties with the International Register of Shipping, one of the classification societies that had classed Belize-registered vessels, which was later determined to have the worst port state control detention record of all classification societies.[75] Belize also began fining ships that did not meet the standards of the registry,[76] created improved reporting systems and an audit system for its vessel surveyors, and added inspectors in major ports to check Belize-registered vessels.[77]

The director of the registry was replaced again in 2001, with a professional ship manager who promised "to accelerate the flag's attempts to become 'whitelisted' at IMO" and with the U.S. Coast Guard.[78] It was at this point that the registry made a serious effort to improve its reputation: the registry immediately removed 668 ships for safety deficiencies and other problems (with more removed the following year), it began requiring that its large ships be classed by members of the International Association of Classification Societies (IACS), and required that all ships have third-party liability and comply with the ISM code. The registry began negotiations with the Belize government in an effort to persuade it to ratify the major international agreements pertaining to ships. In addition, the Belize registry introduced new reductions in taxes for ships with good records.[79] The registry also implemented a 15 percent tax reduction for ships that meet ISO 14001 Environmental Standards and a 25 percent

73. Tokyo MOU, *Annual Report on Port State Control in the Asia-Pacific Region 1999* (Tokyo: Tokyo MOU, 2000).

74. U.S. Coast Guard, *1999 Port State Control Report* (Washington, D.C.: U.S. Coast Guard, 2000).

75. David Osler, "IRS Tops List for Worst Detenion Record in US," *Lloyd's List*, September 6, 1999, 16.

76. "Spotlight on Belize," *Lloyd's List*, September 6, 1999.

77. Michael Grey, "Belize Flag Dismisses Substandard Inspectors," *Lloyd's List*, May 23, 2000, 1.

78. Michael Grey, "Mouzouropoulos: More Than Three Decades' Experience in Commercial Shipowning and Management," *Lloyd's List*, July 25, 2001, 2.

79. Christopher Mayer, "Belize Flag Weeds Out 668 Ships to Polish Tarnished Image," *Lloyd's List*, January 16, 2002, 3.

reduction for ships that go twelve months (or 35 percent for twenty-four months) without detention.[80] When the ISM code entered into force in July 2002, the registry ejected ten vessels that did not comply with the code, and prevented another forty-four from sailing until they met the standards.[81]

The registry also began discussions with Canada, Japan, and the United States. These states had restricted fishery imports (see chapter 7) from Belize-registered vessels that did not adhere to international fishery restrictions. Belize attempted to persuade these states, with some degree of success, that it had undertaken the necessary steps to warrant the removal of trade restrictions.[82]

These efforts have begun to pay off. With a couple of exceptions, the trend in detention rates has been downward since the late 1990s, with particularly notable improvement since 2000. While the detention rate has not fallen below average for any PSC regime except the Coast Guard (and even then the use of rolling averages means that Belize is still targeted for increased scrutiny), it is within reach of the regional averages, something that was not previously true. Belize also worked particularly closely with the United States on the implementation of the new International Ship and Port Facility Security Code, removing ships from its flag that did not meet the new code. This approach, in part, probably helps to account for its recent good record in the U.S. Coast Guard inspection system. After two excellent years it expects to be removed from the Coast Guard black list by 2006,[83] and may be on track to be removed from the Paris MOU black list as well.

The registered tonnage in the registry heavily reflects the decision of the registry to remove low-standard vessels, but has recently rebounded somewhat, suggesting that at least some ships are willing to move to the Belize registry in its new, higher-standard incarnation.

80. "Being Small Is More Beautiful by Belize Flag's Reckoning," *Lloyd's List*, September 7, 2005, 14.

81. Michael Grey, "Belize Puts the Boot into First ISM Code Offenders," *Lloyd's List*, July 2, 2002, 1.

82. "Registers—Belize Flag Weeds Out 668 Ships to Polish Tarnished Image," *Lloyd's List*, January 16, 2002, 3.

83. Michael Grey, "Belize Flag Seeks Removal from USCG Blacklist," *Lloyd's List*, December 7, 2004, 12.

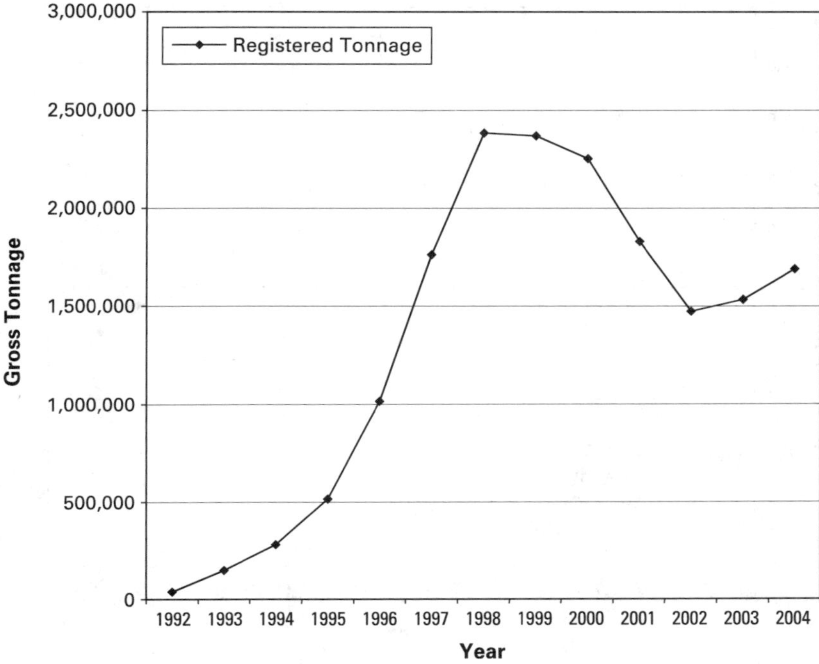

Figure 5.8
Belize registered tonnage. *Source:* Lloyd's Register Fairplay, *World Fleet Statistics 1992–2004* (London: Lloyd's Register, 1993–2005)

Cyprus

Cyprus has run an open registry since the late 1960s.[84] The Cyprus flag is another one that has undertaken a largely successful recent effort to improve its port state control detention rates and attract ship registrations by ensuring that its ships will not be singled out for inspection. It has had some trouble keeping its detention rates low, however. What is particularly interesting is that this increase in detentions has come at the same time that Cyprus has lost some ship registrations (moving from a high of 1,674 registered ships in 1995 to 1,084 in 2004). While it has not yet appeared on any of the inspection black lists, its recent trend is worrisome, because it suggests that the ships that are leaving are the higher-quality ships.

84. Carlisle, 210.

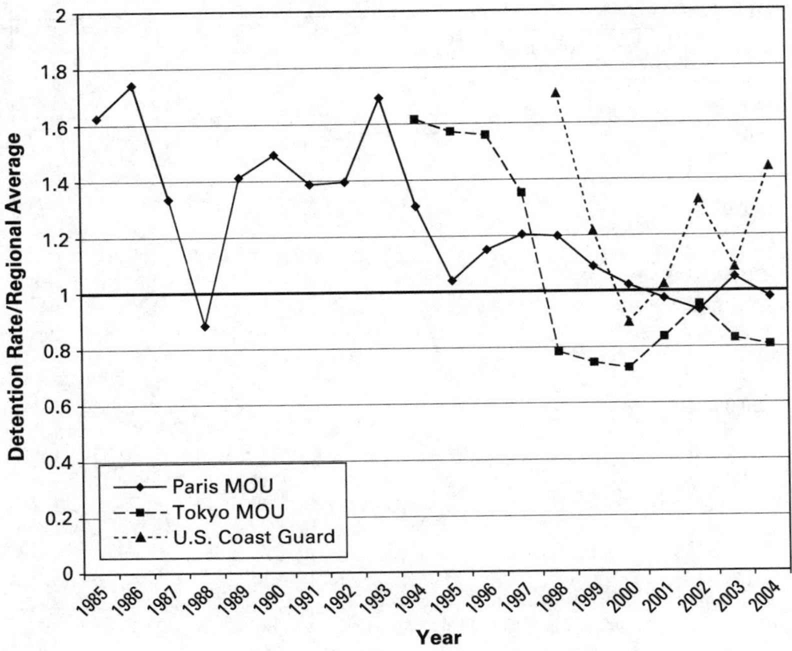

Figure 5.9
Cyprus detention ratios. Calculated from: Paris MOU, *Annual Reports 1985–2004* (The Hague: Paris MOU, 1986–2005); Tokyo MOU, *Annual Reports on Port State Control in the Asia-Pacific Region 1994–2004* (Tokyo: Tokyo MOU, 1995–2005); U.S. Coast Guard, "Port State Control in the United States," *Annual Reports 1998–2004* (Washington, D.C.: U.S. Coast Guard, 1999–2005)

From early on Cyprus generally had a reputation as a "location for reputable ship operators," though was slow to adapt to its rapid growth by adding the levels of administration to oversee such a large fleet.[85] The state was also slow to ratify some relevant agreements; it landed on ITF blacklists in the early 1990s because of a failure to ratify ILO Convention 147, the Merchant Shipping (Minimum Standards) Convention, which it did not ratify until 1995. So from the early years of most of the PSC regimes it had higher-than-average detention rates. In the early years of the Coast Guard system, even before systematic records were publicized, the Cyprus registry was noted as having an above-average detention rate beginning in 1991, and has been targeted for inspection every

85. "Better Control," *Lloyd's List*, March 3, 1992, 8.

subsequent year.[86] It was targeted under the Paris MOU from 1992 to 2000, and once the black list process began it was characterized in the least severe black list category (medium risk) in 2001; it was also noted as having an above-average detention rate under the Tokyo regime in 1996, 1997, and 1998.[87]

Some, in fact, suggested that its poor record of adopting and enforcing international agreements "was one way to attract a certain class of owner." The registry did not (as of the mid-1990s) inspect most vessels other than as required by SOLAS, though it did focus its inspections on older vessels.[88] The ship registry commissioned a survey by management consultants Deloitte Touche Tohmatsu in 1995, which recommended that the Cyprus flag implement tougher standards on ships in order to improve its safety record and thus its overall image.[89]

What seems to have made the ultimate difference in the willingness of the Cyprus registry to increase its standards and attract more reputable ships was its bid for European Union membership. The economic officer for the Cypriot Department of Merchant Shipping, Demos A. Petropoulos, made the incentive clear: "The aim is to join the EU at the turn of the new century, and to do this we must draw closer to the EU on policies and standards." The registry's specific efforts to improve its image manifest themselves as an attempt to decrease port state control detention rates. When it began this effort in the mid-1990s, it added fifty ship inspectors at ports throughout the world.[90] Most importantly, it passed

86. U.S. Coast Guard, "Port State Control Targeted Flag List 1991–1993," "Port State Control 1995 Flag List," "Port State Control 1996 Flag List," and "Coast Guard Publishes Port State Control Flag State and Classification Society Targeting Lists," unpublished documents supplied by CDR Lonnie P. Harrison Jr., Commandant, U.S. Coast Guard Headquarters, Washington, D.C.; U.S. Coast Guard, *Port State Control in the United States*, Annual Reports 1998–2003 (Washington, D.C.: U.S. Coast Guard, 1999–2004).

87. Tokyo MOU, *Annual Report on Port State Control in the Asia-Pacific Region 1996, 1997 and 1998* (Tokyo: Tokyo MOU, 1997, 1998, 1999); Paris MOU Annual Reports for the years in question.

88. Keith Hindell, "Cyprus Makes Rapid Progress," *Lloyd's List*, March 30, 1994, 9.

89. Jim Mulrenan, "Cyprus Shipping Reforms Urged," *Lloyd's List*, November 11, 1995, 10.

90. Robert Ward, "Cyprus Sets Out to Lose 'Bad Boy' Name," *Lloyd's List*, March 27, 1996, 14.

domestic legislation that used foreign port state control detentions as a cause for deleting ships from the Cyprus registry, with the support of the Cyprus Shipping Council, an organization of national shipowners.[91] Cyprus then moved ahead of the curve by undertaking a study of bulk carriers more than twenty years old, requiring all aged bulk carriers in its registry to participate, in an effort to ensure the safety of these otherwise-risky vessels and thereby improve its port state control record.[92] This record did indeed improve—it was no longer on the Paris MOU black list as of 2004 (moving down to grey list), and is not targeted under the Tokyo regime. It is still targeted by the Coast Guard system, however. Cyprus successfully joined the EU in 2004, a move that is expected to draw more ships to the registry.

Malta

Interestingly, Malta, another new EU member as of 2004 and also a major open registry, experienced a more gradual approach to lowering its detention rates, with rates that are only now inching below average. As 2004 EU membership approached, its ship registry was seen as a possible problem for acceptance into EU membership; it therefore worked to raise standards to EU acceptability.[93]

Malta's open registry began attracting substantial foreign ship registrations in the mid-1980s. In the late 1980s in an effort to become even more competitive the Malta registry streamlined registration (so that the entire process can be completed in "a few hours") and changed its rules to better protect mortgage holders.[94] Its levels of registration improved, and by 1990 it was one of the first open registries to register significant numbers of Chinese-owned vessels.[95]

Its initial PSC results were not promising. It landed on the target list for the Paris MOU from the beginning, was noted as having a detention

91. Nigel Lowry, "Cyprus Set to Tighten Up Register: Clampdown on Substandard Ships," *Lloyd's List*, July 21, 1997, 1.

92. Nigel Lowry, "Posidonia: Safety Worries Prompt Cyprus to Launch Bulker Strength Study," *Lloyd's List*, June 6, 2000, 1.

93. Winchester and Alderton, 296.

94. Keith Hindell, "Special Report on World Ship Registers: Malta Becomes One of Major Players," *Lloyd's List*, March 30, 1994, 9.

95. John Prescott, "Maltese Flag to Register Ten Chinese Vessels," *Lloyd's List*, December 27, 1990, 3.

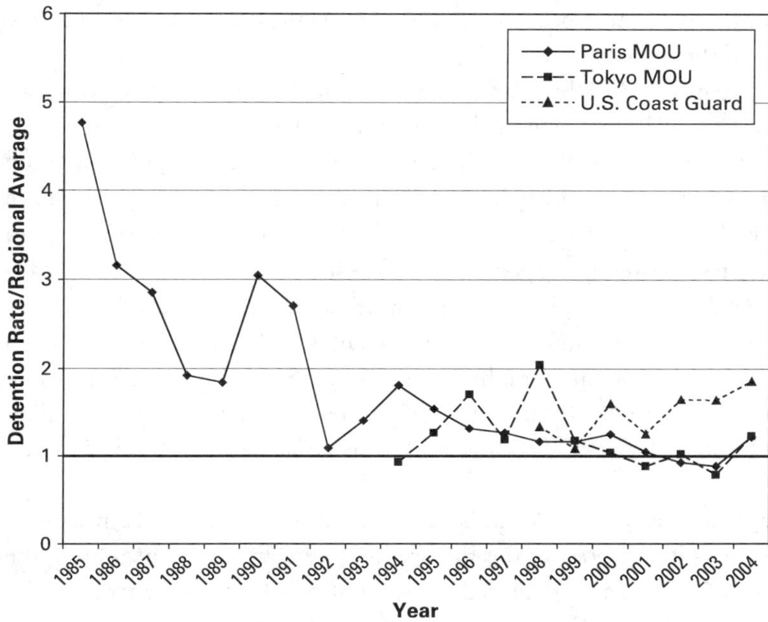

Figure 5.10
Malta MOU detention ratios. Calculated from: Paris MOU, *Annual Reports 1985–2004* (The Hague: Paris MOU, 1986–2005); Tokyo MOU, *Annual Reports on Port State Control in the Asia-Pacific Region 1994–2004* (Tokyo: Tokyo MOU, 1995–2005); U.S. Coast Guard, "Port State Control in the United States," *Annual Reports 1998–2004* (Washington, D.C.: U.S. Coast Guard, 1999–2005)

rate "above average" in the Tokyo MOU between 1996 and 2000, and was also targeted in the early 1990s in the Coast Guard system, before systematic records were publicized.[96] By the early 1990s, however, the registry decided to improve its standards. Malta ratified many of the major IMO ship-related agreements in 1991 (including, most importantly, MARPOL) and the United Nations Convention on the Law of the Sea in 1993.[97] Also in 1993 the registry decided to set up a safety inspectorate (which itself bears the cost of inspections), with the goal of inspecting 25 percent of Maltese-registered ships per year in addition to the already-required annual class inspections. The chair of the ship registry indicated

96. See Appendix D.

97. IUCN et al., "ENTRI Query Service."

that some shipowners became interested in Maltese registration with the advent of the inspectorate.[98]

After a number of high-profile disasters of Maltese-registered ships, and early MOU blacklisting, the director of the Merchant Marine Authority indicated in 1994 that the registry was "endeavoring to upgrade the quality of vessels under the flag."[99] It began removing ships from the registry that had been detained in port state control inspections, and refusing to register other ships that did not meet the prevailing standards.[100] The Malta registry did fall under increased scrutiny at the turn of the century (and suffered a consequent loss of registered tonnage) when the *Erika*, a Japanese-built single-hulled oil tanker registered in Malta, broke in half off the coast of Brittany in December 1999, spilling 12,000 tons of heavy fuel oil and causing a serious environmental disaster.[101]

The main impetus for Malta's efforts to improve standards in its ship registry was its bid to join the European Union. From the beginning the European Commission identified the state of maritime transport in Malta as a key problem in Malta's application. It pointed out in its report on Malta's application for membership in 1999 that, among other problems in that sector, "implementation of international safety and pollution standards lags behind the average for the Community fleet."[102] Malta was called before the European Commission Transport Directorate in November 1999 to defend its record on maritime environment and safety protections. Beginning in 2000 in a specific bid to achieve EU-mandated standards, the registry began refusing registration for a great number of ships, and removing from the registry those that did not con-

98. Clive Woodbridge, "Inspectorate Adds to Island's Appeal," *Lloyd's List*, November 23, 1993, 7.

99. Alan Dickey, "Flag Tightens Up on Inspections," *Lloyd's List*, November 10, 1994, 7.

100. Andrew Spurrier, "Register Growing as Inspections Improve," *Lloyd's List*, November 28, 1996, 6.

101. Clare Garner, "Diesel Oil Tanker Snaps in Two Off the French Coast," *The Independent (London)*, December 13, 1999, 9.

102. Commission of the European Communities, "Report Updating the Commission Opinion on Malta's Application for Membership," COM (1999) 69 (Brussels: EU, 1999), 30.

form to various standards.[103] Malta also ratified five of the most important ILO shipping agreements in 2002, including Convention 147, the Merchant Shipping (Minimum Standards) Convention, and its protocol.[104] It began to employ its own inspectors worldwide to inspect ships in its registry.[105]

Cyprus and Malta together (along with the transport ministers of other states slated for EU accession) met with the transport committee of the European Parliament in October 2003, and pledged that vessels in the registries would fully comply with all EU maritime safety rules at the time of accession. The MEPs expressed concern about implementation of these rules by the two states, noting that they appeared on PSC black lists.[106] In particular, a report from the EU in November 2003 found that the Maltese flag was in need of "serious improvement" before the country would be ready to join the EU.[107] Doing so required earlier implementation of the ban on single-hulled tankers than would otherwise be required by IMO rules. Malta also participated in an IACS-sponsored program to improve its safety record, with an aim to improve port state control inspection statistics, begun in early 2004.[108] Its accession went ahead as planned, in 2004, and by the end of that year it found itself moved from the black list to the grey list under the Paris PSC system.

Honduras

Honduras, identified in chapter 2 as the main ship registry with consistently low standards, finds these reflected in its port state control

103. Giovanni Paci, "Malta Steps Up Policing of Its Euro-Friendly Register," *Lloyd's List*, May 21, 2001, 3.

104. ILO, "ILOLex: Database of International Standards," http://www.ilo.org/ilolex/english/convdisp2.htm.

105. "Cooperation Is Linchpin of Registry's Drive to Maintain High Standards," *Lloyd's List*, October 6, 2005, 13.

106. Roger Hailey, "Cyprus and Malta in Safety Pledge," *Lloyd's List*, October 2, 2003, 3.

107. "An Uphill Task to Meet Tough Demands of EU Entry," *Lloyd's List*, December 29, 2003, 10.

108. Michael Grey, "Blacklisted Flag States Gain Help from IACS," *Lloyd's List*, December 19, 2003, 1.

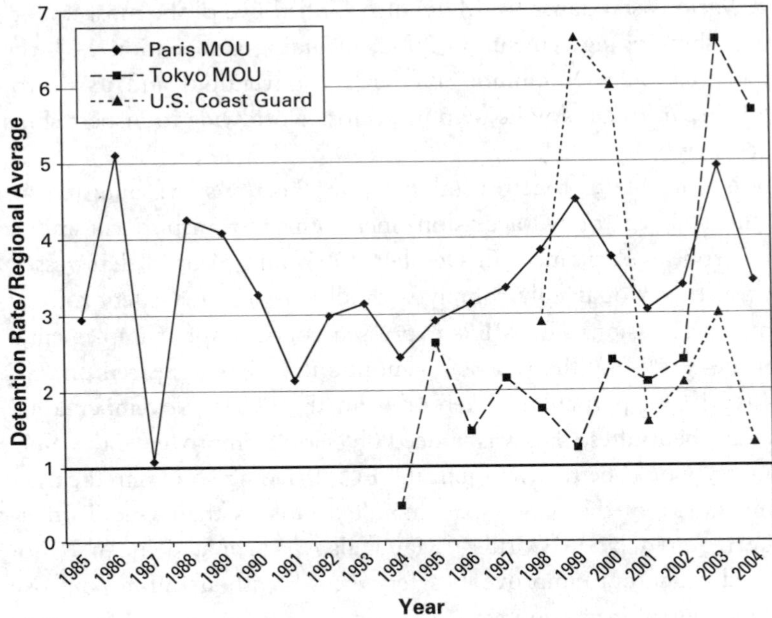

Figure 5.11
Honduras detention ratios. Calculated from: Paris MOU, *Annual Reports 1985–2004* (The Hague: Paris MOU, 1986–2005); Tokyo MOU, *Annual Reports on Port State Control in the Asia-Pacific Region 1994–2004* (Tokyo: Tokyo MOU, 1995–2005); U.S. Coast Guard, "Port State Control in the United States," *Annual Reports 1998–2004* (Washington, D.C.: U.S. Coast Guard, 1999–2005)

detention statistics: it has been regularly above the regional averages of all inspection processes, and on black lists for all inspection regimes. The impact of the port state control system, however, is clear even in this case. While there is no evidence that Honduras aims to be a high-quality registry, even it took some steps after the turn of the century in an effort to avoid the highest levels of scrutiny in the inspection system, and it has had a recent improvement in all three inspection systems.

The Honduran registry is the second oldest open registry, having gotten its start before World War II.[109] From the beginning it has been seen

109. Boleslaw Adam Boczek, *Flags of Convenience: An International Legal Study* (Cambridge: Harvard University Press, 1962), 10.

as a low-standard registry. In part in reaction to the registry's reputation as unable to enforce standards, the state turned over administration of the registry to the Honduran Navy (which still runs the registry) beginning in 1978.[110]

Honduras has been targeted for increased scrutiny in the major MOU regimes from the beginning. It appeared on the Paris MOU target list beginning in 1992, and it was classified as "above average" (in detention rates) by the Coast Guard from 1992 and was placed on the actual Coast Guard target list once it began in 1998. It has also been listed on the Tokyo MOU black list from 1996, the first year of such a designation. In addition, since the Paris regime disaggregated its black list, ranking states within the list, Honduras has been designated "very high risk."

Concerned about the extra attention its ships were receiving in PSC inspections, Honduras started to weed out particularly substandard ships from its registry beginning in 1999. (Figure 5.12 shows Honduran registered tonnage over time.) The director general of the registry removed nearly 2,300 vessels, between 1999 and 2001, in an effort to address what the Honduran merchant marine director termed "continual embarrassment." At the same time, the registry refused to take on ships more than twenty years old, and created a Maritime Training Institute.[111] This cull, representing nearly half (by number) of the ships registered, did have the temporary effect of dropping the detention rates in all three regimes examined above. It was not sufficient to remove Honduran ships from target lists, however, and the effect did not last, with upward trends in detentions since then, though followed by improvements in 2004. At the same time that this purge happened, the United Arab Emirates took the radical step of banning ships from ten low-standard registries, most prominently Honduras, from calling in UAE ports.[112]

Honduras's consistently poor record in inspections suggests that the PSC system is not a panacea for persuading low-standard flags to

110. Winchester and Alderton, 186.

111. "Honduras Lowers Flag on 1500 Problem Ships," *Lloyd's List*, March 26, 2001, 1; Michael Grey, "Honduras Purges Substandard Ships," *Lloyd's List*, November 23, 2001, 6.

112. "Flags of Convenience Hit Back over UAE Port Ban," *Lloyd's List*, June 28, 2001, 22.

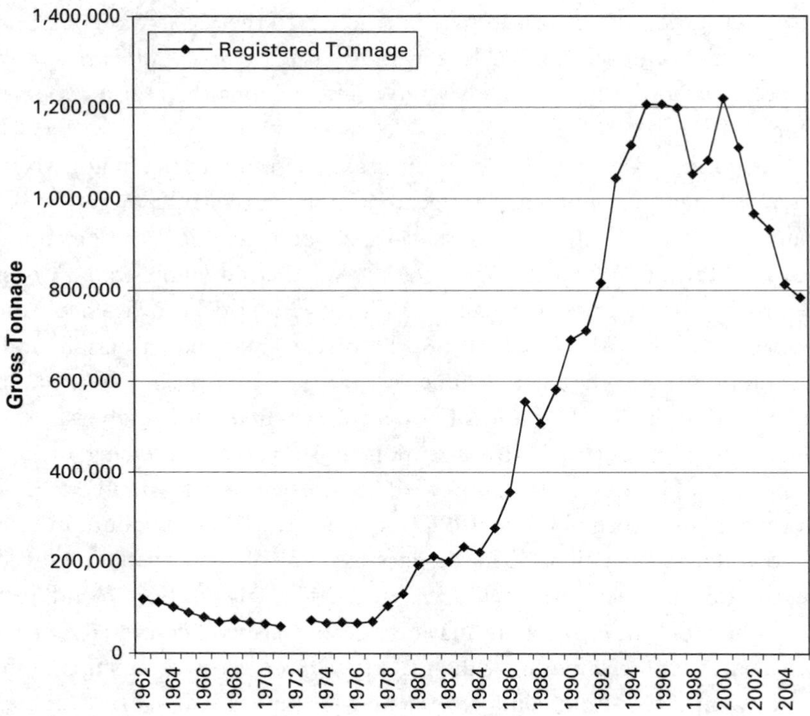

Figure 5.12
Honduran registered tonnage. *Source:* Lloyd's Register Fairplay, *World Fleet Statistics 1948–2004* (London: Lloyd's Register, 1949–2005)

improve. Nevertheless, the fact that when Honduras took action against the lowest-standard ships on its registry, its detention rates decreased dramatically, suggests both that flag states have the power to improve their records should they choose, and that the PSC regime can be a strong incentive to do so. In the case of Honduras, however, it may not be a sufficient incentive. Nevertheless, the drop in registered tonnage is associated with an improving (though still dismal) PSC inspection record, so it is possible that the most recent efforts by Honduras will pay off.

Panama

Panama is the oldest open registry and the largest registry of any kind. There are no limitations on age, size, or type of vessel that may register

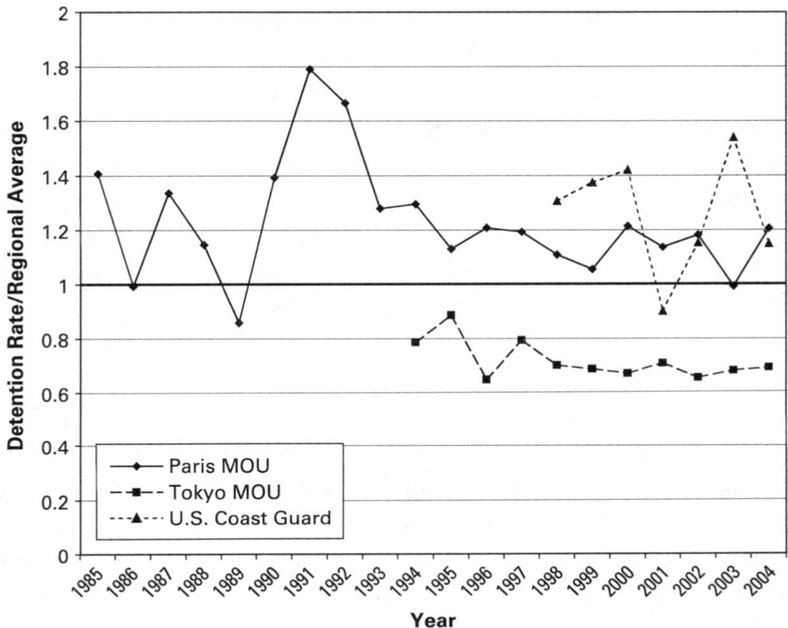

Figure 5.13
Panama MOU detention ratios. Calculated from: Paris MOU, *Annual Reports 1985–2004* (The Hague: Paris MOU, 1986–2005); Tokyo MOU, *Annual Reports on Port State Control in the Asia-Pacific Region 1994–2004* (Tokyo: Tokyo MOU, 1995–2005); U.S. Coast Guard, "Port State Control in the United States," *Annual Reports 1998–2004* (Washington, D.C.: U.S. Coast Guard, 1999–2005)

in Panama.[113] Its experience with port state control inspections reflects the general strategy that has led to its consistent growth. Its approach seems to be not to stand out either with particularly high or particularly low standards. It is thus not surprising that its detention rate (indicated in figure 5.13) is generally close to the average in a given inspection regime (represented here by a detention ratio of 1). Ideally Panama would like to avoid being singled out for increased attention in these inspection processes, but has been unable or unwilling to take dramatic action to prevent that.

Panama's worst record in port state control inspections came in the early 1990s. It was on the first Paris MOU target lists in 1992 and 1993

113. Richard M. F. Coles, *Ship Registration* (London: LLP, 2002), 239.

(though not on the nascent Coast Guard list) and was also targeted for inspection by some individual port states. To try to remove itself from MOU and individual state blacklists, it did undertake several initiatives to attempt to improve its inspection records. In 1992, when notified that Panamanian ships would be singled out for inspection in Norwegian ports, officials from the Panamanian registry met with Norwegian port inspectors to discuss ways that the Panamanian registry could increase environmental and safety standards.[114] Among other responses, the Panamanian registry increased the requirements for classification societies that class Panamanian-registered vessels, though it was still not a requirement for ships to be classed in order to register in Panama. (In 1994 Panama ended recognition of some of the less reputable classification societies it had allowed to class vessels, though it still resisted pressure to use only classification societies that are members of IACS.)[115]

Panama increased inspections of its own ships, and required additional information on the competence of the organizations that inspected Panamanian ships, all in an explicit effort to improve its detention record.[116] The Panamanian Consul General in London echoed this belief in the importance of port state control: "Open registries now have a strong incentive to clean up their act. To risk the targeting of an entire fleet for the short-term gain from one wayward client is akin to killing the goose that lays the golden eggs."[117] Note the difference that remained at this point, however, between Panamanian requirements and higher-standard open registries that demanded more in terms of inspection and classification for ships to register. Officials from the registry in the mid-1990s indicated that Panama had as a goal the idea that all ships should be inspected annually and classed by high-quality classification societies, and that IMO casualty reports should be filed regularly, but as of 2002 there was no evidence that Panama required classification as a condition

114. Sean Moloney, "Norway to Meet on Panama Flag Safety," *Lloyd's List*, February 5, 1992, 3.

115. Sean Maloney, "Panama Rejects Eight Classification Socieities," *Lloyd's List*, May 19, 1994, 16.

116. Tony Gray, "Leading Registry Status Is within Reach," *Lloyd's List*, September 7, 1993, 8.

117. Kevin Harrington-Shelton, "Panama Recognized as a Reliable Long-Term Player," letter to the editor, *Lloyd's List*, November 6, 1996, 5.

for registration.[118] A journalist covering Panama for the daily *Lloyd's List* opined of Panama's growth in number of registered ships: "You can be sure they were not attracted to Panama by high standards of enforcement."[119]

By the end of the 1990s, however, its inspection rates improved at least somewhat. By mid-2003 it was half a percentage point away from appearing on the U.S. Coast Guard white list,[120] and it appeared on the Tokyo white lists in 2002, 2003, and 2004.

Another interpretation of Panama's record is that, as such a large registry, it simply is not able to make sure that all its ships meet high standards. The experience in Liberia, which, until 1993, was the largest registry and nevertheless managed to maintain high environment and safety standards and an impressive port state control inspection history, suggests the flaws with this explanation, however. It is true, though, that Panama's registry has had a much more complex task: even at the time when the two states registered about equal tonnage Panama had more than three times as many ships, since it tended to register smaller vessels.

A more likely explanation, given Panama's reluctance to require inspections and classification by high-quality classification societies, is that Panama simply wants to be the largest ship registry. It accomplishes that end by trying to keep its PSC record sufficiently moderate that its ships will not be unduly singled out, but it is more important to keep the registration process simple enough that all ships can register. Panama demonstrates the classic race to the middle, and the advantage to states and ships of that strategy.

PSC for Labor Standards?

Though labor standards were the original impetus for the creation of the port state control system, they have received short shrift under the system as it is currently implemented. ILO Convention 147, (Merchant Shipping (Minimum Standards)), creates a framework for port state

118. Coles, 243–244.

119. Keith Hindell, "Panama Faces Clean-Up Campaign," *Lloyd's List*, March 30, 1994, 9.

120. Rainbow Nelson, "Panama Flag Detentions Fall," *Lloyd's List*, May 23, 2003, 3.

control inspections to uphold its provisions, but these issues have not generally been integrated into PSC inspection procedures or training. This inattention is unsurprising: enforcing labor standards is a much more time-consuming and intrusive process than checking for required safety or environmental equipment. At the same time, the advantages to the states whose officers inspect at ports with high labor standards are less clear than the advantages of environmental measures, for instance, which may protect a coastal state from an environmental disaster.

A new Consolidated Maritime Labor Convention, under negotiation at the International Labour Organisation since 2001, might bring labor under the PSC process, however. This convention would bring together the major labor obligations under other ILO maritime conventions into one instrument. One of the main proposals to improve enforcement of these measures would be to include these obligations under the port state control process.[121] These negotiations are taking place under ILO processes, in which unions and industry actors (in this instance, shipowners) negotiate alongside states. Enforcement of the resulting agreement has been essential to the unions representing seafarers, but recently there has been some reluctance on the part of shipowners to acquiesce to the use of PSC for enforcement.[122] It remains to be seen whether labor will become a part of the PSC inspection process.

Conclusions

The states examined in detail here are the important open registries for which the port-state inspection system seems to have played some role in decisions about what level of standards to maintain. In general it seems likely that a flag state would prefer not to be singled out for increased scrutiny, and that open registries make an effort to avoid this status if possible. But some are either not able to, or do not prioritize avoiding inspections sufficiently, to undertake the types of regulation and oversight that would be required to escape this scrutiny.

121. Nathan Lillie, "Industrial Regulation by International Regime: Negotiating a Consolidated Maritime Labor Convention in the ILO," unpublished draft manuscript, December 1, 2004, cited with permission.

122. Nathan Lillie, "Industrial Regulation by International Regime."

What can be said more generally about the port state control system? First, as already suggested, it appears to correlate highly with other judgments made about the quality of ship registries—those that have adopted more international agreements (as categorized in chapter 2) fare better in PSC regimes, as shown earlier in this chapter. These flag states also have lower casualty rates (number of ships lost per year, compared to number of ships registered) than those with better PSC results. For example, the states with the highest loss average in the years 1993–1997, according to the Institute of London Underwriters, were Honduras, Belize, and St. Vincent and the Grenadines,[123] all of which had among the ten worst detention rates under the Paris MOU in 1997 (in that year Belize had the worst record, Honduras the fifth worst, and St. Vincent and the Grenadines the ninth worst) and in most preceding years. Since both treaty ratification and casualty rates measure different things than port state control inspections per se, the correlation among these measures suggests that they are good indicators of flag-state quality.

Second, the major national registries fare better in PSC records than do the major open registries. Figure 5.14 shows the average detention ratios for the six largest open registries (left) and the six largest national registries (right) under the Paris and Tokyo MOUs and the U.S. Coast Guard inspection regimes.[124] These numbers record the average detention rate for that state over the entire time frame of the official recordkeeping of each of these inspection regimes. While it is not the case that all open registries fare worse than all the national flags, collectively their record is considerably worse.

Most importantly, the overall record is improving. The port state control inspection systems have increased in stringency over time; the number of things for which they inspect has increased, as new treaty obligations have mandated new equipment, certificates, and training and the MOUs themselves have demanded higher standards. At the same time, the PSC regimes have also passed regulations that require inspectors to focus on inspections of ships with the greatest likelihood of having problems. And in the context of these increasingly stringent

123. Institute of London Underwriters, Chart 7.

124. Hong Kong is omitted because of its changeover in regime during the time period of this study.

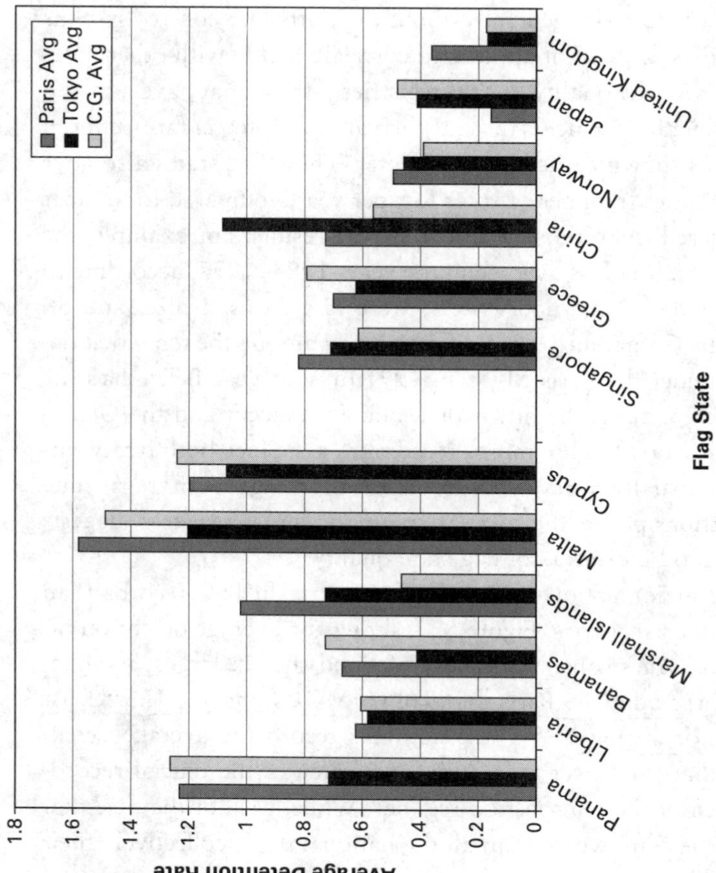

Figure 5.14
Port state control averages for Top twelve flag states Calculated from: Paris MOU, *Annual Reports 1985–2004* (The Hague: Paris MOU, 1986–2005); Tokyo MOU, *Annual Reports on Port State Control in the Asia-Pacific Region 1994–2004* (Tokyo: Tokyo MOU, 1995–2005); U.S. Coast Guard, "Port State Control in the United States," *Annual Reports 1998–2004* (Washington, D.C.: U.S. Coast Guard, 1999–2005)

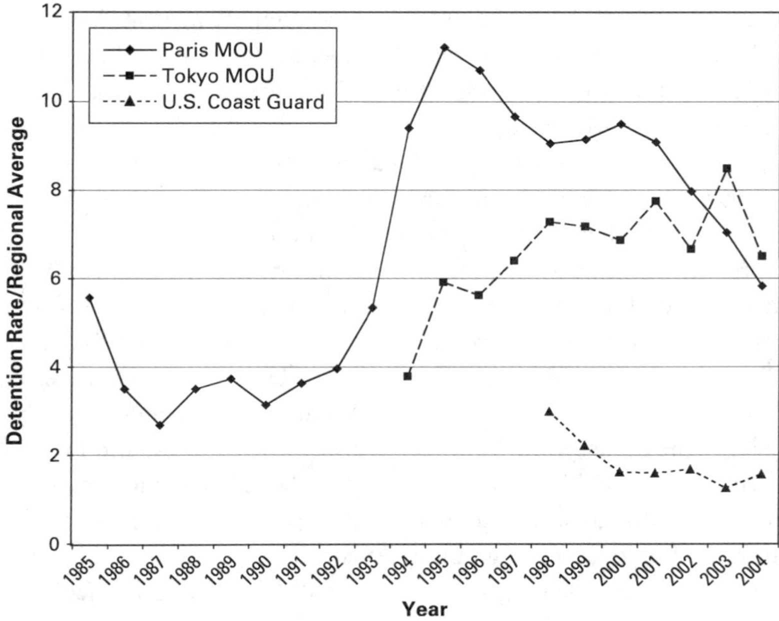

Figure 5.15
Detention rates of major PSC regimes. *Source:* Paris MOU, *Annual Reports 1985–2004* (The Hague: Paris MOU, 1986–2005); Tokyo MOU, *Annual Reports on Port State Control in the Asia-Pacific Region 1994–2004* (Tokyo: Tokyo MOU, 1995–2005); U.S. Coast Guard, "Port State Control in the United States," *Annual Reports 1998–2004* (Washington, D.C.: U.S. Coast Guard, 1999–2005)

inspections, in recent years detentions overall have fallen, beginning in 1996,[125] in the Paris and Coast Guard regimes,[126] suggesting that on the whole the safety and environmental records of ships have improved. Figure 5.14 shows the detention rates over time for all three inspection regimes.

The black lists created by the various regimes are inherently comparative: flag-state detention rates are compared to the regional average. It is thus true in the aggregate that for any state that improves in the

125. Robert Ward, "Detentions Show First Decline in 10 Years," *Lloyd's List*, September 19, 1997, 8.

126. Again, the Tokyo regime is the exception, but this regime has inspected a much larger percentage of ships than the other two regimes, inspecting more than 50 percent of ships, which may account for the differences.

rankings, others will decline. This makes the improvement in detention rates for some of the open registries like Liberia, Vanuatu, and the Marshall Islands all the more impressive, and also means that flag states that have maintained fairly steady detention rates, like Panama, Malta, Cyprus, and Belize, have actually improved over time.

In general, then, the port state control system helps support the general patterns noted in chapter 2: it increases the incentive for flag states (or, more properly, registries) to raise their standards. And, as they do, new registries fill the low-standard void. One important pattern seen in the registries that have worked in recent years to raise their standards is that they have dropped ships—sometimes, as with Honduras and Belize, in large numbers—from their rolls. These low-quality ships, unfortunately, rarely leave the industry. Instead, they register in the newest and lowest-standard registries. This is how Bolivia, Cambodia, and most recently Sierra Leone, Mongolia, and Equatorial Guinea begin the role of ship registration. But over time in these registries—at least the ones that choose to maintain open registries—ships will be exposed to increased standards, and will be detained and forced to fix their most egregious problems before they can sail. In this way, the standards of even the lowest-quality vessels are forced to inch upward over time.

Also interesting is the relationship between port state control detention statistics and number of ships in a registry. While cause and effect must be ascertained individually (for example, in some cases registry numbers decrease because ships are kicked out in an effort to improve the registry PSC records, and in other cases ships leave of their own accord because meeting the new standards would be too costly or difficult), the varying relationships support the argument that flag states are, indeed, attempting to fill different niches with the standards they take on. Some, such as the Marshall Islands and Vanuatu, follow in Liberia's path and attempt to offer moderate-cost shipping with a good reputation for environmental and safety standards. These appeal to shipowners that are willing to adopt reasonably high standards but want to continue to operate with the lower taxes, fees, and wages that exist in open registries. Others, such as Honduras, work to avoid being considered among the absolute worst registries, but want to remain open to shipowners that are not interested in high standards. States like Panama best represent the middle strategy, attempting to avoid the worst reputation, but refusing to implement the types of inspection and oversight systems that the higher-quality open registries require.

These niches to some extent become self-perpetuating. Liberia attracts oil tankers that do not want to be singled out for inspection and are of high enough quality that they can survive the scrutiny its registry requires. As a result, when these ships are inspected under PSC, they are likely to pass, thus continuing the positive Liberian reputation. The same may happen in the other direction with low-standard registries.

Once a number of these open registry states had gained a reputation for high standards, they then made efforts to maintain this advantage. The Marshall Islands registry led an (as-yet) unsuccessful effort to create a "network of quality registers" that could cooperate to prevent substandard vessels from switching from one flag to another.[127] A number of these states also successfully proposed, at the 2002 meeting of the IMO Council, the creation of a voluntary IMO audit that would examine how well flag states implement safety and environmental standards.[128] Interestingly, some of the midquality open registries resisted the creation of such a system: the Bahamas in particular complained that even though the audit system was intended to be voluntary, it could be used to target states for PSC inspections, and complained of the cost of such a system.[129] Some open registry states, like the Marshall Islands and Vanuatu, supported the proposal by traditional maritime states (including Italy, New Zealand, Denmark, Greece, France, the Netherlands, Japan, and Australia) to make such a system mandatory. Panama wanted to keep such a system voluntary.[130]

Port state control was initiated by states concerned about the standards of ships that enter their ports, and implemented via international cooperation. By selecting ships for inspections based in part on their registry state or classification society and its previous record, it creates a

127. Michael Grey, "Rogue Flag States 'Should Face Punishment,'" *Lloyd's List*, July 26, 2001, 3.

128. "IMO to Develop a Model Audit Scheme," *Lloyd's List*, September 3, 2002, 17.

129. "Bahamas—Questions over Need for Voluntary Auditing," *Lloyd's List*, September 3, 2002, 15.

130. Hugh O'Mahony, "Late Bid to Amend IMO Meets Opposition," *Lloyd's List*, November 26, 2003, 1.

club of higher-standard registries that are less likely to be inspected and detained. It has provided an incentive for shipowners to register in states whose vessels are not singled out for increased scrutiny under the system. A number of flag states, in an effort to court ship registrations, have raised their standards, sometimes at the behest of shipowners. While the system does not prevent the existence of poor-quality ships, it does decrease the advantages to low-standard registries, and creates a mechanism to prevent some of the worst ships from sailing until they do not pose an immediate threat.

6

The International Transport Workers Federation and Labor Standards

Labor standards are among the most difficult to create and enforce internationally, particularly on the oceans. Given that one of the main incentives to register ships in open registries is to lower operating costs, and that labor is the most expensive aspect of international shipping, states attempting to attract ship registrations are particularly reluctant to take on or enforce costly labor standards. Moreover, it is particularly difficult to ascertain whether ships are upholding even those labor standards they are required to. Unlike equipment standards that can be checked objectively (often at the point of construction, classification, or insurance of the ship)—and that may need to be checked only once—labor standards are at issue for every ship traveling the oceans and may be upheld or ignored at different points in time. Studies of flag-of-convenience (FOC) ships suggest that vessels often keep false paybooks that crew members are forced to sign, suggesting higher wage rates than they are actually receiving, and that officers may lie about conditions and labor regulations enforced on their vessels.[1]

The efforts by international labor unions to raise labor standards on ships, described in this chapter, must address the issue of how ships operate. Doing so requires a more intrusive approach to monitoring conditions on ships than is the case for port state control, because of the form of standards in question; actors need to be able to determine what ships are doing while on the ocean. Likewise, unions are working without the authority of states and are limited in what they can require of ships. The

1. Parliament of the Commonwealth of Australia, *Ships of Shame: Inquiry into Ship Safety*, Report from the House of Representatives Standing Committee on Transport, Communications, and Infrastructure (Canberra: Australian Government Publishing Service, 1992).

union approach tackles this question strategically at a later temporal point than does port state control: by influencing whether ships will be able to load or offload the goods they carry once they have already come to port.[2]

The flag-of-convenience system globalized labor on ships. Before open registries, nationally flagged ships employed their own nationals, regulated labor by their national rules, and paid their national wage rates. The open registry "brought freedom to hire from anywhere,"[3] since one of the main characteristics of open registries is lack of regulatory oversight. A global market for seafarers has since developed, with ship workers hired from low-wage countries and easily replaced by crews from elsewhere if labor conditions or wage expectations from those locations change.[4] One of the major ways that national registries have attempted to compete with flags of convenience is to relax nationality rules for ship labor; these are relaxed even further in international and second registries. For the most part, seafarers are paid rates, whatever ship they are on, that reflect the norms of the labor markets in their home states, rather than those determined by ownership or registry of the ship.

It is difficult even to characterize the level of labor conditions globally for ship workers, since there are so many different types of standards—hours worked, conditions of work, wages, other benefits—and they may vary in different ways on different ships. One aspect that certainly matters, and that may be easier to compare than other measures of labor protection, is wages. Even that level of comparison is difficult, however. The only existing surveys, by the International Shipowners Federation (ISF) of wage rates, break them down by nationality of worker, rather than nationality of ship. So while it is possible to compare the wages of Indian officers (or Filipino able seamen) from year to year, there exist no systematic data that allow a comparison of wages on ships registered in the Bahamas to those registered in Norway.

2. This process can also work via tugboat pilots that can refuse to service ships without ITF-approved contracts.

3. Nathan Lillie, "Union Networks and Global Unionism in Maritime Shipping," *Relations Industrielles* 60/1 (winter 2005): 88–111.

4. International Labour Office in Collaboration with the Seafarers International Research Centre, *The Global Seafarer: Living and Working Conditions in a Global Industry* (Geneva: International Labour Organisation, 2004).

Existing studies of wage rates by nationality of seafarer suggest that there are enormous differences. A study commissioned by the International Transport Workers Federation in 1996 found that Russian, Ukrainian, Croatian, and Indonesian seafarers have the lowest rates of pay, regardless of the flag state of the vessels on which they serve, followed by Filipino and Chinese seafarers.[5] This study, though small (covering approximately .63 percent of seafarers serving at the time of the study), did find some important differences across flag states in terms of wage rates. At that point the number of ratings paid less than the ITF benchmark salary was highest (among the flag states for which there was a significant response) on ships registered in the Bahamas (80 percent) and Cyprus (79 percent), followed by Liberia (77 percent), Panama (74 percent), Malta (59.5 percent), and Vanuatu (58.5 percent). Importantly, similar (and often higher) numbers were posted for below-benchmark ratings wages for non-FOC registries: Philippines (100 percent), Russia (95 percent), and Greece (83 percent). Other national registries had a better record: New Zealand had only 15 percent of its ratings paid below benchmark, for instance.[6] More generally, seafarers on nationally flagged ships were more likely to be paid what the survey considered "high" wage rates than those on ships flying flags of convenience.[7]

ISF surveys contribute to some recent efforts at establishing what the global average shipping wage is, and this wage appears to have fallen in recent times. For example, the 1999 average rate of pay for an able seaman, the basic crew position on a ship, was approximately three-quarters of what it was in 1992. Bloor, Thomas, and Lane attribute this decline to the hiring of cheaper workers from developing countries.[8]

5. MORI, *Seafarers' Living Conditions Survey: Interpretive Report*, research conducted for the International Transport Workers' Federation (ITF) (London: MORI, 1998), 27.

6. MORI, 32–33.

7. International Labour Office in Collaboration with the Seafarers International Research Centre, *The Global Seafarer*, 111.

8. On the other hand, the most recent surveys show an increase in the median able seaman's wage by 2.7 percent between 1999 and 2000. See D. A. Dearsley, "ISF Shipping Wages Survey 2000," ISF (01) 11 (London: International Shipping Federation, 2001), 2; Michael Bloor, Michelle Thomas, and Tony Lane, "Health Risks in the Global Shipping Industry: An Overview," *Health, Risk & Society* 2/3 (2000): 331.

Even this trend does not give the full picture, however, since one of the additional trends is the downsizing of labor forces on ships in order to cut labor costs, so a smaller crew may be doing the work once done by more workers.[9]

Other changes in shipping practices affect working conditions on board. One trend is the decreased amount of time ships spend in port when unloading their cargo, before heading back out to sea. A study of one British port found that the average time for a ship at port decreased 16 hours between 1970 and 1998. In particular, the percentage of ships that turned around in port in less than twenty-four hours increased from 11 percent in 1970 to more than 70 percent in 1998.[10] This trend held true even though the ships in this latter period were larger and carried more cargo.

Most agree that among the most important influences in raising wages and other working standards on ships is the International Transport Workers Federation (ITF), an international labor union.[11] The ITF, more than a century old, worked actively in the early years of the twentieth century advocating in the International Labour Organisation for the creation of international agreements setting minimum requirements for the protection of seafarers.[12] Once such protections were in place, the ITF has worked to increase the number of states (and thus ships) bound by them. This focus led to a concern with open registries and their frequent use as a way to pay seafarers lower wages and avoid other labor protections. As early as 1933 the ITF brought the issue of open registry ships to the attention of the ILO, arguing that shipowners were transferring their vessels to different flags in order to avoid labor standards and other social protection.[13] The ITF began its focus on this issue in earnest just after World War II, passing a resolution at its 1948 congress urging a

9. Bloor, Thomas, and Lane, 329–340.

10. Erol Kahveci, "Fast Turnaround Ships: Impact on Seafarers' Lives," *Seaways*, March 2000, 8–12.

11. The ISF Deputy Secretary General noted in the 1997 Wages Survey, for instance, that ITF activities would be likely to have an impact on wage trends. See D. A. Dearsley, "ISF Wages Survey 1997," IF(97)47(IF.9) (London: International Shipping Federation, 1997), 2.

12. George C. Kasoulides, *Port State Control and Jurisdiction: Evolution of the Port State Regime* (Dordrecht: Martinus Nijhoff, 1993), 104.

13. Kasoulides, 91.

boycott by seafarers and dockworkers of ships registered in Panama and Honduras.[14]

The newly created Seafarer's Section of the organization initiated a campaign in 1958 to enforce existing labor standards on open registry ships.[15] The stated goal of the campaign is to prevent or reverse FOC registration by decreasing the labor advantages of flying flags of convenience.[16] As Herbert Northrup and Peter Scrase suggest, the ITF campaign is an "attempt to overcome by direct action the market effects of lower costs" and by that process prevent the movement of ship registrations and the jobs associated with them to developing countries.[17] The campaign thus has a state-based focus (working to change the attractiveness of open registries and thereby increase the number of ships registered in the states that are willing to exercise strict labor oversight), but it tries to achieve its goals in large part through working with individual ships. As such, its main impact has been to change the working conditions on ships rather than necessarily altering flag-state behavior. Though there is little evidence that the campaign has diminished the number of FOC-registered ships, it appears to have made a genuine difference in the wage rates and other labor protections on ships that are registered in open registries.

There are two parts to the ITF process: the political campaign and the industrial campaign. The political campaign involves deciding which states will be considered by the ITF to be "flags of convenience." Because there is no universally accepted definition of the term (and even traditional registries currently vary in the extent to which they allow registration of ships by noncitizens or in the requirements to use national labor on board a ship), the decision to label a state as a flag of convenience is a political decision. The primary criterion for this decision is the extent to which beneficial control of a flag state's ships is outside of the flag

14. Kasoulides, 105; the boycott was not implemented after Panama requested an ILO inquiry.

15. Anderson, 166; see, generally, Herbert R. Northrup and Peter B. Scrase, "The International Transport Workers' Federation Flag of Convenience Shipping Campaign 1983–1995," *Transportation Law Journal* 23/3 (1996): 369–423.

16. ITF, "What Are FOCs?", http://www.itfglobal.org/flags-convenience/sub-page.cfm.

17. Northrup and Scrase, 371.

state,[18] but the organization also considers the flag state's ratification history with respect to ILO and IMO conventions, and its general willingness to enforce labor, safety, and environmental standards as suggested by port state control inspection results and other domestic indications of social regulations.[19] The ITF also takes into consideration the wishes of implicated domestic labor unions, which is particularly relevant for international registries, where the wishes of the domestic unions make the difference in whether a registry is listed or not.[20] The decision on which states are to be considered FOCs is undertaken by the Fair Practices Committee of the ITF, which meets annually and consists of equal numbers of affiliates from the seafarers' and dockworkers' sections of the organization. See appendix E for a current list of ITF-designated FOCs. In addition to simply determining which states will be considered FOCs (which has implications for what other actions the ITF takes with respect to ships flagged in those locations), as part of the political campaign the ITF attempts to convince shipowners not to register in FOCs, seafarers not to work on ships registered in these locations, and shippers not to use these ships to ship their goods.

The industrial campaign works to protect and gain rights for seafarers on FOC-registered ships. In addition to acting based on specific complaints lodged by seafarers for mistreatment on a given vessel, the organization attempts to bind individual ships to a set of labor standards by creating a "collective agreement" between the ship and the ITF or a national union recognized by the ITF. Such an agreement covers things like duration of labor, hours of duty, wages (laying out a specific scale of acceptable minimum wages), medical attention, insurance and compensation, food and accommodation, safety, and the rights of seafarers to join unions.[21] Most collective agreements are actually between the na-

18. International Transport Workers Federation, *The ITF Handbook* (London: ITF, n.d.), 13(1).

19. ITF, "What Are FOCs?"

20. Interview with Graham Young, Assistant Secretary, Special Seafarers Division, International Transport Workers Federation, May 2004. The unions may sometimes prefer to hold the prospect of ITF FOC listing as a threat for what would happen if the state creating the international registry does not accede to their wishes.

21. ITF, *ITF Standard Collective Agreement for Crews on Flag of Convenience Ships*, January 1, 2001.

tional union of the state where the shipowner is a citizen (rather than where the ship is registered) and the ship, though the ITF examines these agreements to make sure they conform to ITF standards. In cases where there is no appropriate or available national union, the ITF can negotiate and sign agreements with the ship operators. Ships that have collective agreements with the ITF are given what is known as a "blue certificate" that indicates their status.

The standards contained in the collective agreement are predominantly derived from existing international agreements on labor and safety, under the International Maritime Organization and the International Labour Organisation. The wage rates that must be paid on a ship in order to meet the ITF requirements of the collective agreement have traditionally [illegible] by the ITF alone, through a decision-making process [illegible] tices Committee.[22] More recently, however, the ITF [illegible] d to involve shipowners in the process of designating [illegible]. The International Maritime Employers' Committee [illegible] emerged in 1993 out of a previously existing shipowners' [illegible] concerned with Indian workers on British ships,[23] was [illegible] rt to pressure the ITF on wage rates. Beginning in 1999 [illegible] ITF agreed to collectively negotiate a benchmark wage rate [illegible] ers employed by IMEC members on FOC-registered ships. [illegible] egotiations resulted in an agreed-on schedule of wage increases for the four-year period beginning in 2001, which included a starting wage of $1,200 per month with scheduled increases up to $1,400 per month, for able seamen. Other shipowners agreed to abide by this wage rate and accept it as the basis for an ITF blue certificate, though they had not participated in the negotiations.[24]

This process has more recently been transformed, with the addition of the International Mariners' Management Association of Japan (IMMAJ), into what has come to be called the International Bargaining Forum.[25]

22. Northrup and Scrase, 371–389.

23. Andrew Guest, "Ship Management: IMEC Steps into a Global Market," *Lloyd's List*, July 6, 1993, 5.

24. IMEC, "Agreement with ITF," press release, December 2001, http://www.marisec.org/IMEC/press%20dec%202001.htm.

25. "ITF Set to Open Talks in New Bargaining Forum," *Transport International* 13 (October 2003), http://www.itf.org.uk/TI/13/english/bargainingforum.htm.

While the traditional types of ITF agreements with ships receiving blue certificates continue to be an option for individual shipowners, participating in the IBF process creates a slightly different type of agreement (and a "green certificate" instead of a blue one). Shipowners may apply to affiliate themselves with the organizations that make up the joint negotiating group process (currently consisting of IMEC, representing European shipowners, and IMMAJ, representing Japanese shipowners) for the purposes of bargaining.

While this bargaining forum sets the standards that must be upheld in IBF agreements, these are much more flexible than the in the regular collective agreements. In particular, these agreements do away with precise wage rates for all ship workers based on a specified benchmark. Instead, a certain overall wage for the entire crew is determined, with the shipowner free (within certain parameters) to allocate that collective wage as needed. This process also permits increased flexibility, within the agreed pay rate, about how much of it will be paid in cash versus as pension, other benefits, and training costs, with monitoring by the ITF to ensure that money promised in benefits (rather than in wages) is actually paid to the seafarer. This process means that it is possible that ships with IBF agreements (green certificates) pay lower wages than on the standard or uniform collective agreements, though they would still be considerably higher than average wages on FOC vessels without agreements.[26]

The increased flexibility is included in the agreement not only to create an incentive for shipowners to negotiate these types of agreements, but because the ITF has more confidence that the agreements, once negotiated, will be implemented and maintained over time. The cooperation between shipowners and the ITF suggests that when shipowners enter into IBF agreements the agreement will be upheld and monitored. Initial experience suggest that these agreements, entered into voluntarily, have indeed been well honored, and the ITF hopes that more ships will become a part of this process.[27]

Not all states appreciate the work the ITF does on behalf of their seafarers. The idea of a universal wage rate has been supported more by the

26. Interview with Graham Young, Assistant Secretary, Special Seafarers Division, International Transport Workers Federation, May 2004.

27. Interview with Graham Young, Assistant Secretary, Special Seafarers Division, International Transport Workers Federation, May 2004.

traditional maritime states than by states whose seafarers would receive the highest wage increases under it. Developing countries (and some seafarers from these areas) have expressed two types of concerns that have led them to resist ITF-mandated minimum wages. One is a concern about domestic equity: if seafarers from low-wage countries earn a global wage that is so much higher than the average domestic wage, it may cause domestic inequity and thus political complications in the home state. Of even greater concern to states is the fear that if their seafarers get paid higher wages, they will no longer be attractive employees in the international shipping market. The latter concern is realistic given the implicit ITF agenda, which is working on behalf of its membership of unions in traditional maritime states, trying to prevent "unfair competition" from FOC-registered ships that employ lower-wage seaferers.[28] The method used in the IBF process, in which the total wage for an average ship is agreed on but the shipowners can distribute that wage among the workers, within parameters, as they see fit, is one compromise among these perspectives.

But, also importantly, many of the unions or officials from traditionally low-wage developing countries have come to believe in the advantages of the ITF campaign because it helps them in the global labor market. A concern that their seafarers will lose their comparative advantage in the global labor market if paid ITF wages has been supplanted—especially in the years following the cold war—with a concern that new entrants to the labor market could undercut the low wages these seafarers were earning. As Nathan Lillie puts it, ITF affiliates from countries that supply labor "have an interest in excluding new market entrants, and the FOC campaign allows them the possibility to do this."[29]

A shipowner who signs an ITF-approved collective agreement indicates an intention to be bound by these obligations with respect to the specified ship, which includes allowing the organization to inspect its ships, and allowing the appointment of an onboard safety representative that can inspect the ship and investigate accidents without fear of reprisal.[30] In

28. ITF, "Oslo to Delhi: A Comprehensive Review of the ITF FOC Campaign" (London: ITF, n.d.) 14.

29. Nathan Lillie, "Global Collective Bargaining on Flag of Convenience Shipping," *British Journal of Industrial Relations* 42/1 (March 2004): 58.

30. ITF *Standard Collective Agreement*, Article 34.

addition, the shipowner agrees to contribute an amount of money per seafarer annually to the Seafarers' International Assistance, Welfare and Protection Fund (usually referred to simply as the "welfare fund"). Currently the required contribution to the welfare fund is $230 per seafarer.[31] The money in this fund is used to finance the FOC campaign, including the inspection of ships. The investment income from the welfare fund goes into the Seafarers' Trust, a nonprofit organization that works for the "spiritual, moral, and physical welfare of seafarers."[32] All seafarers on the ship must be enrolled in an ITF-affiliate union (and if a suitable union is not available the shipowner must pay to enroll them in the Special Seafarer's Section of the ITF, which acts as a union for those for whom there are no ITF-affiliated national unions), and the shipowner agrees to pay the union or ITF contributions for the seafarer. Moreover, if the ship has not previously been operating under a collective agreement and has paid wages below the ITF minimum, the ship operator must agree to contribute "back pay." This is calculated as the differential between the rate of pay previously in effect and the higher ITF scale for the time from when the seafarer signed on board the ship. This money is collected by the ITF and given to the individual seafarers.

The organization uses direct action and boycotts to attempt, with some degree of success, to convince ship operators to accept these standards and receive blue certificates (and also, under the IBF process described above, green certificates). ITF inspectors seek to board a FOC-registered ship when it is in port and ask to see its blue—or green—certificate. If it does not have one, it is given the opportunity to agree at that point to uphold the required standards. If the ship does not have an ITF-approved collective agreement and refuses to agree to ITF demands, the organization attempts to convince crew members to leave or ship workers in port to refuse to unload or service the vessel. (If the ship's officers refuse to let it be boarded, the ITF can similarly encourage a work boycott.) Because the type of agreement offered when a ship is boarded in port requires even higher wages and more stringent standards than those entered into

31. Interview with Graham Young, Assistant Secretary, Special Seafarers Division, International Transport Workers Federation, May 2004.

32. ITF, "What Is the Trust?", http://itf.org/uk/seafarers_trust/information/what_is_the_trust.htm.

when a ship is not a target of industrial action, shipowners have an incentive to negotiate agreements before they are targeted for action.

In addition, the ITF keeps a blacklist, on which the names of specific shipowners, managers, and agents who have repeatedly been singled out as responsible for substandard shipping practices are listed; this list is publicized broadly along with the specific complaints for which these actors are cited. Initially this list only contained those operating FOC vessels, but was expanded in 2000 to include those operating vessels flagged in traditional maritime registries as well.[33]

More recently the union has taken to organizing "weeks of action" that focus on ports in particular areas. The ITF focuses on particular ports in a given region, and sends inspectors to check on the labor conditions and regulations aboard ships that come into port. The organization not only targets ships for inspection that are registered in open registries, but also those that have been singled out for other reasons, such as being blacklisted on a regional memorandum of understanding (MOU) on port state control, those that have not been inspected by port state control inspections in the previous six months, those that are more than twenty years old, or specific ships that have a record of violations of labor and safety standards. Such a campaign in Europe in 2000 inspected 520 ships visiting ports in twenty-eight different states during a week. In the process the organization recovered more than US$400,000 in back pay for ship workers.[34]

What impact has this process had on labor standards on ships? Some have referred to the ITF campaign as "the one really effective anti-FOC force."[35] It has clearly not stemmed the tide of open registry ship registrations, but has had some effect on labor standards, both raising them generally and holding shipowners to implementing them. Northrup and Rowan suggest that the threat of ITF boycotts and the associated campaign to sway public opinion "have forced FOC countries to raise their standards, to devote more attention and legislation to safety practices,

33. ITF, *Flags of Convenience Campaign Report 2001/2002* (London: ITF, 2002), 64.

34. Beth Jinks, "ITF Starts Major Drive in Europe," *Business Times Singapore*, September 24, 2001, p. SHIP1.

35. Wiswall, 121.

and have greater concern with the rights, training, and well-being of seafarers." They suggest as well that the ITF's work has influenced open registries to move their standards toward ILO levels of labor protections.[36]

The most important incentive for ships to sign agreements with the ITF comes from those who would hire ships for the purpose of transporting goods. Those who ship goods to or from states with a strong ITF presence will now often demand that the ships they use sign ITF-recognized agreements so that they can be assured that their ships will not be detained.[37] Northrup and Rowan point out that the cost of an ITF-sponsored boycott can be much greater than the cost of paying ITF-acceptable wage rates and contributing to the welfare fund.[38]

At a minimum, the number of ships covered by collective agreements approved by the ITF has increased. The ITF claims that approximately 30 percent of ships registered in states designated as FOCs by the organization now have ITF-approved collective agreements, covering more than 95,000 seafarers.[39] As of May 2004 there were approximately 5,081 total agreements in effect, about 2,000 of which are IBF agreements.[40] This is up from 1,533 as of 1990.[41] Some flag states have better records than others—Liberia has frequently had years where more than 50 percent of its ships had blue certificates, the Cayman Islands and Gibraltar have recently had years with more than 40 percent of their ships covered by agreements, and more than 35 percent of Marshall Islands ships are also under ITF-approved agreements (see appendix F).

The International Shipping Federation wage-rate studies suggest that these agreements do make a difference in wage rates for the seafarers themselves—for example, an able seaman would earn approximately

36. Northrup and Rowan, 134, 150.

37. "Placing a Value on Crew Experience," *Lloyd's Shipping Economist* 18/3 (March 1996): 9; Northrup and Rowan, 133.

38. Northrup and Rowan, 133.

39. ITF, *Oslo to Delhi: A Comprehensive Review of the ITF FOC Campaign* (London: ITF, n.d.), 15.

40. "Total FOC Live Agreements," May 2004, from ITF database; interview with Graham Young, Assistant Secretary, Special Seafarers Division, International Transport Workers Federation, May 2004.

41. Northrup and Scrase, 377.

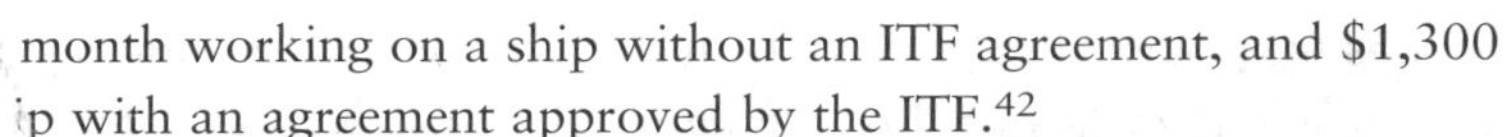

month working on a ship without an ITF agreement, and $1,300 p with an agreement approved by the ITF.[42]

at the ITF indicate that some shipowners with ships flagged in y as well as required by ITF collective agreements but refuse to agreements; if they do not regularly traverse routes that put contact with areas where the ITF has a strong presence they he chance that they will not become a target of industrial ham Young, the Assistant Secretary of the Special Seafarers the ITF, suggests that the existence of ITF agreements has e market rate of pay for well-qualified seafarers, such that a hat wants to operate a quality ship must pay near-ITF- ges (and benefits) in order to be able to hire good seafarers.[43] it do not have ITF agreements peg their pay to ITF rates, so rates increase these seafarers earn more as well.[44]

e ITF is not universally praised. Some seafarers are indig- arge amounts of funding the organization gets from ship- fund that is more likely to underwrite a research institute ns for ports[45] than to pay back wages they might be due ous owners. Owners, understandably, are unhappy about tics (and in particular, the high required donation) used sign up for blue certificates.[46] And some labor unions ith the tactics this megaunion uses to maintain control d labor in international shipping: its control over large ig that can be given to affiliate unions and its broad- signing collective agreements (e.g., the fact that ships agreements approved by the ITF, regardless of what other

42. International Shipping Federation, *The ISF Year* 2001 (London: ISF, 2001), as cited in Lillie, "Global Collective Bargaining." The $800 figure is a fairly rough estimate, estimated in 1999, but probably held constant in 2002, the comparison year.

43. Interview with Graham Young, Assistant Secretary, Special Seafarers Division, International Transport Workers Federation, May 2004; Lillie makes this argument as well in "Global Collective Bargaining," 49.

44. Marcus Hand, "The Great Divide on Minimum Pay Issue," *Lloyd's List*, September 19, 2003, 7.

45. ITF, *The ITF Seafarers' Trust Annual Report 1997/1998* (London: ITF, 1998); see Chapman, 89, for seafarer complaints.

46. Chapman, 90.

unions may be pushing for) make it difficult for national unions to operate outside the aegis of this international union, which prefers to maintain its international influence.[47] Moreover, despite its dependence on ILO standards as the basis for many of the obligations under its collective agreements, the ITF will sometimes negotiate agreements that allow for wages lower than ILO standards (as is possible under the new IBF system), which has irritated some affiliate unions.[48]

Nevertheless, its influence on wage rates and labor standards both on the individual ships with which it negotiates collective agreements and on the overall level worldwide is impressive. Even those who consider the overall FOC campaign a failure (since it has clearly had little impact on level of FOC registration) concede that the organization has "come close to imposing a worldwide minimum wage ten times higher than some local rates."[49]

It is also possible that the ITF may begin to have some success at moving ship registrations by higher-standard shipowners back to traditional registries. One of the impacts of the success of ITF-approved agreements with FOC ships is that the standards, particularly wage rates, are now higher than on many national-flagged vessels. It is possible that the raising of wage rates on these FOC vessels may ultimately have some success at pushing ships back to national registries, where the wages and benefits may be less costly, and where the shipowner would not be required to contribute to the ITF welfare fund. A particular irony of this success, should it materialize, is that the ITF would lose its major source of income.

The negotiation of a Consolidated Maritime Labor Convention under the International Labour Organisation, as discussed briefly in chapter 5, would have the effect of making the union labor efforts part of the official port state control process. The PSC process would then support the opportunity of unions to enforce labor standards. This system would take some of the pressure off the ITF by removing it as the primary inspectorate for labor standards, and decreasing the odds that those

47. Chapman, 88–94.

48. Chapman, 89.

49. "Shipping: Follow the Flag of Convenience," *The Economist*, February 22, 1997, 75.

with ITF-approved agreements would cheat. These efforts, if they succeed, will do so because shipowners that adopt higher labor standards have an interest in evening the playing field so that they do not have to compete with those with the lowest standards.[50] But the recent reluctance on the part of shipowners, which may scuttle the inclusion of labor standards in a port state control process, may not be that surprising. Under the current ITF system shipowners can determine whether it is cost-effective to maintain low labor standards and run the risk of labor action or increase standards to avoid it, based on whether their ships travel to ITF strongholds.

Organized labor has made efforts to raise labor standards on ships at least in part so that seafarers from traditional maritime states with strong labor protections are not closed out of the global labor market for seafarers. The ITF has done so by using the point of access available to unions: the labor to load, unload, or service ships. It creates a club of ships that have accepted high labor standards, who gain access to ship services in ports from which low-standard ships are excluded. By labor boycotts of those ships in port that have refused to take on the level of labor protections demanded, the ITF has created a context in which large numbers of ships take on labor standards higher than those required by their flag states. While the stated objective of the ITF campaign, to prevent the registration of ships in open registry states, has clearly failed, the overall increase in wages and labor protections on ships comes from changing the economic calculation of shipowners; it becomes less costly for them to raise labor standards to gain access to this club than to run the risk of a labor boycott.

50. Nathan Lillie, "Industrial Regulation by International Regime: Negotiating a Consolidated Maritime Labor Convention in the ILO," unpublished draft manuscript, December 1, 2004, cited with permission.

7

Regional Fisheries Management Organizations and Trade Restrictions

The practice of shipowners choosing a flag in order to avoid conservation-related regulations has had a significant impact on the efforts to protect fisheries or other ocean resources from overharvesting. Fishery regulation is made more difficult by the opportunity for ships to fly flags of convenience. To an even greater degree than in other shipping issues, the extent of regulation adopted by a flag state is likely to be the primary basis on which owners of fishing vessels choose where to register. When faced with either domestic or international fishery regulations, some fishing vessels choose to flag in states that do not belong to the relevant international agreements or are unlikely to uphold them. They can thereby harvest as much of the resource in question as they are able to. In doing so, they make conservation potentially impossible for other states, and undermine the advantages to those who have agreed to limit their resource extraction. Unregulated fishing also drives down the price for legally caught fish, thus restricting the earnings of legitimate fishers and even decreasing their ability to invest in costly monitoring activities.[1]

Efforts to persuade ships flagged in open registries to uphold international fishery conservation rules come from a set of collectively adopted measures within international fishery management organizations to refuse to allow the fish caught on such ships to enter domestic fishery markets unless they have been caught within the rules. These efforts are thus implemented after ships have been allowed into port and have been unloaded: if it cannot be shown that they have followed international rules, their cargo cannot be bought and sold in states that do accept these standards.

1. Liza D. Fallon and Lorne Kriwoken, "International Influence of an Australian Nongovernmental Organization in the Protection of Patagonian Toothfish," *Ocean Development & International Law* 33 (2004): 232.

In 2002 just under 10 percent of the world's fishing vessels were registered in open registries.[2] But the number is increasing: of new fishing vessels built in the period 2000 to 2003, 14 percent were registered in open registries at the end of 2003.[3] The numbers are almost certainly higher. Some have estimated the percentage of open registry fishing vessels at 21.5 percent,[4] and studies have found that most fishing vessels whose registry is listed as "unknown" by the major record-keeping organizations are actually registered in open registries.[5] FOC-registered fishing vessels also tend to be larger than nationally registered ones;[6] a higher proportion of those fishing on the high seas in lucrative fisheries are thus flying flags of convenience.

The four top open registry fishing states recently have been Belize, Panama, Honduras, and St. Vincent and the Grenadines. Others identified in OECD documents as up-and-coming FOC fisheries registries include Georgia, Cambodia, Vanuatu, and landlocked Bolivia.[7]

To those who operate them, fishing vessels flagged in open registries can be particularly lucrative, especially if the owner intends to flout international standards. Crew costs, which account for up to 30 percent of total catch value in most major high-seas fisheries for nationally registered vessels,[8] are considerably lower on ships in open regis-

2. Judith Swan, *Fishing Vessels Operating under Open Registers and the Exercise of Flag State Responsibilities—Information and Options*, FAO Fisheries Circular 980, FITT/C980 (Rome: FAO, 2002), 3.

3. Matthew Gianni and Walt Simpson, *Flags of Convenience, Transshipment, Re-Supply and at-Sea Infrastructure in Relation to IUU Fishing*, AGR/FI/IUU(2004)22, (Paris: OECD, Fisheries Committee, Directorate for Food, Agriculture and Fisheries, April 2004), 7.

4. ICFTU, Trade Union Advisory Committee to the OECD, ITC, and Greenpeace International, "More Troubled Waters: Fishing, Pollution and FOCs," Major Group Submission for the 2002 World Summit on Sustainable Development, Johannesburg, August 2002.

5. Gianni and Simpson, 6.

6. Gianni and Simpson, 11.

7. Gianni and Simpson, 6; see also ISL, *Shipping Statistics Yearbook 2003* (Bremen: ISL, 2003), 103.

8. OECD, "Draft Chapter 2—Framework for Measures against IUU Fisheries Activities," OECD, Fisheries Committee, Directorate for Food, Agriculture and Fisheries, AGR/FI/IUU(2004)5/PROV, March 23, 2004, 21.

tries.[9] Taxes are lower, too, and many states that offer flags of convenience operate as tax havens as well, decreasing even further any tax burden. Most important, however, is the opportunity to fish without having to abide by national or international limits.

Those that truly want to operate outside the international regulatory system can change their flag repeatedly, without even having to enter port to do so. Modern factory fishing vessels can stay away from ports almost indefinitely; not only do they have all they need to process and freeze catches at sea, but those that prefer to remain away from rules and inspections can resupply and offload their catches at sea to other vessels.[10] Reflagging fishing vessels has been estimated to cost as little as $1,000.[11]

The decision by some owners of fishing vessels to choose ship registration as a way to evade fishery conservation measures is not new. One of the earliest examples came more than a century ago when the owners of British fishing trawlers reregistered their vessels in Norway (employing a Norwegian crew member to circumvent Norwegian prohibitions on foreign registration) in order to avoid being bound by British law restricting fishing in the Moray Firth.[12]

Another early instance of vessel registration being used to systematically skirt international fishery regulation came in the 1950s from the Olympic Whaling Company, run by Aristotle Onassis. The company's main whaling vessel, the *Olympic Challenger*, was registered in Panama; other whaling vessels run by the company were registered in Honduras. The company itself was incorporated in Uruguay. Since none of these states were International Whaling Commission (IWC) members, the vessels were not bound by IWC regulations. In the early 1950s the *Olympic*

9. David J. Agnew and Colin T. Barnes, "Economic Aspects and Drivers of IUU Fishing: Building a Framework," OECD, Fisheries Committee, Directorate for Food, Agriculture and Fisheries, AGR/FI/IUU(2004)(2), March 2004, 13.

10. Gianni and Simpson, 14–15.

11. Agnew and Barnes, 17.

12. Boleslaw Adam Boczek, *Flags of Convenience: An International Legal Study* (Cambridge: Harvard University Press, 1962), 7; see also Herbert Whittaker Briggs, *The Law of Nations*, 2nd ed. (New York: Appleton-Century-Crofts, 1952), 52–53, and Thomas Wemyss Fulton, *The Sovereignty of the Sea* (Edinburgh: W. Blackwood, 1911), 729.

Challenger and its associated whale catchers caught whales while flouting nearly every IWC rule.[13]

More recently, when the United States passed regulations in the 1970s under the Marine Mammal Protection Act requiring that U.S. tuna fishers refrain from killing dolphins in the process of tuna fishing, a number of shipowners reflagged their vessels in states that did not regulate dolphin mortality, where they would not be bound by the costly U.S. restrictions.[14] There are related current concerns about European ships—especially Spanish-owned ships—"flag hopping" to get access, under European fishing regulations, to quotas from other member states. In an effort to prevent this type of activity, the UK passed regulations in 1988 that required that vessels not only be British registered but that the owner also be a UK resident in order to participate in the British quota. But the European Court of Justice overturned this measure in 1991 as contravening Article 52 of the EEC treaty.[15]

Other states have made rules to try to prevent their citizens from participating in open registry fishing as an effort to stem the phenomenon of flagging out. New Zealand citizens are prevented by national law from taking or transporting fish on foreign flagged vessels unless such activity happens under the authority of a state that is party to international fisheries agreements. Japanese law requires Japanese nationals to obtain permission of the Japanese government before they can work on non-Japanese-flagged vessels fishing for Atlantic and southern bluefin tuna. The law also is intended to prohibit Japanese nationals from fishing in any fishery on vessels flagged in states that are not party to the relevant regional fishery conservation organizations.[16] Spain has declared that its national penalties for breaking fisheries laws can apply to its nationals

13. J. N. Tønnessen and A. O. Johnsen, *The History of Modern Whaling* (Berkeley: University of California Press, 1982), 534–538.

14. Between 1981 and 1985 thirty-four U.S. tuna boats transferred to other flags to continue to fish for tuna. See Alessandro Bonanno and Douglas Constance, *Caught in the Net: The Global Tuna Industry, Environmentalism, and the State* (Lawrence: University Press of Kansas, 1996), 156, 183.

15. Rachel Davies, "Fishing Boat Registration Rules Contravene EC Law," *Financial Times*, August 14, 1991, 21.

16. David A. Balton, "IUU Fishing and State Control over Nationals," OECD, Fisheries Committee, Directorate for Food, Agriculture and Fisheries, AGR/FI/IUU(2004)2, April 6, 2004, 3.

fis ng f eign-flagged ships.[17] Such regulations are intended to re- du itives for a nationally owned ship to reflag elsewhere. But sh to flag out, and open registry vessels catch fish in all the m is fishing areas where regional fisheries management orga- ni npt to restrict the catches of member states.

l organization efforts simply to convince open registry sta he relevant fishery management agreements, so that ships th ill be legally bound by the agreements, have had little im- pa wn. The most effective efforts at persuading these states to jo s, or individual shipowners to uphold them regardless of th ation to do so, has come through the use of trade restric- t ites or international organizations have restricted access t nly those who agree to uphold the relevant conservation a incentive for ships to operate outside the regulatory inishes considerably. The experiences in reducing the ates to remain outside international fishery regulation in ship registrations illustrate the ways the problems caused es can be decreased and shed light on the broader pro- ng to maintain international standards in the face of

International Agreements

Issues of overfishing on the open ocean are generally addressed by international conservation agreements. They are most frequently negotiated based on a species, a geographic region, or both. Fishing activity is regulated by imposing fishing seasons, fishing catch limits, or equipment standards (often prohibiting certain types of equipment, such as driftnets). Every effort is made to ensure that all the states whose vessels are likely to be fishing in the area participate in the negotiation of an agreement or join, but there are certainly some that prefer not to.

International attempts have been made to address this nonparticipation. The 1995 Agreement for the Implementation of the Provisions of the United Nations Convention on the Law of the Sea Relating to the

17. OECD, "National Measures against IUU Fishing Activities," OECD, Fisheries Committee, Directorate for Food, Agriculture and Fisheries, AGR/FI/IUU(2004)6/PROV, April 12, 2004, 58, 88.

Conservation and Management of Straddling Fish Stocks and Highly Migratory Fish Stocks requires that a state not party to fisheries management organizations not "authorize vessels flying its flag to engage in fishing operations for the straddling fish stocks or highly migratory fish stocks" that are the subject of those organizations.[18] The converse is also elaborated: states (which under UNCLOS have a duty to cooperate in fisheries management) are instructed to become members of these organizations or at least to apply the conservation measures they create.[19]

A number of other international agreements also mandate flag-state control over fishing vessels to ensure that they do not fish in otherwise-regulated areas. The FAO Compliance Agreement (1993), which entered into force in 2003, requires that flag states license fishing vessels before they can fish, conditional on abiding by international conservation measures.[20] Two nonbinding agreements, the FAO Code of Conduct for Responsible Fisheries (1995) and the FAO International Plan of Action on IUU Fishing (2001), also ask flag states to make sure that their vessels only fish after receiving authorization to do so by the relevant conservation organizations or states. The plan of action, in particular, encourages flag states to prevent flag hopping for the purpose of avoiding fisheries regulations. But the major open registries used by fishing vessels have not joined the binding agreements and do not participate in the nonbinding ones. The same legal rules that allow for open registry states to remain outside of fishing agreements allow them to avoid the cooperative agreements to address the fact that they remain outside of fishery agreements.

The most obvious way to deal with the threat of ships flagged in a state that is not a member of an international fisheries agreement or organization is to convince it to join. Most fisheries commissions have a long history of efforts to gain membership by states whose vessels are fishing in a given regulatory area or for a protected fish stock. Between the mid-1980s and mid-1990s the Northwest Atlantic Fisheries Organization (NAFO), for example, faced an annual average of between thirty and forty vessels that were flagged in nonmember states (most frequently Panama and Honduras) and were fishing in the NAFO regulatory area.

18. Article 17(2).

19. Article 8.

20. Agreement to Promote Compliance with International Conservation and Management Measures by Fishing Vessels on the High Seas (1993), Article III.

Each year the commission would ask the states in question to join or prevent their ships from fishing in the area. They did not join the organization, and when diplomatic pressure increased, a large number of the ships simply reflagged in Belize.[21]

The International Whaling Commission encountered a similar problem in the 1950s. The organization repeatedly discussed how to prevent what it called "pirate whaling," by ships flagged in nonmember states, with specific reference to the *Olympic Challenger*. Most efforts were aimed at convincing Panama, the state under which this ship was flagged, to join the commission, or to at least enforce IWC provisions. The IWC had little success, however, and it is likely that had Panama joined at the time, Onassis would simply have registered his operations elsewhere. In 1956 the Peruvian Navy seized the vessel for fishing in Peruvian waters and sold it to the Japanese,[22] ending the most serious case of FOC whaling.

While this particular situation may have been solved in an unusual way, two underlying observations are useful. First, fisheries commissions in general seem to have little success in persuading FOC states to join fishery conservation agreements. Second, if vessels have flagged in one state to avoid regulation, they are likely to reflag elsewhere if their flag state takes on the regulations they are trying to avoid, as long as doing so does not block other advantages they seek. The number of fishing vessels registered in recently opened registries supports this contention. The regional fisheries management organizations can only succeed in protecting the stocks they address if all those who fish in the area are bound by the relevant conservation regulations. Finding a way to persuade states that register fishing vessels to belong to these agreements is thus essential if the fishery organizations are to succeed at their conservation goals.

Trade Restrictions

What has succeeded in convincing open registries to join fisheries agreements or persuading individual fishing vessels to uphold them is tying

21. Agnew and Barnes, 10.

22. Ronald B. Mitchell, "Membership, Compliance, and Non-Compliance in the International Convention for the Regulation of Whaling," October 1992, unpublished paper, 19.

access to international markets for fish products to participation in the relevant conservation measures. The threat or imposition of trade restrictions has been used in efforts to convince open registry states to join international agreements relating to ocean resources. In the cases where ships have reflagged in order to avoid these restrictions, they may find that their new state of registry decides to take on these international regulations, or that they are prohibited from selling to their primary markets if they do not accept them.

The United States had been the biggest practitioner of this method; it has refused to import tuna from states that do not protect dolphins in the process of tuna fishing, or do not uphold the major tuna-fishing conventions. The United States has also threatened not to accept fish exports from states that do not uphold international standards on driftnet fishing or do not participate in the regulation of whaling.[23]

Initially this method was implemented by individual states. But given the multilateral nature of fishery conservation efforts and the multiple markets for fishery products, involvement of international organizations made success more likely. Such an approach has coordination advantages and also makes scrutiny from the World Trade Organization less likely.[24] More recently, a number of regional fishery management organizations are requiring that their members restrict trade in regulated species, only importing or transshipping fish caught by members of the agreements or by vessels that can otherwise demonstrate that they are operating within their restrictions.

The regional fisheries management organizations that have experienced significant levels of fishing by ships flagged (often intentionally) in nonmember states have created an array of mechanisms that restrict the options of these ships. These programs aim to diminish the advantage to open registry–flagged vessels and others that attempt to catch protected species outside the regulatory regime. These mechanisms have generally been adopted at different points within a several-year period and often

23. Elizabeth R. DeSombre, *Domestic Sources of International Environmental Policy: Industry, Environmentalists, and U.S. Power* (Cambridge: MIT Press, 2000).

24. Elizabeth R. DeSombre and J. Samuel Barkin, "Turtles and Trade: The WTO's Acceptance of Environmental Trade Restrictions," *Global Environmental Politics* 2/1 (February 2002): 2–18.

work in tandem. They have been used, with small variations, across a number of fisheries organizations attempting to address the same types of problems. Often this similarity is intentional, because fisheries organizations attempt to replicate successful efforts, or because they recognize the possibility that ships chased off from one fishing area may move to another. The FAO has explicitly tried to coordinate the imposition of catch certification schemes to ensure that the various documentation efforts do not conflict with each other.[25]

The set of strategies used usually includes the creation of a blacklist of ships (or flag states) not authorized to fish in the regulatory area, often followed by the creation of a whitelist of ships that are specifically allowed to fish. Also commonly implemented is the requirement of some kind of catch documentation that accompanies traded fish from the regulatory area (or landed in or transshipped through member states) to allow member states to distinguish between fish caught legally and within the regulatory framework and those caught by ships not bound by regulations. This type of measure also allows fishery organizations to gather statistical information that assists in scientific assessments of catches and stocks. Most organizations have also augmented these measures by some sort of vessel-monitoring system that allows flag states (at a minimum) or fisheries commissions (more intrusively) to keep track of where ships are fishing. Finally, and most successfully, these measures in combination may lead to an actual requirement by the relevant commission that members refuse to accept imports of fish from ships or states that have kept themselves outside of the regulatory framework.

The fisheries organizations that have faced the biggest threats from unregulated fishing by ships flagged in nonmember states have primarily been those focused on high-value, high-seas (and sometimes highly migratory) species such as tuna, swordfish, and Patagonian toothfish. The fisheries commissions that have adopted these types of measures have been the International Commission for the Conservation of Atlantic Tunas (ICCAT), followed by the other tuna commissions: the Commission for the Conservation of Southern Bluefin Tuna (CCSBT) and the Indian Ocean Tuna Commission (IOTC), plus the commission in charge of the

25. FAO, *Report of the Expert Consultation of Regional Fisheries Management Bodies on Harmonization of Catch Certification*, FAO Fisheries Report 697, FIIT/R697 (La Jolla: January 9–11, 2002).

Convention on the Conservation of Antarctic Marine Living Resources (CCAMLR). Other commissions, including the Northwest Atlantic Fisheries Organization (NAFO) and the Inter-American Tropical Tuna Commission (IATTC), have experienced the same problems and are beginning the process of implementing these types of measures.

International Commission for the Conservation of Atlantic Tunas

The conservation measures of the International Commission for the Conservation of Atlantic Tunas (ICCAT) have frequently been undermined by fishing undertaken by ships registered in nonmember states. The organization suggests that about 10 percent of the total catch in the fisheries it oversees is taken by unregulated fishers,[26] mostly those flagged in open registry states. ICCAT followed the standard practice of asking nonmember states whose vessels were seen fishing in the regulatory area to join the agreement, with little success. The organization decided that restricting access to markets so that only fish caught within the regulatory process could be traded would be the most effective way to curb the incentive to fish outside the regulatory structure.

In 1992 the organization created the Bluefin Tuna Statistical Document (BTSD) Program. Under this program, any bluefin tuna imported by ICCAT member states must be accompanied by a document explaining where, when, and how it was caught; this document must be validated by an official of the flag state whose vessel caught the tuna. (The organization allows for any equivalent documentation program to be followed, provided that states indicate in advance that they will be using an alternative.)[27] All ICCAT members are now required to refuse landings of tuna (or reexport of tuna) without a BTSD or the equivalent or tuna caught outside the ICCAT regime. As of 2002 this process was extended to cover bigeye tuna and swordfish as well.[28] This information is used to ensure that member states can refuse entry to improperly caught (or documented) fish, and also that statistical information can be compiled on catches and trade.

26. OECD, "Draft Chapter 2," 22.

27. ICCAT Recommendation 92-1, "Recommendation by ICCAT Concerning the ICCAT Bluefin Tuna Statistical Document Program."

28. ICCAT Recommendation 01-21, "Recommendation Establishing BET Statistic Program," and ICCAT Recommendation 01-22, "Recommendation Establishing a SWO Statistical Documentation Program."

ICCAT decided to go further than simply requiring documentation, to ensure that member states would penalize states operating outside the regulatory framework. In 1996 the organization began passing recommendations (legally binding on its member states), calling for the restriction on imports of regulated species from nonmember states whose vessels fished regularly for these species in the convention area.

In 1996, recommendations required the prohibition of bluefin tuna imports from Panama, Belize, and Honduras. Panama became an ICCAT member in 1998 and also took measures to reduce the activities of its fishing vessels, and the organization lifted restrictions on imports by a 1999 recommendation.[29] Honduras was also targeted by recommendations in 1999 prohibiting imports of Atlantic swordfish. Honduras joined ICCAT effective in 2001, and these measures were removed.[30] It was still targeted in 2002 with import prohibitions on Atlantic bigeye tuna because it had not sufficiently addressed the problems of Honduran-flagged ships fishing for bigeye tuna in the convention area, but after the Honduran government communicated to the ICCAT secretariat the specific measures it had taken, including a large reduction in the number of registered fishing vessels, these restrictions were removed.[31] Honduras claimed that it would close its registry to fishing vessels until it could be sure of ICCAT compliance.[32]

Recommendations in 1999 and 2000 added prohibitions on the import of Atlantic swordfish and bigeye tuna to the existing prohibitions on bluefin tuna from Belize. The restrictions on imports were lifted in 2004 after Belize began attending ICCAT meetings and undertook "a broad program of reform to achieve full compliance with ICCAT measures" (despite not joining the organization), including deleting a large number of fishing vessels from its registry.[33]

29. ICCAT Recommendation 99-9, "Panama: Lift BFT Import Prohibition."

30. ICCAT Recommendation 01-15 "Lifting of BFT and SWO on Honduras."

31. Of 269 fishing vessels registered to Honduras in 2000, 41 were suspended and 228 removed (Swan, 29). Also see ICCAT Recommendation 02-18, "Recommendation by ICCAT Concerning the Importation of Bigeye Tuna and Its Products from Honduras."

32. Swan, 29.

33. ICCAT Recommendation 02-16, "Recommendation by ICCAT Concerning the Importation of Atlantic Bluefin Tuna, Atlantic Swordfish, and Atlantic Bigeye Tuna and Their Products from Belize."

St. Vincent and the Grenadines was identified in 1999 as a state that diminished the effectiveness of ICCAT measures by unregulated tuna fishing in the area. A recommendation in 2000 restricted imports of St. Vincent–caught Atlantic bigeye tuna. This prohibition was slated to be lifted as of 2003 by a recommendation passed in 2001, when St. Vincent indicated that it had undertaken efforts to reform its registry and to curtail efforts by fishing vessels in the area.[34] ICCAT member states, however, expressed concerns that the state had not fully planned for the oversight of fishing vessels under its flag, and postponed the removal of the sanctions until the beginning of 2004.[35]

Even some of the most recently targeted states have managed to take the necessary steps to remove sanctions. Equatorial Guinea was targeted in 1999 and 2000,[36] and the ICCAT Commission was sufficiently concerned about Equatorial Guinea's lack of action after several years of ICCAT pressure that it reiterated the trade restrictions for all three species for which the state was targeted (bluefin tuna, swordfish, and bigeye tuna) in 2003.[37] Equatorial Guinea issued Decree No. 33/2004 in May 2004, canceling the licenses and flags of fishing vessels of concern to ICCAT and notified the ICCAT Secretariat that it had passed a number of measures to ensure compliance with ICCAT regulations. ICCAT lifted the trade restrictions in late 2004.[38]

Cambodia (targeted in 2000)[39] also responded to criticisms. It deregistered vessels identified as engaged in illegal or unregulated fishing in the ICCAT convention area, and indicated that it would not authorize any

34. ICCAT Recommendation 01-14, "Recommendation by ICCAT Concerning the Importation of Bigeye Tuna and Bigeye Tuna Products from St. Vincent and the Grenadines."

35. ICCAT Recommendation 02-20, "Recommendation by ICCAT Concerning the Trade Sanctions against St. Vincent and the Grenadines."

36. ICCAT Recommendation 99-10, "Equatorial Guinea Pursuant to 1996 Compliance Recommendation—BFT and N SWO Fisheries," and ICCAT Recommendation 00-16, "Equatorial Guinea Pursuant to 1998 IUU Resolution."

37. ICCAT Recommendation 03-17, "Recommendation by ICCAT Concerning the Continuance of Trade Measures against Equatorial Guinea."

38. ICCAT Recommendation 04-13, "Recommendation by ICCAT Concerning the Lifting of Trade Sanctions against Equatorial Guinea."

39. ICCAT Recommendation 00-15, "Belize, Cambodia, Honduras, St. Vincent and the Grenadines Pursuant to 1998 IUU Resolution."

Cambodian-registered ships to fish in the regulatory area. It also canceled the contract of the Singapore-based firm that had been providing its registry services.[40] ICCAT lifted the trade restrictions in late 2004.[41]

Sierra Leone (targeted in 2002)[42] took steps to respond to the Commission's concerns, by developing a plan for monitoring and control, reporting data, and removing from its registry a vessel that ICCAT had identified as fishing illegally. As a result, ICCAT lifted the trade restrictions in 2004.[43]

Not all recently targeted states have addressed ICCAT's concerns, however. Bolivia (targeted in 2002)[44] and Georgia (targeted in 2003)[45] have not sufficiently changed their behavior to be allowed to export tuna and tunalike products to ICCAT members.

In an effort to expand these measures, ICCAT in 2002 decided to create a "whitelist" and "blacklist." The organization had begun this process in 1994 with a resolution calling for the creation of a list of vessels authorized by member states to fish in the regulatory area, followed in 1999 by publication of a list of longline tuna-fishing vessels flagged in open registries that were conducting unauthorized fishing in the convention area.[46] These lists were formalized in 2002 (to take effect in mid-2003) with the requirement that member states prevent landings or transshipment of regulated species by ships not on the positive list, and in particular refuse to do anything that would help ships on the negative

40. Tony Gilotte, "Cambodia Claims Its Register Has Turned Corner," *Lloyd's List*, February 13, 2004, 3.

41. ICCAT Recommendation 04-15, "Recommendation by ICCAT Concerning the Lifting of Bigeye Tuna Trade Restrictive Measures against Cambodia."

42. ICCAT Recommendation 02-19, "Recommendation by ICCAT for Trade Restrictive Measures on Sierra Leone."

43. ICCAT Recommendation 04-14, "Recommendation by ICCAT Concerning the Lifting of Bigeye Tuna, Bluefin Tuna, and Swordfish Trade Restrictive Measures against Sierra Leone."

44. ICCAT Recommendation 02-17, "Recommendation by ICCAT Regarding Bolivia Pursuant to the 1998 Resolution Concerning the Unreported and Unregulated Catches of Tuna by Large-Scale Longline Vessels in the Convention Area."

45. ICCAT Recommendation 03-18, "Recommendation by ICCAT for Bigeye Tuna Trade Restrictive Measures on Georgia."

46. OECD, "Draft Chapter 2," 23.

Table 7.1
ICCAT trade restrictions

RES #	In force	Import prohibition	Target state	Lifting res #	Year lifted	Target action taken
96-12	1/1/98	Bluefin tuna	Panama	99-9	1999	Became ICCAT member; reduced fishing
96-11	8/4/97	Bluefin tuna	Belize	02-16	2004	Deregistered vessels
96-11	8/4/97	Bluefin tuna	Honduras	01-15	2002	Joined ICCAT 1/30/00
99-8	6/15/00	Atlantic swordfish	Belize	02-16	2004	Deregistered vessels
99-8	6/15/00	Atlantic swordfish	Honduras	01-15	2002	Joined ICCAT 1/30/00
99-10	6/15/00	Bluefin tuna	Eq. Guinea	04-13	2004	Deregistered vessels; other compliance
99-10	6/15/00	Swordfish	Eq. Guinea	04-13	2004	Deregistered vessels; other compliance
00-15	10/15/01	Bigeye tuna	Belize	02-16	2004	Deregistered vessels
00-15	10/15/01	Bigeye tuna	Cambodia	04-15	2004	Deregistered vessels
00-15	10/15/01	Bigeye tuna	Honduras	02-18	2002	Joined ICCAT; took action
00-15	10/15/01	Bigeye tuna	St. Vincent	01-14; 02-20	2004	Took measures to comply
00-16	6/26/01	Bigeye tuna	Eq. Guinea	04-13	2004	Deregistered vessels; other compliance
02-17	6/4/03	Bigeye tuna	Bolivia			
02-19	6/4/03	Bluefin tuna	Sierra Leone	04-14	2004	Deregistered vessel; monitoring plan
02-19	6/4/03	Bigeye tuna	Sierra Leone	04-14	2004	Deregistered vessel; monitoring plan
02-19	6/4/03	Swordfish	Sierra Leone	04-14	2004	Deregistered vessel; monitoring plan
03-18	6/19/04	Bigeye tuna	Georgia			

list fish for regulated species.[47] The blacklist of vessels, however, has had mixed success so far. The Japanese representatives to the International Conference on Illegal, Unreported and Unregulated Fishing in 2002 indicated that forged documents have made enforcing these measures difficult.[48] ICCAT has begun to develop a vessel-monitoring system as well. The ships of each member state will be required to use satellite tracking systems that report data continuously to the state.[49]

In addition to these specific recommendations, individual ICCAT member states undertook related actions to support and expand the effect of ICCAT measures. Japan restricted the import of tuna from all fishing vessels that are not registered in ICCAT member states.[50] The United States, even before official ICCAT recommendations required it, refused to import tuna from states identified by the organization as diminishing the effectiveness of ICCAT.[51] South Africa also banned landings of fish by vessels listed by ICCAT as engaging in IUU fishing.

There is some evidence that these measures are having an effect. ICCAT estimated that unregulated catch (primarily by vessels flying flags of convenience) had declined by about two-thirds between 1998 and 2001. But a study by Japan presented in 2002 indicated that unregulated tuna fishing accounts for 25,000 tons of tuna annually, a figure close to the 1998 ICCAT estimate.[52] In addition, some fishing vessels that left ICCAT-targeted flag states during the time when sanctions were imposed

47. ICCAT Recommendation 02-22, "Recommendation by ICCAT Concerning the Establishment of an ICCAT Record of Vessels over 24 Meters Authorized to Operate in the Convention Area," and ICCAT Recommendation 02-23, "Recommendation by ICCAT to Establish a List of Vessels Presumed to Have Carried Out Illegal, Unreported and Unregulated Fishing Activities in the ICCAT Convention Area."

48. OECD, "Draft Chapter 1—Economics of IUU Fishing Activities," OECD, Fisheries Committee, Directorate for Food, Agriculture and Fisheries, AGR/FI/IUU(2004)3/PROV, March 12, 2004, 29.

49. ICCAT Recommendation, "Recommendation by ICCAT Concerning Minimum Standards for the Establishment of a Vessel Monitoring System in the ICCAT Convention Area."

50. "Japan to Ban Tuna Imports from Panama, Honduras, Belize," *AP Worldstream*, December 3, 1996 (Lexis/Nexis).

51. DeSombre, *Domestic Sources*, 216–217.

52. Agnew and Barnes, 10.

(because they would not be able to sell their tuna to their primary markets) returned once the restrictions were lifted and in some cases engaged in unregulated fishing.[53]

There have clearly been some changes by targeted states: Panama and Honduras joined ICCAT, and Belize and St. Vincent and the Grenadines took measures to reduce their fishing fleets and to make sure their ships were not fishing against ICCAT regulations. Honduras also requires that, before they can be registered, fishing vessels sign an affidavit that they will not fish for tuna.[54]

But the most recently targeted states, Cambodia, Bolivia, Sierra Leone, and Georgia, are among those open registries with the greatest increase in fishing vessels. It seems clear that ships that did not want to meet the standards their previous registries decided to take on have instead moved their registration elsewhere. ICCAT has limited their access to the most lucrative markets, however, and in doing so has removed at least some of their incentive to fish outside the regulatory scheme.

Commission for the Conservation of Southern Bluefin Tuna

The Commission for the Conservation of Southern Bluefin Tuna (CCSBT) has also faced increasing fishing by ships flagged in nonmember open registries. The organization estimated that in 1999 15 percent of the catch was being taken by these vessels;[55] later estimates put the catch at nearly one-third of the total.[56] In June 2000 the organization created a Trade Information Scheme (TIS) to combat this problem. Under this program, member-state imports of southern bluefin tuna require a CCSBT Statistical Document, providing details on where, when, and how the tuna was caught, attested to by a state authority. The program requires that member states refuse tuna caught outside the regulatory system or without proper documentation. Some nonmember states, most importantly the United States and the Philippines, have agreed to cooperate. The organization has also begun, in July 2004, the creation of a list of vessels authorized to fish in the regulatory area, and member states (and

53. ICFTU et al., 17.
54. Swan, 26.
55. Swan, 36.
56. OECD, "Draft Chapter 2," 22.

cooperating nonmember states) are not allowed to import tuna caught by vessels not on the list.[57]

Since Japan, a member state, is by far the largest market for southern bluefin tuna, this mechanism has been reasonably successful. Trade with nonparty states has decreased significantly since the program was introduced.[58]

Indian Ocean Tuna Commission

The Indian Ocean Tuna Commission, established in 1996, has had to deal with the problem of fishing by open registry flagged vessels since almost the beginning of its existence. The organization has estimated that approximately 10 percent of the landings of tuna under its regulatory purview is taken by vessels registered in nonmember states.[59] The commission adopted a resolution in 2001 requiring member (and cooperating) states to inspect the ships from any noncontracting party that enter their ports, and prevent these vessels from landing or transshipping fish until such an inspection has happened. If a ship flagged in a nonmember state has fish on board from species regulated by IOTC it is not allowed to land or transship fish unless it can demonstrate that they were caught outside of the regulatory area.[60] A resolution adopted the following year mandates the creation of a list of ships flying the flags of noncooperating states. Members (and cooperating nonmembers) are then required to take a variety of steps to ensure that no tuna be imported, landed, or transshipped from these vessels.[61] The IOTC also adopted, in 2002, a positive listing process, which created a list of large-scale fishing vessels

57. CCSBT, "Management of SBT," http://www.ccsbt.org/docs/management.html.

58. Swan, 37.

59. OECD, "Draft Chapter 2," 22.

60. IOTC, "Resolution 01/03 Establishing a Scheme to Promote Compliance by Non-Contracting Party Vessels with Resolutions Established by IOTC," at http://www.iotc.org/English/resolutions/reso_detail.php?reso=14.

61. IOTC, "Resolution 02/04 on Establishing a List of Vessels Presumed to Have Carried Out Illegal, Unregulated, and Unreported Fishing in the IOTC Area," http://www.iotc.org/English/resolutions/reso_detail.php?reso=17&apndx=1; this resolution was superceded by an expanded version: IOTC, "Resolution 05/02 Concerning the Establishment of an IOTC Record of Vessels Authorized to Operate in the IOTC Area."

authorized to fish for tuna in the IOTC regulatory area. Member and cooperating states must then take actions to prohibit the import of tuna from vessels not on the list.[62] This policy, mirroring that used in ICCAT, was adopted at least in part to prevent unregulated fishers from moving ships from the Atlantic to the Indian Ocean.

In 2001 the organization also created an IOTC Bigeye Tuna statistical document that members were asked to require from states from which they imported tuna. This document needs to be authorized by an official of the flag state that caught the tuna, and must include information on the ship that caught or is transshipping the tuna, the area and method of catch, and a description of the fish product. Member states must refuse imports of tuna not accompanied by such a document. They must also refrain from importing tuna when the accompanying document shows that the catch was not acceptable under IOTC rules.[63] This process was expanded by a 2003 resolution that grants to the commission the right to impose ICCAT-like trade sanctions against nonmember flag states who consistently let their ships fish in the regulatory area.[64] As of 2005 such measures have not been taken.

In addition, IOTC member states Seychelles, Vanuatu, and Japan adopted their own joint effort to eliminate tuna longline vessels operating outside of the IOTC regulatory process, by either registering or scrapping longline tuna vessels previously noted as engaging in unregulated fishing.[65]

Industry actors have also joined the effort against fishing by vessels not involved in international conservation measures. Longline tuna fishers in

62. IOTC, Resolution 02/05 Concerning the Establishment of an IOTC Record of Vessels Over 24 Metres Authorised to Operate in the IOTC Area," http://www.iotc.org/English/resolutions/reso_detail.php?reso=23.

63. IOTC, "Resolution 01/06 Concerning the IOTC Bigeye Tuna Statistical Document Programme," http://www.iotc.org/English/resolutions/reso_detail.php?reso=22.

64. IOTC, "Recommendation 03/05 Concerning Trade Measures," 2003, http://www.iotc/English/resolutions/reso_detail.php?reso=32.

65. Delegation of Japan, *Report on the Progress in the Measures to Eliminate IUU Large Scale Tuna Longline Fishing Vessels*, Preparatory Conference for the Commission for the Conservation and Management of Highly Migratory Fish Stocks in the Western and Central Pacific, 4th session, WCPF/PrepCon/DP.11, May 9, 2003.

Japan and Taiwan, along with distributors, and consumer and trade organizations in Japan, created the Organization for the Promotion of Responsible Tuna Fisheries (OPRT) in December 2000. Fishing-industry actors in Korea, Indonesia, the Philippines, China, and Ecuador have since joined. As of March 2004 the organization counted 1,460 fishing vessels as members.[66] The organization was founded by those concerned that open registry vessels were catching tuna outside of the relevant regulatory frameworks and exporting their tuna to Japan. The organization works to reduce tuna-fishing capacity. In particular, OPRT hopes to prevent secondhand tuna vessels from being registered elsewhere, by making sure they are scrapped instead. At OPRT's initiative, forty-three out-of-service Japanese tuna vessels were scrapped between 2001 and 2003.[67] The organization also compares tuna landing statistics with catch data, to check the accuracy of self-reported catches.[68]

Commission for the Conservation of Antarctic Marine Living Resources

The Convention for the Conservation of Antarctic Marine Living Resources and its associated commission (CCAMLR) have also experienced the impacts of widespread fishing by ships flagged in nonmember states. The organization estimates that between 1996 and 1999 illegal, unregulated, and unreported (IUU) fishing, done primarily by vessels flying flags of convenience, accounted for more than twice the amount of regulated fishing.[69] Estimates from other organizations put this number much higher.[70] Panama and Belize have been singled out as the primary FOC registries for vessels wishing to avoid CCAMLR catch limits.[71]

66. Hiroya Sano, "Are Private Initiatives a Possible Way Forward? Actions Taken by Private Stakeholders to Eliminate IUU Fishing Activities," OECD, Fisheries Committee, Directorate for Food, Agriculture and Fisheries, AGR/FI/IUU(2004)13, April 8, 2004, 2.

67. Sano, 2.

68. OECD, "Draft Chapter 2," 18.

69. CCAMLR, "Explanatory Memorandum on the Introduction of the Catch Documentation Scheme (CDS) for Toothfish," n.d., http://www.ccamlr.org/pu/E/cds/p2.htm.

70. TRAFFIC suggests that IUU fishing may account for four times that of legal fishing. See M. Lack and G. Sant, "Patagonian Toothfish: Are Conservation and Trade Measures Working?", *TRAFFIC Bulletin* 19/1 (2001): 1.

71. TRAFFIC, 4.

Additionally, it appears that fishing vessels from traditional maritime states (such as Spain) were registering in open registries that were CCAMLR parties, with low capacity for oversight (such as Uruguay).[72] This registration allows them to operate within the CCAMLR system but in a way that decreases the odds that noncompliance will be detected. This unregulated fishing poses a problem not only for conservation but also for the scientific research associated with the commission, because the location and amount of fish caught by nonmember states cannot be factored into scientific evaluation of stocks.

After these states ignored requests to join the organization, CCAMLR created a "Catch Documentation Scheme" for Patagonian toothfish (also known as Chilean seabass) to dissuade unregulated fishing by blocking access to markets in CCAMLR member states for vessels whose ships continue to operate outside the regulatory framework. This scheme works to monitor and track catches of toothfish. Member states have an obligation to prohibit the import of fish caught in an inappropriate manner, or not otherwise documented. Flag states that are not members of CCAMLR may still participate in the program as long as they are able to document that their catches were caught within the conservation regulations.[73] This aspect of the mechanism is designed, at least in part, to avoid a World Trade Organization challenge to the legality of the trade restrictions, by making them nondiscriminatory.

Those who wish to land or transship toothfish must present this document to the officials in the port in which the fish are landed. States participating in the scheme may only allow the entry of toothfish with a complete and authorized document; otherwise the fish must be detained. CCAMLR also passed an associated measure enabling port states to inspect all vessels (whether they are from CCAMLR parties or not) that wish to land toothfish in their ports.[74]

As per the usual process, the policy instructs the commission to contact nonmember states whose vessels have fished in the convention area

72. "Rogues Gallery: The New Face of IUU Fishing for Toothfish," *COLTO Brochure*, October 2003, 2, http://www.colto.org.

73. CCAMLR, "Catch Documentation Scheme," http://www.ccamlr.org/pu/E/cds/intro.htm.

74. Julia Green and David Agnes, "Catch Documentation Schemes to Combat Illegal, Unreported, and Unregulated Fishing: CCAMLR's Experience with Southern Ocean Toothfish," *Ocean Yearbook* 16 (2002): 171–194.

(particularly if "implicated in" illegal, unregulated, and unreported fishing) to ask them to attend commission meetings and consider joining the convention. But these states are also to be informed of the Catch Documentation Scheme and "the consequences for them of not participating."[75] The process laid out requires some participation by the flag state—an official of the state the ship is registered in must attest to the validity of the document filed when fish are traded—but can otherwise be undertaken by individual vessels that wish to participate, even if their flag state does not want to join CCAMLR. Those vessels registering in open registries specifically to avoid being bound by fishing restrictions are, however, unlikely to take advantage of this provision.

CCAMLR has also created a Catch Documentation Scheme Fund, to be used for projects to improve the effectiveness of the CDS, including assistance for states wishing to implement the CDS. States are encouraged to put the money gained from sales of confiscated toothfish into this fund.[76]

The CCAMLR Catch Documentation Scheme faces some hurdles that those implemented by the various tuna commissions do not. Because CCAMLR focuses on a location, rather than on particular species, there is legal fishing for toothfish that can take place outside the CCAMLR regulatory area. Distinguishing between legally caught and illegally caught toothfish can be difficult, and depends entirely on where it was caught.

For this reason, CCAMLR required that as of 2001 satellite tracking equipment be installed on ships fishing for toothfish to enable their flag states to track their location. But since this mechanism depends on flag-state oversight, it has been subject to abuse. Member states with little regulatory oversight capacity lack either the will or the ability to track their vessels. There is evidence that some vessels have falsified their location reports. Many CCAMLR member states hoped to augment this system with a centralized electronic-tracking mechanism that would allow the organization to track vessels, but such a measure was vetoed by Argentina at the 2003 CCAMLR meeting.[77] CCAMLR did authorize a

75. CCAMLR, "Policy to Enhance Cooperation between CCAMLR and Non-Contracting Parties," n.d., http://www.ccamlr.org/pu/E/cds/p4.htm.

76. CCAMLR Conservation Measure 10-05 (2004).

77. "Snag in Toothfish War," *The Mercury (Australia)*, November 8, 2003 (Lexis/Nexis).

seven-state test of such a system, however. The organization also created a blacklist of vessels known to be illegally fishing, so that they can be tracked. Member states agreed to refuse to accept any toothfish caught on blacklisted ships.[78]

There is evidence that the scheme is having a variety of impacts, at least some of them consistent with its goals. Immediately after it began, the price paid for toothfish at the point of landing in the ports of contracting parties was double that of nonparties.[79] Since then, a more consistent price differential has been estimated, with shipments without documentation fetching a price 20 to 40 percent lower than documented catches,[80] though some still estimate the amount paid for documented fish is more than double than for undocumented.[81] This differential certainly suggests that well-documented catches could fetch a premium in member states.

Since the costs of fishing legally have not increased while the relative price to be gained by selling fish within the regime has, the system is doing what it intended to do by making legal fish more lucrative than previously. Whether that will fully address the problems of vessels fishing outside the regulatory system remains to be seen. Fish caught by nonmember states (or those that did not follow the conservation regulations) can clearly still find a market—as Stokke and Vidas put it, "there is always some other port"[82]—but not one that is as lucrative. And it is generally agreed that the CDS has ended landings in member states of fish caught in an unregulated way.[83]

78. CCAMLR Conservation Measures 10-06, 10-07, and Resolution 19/XXI; http://www.ccamlr.org/pu/E/cds/cds-ops.htm.

79. D. J. Agnew, "The Illegal and Unregulated Fishery for Toothfish in the Southern Ocean, and the CCAMLR Catch Documentation Scheme," *Marine Policy* 24/5 (2000): 368.

80. Olav Schram Stokke and Davor Vidas, "Regulating IUU Fishing or Combating IUU Operations?", OECD, Fisheries Committee, Directorate for Food, Agriculture and Fisheries, AGR/FI/IUU(2004)(8), March 30, 2004, 54; Agnew and Barnes, 15.

81. Stokke and Vidas, 22.

82. Stokke and Vidas, 13.

83. TRAFFIC; U. R. Sumaila, "The Cost of Being Apprehended Fishing Illegally: Empirical Evidences and Policy Implications," OECD, Fisheries Committee, Directorate for Food, Agriculture and Fisheries, AGR/FI/IUU(2004)11, April 6, 2004, 12.

More important is the impact of the measures on fishing behavior. There is certainly evidence that it is having an effect, at least some of it positive. CCAMLR itself suggests that there has been a decrease in toothfish catch over the first four years of the program.[84] The largest decrease appears to have been in the 1999–2000 fishing season, when the program had been created but was not yet fully operational. TRAFFIC suggests that in that year IUU catches declined by 21 percent,[85] and CCAMLR charts show a large drop in that year followed by a gradual (but small) increase since then, falling again slightly in the 2002–2003 fishing season.[86]

Also relevant, and less promising, are changes in the location of fishing. Since the beginning of the Catch Documentation Scheme more fishing catches have been reported as coming from just outside the CCAMLR regulatory area. Stock estimates cast doubt as to whether toothfish could even be found in abundance in areas from which these reports come. Some fishing has probably moved outside the CCAMLR regulatory area[87] (hardly a victory for stock preservation), and other fishing activity has likely simply been reported as having moved.

At a minimum, it does seem that the Catch Documentation Scheme has successfully created a record of the legal trade,[88] and has allowed CCAMLR members to discriminate in favor of fish that have been caught within the regulatory framework. CCAMLR officials suggest that the CDS now covers more than 90 percent of the world market for toothfish.[89]

The most promising indications are the behavior by flag states. Two states have joined the agreement since the Catch Documentation Scheme and its associated membership push began. Namibia, which is not an open registry but which has been a major landing and transshipment location for toothfish, joined as a full-fledged member of the commission in

84. Denzil G. M. Miller, "Patagonian Toothfish—the Storm Gathers," OECD, Fisheries Committee, Directorate for Food, Agriculture and Fisheries, AGR/FI/IUU(2004)7, April 1, 2004, 10.

85. TRAFFIC, 5.

86. Miller, 39.

87. Stokke and Vidas, 23.

88. "Rogues Gallery," 3.

89. Miller, 18.

June 2000. Vanuatu, which is an open registry, joined as a noncommission member in June 2001.[90]

In addition, Belize, an open registry that has until recently drawn large numbers of fishing vessels, has begun cooperating with the commission.[91] It deregistered four vessels (and warned one other) specifically identified by CCAMLR as fishing in the regulatory area.[92] Panama has declined to join the agreement, but has said that it will provide the commission with a list of its vessels licensed to fish internationally. China, Mauritius, the Seychelles, and Singapore are all officially cooperating with the Catch Documentation Scheme, though they have not signed the convention.[93] Canada, which is a CCAMLR signatory but not a commission member, has not yet agreed to participate in the scheme, which causes potential problems, because it is a large market for toothfish. Most observers expect that it will participate eventually, however.[94] The commission has also taken steps to urge member states to only authorize their vessels to land catches in states that implement the CDS.[95]

The flagging of rogue ships in open registries that are members of CCAMLR is a trend that bears watching. Uruguay's registration, after declining noticeably between 1998 and 1999, has been increasing since

90. *Report by the Australian Delegate in His Capacity as Representative of the Depository Government for the Convention on the Conservation of Antarctic Marine Living Resources to the Twenty-Fifth Antarctic Treaty Consultative Meeting*, ATCM XXV, Information Paper IP-111, 2002. Under CCAMLR, states that newly join the treaty may only become members of the commission, the decision-making body of the organization, if they are "engaged in research or harvesting activities" pertaining to CCAMLR-restricted stocks (Convention for the Conservation of Antarctic Marine Living Resources, Article 7(2)(b)).

91. TRAFFIC, 6–7.

92. Swan, 38.

93. CCAMLR, "List of Parties Implementing the CDS," http://www.ccamlr.org/pu/E/cds/list-of-parties.htm.

94. Eugene N. Sabourenkov and Denzil G. M. Miller, "The Management of Transboundary Stocks of Toothfish, *Dissostichus spp*., under the Convention on the Conservation of Antarctic Marine Living Resources," in A. I. L. Payne, C. M. O'Brien, and S. I. Rogers, eds., *Management of Shared Fish Stock* (Oxford: Blackwell, 2004), 84–86.

95. CCAMLR Resolution 15(XXII), "Use of Ports Not Implementing the Catch Documentation Scheme for Dissostichus spp." (2003).

then, moving from 61,800 GT registered in 1999 to 76,000 GT registered in 2004.[96] Those within the CCAMLR system, especially if willing to falsfify satellite position data (as has been the case with a number of Urguayan-flagged vessels), can participate in the Catch Documentation Scheme while actually circumventing the rules.

Other nonstate actors, most prominently those from the fishing industry, have played important roles in this process as well. Following the 1997 CCAMLR Commission meeting a group of interested environmentalists formed the International Southern Oceans Longline Fisheries Information Clearing House (ISOFISH). The organization received initial funding from fishing and trading companies within CCAMLR member states, as well as from the Australian government. During its 3-year existence the organization focused on transparency: it reported on unlicensed fishing and the trade resulting from it within the CCAMLR regulatory area, and made an effort to raise awareness of, and disseminate information about, illegal and unregistered fishing. In particular, this involved publicizing lists of vessels fishing outside the CCAMLR regulatory process, and those states or ports that facilitated this practice.[97] After much success at publicizing the issue, the organization ceased to exist in 2000.

After the decline of ISOFISH, fishing interests that wanted to operate within the rules formed their own organization: the Coalition of Legal Toothfish Operators (COLTO). They recognize that their livelihoods over the long term would be negatively impacted by unregulated fishing that threatens to deplete the fish stock on which they depend, and so created an industry organization to aid CCAMLR and its member states in combating unregulated or illegal fishing. Among other functions, the group maintains a list of fishing vessels known to be fishing in an illegal or unregulated way in the area, along with photos and information about registry. It began a "Wanted" program in 2003, which offers rewards of $100,000 for information leading to the arrest and conviction of those illegally fishing for toothfish.[98]

96. Lloyd's Register Fairplay, *World Fleet Statistics 2004* (London: Lloyd's Register Fairplay, 2005).

97. Fallon and Kriwoken, 221–266.

98. COLTO, "The Wanted Campaign," http://www.colto.org/Wanted_Campaign.htm.

Other Schemes

Several other fisheries organizations have developed some aspects of the schemes discussed above. The Northwest Atlantic Fisheries Organization (NAFO) actually created one of the earliest port state control obligations, with a 1997 plan that presumes that nonparty vessels fishing in the NAFO regulatory area are undermining NAFO efforts. NAFO members are required to inspect such vessels that enter their ports, and they may not allow landings or transshipments of fish on board unless the vessel can demonstrate that the fish were caught outside of the NAFO regulatory area. Member states report the results of such inspections to the NAFO secretariat and members, and to the flag state of inspected vessels.[99] The North East Atlantic Fisheries Commission (NEAFC) has a similar port state inspection process,[100] as well as lists of ships registered in noncontracting states fishing in the regulatory area. Member states are not supposed to allow these ships to land or transship fish in their territory.[101]

Individual states have gone further than some of the fisheries commissions have required. For example, Norway has created a prohibition on landing of fish catches in contravention of fisheries agreements, even if the ship's flag state is not a member of these agreements.[102] New Zealand requires that any fish landed in New Zealand be approved in advance by the Ministry of Fisheries. Approval is contingent on evidence that no fish has been caught outside of international conservation processes; usually the vessel is required as well to use a vessel-monitoring device during the time it is fishing.[103]

What about the WTO?

One concern about the mechanisms described here is their compatibility with international trade rules. At first glance, provisions requiring that

99. Terje Lobach, "Port State Measures," OECD, Fisheries Committee, Directorate for Food, Agriculture and Fisheries, AGR/FI/IUU(2004)9, April 8, 2004, 5.

100. NEAFC Secretariat, "IUU Fishing in NEAFC: How Big Is the Problem and What Have We Done?", OECD, Fisheries Committee, Directorate for Food, Agriculture and Fisheries, AGR/FI/IUU(2004)5, April 15, 2004.

101. NEAFC, "Non-Contracting Party Scheme," January 2005.

102. Terje Lobach, *Port State Control of Foreign Fishing Vessels*, FAO Fisheries Circular 987, FIP/C987(Eng), 2003, 15–16.

103. OECD, "National Measures," 71.

states discriminate in trade based on conservation concerns seem likely to run afoul of the World Trade Organization requirements that member states refrain from using nontariff barriers to trade. Some suggest that decisions by the dispute-settlement mechanisms of the WTO (and its predecessor under the General Agreement on Tariffs and Trade) mean that the organization will disallow trade restrictions for environmental purposes. The most notorious of these are the findings against the United States in 1991 and 1994 for its unilateral restrictions on imports of tuna not caught in ways that protected dolphins,[104] and in 1998 and 2001 for its restrictions on imports of shrimp caught in ways that harmed sea turtles.[105] But within its findings against these particular trade measures, the dispute-settlement process elaborated an increasing acceptance of environmental protection as a legitimate reason for restricting trade, as long as restrictions on trade are applied in a nondiscriminatory way, are designed specifically for environmental protection, and are accompanied by multilateral attempts to address the environmental issue.[106]

In part due to these rulings, the sanctions described here against fish caught by vessels flagged in nonmembers of fisheries organizations have been more carefully targeted to allow individual vessels that can prove they meet standards to export fish to the states that otherwise would exclude fishery imports from their flag state, since the measures do not discriminate against individual vessels that meet standards even when

104. General Agreement on Tariffs and Trade, 1991, "Dispute Settlement Report on United States Restriction on Imports of Tuna," *International Legal Materials* 30: 1594–1623; General Agreement on Tariffs and Trade, 1994, "Dispute Settlement Panel Report on United States Restrictions on Imports of Tuna," *International Legal Materials* 33: 839–903.

105. World Trade Organization, *United States—Import Prohibition of Certain Shrimp and Shrimp Products: Report of the Panel*, WT/DS58/R, May 15, 1998; World Trade Organization, *United States—Import Prohibition of Certain Shrimp and Shrimp Products: Report of the Appellate Body*, WT/DS58/AB/R, October 12, 1998; World Trade Organization, *United States—Import Prohibition of Certain Shrimp and Shrimp Products: Recourse to Article 21.5 by Malaysia: Report of the Panel*, WT/DS58/RW, June 15, 2001; World Trade Organization, *United States—Import Prohibition of Certain Shrimp and Shrimp Products: Recourse to Article 21.5 of the DSU by Malaysia*, WT/DS58/AB/RW, October 22, 2001.

106. Elizabeth R. DeSombre and J. Samuel Barkin, "Turtles and Trade: The WTO's Acceptance of Environmental Trade Restrictions," *Global Environmental Politics* 2/1 (February 2001): 12–18.

their flag states have not taken them on. The organizations are careful to avoid running afoul of the WTO. A recent ICCAT resolution makes a point of noting that these restrictions should only be used as a last resort, and that they "should be adopted an implemented" in accordance with international law and the WTO, and be implemented "in a non-discriminatory manner."[107] The IOTC, similarly, indicates in its recommendation on trade measures that trade measures should be "adopted and implemented in accordance with international law including ... obligations established in WTO Agreements."[108] The WTO Secretariat has indicated that the ICCAT and CCAMLR trade restrictions "provide examples of appropriate and WTO-consistent (i.e. non-discriminatory) use of trade measures in multilateral environmental agreements."[109]

The success of economic sanctions at gaining adherence to fishery agreements comes from the creation of a trading club. Those that want to sell fish to the large American or Japanese markets must live up to certain fishery regulations in order to be able to do so. This requirement has caused some open registry states to join fishery conservation agreements and other individual fishing vessels to lose their incentive to flag in states that do not uphold the regulations. Since the trading club created is around fishing regulations, it is the state rather than the individual vessel that is held to the standard. It is thus even more difficult for an individual vessel to gain admission to the club if it is flagged in an open registry.

Exclusion of fish from a market also requires a willingness to undertake fairly intrusive action, since it would not be apparent from the shipment of fish itself whether it had been caught in compliance with fishery regulations.[110] The states that are willing to require of others that they document their adherence to fishery agreements in order to be able to export fish do so frequently because their domestic fishers compete internationally with FOC fishers, and would gain directly from raised stan-

107. ICCAT Resolution 03-15, "Resolution by ICCAT Concerning Trade Measures."

108. IOTC, "Recommendation 03-05 Concerning Trade Measures," 2003.

109. WTO, *The Environmental Benefits of Removing Trade Restrictions and Distortions: The Fisheries Sector*, Note by the Secretariat. (Geneva: WTO, October 16, 2000); WT/CTE/W/167.

110. It is precisely for this reason that these types of sanctions have frequently been found to be in violation of international trade law.

dards.[111] More recently, in part due to rulings by international trade bodies, sanctions have been more carefully targeted to allow individual vessels that can prove they meet standards to export fish to the states that otherwise would exclude fishery imports from a given state.

Several important observations should be made about the efforts to hold flag states to international fishing standards. The first is that the states targeted by the measures examined here that improved their behavior and signed international fishery agreements are most frequently those that were working to improve their registries more generally. Belize and St. Vincent and the Grenadines worked to improve the records of their fishing vessels at the same time they were attempting to avoid being singled out for scrutiny under the port state control inspection regime. They also removed a large number of vessels from their registry during this time period. Panama, while not aiming for the highest standards, is generally concerned with at least maintaining a reasonable reputation. Honduras provides a more interesting case, since it has been more responsive to incentives from fish-trade restrictions than port state control, being willing to change its behavior sufficiently to avoid being excluded from major fish markets. Whether this behavior indicates that economic sanctions are more powerful than the threat of added inspections in port, or simply that fishing is not that important to the Honduran registry, is unclear.

Second, a number of these states—Belize as the most extreme example—manage to increase fishing standards by removing fishing vessels from their registries. (Panama, Malta, Mauritius, and Honduras also removed fishing vessels from their registries.)[112] Since it is highly unlikely that these fishing vessels simply cease fishing, they almost certainly find somewhere else to reregister, and continue depleting world fisheries under a different flag. The list of states targeted under ICCAT provides an excellent example of this process. The most recently targeted flags are the low-standard newcomers to ship registration: Cambodia, Equatorial Guinea, Bolivia, and Sierra Leone. There is even evidence that if

111. Elizabeth R. DeSombre, "Baptists and Bootleggers for the Environment: The Origins of United States Unilateral Sanctions," *Journal of Environment and Development* 4 (winter 1995): 53–75.

112. International Transport Workers Federation, *Steering the Right Course* (London: ITF, June 2003).

these ships cannot find suitable flags they will avoid registration altogether. This strategy is most likely followed by those operating the furthest outside the bounds of law; not only are ships required by international law to be registered, but "stateless vessels" have few rights. Fishing vessels flying an "unknown flag" increased from 14 in 1994 to 1,602 in 2003.[113]

Nevertheless, the innovation in these fishery conservation measures is that they involve the markets for fish. There is a limit to the number of vessels that could continue to fish profitably when the major markets for fish products are closed to them. So the number of fishing vessels that can fish outside these regimes is increasingly small.

Finally, it is interesting to observe that these economic measures do not target open registries as open registries. All nonmember states fishing outside the regulatory structure (and, to a lesser extent, member states that are not fully implementing the convention requirements) are affected by the CCAMLR system and the related ones on tuna. At a minimum this suggests that the open registry system, while certainly problematic for fishery conservation, does not need to be ended to make progress on the issue.

113. ICFTU et al., 18; Lloyd's Register Fairplay 2003, 52.

8

Industry Self-Governance

In addition to the mechanisms of exclusion already discussed in this book, there are a number of examples of collective action by shipping-industry actors that create clubs with the effect of raising shipping standards. Ship owners hire classification societies to class their ships, and subscribe to Protection and Indemnity insurance clubs to insure against liability. Both of these are technically voluntary on the part of shipowners, but ships that are not classed or do not have insurance are excluded from a wide range of access within the regulatory processes described generally in this book. Both classification and insurance groups have followed clublike approaches to increasing the standards—and thus access—of those within the group, by discriminating in membership. Those that own, operate, or hire the services of ships have also begun to use existing industry organizations. In addition industry organizations abound in the shipping issue area; many of these have begun to undertake clublike self-regulation to better face some of the incentives examined in the preceding chapters.

This type of "industry self-governance," as Franco Furger terms it in the context of the maritime industry,[1] follows processes similar to those undertaken by states, nongovernmental organizations, and international organizations, as described in previous chapters. Those processes all impact shipowners (or operators or charterers)—whose decisions about what regulations to take on are the ultimate determination of ship standards. But in responding to port state control inspections, labor union action, or fishery organization–mandated trade restrictions, shipowners

1. Franco Furger, "Accountability and Systems of Self-Governance: The Case of the Maritime Industry," *Law and Policy*, 19/4 (October 1997): 445–476.

make decisions in order to gain access to clubs created by others. Here the clubs they face are their own.

The first important example of this industry self-governance can be found in the action by Liberian-registered tanker owners in the early 1980s, discussed in chapter 5. Tanker owners, afraid that oil spills by Liberian-registered tankers would undermine support for the FOC system, encouraged the Liberian state to adopt international standards and the Liberian registry to create an inspection system to ensure that the ships in the registry maintained high environmental and safety standards. They were instrumental in increasing the standards to which they were held, and ensuring that they upheld them. As a result, the "club" of Liberian-registered tankers grew smaller but more reputable. In this instance, done in the context of the nascent port state control process, it was the registry and the flag state that undertook the action, after pressure from tanker owners. More recently it has been organizations of shipowners or other industry groups that have created their own systems of inspections to limit the possibility that group members would be singled out, and to increase the influence of the group as a whole.

Classification

Classification societies inspect ships and classify them based on design factors, the type of equipment they have, and the condition they are in. Numerous classification societies exist, so if one society will not class a vessel, another might. Classification societies arose during the seventeenth and eighteenth centuries to provide technical advice to shipowners and to the insurance industry, both of which wanted to make sure that a given ship was seaworthy. The initial classification societies—Lloyd's Register, Bureau Veritas, American Bureau of Shipping (ABS), and Det Norsk Veritas (DNV)—created a set of design standards and then monitored ships to determine whether these standards were followed. Initially, classification societies were employed by insurance agents. The system evolved toward the end of the nineteenth century into one in which the societies were instead hired by shipowners, who would class a ship for a given period of time.[2] That system is more or less in effect today.

2. Philippe Boisson, "Classification Societies and Safety at Sea," *Marine Policy* 18/5 (1994): 363–377.

While originally classification societies used a rating system to indicate the quality of the ship construction and equipment, the current system is binary: ships are either in class or out of class.[3] Classification covers the physical characteristics of the ship, and not anything about how it is crewed or operated. The characteristics on which a ship is inspected come from two main sources: international agreements generally overseen by the International Maritime Organization (such as SOLAS, MARPOL, and the International Load Lines Convention), and rules created by the classification society or mandated by the international organization of classification societies to which it belongs.[4] This latter category means that different societies have different standards they require or look for in a ship,[5] and allows for the possibility of "class hopping" to find a society that will class a ship that might otherwise not be accepted. To take a prominent example mentioned earlier, the *Erika*, a Maltese-registered oil tanker that gained infamy by causing an enormous oil spill as it sank off the coast of France in 1999, had failed port state control inspections shortly before its accident. Bureau Veritas, its classification society, demanded that a full inspection be carried out, but instead of submitting to the inspection, the ship changed classification society to the Registro Italiano Navala, which classed it without a complete inspection.[6]

The ten most reputable classification societies (of a world total of more than fifty) have formed the International Association of Classification Societies (IACS), which collectively classes up to 92 percent of the ocean-going vessels as measured by tonnage (though only half as measured by number).[7] While individual IACS members are free to set higher standards, the IACS sets uniform minimum standards that all member

3. IACS, "What Are Classification Societies?", at http://www.iacs.org.uk/.

4. These rules have evolved over time and come at least in part from knowledge about how materials and structures in ships function over time. Interview with Alan G. Gavin, Marine Director, Lloyd's Register, London, June 2003.

5. Hannu Honka, "The Classification System and Its Problems with Special Reference to the Liability of Classification Societies," *The Maritime Lawyer* (winter 1994).

6. Nathan Lillie, *A Global Union for Global Workers: The International Transport Worker's Federation and the Representation of Seafarers on Flag of Convenience Shipping*, doctoral dissertation, Cornell University, 2003, 53.

7. John Braithwaite and Peter Drahos, *Global Business Regulation* (Cambridge: Cambridge University Press, 2000), 422.

societies must accept. Another organization of classification societies, the International Federation of Classification Societies (IFCS), is composed of an additional set of societies,[8] though they are much less well known and less favorably regarded.

Initially, classification societies were largely nationally based; a British ship would be classed by Lloyd's Register, a Norwegian one by Det Norsk Veritas, and so on. This process began to change in the mid-twentieth century, and now shipowners are generally free to hire whichever classification societies they want. Registries do lay out which classification societies they will accept to class their vessels, however.[9]

The role of classification societies ideally begins even before a ship is constructed; the person contracting to have a ship built chooses a classification society, which mandates the standards to which the ship must be built and oversees all aspects of the construction, ultimately classing it before it gets put to sea. Once the ship has entered service, the classification society inspects it at a variety of intervals to make sure that it still qualifies as meeting the requirements to be considered in class.[10]

Ships that meet international standards can get classed; classification—by certain classification societies—may represent the difference between being able to register in a given registry and being excluded. It may influence the type or cost of insurance a ship will be able to obtain.[11] Moreover, port states may refuse entry to ships that are not classed, so the ability of classification societies to determine whether ships have the proper equipment in working order can provide an important incentive to shipowners to use such societies, regardless of the standards required by their flag states. It is certainly possible for a ship not to be classed, but that would severely restrict its options. Such a ship would almost inevitably be substandard.

8. IFCS, "IFCS Member Societies," http://www.classification-society.org/memsocs.html.

9. Richard M. F. Coles, *Ship Registration* (London: LLP, 2002).

10. Alan G. Gavin (Marine Director, Lloyd's Register; Chair, IACS), speech before the 12th International Command Seminar, May 21–22, 2003.

11. International Registries, at the time the registry for both Liberia and the Marshall Islands, undertook an ultimately unsccessful public campaign to persuade insurance underwriters to only insure IACS-classed vessels, or to grant a rate reduction for them. See Andrew Guest, "Liberia Calls for IACS Backing," *Lloyd's List*, July 6, 1992, 1.

Classification societies play an essential role in enforcing equipment standards through refusing to classify vessels that do not meet international standards. For some environmental or safety problems, then, mandating the use of certain types of equipment (through international agreement) may make it more difficult for ships to avoid international regulations, because classification societies can ensure that they are held to the requirements. The two cases in which this solution has shown the most promise relate to oil pollution and safety standards. Intentional oil pollution has been tackled through several types of equipment standards. For oil tankers, the International Convention for the Prevention of Pollution from Ships (MARPOL) in 1973 required the use of segregated ballast tanks (SBTs) on all large new tankers, and a 1978 revision included additional equipment requirements for existing tankers.[12] For ships not engaged in transporting oil, equipment standards have also been used. Devices are required to catch the oil used in passenger and shipping vessels so that it will not be dumped overboard. More recently the use of double hulls on tankers, to decrease the risk of accidental oil spills, has been required for new ships and phased in for existing ones.

Equipment standards have also been mandated for safety issues.[13] In addition to general structural integrity, ships are required to have dividing walls between bulkheads, to prevent flooding of the entire ship when water enters the ship. One of the main advantages of equipment regulations of the type discussed here is that they can make it nearly impossible not to comply with the standards they are designed to implement.[14] These standards are monitored almost entirely by classification societies.

Classification societies have developed reputations about how stringent they are. Generally IACS members are considered particularly reputable (and the IACS audits its members to ensure reliability), though even within that group there is variation. For instance, the Tanker Advisory Center determined that in the 1980s Bureau Veritas had double the loss

12. Mitchell, 172.

13. Some of the regulations discussed under safety mandate equipment—like lifeboats or fire-suppression equipment. But that is a different type of equipment standard than the ones discussed here that are designed to make noncompliance difficult.

14. See, generally, Mitchell.

record of other IACS members.[15] IACS has maintained its prominent reputation by excluding member societies whose records are not sufficiently good. Most recently the Polish classification society Polski Rejestr Statkow was expelled from IACS associate membership in 2000 after a ship it classed sank. The IACS argued that the society showed "serious shortcomings" in its work with the ship in question, which warranted explusion.[16]

Recently port state control inspections have calculated not only the number of detained ships per flag state, but also per classification society. Examining these numbers suggests that even the most reputable classification societies have quite varied records for classing ships that will be able to avoid detention. For instance, in 2001 Paris MOU inspections, ships classed by Bureau Veritas were detained thirty-two times, compared to those classed by Det Norsk Veritas, which were detained twenty times.[17] And some classification societies, especially non-IACS members, have developed a reputation for classification that is both cheap and permissive.[18]

Classification societies thus are in competition with each other (in much the same way flag states are), based on reputation and cost. Classification societies vying for high status will therefore take on stricter requirements and be willing to refuse to class questionable ships (as DNV and ABS reportedly did in 1992 when they refused to class more than 600 ships).[19] In addition, they may even choose to refuse to class ships in registries considered disreputable; Lloyd's Register in 2003 sent letters informing the registries of Cambodia and Mongolia that they would not class ships registered in these states.[20] Det Norsk Veritas also

15. Cited in Braithwaite and Drahos, 422.

16. "PRS Must Shake Off Taint Left by IACS Explusion," *Lloyd's List*, January 7, 2005, 12.

17. Paris MOU, *Annual Report 2001* (Paris: MOU, 2002), Annex 4, 33. It is important to note that these initial statistics do not indicate the percentage of inspected ships that were detained, and thus it is possible that more BV ships than DNV ships were inspected. Nevertheless, the classification-society chart indicates large variation by classification society.

18. Braithwaite and Drahos, 422.

19. Braithwaite and Drahos, 422.

20. Christopher Mayer, "LR Warns Registers to Seek IACS Role," *Lloyd's List*, March 17, 2003, 1.

gave notice that it would cease classifying ships registered in Cambodia, and other IACS member societies appear to be considering that option as well.[21] These societies will be chosen by the most responsible shipowners, mandated by the most stringent flag states, and required by the best insurance companies.

Some have pointed to the conflict of interest inherent in the current classification system, which helps maintain the less reputable end of the spectrum. Because shipowners hire and pay the classification societies, those societies that then demand costly repairs or upgrades may be less favored by shipowners, whose profits will be lowered if they must undertake expensive work on their ships before they can be classed.[22] Those competing for the lower end of the market will impose only the barest obligations. The European Union referred to these as "classification societies of convenience."[23] Recently there have been some proposals in the EU to separate out the public- and private-sector roles of classification societies, and reform the way they are paid, to try to address these perverse incentives,[24] though such a policy would surely face strong opposition.

The competition can be problematic on the other end of the quality spectrum as well. Classification societies that raise their standards unilaterally are likely to lose business if there are other high-quality societies still accepted by those who discriminate based on class. When the American Bureau of Shipping introduced stricter survey requirements for tankers and bulk carriers before the other IACS members mandated such rules, twenty owners of single tankers, registered in fifteen different flag states, left that classification society. As ABS Europe vice president Robert Vienneau concluded, "the owners have gone shopping," attributing their departure to "the dangers of starting first."[25] Recently the

21. "Class Societies Get Tough on Flag States as IACS Pair Drop Cambodia," *Lloyd's List*, September 30, 2002, 1.

22. Boisson, 373; Honka.

23. Sean Moloney, "Societies Force Ship Fault Move," *Lloyd's List*, February 7, 1997, 3.

24. Justin Stares, "Brussels in Regulatory Clampdown on Classification Industry," *Lloyd's List*, February 22, 2005, 1.

25. Marion Welham, "Tanker Owners Quit ABS After Rules Tighten," *Lloyd's List*, June 3, 1993, 16.

IACS has created some common rules on building standards to avoid competition among the high-end registries,[26] though the process was contentious.

The system for assessing liability against classification societies when problems occur with ships they have classed has been uneven. Though previously the few cases that were brought against classification societies had been dismissed or decided in the societies' favor,[27] recent high-profile oil spills (including by the *Erika* and the *Prestige*) have resulted in lawsuits against their classification societies.[28]

There are also some indications of increasing transparency for the responsibility of classification societies in ship quality. Responding to a request by IACS, the Paris MOU moved in 1997 to explicitly state in its annual reports whether or not a ship's classification society should be considered responsible for any given vessel deficiency.[29] In 2004 the Paris MOU took this designation even further, creating a performance ranking of classification societies generally, examining class-related detentions per classification society compared to the number of inspections in the previous 3 years. All IACS member appeared on the high end of the ranking scheme, though two IACS societies were ranked in the "medium-performance" section. The highest-ranked society was Germanischer Lloyd, and the lowest was Albania's Register of Shipping.[30]

In addition to the clublike nature of classification societies generally, the club of high-quality classification societies hopes to increase the advantage of belonging to their club, by disadvantaging lower-quality societies. Because some states and some industry organizations (discussed below) require that ships be classed by IACS member societies, membership in the organization is valuable to a classification society. Moreover, with increased transparency about the PSC records of classification societies, flag states may choose which classification societies their ships may use, based on quality. All these factors likely lead to a push upward for

26. Julian Bray, "IACS Clinches 'Peace in Our Time,'" *Lloyd's List*, June 14, 2005, 1.

27. Honka.

28. Justin Stares, "IACS Alarmed over Barrot Threat," *Lloyd's List*, February 7, 2005, 1.

29. Moloney, "Societies Force Ship Fault Move," 3.

30. Brian Reyes, "IACS Members Rate Well in Paris MOU List," *Lloyd's List*, July 9, 2004.

shipping standards in the context of the other incentives discussed in this book.

Insurance

Most ships choose to have insurance; in some instances it is required before ships can travel through certain waters. Traditional insurance generally covers the ships themselves, but most of the world's ships have additional liability insurance, insuring against liabilities that arise from catastrophic damage, death or injury to crew or passengers, pollution or other environmental damage, loss of cargo, and collision. What is notable about this type of insurance is that for most of the shipping industry it is provided by Protection and Indemnity (P&I) clubs that operate by attempting to limit membership to ships deemed least risky.[31]

In this type of insurance, the group insures itself.[32] In other words, shipowners put money into a collective fund from which each draws in case of an accident. Because it is the group that is responsible, shipowners only know in advance what proportion of the overall year's costs they will have to pay; the actual amount depends on the extent to which shipowners collect from the fund during the year. For that reason, shipowners within a P&I club have an incentive to admit only those to the club who do not pose a particularly high risk of accident or other liability. To do this, most club managers interview representatives of the shipowner, find out the credit rating of the owner, and gather information from current club members. Most also hire inspectors to inspect ships that are more than ten years old,[33] and refuse to insure passenger ships, oil tankers, and bulk carriers that are not certified as complying with the International Maritime Organization's International Safety Management (ISM) code.[34] The head office for the club also keeps records of accidents and their costs.

31. See, generally, Paul Bennett, "Mutual Risk: P&I Insurance Clubs and Maritime Safety and Environmental Performance," *Marine Policy* 25 (2001): 13–21.

32. It should be noted, however, that legally P&I clubs are now actually corporations.

33. Regular inspections are done in most cases of members' ships on some kind of schedule as well.

34. Paul Bennett, "Mutuality at a Distance: Risk and Regulation in Marine Insurance Clubs," *Environment and Planning A* 32(2000): 155.

The managers of a given P&I club have the authority and the ability to inspect the ships covered by the club, and they do with a degree of regularity that depends on the size of the club. Some, like the London Club (the P&I coverage for the *Prestige*) inspect as frequently as once a year; others do so more like every two or three years or after the ship reaches a certain age.[35]

Many of the P&I clubs work together in an organization called the International Group of P&I Clubs. This club of clubs has several functions, one of which is to serve as a clearinghouse for information. If a shipowner from one P&I club in the International Group applies to join a different club, the club it previously belonged to is obligated to tell the new club what the rates and performance of the ship were. Since nearly 90 percent of new members in a club come from another club within the International Group, this policy can make it difficult to hide bad performance records by moving to a new club. In addition, as Paul Bennett has pointed out, social networks among managers of clubs within this group lead to the additional exchange of opinions about the riskiness of ships or owners.[36] P&I groups seek to become members of the International Group (the China Shipowners' Mutual Assurance Association is the latest seeking membership) because of the reputational advantages that will allow them to seek high-quality ships for their group, especially as industry groups (discussed further below) have begun to require that members maintain P&I coverage with a member of the International Group.

In addition to deciding whether shipowners may enter the club at all, the club managers also currently decide what share of the overall group costs that shipowners will pay. To do that, they attempt to estimate the risk posed by a given ship, generally by examining eight to ten years of the ship's history. The sector in which the ship is operating (bulk transport or oil shipping, for instance) also influences the costliness of the premium, since some sectors—like passenger shipping—are more prone to liability claims. Because payments required by a P&I club are frequently assessed to the shipping company (the firm that actually owns the ships) on its collection of ships rather than determined by individual ship, ship-

35. Interview with Nigel Hartley, A. Bilbrough and Co., Managers for the London Club, London, June 2003.

36. Bennett, "Mutuality at a Distance," 155.

ping companies have the same incentive flag states do to improve their records in the hope of lowering their fees.[37]

Historically these clubs did not differentiate on costs; all shipowners who were accepted paid the same amount per ton to belong to the group. But, as an indication that these are imperfect clubs in the game-theoretic sense of the term, they had problems with the costs from lower-quality ship operators creating too much of a drain on the resources of the better-quality operators. In addition, with the rise in open registries and larger variation in types of ships, there were other reasons to differentiate in premiums, since ships became less comparable based only on tonnage.[38] Some clubs, additionally, have examined overall records to determine which types of ships generate the greatest costs. Their conclusion was that the riskiest ships are those between ten and fourteen years of age, bulk carriers or tankers, and ships that are registered in Panama or Cyprus.[39] Some clubs have targeted inspections to particularly high-risk ships because of this analysis, which may decrease risks. Despite this information, however, little seems to have been done by these clubs to discriminate in membership or rates based on these statistics.

Another imperfection in the clublike nature of P&I clubs is that it appears that clubs infrequently terminate membership of those who have been found to represent particularly high liability. They can do so with as little as two weeks' notice, and sometimes they will.[40] But because most shipowners know that they, too, could have a run of bad luck and run up large insurance liability, they are inclined not to push to remove other such ships from their club's roster.

P&I clubs will nevertheless terminate coverage for those who have been found to be substandard, including (for instance) not complying with classification-society requirements. Clubs also have the power to end coverage retroactively.[41] And the unwillingness to remove members may be changing. In 2005 the UK P&I club required that ships renewing

37. Nigel Hartley interview, June 2003.

38. Christopher Hill, Bill Robertson, and Steven J. Hazelwood, *An Introduction to P&I* (London: Lloyd's of London Press, 1988), 31–35.

39. Bennett, "Mutuality at a Distance," 159.

40. Nigel Hartley interview, June 2003.

41. A. D. Couper, *Voyages of Abuse: Seafarers, Human Rights, and International Shipping* (London: Pluto Press, 1999), 161.

policies that year provide International Ship Security Certificates or not be allowed to reenroll.[42] Others involved with the industry have argued that the clubs need to refuse to cover ships that "just scrape over the safety standards bar."[43] On the other side of the equation, shipowners may choose their P&I club based on its record, with the increase in insurance rates recently varying dramatically across clubs depending on the previous records of ships they insure.[44]

Nevertheless, it has been estimated that as many as 5 percent of ships engaged in international shipping have no P&I insurance.[45] The inability of ships to obtain P&I coverage is both a strength and a weakness of the club system: that substandard ships are excluded means in part that the clubs are successful at identifying—both to themselves and to others involved in the shipping industry—which ships are too risky to insure. Or it has put insurance rates for such ships out of their reach, accurately reflecting their riskiness.[46] But the existence of a number of ships without liability insurance increases the chances that, in case of a major disaster, no one will contribute to the costs of recovery.

Shipping-Industry Clubs

Classification and insurance are considered industry-related activities because they are contracted for by shipowners. But other industry actors are even more directly involved in choosing the regulatory approach of a given ship: those who own ships or use them to transport goods. Both sets of actors have conflicting goals for the international regulatory structure. They would like to be able to keep shipping costs low, which suggests a preference for avoiding costly standards. But they also would like

42. "UK P&I Club Mandates Security Certification for Annual Policy Renewal," *Lloyd's List*, January 31, 2005, 19.

43. "We Must Take a Hardline on Substandard Vessels, Says Coughlin," *Lloyd's List*, January 31, 2005, 16.

44. James Brewer, "P&I Clubs Look High and Low on Renewals," *Lloyd's List*, October 20, 2005, 1.

45. Couper, 161. Some of these are likely big enough to self-insure in other ways, but that still leaves approximately 3 percent of ships uncovered with respect to liability.

46. Some ships may simply prefer to remain outside of the system at almost any price; these are almost certainly low-standard ships.

to ensure that they do not run afoul of the programs described elsewhere in this book that attempt to increase standards. They see the competitive aspects of regulation, too, and within a given regulatory system would like to increase the odds that the ships they use or own can avoid being excluded from access to ports or markets. For the most part, these organizations would like to be able to meet mandated standards and would like to see strict enforcement of standards at the level they can reasonably achieve but that their competitors may not be able to. A number of existing groups of shipowners or operators are beginning to use these organizations to increase the odds that members of these clubs will be able to successfully navigate the regulatory environment created by the reaction to the growth of flag-of-convenience shipping.

Producer Clubs

Producer groups provide many services for their members, but important among them are recently created inspection systems, to increase the odds that the ships they use will be able to safely deliver their cargo without sinking, creating environmental disasters, or being the subject of labor action. In particular, industrial organizations such as groups of oil companies and chemical companies have required that the ships they use undergo inspections in addition to those required by insurers, classification societies, flag states, or port state control.

Most of these programs began in the early- to mid-1990s. The Oil Companies International Marine Forum (OCIMF), "a voluntary association of oil companies having an interest in the shipment and terminalling of crude oil and oil products," formed in 1970 in the wake of the Torrey Canyon oil spill in response to increasing public concern about oil pollution. In 1993 the organization, currently comprising forty-seven companies, created a Ship Inspection Report Program (SIRE). This program mandates a uniform inspection process in which information is collected electronically and made available to member organizations (as well as governmental organization such as port-state inspectors and MOUs) so they can ascertain how well maintained and managed a given tanker is.[47]

47. OCIMF, "Oil Companies International Marine Forum," n.d. http://www.ocimf.com/index.cfm?pageid=10; OCIMF, "SIRE Introduction," n.d. http://www.ocimf.com/index.cfm?pageid=8.

Similar programs have been created by chemical organizations.[48] The Chemical Distribution Institute now has an audit process, revised in conjunction with the International Association of Classification Societies and other inspection processes created by chemical associations, and taking into consideration the most recent IMO rules.[49] This program does not give ships a passing or failing grade, but rather makes available to those considering using shipping services the information about what equipment and procedures the ship has in place. This information is loaded into a CDI database that can be accessed by member organizations. These types of inspection processes give those who use the services of ships the opportunity to choose ships that are likely to be in good condition and that are unlikely to be stopped by one of the other inspection processes like port state control.

Shipowner Clubs

Shipowners have similar organizations that maintain clublike aspects to increase the odds that their ships will successfully navigate the international maritime standards they face. The two most prominent organizations of this type are constituted by the type of ship owned. The International Association of Independent Tanker Owners (most frequently referred to as INTERTANKO) and the International Association of Dry Cargo Ship Owners (called INTERCARGO) provide a wide range of services to members, but have more recently begun to self-regulate in an attempt to ensure that their owners are recognized as posing a lower degree of risk than the ships belonging to nonmembers.

INTERTANKO began operations in 1970. Membership is open to independent operators and owners of oil and chemical tankers (company- or state-owned tankers are excluded from full membership, though they may be associate members). The organization works to increase the bargaining position internationally for its membership within international organizations and with respect to states, and provides legal services, training, and other services. For example, the organization holds regular "vetting seminars" to help members learn more about how to successfully navigate the port state control inspection process.

48. Boisson, 374.

49. Chemical Distribution Institute, "Ship Audit Report, Marine Pack Cargo, Ship Questionnaire," 1st ed., June 1, 2002, http://www.cdi.org.uk.

But members must meet the membership criteria of the organization, and these have become increasingly strict. The organization faced enormous pressure following the 1989 Exxon Valdez oil spill, and it began to work to improve the environmental reputation of its membership. Beginning in 1994, the organization required that new members be approved by classification societies that are members of IACS; this requirement was extended to existing members the following year.[50] It also began to require members to carry pollution insurance for at least $500 million per tanker via P&I clubs.[51] The organization then began to remove members that did not comply with these new requirements; the first of these was the twelve-tanker Adriatic Tankers Shipping Company, which refused to provide details of the classification or insurance status of its ships.[52] The organization mandated that members meet International Ship Management (ISM) Code requirements by 1998, regardless of what their flag states required, expelling those that did not meet the deadline.[53]

Current membership requirements call for members to have a certified ISM system, be classed by an IACS classification society, belong to a P&I club and have other insurance, and have a "satisfactory oil pollution response plan."[54] There are 235 members, who own a total of 2,230 tankers. Members comprise 70 percent of the independent tanker fleet worldwide,[55] down from more than 80 percent before the organization began to institute the safety and insurance requirements.

The dry-cargo shipowners' organization, INTERCARGO, has followed a similar trajectory. The organization formed in 1980 to address issues of concern to dry-cargo shipowners. Members receive technical

50. Janet Porter, "INTERTANKO to Discuss Stricter Guidelines," *Journal of Commerce* 5 (May 1994): 8B.

51. Alan Abrams, "Tanker Association Seeks to Require Pollution Insurance," *Journal of Commerce*, May 12, 1994, 7B.

52. Janet Porter, "INTERTANKO Expels Greek Tanker Owner," *Journal of Commerce*, May 24, 1995, 8B.

53. Allison Bate, "INTERNANKO: Most Tankers Will Meet Standards by Deadline," *Journal of Commerce*, February 23, 1998, 3B.

54. INTERTANKO, "Mission Statement," http://www.intertanko.com/about/mission/.

55. INTERTANKO, "General Information," http://www.intertanko.com/about/.

information, assistance from the organization in the case of commercial disputes and in assessing charterers or business partners, and advice on meeting PSC requirements, among other services.[56] INTERCARGO also works to represent the interests of its members in the International Maritime Organization and other international forums.

Following a similar timeline to INTERTANKO's increased standards for membership, INTERCARGO in 1995 indicated that membership should be seen as "a seal of quality operation."[57] New members were required to be classed by an IACS-member classification society as of 1994, a requirement later extended to existing members. The organization also required members to meet the ISM code as soon as it entered into force in July 1998.[58] The organization explored setting up its own inspection system,[59] but appears not to have done so.

Membership is currently open to the owners and operators of dry-bulk ships that are classed by IACS-member classification societies and that have P&I insurance from a member of the International Group. The membership guidelines specify that members must have "quality ships and operation" without specifying the determination of quality. The organization does reserve the right to expel members or turn down applicants by unilateral decision of the organization's Executive Committee if "the member's operation is adjudged to be of insufficient standing or quality."[60] There are currently 62 full members of the organization and 53 associate members; collectively they own and operate 750 dry-cargo ships,[61] approximately 12.5 percent of the world's bulk carriers. This number too represents a decrease from the era before tightened standards, when a membership of 185 owners collectively owned more than 1,250 bulk carriers, accounting for 30 percent of the industry.[62]

56. INTERCARGO, "Members Charter," http://www.intercargo.org/.

57. Janet Porter, "Bulker Group to Tighten Membership Conditions," *Journal of Commerce*, June 22, 1995, 13B.

58. Anthony Poole, "Intercargo Gives Pledge on ISM Code," *Lloyd's List*, November 19, 1997, 3.

59. Julian Bray, "Intercargo Poised to Set Up Safety Scheme," *Lloyd's List*, June 11, 1997, 1.

60. INTERCARGO, "Members Charter."

61. INTERCARGO, *2004–2005 Review*, http://www.intercargo.org/.

62. David Osler and Jennie Harris, "Intercargo Opts for Shake-Up to Lift Membership," *Lloyd's List*, March 30, 1998, 3.

All of the major industry (both producer- and owner-based) groups have additionally begun to work together to increase (or at least better designate) flag-state standards. The major organizations of shipowners created the "Shipping Industry Guidelines on Flag State Performance," at the end of 2003, which ranks flag states based on port state control records, use of recognized classification societies, and ratifications of international agreements. Eighteen factors are listed as possible "negative performance indicators," and flag states with twelve or more are singled out. Those behind the ranking system suggest that it would encourage shipowners to pressure the registry operators to improve their records,[63] and allow shipowners the opportunity to choose registries that meet their needs for level of regulation.

This process represents an interesting twist on the more state-centric processes such as port state control, in which port states attempt to influence the choices of shipowners about where to register, by singling out substandard flag states. In this shipping-industry Flag State Performance designation it is the shipowners and operators themselves that are working to pressure flag states to increase standards, by increasing the transparency of flag states' records with respect to the major mechanisms of exclusion.

That the industry-based actions described in this chapter are less well developed and less onerous than those discussed in the previous three should not be surprising: industry actors have mixed motives when it comes to increasing the standards on, and thus the cost of operating, their vessels. Nevertheless, the mechanisms depicted in this chapter follow the same process of using mechanisms of exclusion—from classification, insurance, and membership in reputable industry organizations—seen elsewhere. It is important that these efforts to raise standards within particular clubs of shipowners or operators happen in the broader context of actions by states, civil-society actors, and international organizations, because most of the industry-based efforts are targeted at avoiding exclusion from these other mechanisms.

63. Michael Grey, "Shipowners Launch Their Own Guide for Assessing Flag 'Respectability,'" *Lloyd's List*, November 25, 2003, 1; BIMCO, INTERCARGO, International Chamber of Shipping, International Shipping Federation, INTERTANKO, *Shipping Industry Guidelines on Flag State Performance* (London: Maritime International Secretariat Services, 2003). A 2004 updated table is also available at http://www.marisec.org/flag-performance.

The actions of the shipowners are perhaps the most telling. They are the actors who benefit most proximately from the open registry system and the opportunities it presents for lower operating costs, low fees, and tax avoidance. That they are working on collective arrangements to single out higher-quality registries suggests that the incentive to maintain the system but operate within it in a way that avoids being singled out negatively is strong.

9

Ships, States, and Sovereignty

One of the central theoretical concerns about globalization is the question of its implications for state sovereignty and the regulatory capacity of states. Saskia Sassen, for example, argues that changes in the global economy have "the capacity to undo the particular form of the intersection of sovereignty and territory embedded in the modern state and the modern state system."[1]

In particular, many offshoots of the globalized economy, often lumped together under the term *offshore*,[2] are seen as indications that states can no longer control economic activity or even regulate the actions of their citizens in a way they might previously have been able to. When currencies can be traded without oversight from central banks, Internet sites can provide services deemed illegal in states from which they can be accessed, and citizens can earn income out of reach of the taxation processes of their states, it appears that states have lost their regulatory capabilities and no longer have a powerful hand in the shape of the global economy. Sassen agrees, arguing that "offshoring creates a space economy that goes beyond the regulatory umbrella of the state."[3] That most of the world's ships are registered in states with scarcely the population to work them, with lower standards than the home states of the owners would require, suggests that flags of convenience indeed challenge some aspects of the sovereignty of the traditional maritime states.

1. Saskia Sassen, *Losing Control? Sovereignty in an Age of Globalization* (New York: Columbia University Press, 1996), 5.

2. See, for example, Ronen Palen, *The Offshore World: Sovereign Markets, Virtual Places, and Nomad Millionaires* (Ithaca: Cornell University Press, 2003).

3. Sassen, 8.

Indeed, many discussions of the relationship between globalization and sovereignty make precisely this point. Kenichi Ohmae argues that nation-states have become subject to economic choices made by "people and institutions over which they have no practical control."[4] Joseph Calmilleri and Jim Falk suggest that "global processes and institutions are invading the nation-state and as a consequence dismantling the conceptual and territorial boundaries" that have formed the basis for sovereignty.[5] In the specific context of shipping, William Langewiesche echoes many when he suggests that ocean governance "constitutes an exact reversal of sovereignty's intent and a perfect mockery of national conceits," and that the result of this evolution has been "to place the oceans increasingly beyond governmental control."[6]

Others argue, however, that while these offshore activities are indeed the result of globalization, their consequences for sovereignty or state regulatory oversight are less dire. Geoffrey Garrett suggests that "globalization and national autonomy are not mutually exclusive"—in other words, that states can benefit from globalization without undermining their sovereignty.[7] It is precisely the ability of governments to choose how to address the dislocations caused by a globalized economy that gains them a double advantage: they receive both the benefits of international markets and the political allegiance from mediating the difficulties globalization creates.

Stephen Krasner points out that state control over international economic activity has never been absolute, and that states may, in fact, be better positioned to address the issues of the current forms of globalization than was previously true. The social welfare policies of national governments shield many workers from the worst of the effects of international competition.[8] Importantly, he concludes that "there is

4. Kenichi Ohmae, *The End of the Nation State: The Rise of Regional Economies* (New York: Free Press, 1995), 12.

5. Joseph Camilleri and Jim Falk, *The End of Sovereignty?* (Cheltenham: Edward Elgar, 1992), 98.

6. William Langewiesche, *The Outlaw Sea: A World of Freedom, Chaos, and Crime* (New York: North Point Press, 2004), 6–7.

7. Geoffrey Garrett, *Partisan Politics in the Global Economy* (Cambridge: Cambridge University Press, 1998), 6.

8. Stephen Krasner, "Sovereignty," *Foreign Policy* 122 (January–February 2002): 20–29.

no evidence that globalization has systematically undermined state control."[9]

The most nuanced form of this argument is that offshoring is in some ways the process that allows for globalization to happen within the existing state system, mediating between the twin state goals of territorial nationalism and globalization. As Ronen Palen puts it, "offshore provides the perfect legitimization of the goals of neoliberalism,"[10] while preserving the sovereign state system by providing an outlet where all the activities that cannot otherwise be subsumed under a state system in a globalized world can operate. Thus, "far from being an opportunistic development at the margins of the world economy, the rise of offshore is an inherent tendency of an internationalizing economy operating within a particularistic political system."[11] John Gerard Ruggie points out that territorial states have always needed to deal with the aspects of life that did not fit neatly into territories, whether because of transboundary waterways or the concept of diplomatic immunity. He argues that states addressed this through the idea of "unbundling" territoriality, suggesting that long before the current era the functions of states took place in "nonterritorial functional space."[12] This unbundling of territory from the functions of states is, in fact, precisely the way that states have chosen to "compensate for the 'social defects' that inhere in the modern construct of territoriality."[13] In neither of these explanations is the offshore economy unimportant, but it supports rather than undermines the role of the state in the evolving global economic system.

Leaving aside the broader discussions of the extent to which sovereignty more generally has changed over time,[14] an investigation into the evolution of standards in the global shipping industry can contribute

9. Stephen Krasner, *Sovereignty: Organized Hypocrisy* (Princeton: Princeton University Press, 1999), 223.

10. Palen, *The Offshore World*, 15.

11. Palen, *The Offshore World*, 9.

12. John Gerard Ruggie, "Territoriality and Beyond: Problematizing Modernity in International Relations," *International Organization* 47/1 (winter 1993): 165.

13. Ruggie, 171.

14. See, for example, J. Samuel Barkin, "The Evolution of the Constitution of Sovereignty and the Emergence of Human Rights Norms," *Millennium* 27 (summer 1998): 229–252.

to a broader understanding of the role of the state in the process of responding to the potentially contrasting economic and social demands of globalization. Because of the central role of ships in globalized trade, the standards adopted by ships, and the role of states in the process of determining these standards, should be able to illuminate the relationship between sovereignty and globalization.

Scholars of shipping acknowledged this relationship early on in the use of open registries. For example, Rodney Carlisle noted that the rise of the Panamanian flag in the 1920s and 1930s was one of the ways around "the conflict between national interest and social justice" that plagued American shipping.[15] Carlisle, however, does not see the design of open registries as an intentional effort to reconcile these competing elements in the light of globalization, though he argues it eventually did so. Rather, he suggests that U.S. shipowners simply considered short-range concerns: "how to compete and make a profit in the glutted world market when 'hampered' by reforms."[16]

In attempting to examine the impacts on sovereignty from globalization in the shipping industry, there are several elements to consider. First, and most centrally, to what extent do traditional maritime states (the advanced industrialized states that used to dominate the shipping industry) have the ability to control and profit from the maritime activities undertaken by their nationals? Do they want a more regulated international maritime regime? Are they pushing for higher standards and greater oversight? Evidence suggests that, contrary to the public statements by officials in these states, there are broader economic and political advantages to the current system for the traditional maritime states, and that they acquiesce in the overall international registry system, even as they may try to tinker at the margins of the system to improve their advantages from it.

Second, what is the impact of the open registry system on those states that choose to offer their flags for sale internationally? Certainly states that enter the market for ship registration exercise their sovereignty in making the decision to do so, but what are the implications for these

15. Rodney P. Carlisle, *Sovereignty for Sale: The Origins and Evolution of the Panamanian and Liberian Flags of Convenience* (Annapolis: Naval Institute Press, 1981), 35.

16. Carlisle, 37.

states? Do they, as many may hope, increase their domestic control and international influence through the act of selling the rights to fly their flag? In some cases, both of these results are possible. But in others, states—whose flags are attractive often precisely because of the lack of control they have over ships flying them—may run afoul of the interests of the traditionally powerful maritime states in ways that demonstrate or augment their lack of full sovereignty.

Traditional Maritime States and the Open Registry System

The relationship between open registries and traditional maritime states is complex. While powerful maritime states decry the existence of open registries and fight the lowered standards that allow FOC-registered vessels "unfair" advantages in competition with ships in traditional registries, the willingness of these states to use political pressure to end such registries has been limited. The broader argument can be made that the existence of flags of convenience is not a phenomenon distinct from or as a result of national regulation, but one that evolved jointly with, and to allow for, the simultaneous growth of industrial capitalism and national sovereignty.

It could easily be argued that the most powerful states in the international system could prevent most FOC registration, or could determine the extent to which that registration influences international standards, if they wanted to. Daniel Drezner argues that it is states, at least the most powerful ones, that are the central actors in deciding the level of standards that exist under globalization.[17] That most open registries are not only in developing countries but arguably in marginal or even failed states supports the contention that if the most powerful states in the international system wanted to end the phenomenon of open ship registration they would have the ability to change the behavior of the major flag-of-convenience states.

It can thus be inferred from the at least passive complicity of the major maritime states in the current structure that, despite protestations to the contrary, they benefit in some way from the FOC system and have no real interest in fundamentally altering it. To the extent that they benefit

17. Daniel W. Drezner, *All Politics is Global: Explaining International Regulatory Regimes* (Princeton: Princeton University Press, 2007).

from the cheaper trade made possible by flags of convenience, while being able to keep their domestic standards high, there is little incentive to change the broader structure within which open registries exist. In fact, though states like Spain that are the victims of major oil spills cry foul whenever they happen (and generally new safety and environmental regulations are passed in the wake of these events), these states nevertheless benefit from participation in the broader economic globalization made possible by such a system. Moreover, since states (or individual communities or economic entities within them) do not know in advance that they will be the ones to suffer from a major shipping-related disaster, there is generally not a mobilized segment of society strongly in favor of fundamentally reforming the way shipping standards are upheld.

The major industrialized states, to the extent that they benefit from global trade, benefit from the entire system of flags of convenience and the cheap shipping this system makes possible. Within these states, there are two groups that benefit from cheap goods via ocean transport. Industry actors gain from access to cheaper inputs. The general population of consumers prefers less expensive goods.[18] Neither group would choose to pay more for goods in exchange for the remote chance that doing so could someday decrease their likelihood of having to endure a major oil spill or other maritime disaster. In other words, it should be no political surprise that states have been unwilling to change the fundamental system of shipping regulation, preferring instead to improve standards at the margin.

This explanation would expect high standards only in the case where major maritime powers gain from harmonization upward, and not otherwise. There is some evidence to support this contention. The major fishing states, who lose the most from fishing done by open registry ships that refuse to abide by conservation agreements, have recently been willing to undertake fairly radical measures to either persuade flag states or individual ships to follow the international rules. Doing so has been more costly for the high-standard states: they have agreed to intrusive and expensive monitoring of their own ships, and to high-transaction-cost trading systems that increase the price of seafood. But they have deemed it sufficiently important to undertake these actions, and fisheries,

18. David Vogel and Robert A. Kagan, eds., *Dynamics of Regulatory Change* (Berkeley: University of California Press, 2004), 20–21.

arguably the most difficult ocean issue to regulate, have become better protected from the open registry system.

We also see movement upward of standards, and renewed efforts to ensure that they apply to open registry states, in the wake of major environmental disasters from shipping that impact the powerful developed states. The *Prestige* disaster with which this book began resulted in an immediate call for changes in ship standards. Though these have been watered down, activity following this disaster has led to a faster phase-out of single-hulled tankers than would have previously been the case. European Union regulation 1726, which took effect in October 2003, prohibited the transport of heavy fuel oil on single-hulled tankers entering or leaving EU ports, and accelerated the IMO schedule on the phase-out of single-hulled tankers for those entering EU waters, as well as setting up an inspection process for tankers older than fifteen years.[19] Similar results followed the crash of the Maltese-flagged *Erika* off the coast of France in December 1999. In both cases, immediately following the disasters states in the European Union called for banning flag-of-convenience ships from EU ports, but this idea was never seriously debated in the political process. Almost all of the IMO rules that guard against oil spills or increase the safety of ships have passed in the wake of major shipping disasters that affected powerful states.

In addition, states themselves are responsible for some of the actions taken to create mechanisms of exclusion and thus increase regulatory standards for shipping, suggesting that they do participate in changing the system (albeit through the exclusionary mechanisms identified here) when it is to their advantage to do so. That they are not always willing to stop ships in port or use trade restrictions suggests that they are selective about which standards they want to take the trouble to increase globally. That they *are* willing to do these things sometimes suggests that they can do so when they choose.

The types of mechanisms used in successfully raising open registry standards also give some indication of when it will be that states choose to push for higher levels of regulation. In all of the mechanisms described

19. European Union, "Regulation (EC) No 1726/2003 of the European Parliament and of the Council Amending Regulation (EC) No 417/2002 on the accelerated phasing-in of double-hull or equivalent design requirements for single-hull oil tankers," July 22, 2003, L 249/1.

in this book, the creation of a process of exclusion came at the behest of those actors that compete with low-standard shipping and fear that their higher standards put them at a disadvantage. Regional fishery management organizations take up trade restrictions on fish caught outside the regulatory process because fishers flagged in states that follow the rules suffer in international trade when competing with those who do not. These fishers put pressure on their states to do something, and initially the United States and Japan, which have the dual role of being major fishing states and major importers of fish, began to implement unilateral trade restrictions. But additionally problematic is that the conservationist behavior does not have a positive effect on the fishery if it is undermined by those who do not participate; fishers who work within the regulatory system thereby harm themselves competitively in the short run and fail to protect the fishery in the long run. Aware of this incentive structure, the states in which these cooperating fishers are flagged push the fishery organizations to create multilateral trade restrictions.

It would be difficult to demonstrate empirically that the reason we have not seen a fundamental change in the open registry system and the lowered standards that result is that the industrialized or major maritime states do not want such a change, though circumstantial evidence exists to support this contention. It is true that most of the most powerful states rely heavily on ships to transport goods to and from their shores.[20] It is also the case that shipping is by far the least expensive mode of transportation.[21] And it has been conclusively and repeatedly shown that the ships flagged in open registries have significantly lower operating costs than those flagged in traditional maritime states; this cost differential increases when the open registry states have not adopted the major international environment, safety, and labor standards.[22] So it is clear

20. John Braithwaite and Peter Drahos, *Global Business Regulation* (Cambridge: Cambridge University Press, 2000), 418–437.

21. J. Samuel Barkin, "The Counterintuitive Relationship between Globalization and Climate Change," *Global Environmental Politics* 3/3 (August 2003): 10.

22. OECD, *Competitive Advantages Obtained by Some Shipowners as a Result of Non-Observance of Applicable International Rules and Standards*, OECD/GD(96)(4) (Paris: OECD, 1996); OECD, *Cost Savings Stemming from Non-Compliance with International Environmental Regulations in the Maritime Sector*, DSTI/DOT/MTC(2002)8/FINAL (Paris: OECD, 2002); SSY Consultancy & Research Limited, *The Cost to Users of Substandard Shipping*, report prepared for the OECD (OECD: Paris, 2001).

that the most powerful states internationally benefit from having access to the cheap shipping made possible by this system.

At the same time, the traditional maritime states do not suffer particularly from the negative impacts of the cost-saving elements present in the system. One can argue that overall environmental standards on the oceans are lower under an open registry system than they would be otherwise. And it is even the case that those states that import the greatest quantities of goods that can cause pollution in case of accidents (such as oil) are more likely than others to suffer from the pollution should there be an accident, since the likelihood that a spill will happen near their shores is somewhat greater. But for issues like the low wages that are made possible by the open registry system, the advanced industrialized states simply do not have many seafarers employed in the low-wage end of the industry, and thus are less likely to suffer comparatively from a system that keeps wages and benefits low. These states benefit in the aggregate much more from inexpensive shipping than they would from the expansion of slightly higher low-wage shipping jobs that might exist in a world with primarily national registries.

It is also useful to consider the alternatives that the most powerful states could choose instead of acquiescing to the open registry system. The British Navigation Acts passed during the height of British colonialism serve as a model of what the traditional maritime states could implement if they so chose. In a number of laws beginning in 1651 designed to increase British control over international trade, the British created a system in which goods transported to Britain from the colonies, and exports from Britain, could only be carried on British ships. Imports from European countries could only be carried on British ships or ships from the country of origin of the import. Non-British ships could also not carry any goods from the British colonies. These measures had the intended effect: they increased British dominance of the seas in an era when the Dutch had been expanding their shipping empire (and could ship goods much more cost-effectively than Britain).[23] These measure did provoke conflict, including the first war between the British and Dutch, and later resentment in the American colonies. But they showed that a powerful state could in fact control international trade on ships.

23. Peter J. Hugill, *World Trade Since 1431: Geography, Technology, and Capitalism* (Baltimore: Johns Hopkins University Press, 1993), 58.

On the other hand, a mercantilist strategy is to a large extent a zero-sum game. Such a strategy could only be successfully followed by at most several states at a given time, since any state that used it could not trade with any other state that was using it. Diluted versions (e.g., states will only import goods on vessels flying their flags) would still be incredibly inefficient economically. Any such large-scale effort to undermine global trade would have enormous economic impacts domestically, most of them negative. Most of the advanced industrialized states have clearly indicated that they value global trade over protecting the health of minor industries within their borders, and an overall economic calculus supports this decision.

Nevertheless, most of these traditional maritime states have some kind of limited cabotage rules, suggesting that they would prefer to tinker at the margins of the system to gain whatever advantages they can. Ships are not required to register in their home state, but if they do not they will not be eligible for certain types of activities. In the United States, the Jones Act dating from 1920 (modeled on earlier incarnations from 1789) requires that port-to-port traffic be carried only on U.S.-flagged ships.[24] This law generally prohibits ships registered outside the United States from stopping more than once in the United States on a given trip. While there are increasing numbers of exceptions, most cruise or cargo ships make only one stop in the United States before going elsewhere. This rule is responsible for some quirky side effects, such as the development of an enormous tourism industry on Fanning Island, in Kiribati, the closest island to Hawaii. Cruise ships flagged outside of the United States that want to make multiple stops in the Hawaiian Islands can only do so if they stop at a destination outside of the United States in between stops in U.S. territory; Fanning Island has served that purpose.[25]

European states have likewise had laws restricting domestic sea transport to nationally registered ships. European Union regulations, agreed to in 1992 and 1996, broadened existing national cabotage rules to include mutliple-port ship traffic from ships registered in any EU member

24. 46 U.S.C. 833; 19 C.FR 4.80 and 4.80b; Northrup and Scrase, 389, note 62; Carlisle, 5.

25. Arthur Frommer, "A Hawaiian Cruse, Detour Not Required," *Los Angeles Times*, April 4, 2004, L6. Recently some exceptions have been granted for foreign-flagged cruise ships that hire largely American crews.

state.[26] Some EU states, most notably Greece and Spain, resisted this expansion and were given additional time to open their cabotage systems. The system, overall, still allows states to discriminate (albeit now only against non-EU-flagged ships) in transportation that stops more than once in a given state. This regulation has opened new opportunities for open registries within the EU system. Gibraltar markets itself as an open registry that, because it is a British second registry, confers EU status on ships that fly its flag, thereby allowing them to fall within EU cabotage restrictions.[27]

These states occasionally consider increasing the stringency or reach of their cabotage rules. In the United States, Congress has periodically considered, though never implemented, legislation that would require that a certain percentage of goods shipped to the United States be carried on U.S.-registered ships. For example, the proposed Energy Transportation Security Act of 1974 would have mandated that 50 percent of oil the U.S. imported be transported aboard U.S.-flagged vessels. The proposed Energy Transportation Security Act of 1977 lowered the requirement to 30 percent, to be accomplished in stages. The first effort passed in Congress but was vetoed by President Gerald Ford; the second did not pass Congress.[28] These examples stand out for having come as close to passage as they did. Most such measures make little headway.

Rather than expanding the rules requiring that shipping be conducted on nationally flagged vessels, the trend internationally is to reduce them. In a move similar to the EU expansion of cabotage rules, there are now proposed measures to expand the U.S. system to include ships registered in NAFTA partners Mexico and Canada.[29] Moreover, the World Trade Organization has indicated an interest in addressing the trade implications of cabotage rules in new negotiations, though the United States has

26. Hannu Honka, "European Shipping Policies," in William A. Lovett, ed., *United States Shipping Policies and the World* Market (Westport, Conn.: Quorum Books, 1996), 136; European Council Resolution 4055/86, December 22, 1986 and European Council Resolution 3577/92, December 7, 1992.

27. Hassans, "The Registration of Ships and Yachts in Gibraltar," http://www.gibraltarlaw.com/registration_ships_yachts_gibraltar.htm.

28. Carlisle, 186–187.

29. "Box Hopes Are Pinned on Keeping Up with the Jones Act," *Lloyd's List*, January 23, 2004, 13.

thus far prevented such consideration.[30] The existing rules in which states restrict some access of foreign-flagged vessels to domestic shipping routes indicate that states can and do use their sovereignty to moderate the effects of the pure open registry system. But their unwillingness to create a system anything like the British Navigation Acts again indicates a basic acceptance of the current approach. Daniel Drezner's study of the regulation of globalization argues that it is major-power governments that have the greatest degree of influence in determining international regulatory standards.[31] In the case of shipping, it appears that they have little interest in changing the underlying structure of ship registration and instead prefer to work within the system to limit the difficulties it causes.

Sovereignty for Sale?

The system of open registration also intersects with issues of sovereignty for states that offer their flags internationally. While most states choose to operate open registries to generate income, there are sovereignty implications and effects from these decisions. States that offer flags of convenience sometimes do so not only for the income but for the international influence and image of control it can provide, though income generation can itself be an important aspect of a poor state's effort to gain control of its political future. Owners, however, may choose to flag in these locations precisely because these states do not have the kind of capacity for regulatory oversight that sovereignty would usually imply. In fact, in a number of these states the functions of the registry are contracted out, so that external firms make decisions about what is required for a ship to fly a given flag, which is about as symbolic an abdication of sovereignty as one could imagine. And operating an open registry may provide a demonstration of the very lack of control flag states are hoping to overcome, especially if their actions run afoul of the interests of the most powerful maritime states. The title of Carlisle's book, *Sovereignty for Sale*, suggests his view that open registry states are giving up control of their own political sphere in return for the income that ship registration offers.

30. Aviva Freudmann, "U.S. Resists Deal in Maritime Services," *Lloyd's List*, January 13, 2000, 1.

31. Drezner, *All Politics is Global*.

This lack of control was illustrated early in the era of open registration in the interactions between the U.S. government and Panamanian-flagged ships over Prohibition. The United States negotiated agreements with nearly twenty states, Panama among them, to allow the United States to board vessels within 14 to 21 miles of the U.S. shore (or one-hour's steaming time outside of territorial waters), when officials suspected the ship to be in contravention of Prohibition laws. Panama also passed, under pressure from the United States, a law allowing it to cancel registration of ships engaged in smuggling. The way these laws would be interpreted faced difficulty in 1927 when the U.S. Coast Guard turned its attention to four suspected Panamanian-flagged rumrunners. The Coast Guard seized the first one, the *Federalship*, 270 miles from the U.S. coast, claiming that the registration was false because the ship was engaged in smuggling. A U.S. Federal Court eventually ruled the seizure illegal, but before the ship was released the Coast Guard seized another Panama-flagged ship 64 miles outside of U.S. jurisdiction. This seizure too was ruled illegal. The Coast Guard then resorted to negotiation to attempt to persuade Panama to cancel the registration of the four ships it suspected of transporting liquor. Panama eventually canceled three of the four, and the owners of the *Federalship* decided to cancel their own registration, without paying fees and taxes owed to Panama.[32]

Panama found itself in a difficult position; allowing the United States to seize Panamanian-registered vessels on the high seas or to force Panama to cancel their registration would pose political difficulties within Panama, particularly in the context of other unresolved issues between the United States and Panama. But to resist U.S. pressure was to increase the odds of, at worst, U.S. intervention. As Carlisle put it, "assertion of Panamanian sovereignty was essential for local political reasons, yet too great an assertion of that sovereignty was inadvisable, also for local political reasons."[33]

A much more recent example comes in the context of the U.S. Proliferation Security Initiative, in which the United States negotiates bilateral agreements with various states to allow for activities designed to prevent proliferation of weapons of mass destruction. One central element of that

32. Carlisle, 21–27.

33. Carlisle, 29.

effort includes the inspection, by the United States and its allies, of planes and ships to determine whether their cargo contributes to WMD proliferation. The United States has pressured major flag states to sign agreements allowing it to board and search their vessels on the high seas if they are suspected of carrying weapons of mass destruction or related cargo. Panama, Liberia, and the Marshall Islands have done so.[34] While technically these agreements allow for reciprocal rights of inspection, no one actually expects the Marshall Islands to attempt to board and inspect U.S.-flagged ships on the high seas. And though the quid pro quo for these open registry states agreeing to U.S. terms is not clear, the lack of effective sovereignty on the part of these states certainly contributed to their willingness to yield to U.S. pressure.

As the phenomenon of open registration grew in the early years after the Second World War, the traditional maritime states were similarly wary of allowing new registries the influence on international legal governance of maritime issues that their growing registration profile would entitle them to. In particular, the International Maritime Organization,[35] the primary standard-setting organization for shipping, initially allocated membership on its Maritime Safety Commission (MSC) by designating eight of fourteen positions to representatives of the eight largest shipowning nations.[36] By the time the agreement entered into force in 1959 (eleven years after the charter was originally drafted), the growth in open registry shipping meant that Liberia and Panama were among the eight largest registries (at third and eighth respectively). These states attempted to claim their place on the MSC. Their bid was opposed by the traditional maritime states, however, and neither was elected to the commission. This dispute was eventually decided by the International Court of Justice the following year in favor of Liberia and Panama. The ICJ concluded that under international law the "largest ship-owning nations

34. David Osler, "Marshall Islands/US in Flag Security Pact," *Lloyd's List*, August 18, 2004, 3; "Panama to Allow US to Search Its Ships," *Lloyd's List*, May 12, 2004, 12.

35. At that time the organization was still called the International Maritime Consultative Organization (IMCO).

36. Convention on the International Maritime Organization (1948), Article 28(a). Note that the original name of the organization was the International Maritime Consultative Organization; the name was shortened in 1982.

were those having the largest registered ship tonnage," rather than the largest beneficial ownership as the traditional maritime states had claimed.[37] Perhaps as a result the MSC was expanded first to sixteen members by the 1965 Amendments (which entered into force in 1968) and then to the entire IMO membership by the 1974 Amendments (which entered into force in 1978).[38]

A number of states that offer flags of convenience do so in a context of broader offshore industries as well. Most of the major open registries also offer corporate registry and banking services and are tax havens. In some cases it seems that states use ship registration as a loss leader to lure industries to their tax havens and other offshore activities. For example, the Isle of Man ship registry (a British second registry) is, as one scholar notes, "set up in a way that virtually ensures that it will lose money,"[39] serving to lure other offshore business to the island. Offering both a tax haven and a ship registry can be attractive to shipping companies that can incorporate in the same location in which they register, and thereby avoid taxes on all their business.

This strategy has run ship registries into some trouble, however, as the major developed states have attempted to decrease the use of tax havens. The Organisation for Economic Cooperation and Development (OECD) in 2000 crafted a list of thirty-five tax havens (all of which also run open ship registries), identified as those states with nominal or no taxes that advertise internationally for business incorporation while promising some degree of secrecy for the businesses that locate there. The OECD gave these states one year to reform their systems and increase transparency or be subject to economic sanctions, including those that would affect their ship registries. At the same time, the G7 Financial Task Force singled out an overlapping set of states (also mostly, but not entirely,

37. International Court of Justice, "Case Summaries: Constitution of the Maritime Safety Committee of the Inter-Governmental Maritime Consultative Organization," Advisory Opinion as of June 8, 1960, http://www.icj-cij.org/icjwww/idecisions/isummaries/imscsummary600608.htm; Olav Knudsen, *The Politics of International Shipping* (Lexington, MA: Lexington Books, 1973), 81–82.

38. IMO, "Convention on the International Maritime Organization," http://www.imo.org/Conventions/mainframe.asp?topic_id=771.

39. Jessica Bernfeld, *Changing Tides: The Effects of Globalization on the Shipping Industries of Traditional Maritime States*, Wellesley College Honors Thesis, Wellesley, Mass., 2004, 35.

open ship registries) for money laundering.[40] Many of the major ship registries took some actions to moderate their tax-haven practices (usually through increasing transparency so that OECD states could track down revenues of their own citizens for taxation purposes), but seven that did not—Liberia, the Marshall Islands, and Vanuatu as major ship registries among them—were listed in 2002 as "uncooperative tax havens." Panama almost made this list, but wrote a last-minute letter of intent agreeing to reform its laws on tax and banking.[41] Though a few holdouts are willing to test the OECD's resolve, the major open ship registries have demonstrated that their domestic policies can be influenced by the powerful states that have an interest in moderating the impact of their offshoring behavior.

And it may be, as well, that the lack of full sovereignty makes the actions of these open registries more palatable to the advanced industrialized states that tolerate their presence on the international scene. The fact that, when they so choose, the traditional maritime states can still exert influence over the shipping and taxation policies of many of these states makes them much less of a threat to the most powerful states than an open registry system run by industrialized states would be. (The fact that when these powerful states do exert an influence they tend to tinker at the margins of the system rather than radically overhauling it supports the earlier contention that they have no interest in undermining it.)

Second registries fall into an interesting intermediate arena; they explicitly lack certain aspects of sovereignty by virtue of being dependent territories, which is a large part of their appeal. Ships registered in most of these locations benefit from the presumed protections of the home country should they need them, but in most cases the home country does not mandate specific regulatory approaches.

Other open registry states have a similarly reduced degree of sovereignty. Most important of these is the designation of Effective U.S. Controlled (EUSC) fleet for some registries: Panama, Liberia, the Bahamas, Honduras, and the Marshall Islands are considered EUSC registries. Ships majority-owned by U.S. citizens and registered in these locations

40. "Regulation—OECD Cracks Down on Alleged Tax Havens," *Lloyd's List*, June 27, 2000, 2.

41. James Brewer, "OECD—Shipping Nations Under Fire in Tax Haven Probe," *Lloyd's List*, April 22, 2002, 1.

may be called into service by the U.S. government in case of war or national emergency. This provision dates back to the U.S. Merchant Marine Act of 1936, though it technically applies to any ships owned by U.S. citizens and is not limited to ships registered in particular registries.[42] As of 2001 this fleet was considered to consist of approximately 175 commercial ships,[43] a number similar to the number of large U.S.-flagged commercial ships. The advantages of such a system for the United States are obvious, and the shipowners involved may assume that they will enjoy greater U.S. protection should the need arise. But from the perspective of the ship registries, another state has, without consultation, reserved the right to take control of some of their theoretically sovereign resources when it so chooses. There are, in fact, no formal or even informal agreements between the United States and these registries; it is simply assumed that they will willingly give over control of their vessels to the United States.[44] To the extent that these states are willing to put up with this diminution of their control, it is likely because they recognize that it is the price for the willingness of the most powerful states not to undermine the system even more radically.

The distinction between the state and its registry is also relevant for examining the sovereignty impacts for states that run open registries. Sometimes this distinction between state and registry can have beneficial shipping-related impacts. In a number of instances involving responses to port state control discussed in chapter 5, the registry was able to advocate that the state adopt higher standards in order to become a more attractive flag of convenience. The Liberian registry was the first to do this, at the behest of the shipowners using the registry, and the Liberian state was willing to adopt a number of international environmental agreements and to acquiesce in a ship inspection process undertaken on its behalf by the registry, in order to raise the reputation of Liberian-flagged ships. The registries of the Marshall Islands and Vanuatu have undertaken similar campaigns.

42. U.S. Merchant Marine Act, 1936; 49 Stat. 2015, June 29, 1936.

43. Hans Binnendijk and Richard L. Kugler, "Managing Change: Capability, Adaptability, and Transformation," *Defense Horizons*, June 2001, http://www.ndu.edu/inss/DefHor/DH1/DH1.html.

44. William G. Schubert, Maritime Administrator, Department of Transportation, Statement before the Special Oversight Panel on the Merchant Marine, U.S. Congress, House Armed Services Committee, June 13, 2002 (Lexis/Nexis).

But it can also lead to conflicts for the state whose flags these registries offer. The most public of these came in 1997 when Liberia accused its registry company, International Registries, of encouraging ships to flag in the Marshall Islands, another International Registries client, rather than in Liberia. This conflict led to years of litigation and Liberia's eventual split from International Registries to set up it own registry company (which still remains independent of the Liberian state).[45]

Similarly, Vanuatu created a government agency, the Vanuatu Maritime Authority, in an effort to have greater control over its ship registry by overseeing state shipping policies. The head of this agency had open conflicts over quality with the head of the registry, who was ultimately forced to resign.[46] In the case of Belize, the state authorities have replaced the registry officials a number of times, out of frustration that the registry was not attracting as many ship registrations as quickly as the state hoped. The various new directors of the registry have made efforts to increase ship standards in order to increase its attractiveness to shipowners who want a low-cost registry, with mixed results in terms of the state's willingness to take on international obligations. The Liberian shipowners have had similar difficulties making sure that the Liberian state paid IMO dues.[47] While the open registry states clearly have the final say about what they decide to do on ship registration, or on hiring or firing ship-registry firms, the fact that most contract out the day-to-day operations is a decision on their part to "sell" part of their sovereignty.

Finally, when attempting to understand the implications of the open registry system for sovereignty and state control more generally, it is important to remember that ship registration is still happening in *states*. While the number and characteristics of places an individual can choose to register a ship have grown, they are all legally sovereign entities; we have not moved to a system where registration can happen in corporations or substate locations. The small states that offer open registries are certainly

45. "Special Report on Ship Registries: Liberian Registry All Set to Change Hands After Parties Settle 'Restongate' Dispute," *Lloyd's List*, September 6, 1999, 8.

46. Specific details are discussed in chapter 5.

47. "Special Report... Liberian Registry," 8.

cognizant of their ability to use (and, ideally, augment) their sovereignty in this way; as Daniel Drezner puts it, "it has never been so profitable to be a nation-state."[48] But the most powerful states must be aware of this implication as well. To the extent that they are worried about a loss of control in a globalizing economy, ship registration in smaller states preserves the broader system of sovereign control over the rules of maritime transport. It is as though the phenomenon of offshoring (even if it means giving control to marginal states) is the price the most powerful states are willing to pay to maintain what might be termed a "sovereignty cartel," in which states maintain the ultimate legal control over maritime activities. These powerful states may not have sovereign control over everything that happens in the shipping arena, but the system as it operates preserves the principle that states, rather than corporations, are the entities in charge of overseeing this aspect of the international economy. This, then, is the ultimate club good: states have the right and the ability to exclude others from the business of ship registration. For the powerful states, acquiescing in the participation of marginal states in the enterprise of ship registration is the price of creating and upholding a sovereignty club.

Conclusions—The IPE of the Open Registry System

Flags of convenience are manifestations of international free riding in a way that is particularly obvious. As long as flag states gain income from running open registries, shipowners benefit from avoiding international standards, and powerful states benefit from trade made lucrative by cheap ocean transport, the phenomenon is not going to disappear. The initial experience with open registries demonstrates the existence of locations that intentionally keep environmental, safety, and labor standards low to attract industrial actors. Most international trade is now conducted on ships registered in these locations. This phenomenon has had at least an initial impact in lowering the overall level of regulation on these issues by ships that registered in open registries. The improvements we can expect to see in addressing flag-of-convenience issues may therefore be modest.

48. Daniel W. Drezner, "Sovereignty for Sale," *Foreign Policy*, 125 (September/October 2001): 76–77.

Competing pressures on international standards in this context help push standards globally toward a middle range of regulation. The most prominent one is the pressure downward: it is less expensive to run a ship with lower labor standards, less safety equipment, and without regard to environmental impact. As shipowners seek ways to lower their costs of operation, states seek income from running open registries that would allow shipowners to avoid costly international standards. At the same time, traditional maritime states, afraid of losing their entire fleet of nationally registered ships, create (with new ones appearing regularly) second and international registries that lower some requirements for ships and involve less oversight than in the home registry. This situation is ripe for a race to the regulatory bottom, and the migration of large numbers of commercial ships to open registries is at least the first step in such a race. In a world in which shipping runs on increasingly small profit margins, anything shipowners can do to cut costs will help their competitiveness.

Unless, of course, their lowering of standards prevents them from being able to access the advantages of the globalized market. This process does not happen automatically, but comes from collective action by those who take on higher standards and do not want to lose out, competitively, to those who work outside the system. We have thus seen a general raising of labor standards, increased compliance with fisheries agreements, and gradually increasing adoption of safety and environmental regulations by vessels, even those that fly flags of convenience. The changes come largely through collective action to increase the cost to open registry vessels of not adhering to international standards. This can be done through direct action by ship workers who will not service ships that do not pay their crew members adequately, by states singling out for inspection ships flagged in registries that have a particularly bad safety record, or by international organizations that exclude those who do not participate in the management of a protected resource from trade with those who do. It can even come from the classification societies or insurance clubs hired by shipowners to certify or insure their vessels, or by the professional organizations to which they belong.

How this process works goes back to the nature of club goods and the process of international cooperation. There are two characteristics discussed here that determine how to classify a particular good in this context: whether it is excludable and whether it is rival. Most of the collective-action problems faced with respect to environmental issues (and some environmentally related safety issues) are common-pool resource problems,[49] pertaining to goods that are not excludable but are rival, the exact opposite characteristics of club goods. Cooperation to address common-pool resource problems is especially difficult because of both of these characteristics. The beauty of the club-goods approach to management in the mechanisms that have succeeded in nudging shipping standards upward is that actors find ways to change the structure of an issue area so that successful cooperation becomes more likely.

In the case of management of a fishery, for example, both the non-excludability and the rivalness of the resource make successful cooperation extremely difficult. The fact that few global fisheries resources have been successfully managed supports this contention.[50] Creating a club good pertaining to fishery management turns the issue completely on its head. Because it is impossible to prevent access by fishers to fish on the open ocean, the way to create a club good is to figure out where it *is* possible to exclude: in this case, from the markets for fish. Similarly, while fish stocks themselves are rival, markets are not; the advantages of a trading club do not diminish notably as it gains more participants. Interestingly, David Vogel and Robert Kagan specifically point to fisheries agreements (along with shipping standards more generally) as an area without harmonization upward because of a lack of restriction of market access.[51] The clubs described in this book are imperfect and are recent enough that these authors may not have fully considered them. But these mechanisms of exclusion, such as from markets, appear to have made great strides in encouraging upward harmonization, in the case of fisheries, through restricting market access.

Not all the issues addressed here are common-pool resources. Labor issues and labor-related safety concerns are not as rival as environmental

49. J. Samuel Barkin and George E. Shambaugh, eds., *Anarchy and the Environment: The International Relations of Common Pool Resources* (Albany: SUNY Press, 1999).

50. Emma Young and James Randerson, "Mauraders of the High Seas," *New Scientist* 5 (November 2005): 12.

51. David Vogel and Robert A. Kagan, eds., *Dynamics of Regulatory Change: How Globalization Affects National Regulatory Policies* (Berkeley: University of California Press, 2004).

issues and therefore have the characteristics of public goods. Whether or not a specific ship enacts labor protections does not inherently decrease the ability of others to provide labor protections should they choose to. But the market for labor on ships is global, and labor costs are among the most expensive aspects of operating a commercial ship. The lowering of standards on some ships, therefore, may create a competitive pressure to lower standards more generally. In addition, some labor issues contribute to potential environmental and safety problems. Overtired crews that do not speak a common language are less likely to be able to respond to a crisis that arises, increasing the odds of a ship disaster. Even when an issue is not considered rival, however, creating a club to address it may solve some of the problems of the underprovision of successful regulation. Clubs enable the benefits of cooperation to be limited to those who participate in providing it, and thereby decrease the free-rider problems experienced in addressing both public goods and common-pool resources.

How such a club is created depends on characteristics of the issue in question, including the location of the harm, the actors that are most concerned about it, and who they are able to target. We see involvement of states, labor unions, international organizations, and industry groups in these processes, creating and enforcing clubs with variation in type, focus, and strength.

The first aspect of clubs to consider is the question of which actors are most concerned about responding to potential low standards on ships. An important determinant of which actors will be concerned is where the harm caused by low ship standards is felt. Even though the problems examined here are caused on the ocean, in some cases the harm is felt primarily in the territory of states. The kinds of environmental and safety issues that are the focus of port state control efforts affect states in a localized, geographically based way. Though oil pollution on the oceans happens worldwide, its effects are felt primarily on coastlines. Major accidental oil spills are most likely to happen near coastlines, where ships are most likely to run into obstacles, and the coastlines near which oil tankers spend the most time are those of the states to (and from) which they are transporting oil. It is these states that are most likely to feel the effects of low standards that increase the likelihood of accidents. Similar arguments can be made for other types of ocean pollution from ships.

It is therefore not surprising that the port state control system is primarily a state-based enterprise. Though its inspection processes focus on a wide range of environmental and safety standards, many of them pertain to the prevention of the types of disasters that would affect states as territorial entities. Moreover, the system focuses on detaining ships with deficiencies that threaten the marine environment in an imminent way. These ships are required to remedy these deficiencies before they are allowed to put to sea.

Harm to fisheries is also based on location, to some extent. Regional fisheries management organizations work to protect species based on location. That location is (for most agreements) by definition outside of the jurisdiction of states, which means that it is only international organizations that have the ability (with the cooperation of states) to create and enforce regulations. More importantly, however, the markets for fish are territorially based, and it is there that fishers who follow international rules face the biggest competitive disadvantage with respect to those who do not. Regulations on fisheries are therefore created in the context of an international organization, but the option for creating a club comes from the physical location of the fish as they are sold. It is the states that buy fish that have the ability to create trade restrictions and the interest in doing so.

It is also worth noting the actions of some nonstate actors on fisheries. Recently nongovernmental environmental organizations have undertaken efforts to persuade the public to avoid eating fish from overharvested fisheries, and to persuade chefs to refuse to serve these fish.[52] While not sufficiently widespread at this point to have a major impact, there could be clublike elements to these measures, particularly those by chefs and restaurateurs, which could function as a nonstate way to reduce access to fish not caught sustainabily. For the most part, though, those cooking or consuming fish do not have the ability to determine whether a specific fish was caught within a sufficiently regulated process (e.g., by a fisher operating within the restrictions of the relevant management organization), only whether the fish species as a whole is threatened. As such it does not yet function as the type of club examined

52. J. Samuel Barkin and Kashif Mansori, "Backward Boycotts: Demand Management and Fishery Conservation," *Global Environmental Politics* 1/2 (May 2001): 30–41.

here, capable of providing incentives to fishers to work within the management system in order to gain access to markets. These types of consumer-based measures likely did have an impact in persuading fishers to protect dolphins in the course of tuna fishing (an early fishing problem in which ships reflagged to avoid regulations).[53] Protecting dolphins gave fishers the ability to market their tuna in the United States and elsewhere as "dolphin-safe," a club to which overwhelming consumer demand made access profitable.

In some cases, mostly pertaining to labor standards and some labor-related safety standards, the harm itself happens on the ship. It is there that wages are kept low, worker rights not upheld, or safe working conditions not met. These types of harms do not impact states directly, and do not even indirectly affect states whose nationals are not a major source of labor on ships. At this point nearly 70 percent of the labor on ships is supplied by ten states: the Philippines, Russia, Ukraine, China, India, Indonesia, Poland, Greece, Turkey, and Myanmar.[54] Most of these are not traditionally powerful maritime states. The most powerful states in the international political economy, moreover, do benefit indirectly from low labor standards on ships to the extent that they allow costs for international transport to be kept low. It is not surprising, therefore, that states have not created a club for the enforcement of labor rights.

Instead, it is labor unions (organized collectively by the International Transport Workers Federation, a global union organization) that have had to innovate ways to create mechanisms of exclusion to persuade ships to take on and uphold international labor standards. Their club is formed by those who work in the maritime industry, on ships, or servicing them. Rather than denying substandard ships access to ports, they deny them access to the services they need in ports. These unions gain from the benefits to their members whose wages and working conditions are improved when ships agree to take on higher labor standards. Also important in providing an incentive for collective action by the unions is

53. Alessandro Bonanno and Douglas Constance, *Caught in the Net: The Global Tuna Industry, Environmentalism, and the State* (Lawrence: University Press of Kansas, 1996): 156, 183.

54. Minghua Zhao and Maragtas S. V. Amante, "Chinese and Filipino Seafarers: A Race to the Top or the Bottom?", *Modern Asian Studies* 39/3 (2005): 537.

that the agreements ships are forced to sign include provisions requiring them to pay the union dues of their seafarers and pay into the ITF's welfare fund. The club is thus advantageous both for the individual union members and for the union organizations themselves, who are the ones to create the club.

A second, and related, factor in evaluating the type of club created is the characteristics of the resource to be regulated. This issue relates to the type and extent of benefit flag states (or individual ships) gain from remaining outside of the regulatory structure. When ships avoid participating in international fishery management systems, for instance, they benefit in two different ways. They avoid any restrictions on their fishing activity, which confers its own advantages. But they also benefit from the existence of the regulatory structure that keeps others from overfishing the resource and thus increases the availability of fish overall. This type of free riding is the most valuable to those who engage in it (and, conversely, the most harmful to those who are attempting to manage the resource). The more rival the good, the more important it is to bring free riders into the club, and the stronger the club needs to be to compensate for the disadvantages to the group of those who stay outside it. It should not be surprising that the clubs created to prevent environmental problems, as enforced through port state control detention and through fishery trade restrictions, contain reasonably powerful mechanisms of exclusion, at least compared to those addressing other issues.

On the other end of the spectrum are issues like classification and insurance. Ships benefit from having both. They benefit from classification partly because it decreases the chances of ship disasters but mostly because it allows them access to other clubs (such as ports and in some cases even ship registration). They gain from protection and indemnity insurance, which helps pay expenses if disasters do happen. But the issue is not rival: the lack of participation in these clubs by others does not harm those who participate. In other words, the type of problem addressed by insurance and classification has both private and public goods, but not common-pool resource, characteristics.

Recent actions within these industries have created increasingly club-like characteristics in classification and insurance, however. Classification societies, for instance, have refused to class ships flagged in certain open registry states (or have removed low-performance classification societies from the larger club of high-standard societies). The societies with the best reputations have demanded additional higher standards from the ships they class in order to improve their reputations and thereby decrease the odds that the ships they class will be singled out for port state control inspections. Nevertheless, both the classification and insurance clubs are fairly weak, because they do not have to try to bring all of the major players inside of the club in order to have the effect they seek. To some extent, the industry clubs benefit most if there are those that remain outside their clubs, which increases the reputational advantages to belonging.

A third type of variation we see across clubs is variation on who the targets of the mechanisms of exclusion (and push for increased standards) are. There are two different possible targets for raising shipping standards: the flag states, which determine what standards ships are legally bound by, and the ships themselves. Both are important. While the ships are the ones whose ultimate behavior is the most important, focusing on individual ships is inefficient; there are currently approximately 90,000 ships larger than 100 GT registered in states worldwide,[55] and addressing their standards ship by ship is difficult. Changing the standards mandated by flag states affects large numbers of ships at a time, but only if the flag states are willing or able to enforce these standards. More importantly, though, the different actors who create the clubs examined in this book have differing abilities to influence ships or states.

For the most part, the civil-society actors, such as the labor unions that call for ship-worker boycotts or the classification or insurance organizations that mandate specific standards in order to class or cover a ship, target individual ships because that is their only locus of influence. They simply do not have the ability to influence flag-state behavior directly. Not that they do not ever try. The efforts by Lloyd's and other classification societies informing Cambodia and Mongolia that they would no longer class ships registered there can be seen as an effort to influence the behavior of those registries. If it were simply a business decision ("we will no longer class those ships because they represent too great a risk and therefore are not good for our operations"), there would be no need to publicly inform the registry or others.

55. And many more that are smaller; see Lloyd's Register Fairplay, *World Fleet Statistics 2004* (London: Lloyd's Register Fairplay, 2005).

Similarly, the ITF maintains that the underlying purpose of its flag-of-convenience campaign is to reform the flag system and return to a system in which states only register ships belonging to their nationals. But its ability to accomplish that end is limited by its status as a nonstate actor. The only way it could succeed in reforming the flag-state system would be by making individual shipowners sufficiently inconvenienced by the labor action that results from their registration choices that they choose to reflag back in their home states. But even there the ITF faces a trade-off: if it wants to raise standards on individual ships (and also gain the revenue it needs to continue its operations by collecting funding from the ships that adopt ITF-approved collective agreements), it must discriminate by ship rather than by flag state. Doing so has resulted in a great number of ships that adopt higher labor standards than they would be required to by their flag states. But these choices by individual ships reduce the pressure on open registry states to mandate increased standards. The ITF, then, makes important improvements in the actual wages and working conditions on ships, but has little effect on flag states.

Both states and international organizations, the main actors with respect to port state control and trade restrictions, primarily target flag states. The discrimination based on flag state in determining which ships to inspect is an intentional effort to influence the standards of the flag states more generally, by indicating to states in substandard flags that they run a greater risk of inspection. Flag states are then faced with the decision of whether to raise standards to attempt to keep registrations from reputable ships, or to keep standards low and register ships that choose to avoid standards to the extent possible. As chapter 5 demonstrates, many flag states choose to mandate higher standards. Similarly, trade restrictions on fisheries products are determined by whether a flag state is a member of the relevant regional fishery management organization, and a number of open registry states have joined these organizations in response to trade restrictions.

Both mechanisms, however, do ultimately focus on ships more directly. That is the most obvious in the case of port state control. No matter how it is that a ship comes to be singled out for inspection, once it is inspected it passes or fails on its own merit, and is detained, if its deficiencies are particularly egregious or harmful, until they can be remedied. In the case of trade and transshipment restrictions on fish products, the decision made is whether an individual ship may offload fish. While the first stage of that decision is to determine whether the ship's registry state is a member of the relevant fisheries agreement, in most cases it is possible for a vessel whose flag state is not a member to undertake the obligations on its own and demonstrate that it is meeting the obligations of the agreement even if it is not bound under its flag state. These measures may have been put into place largely to avoid charges of contravening World Trade Organization rules, but they nevertheless provide individual ships with the option of adopting higher standards than their flag states require, and thereby gaining entrance to the trading club that otherwise focuses on states.

Behind all of these mechanisms are sets of standards created collectively in international organizations. The labor standards are formed in the ILO, many of the safety and environmental agreements under the IMO, and fishery conservation agreements under a range of regional fishery management organizations. Though states are free to choose their own domestic standards (and, by extension, which international standards they adopt as domestic standards through ratification), the globalization of shipping and ship registration requires international standards to function smoothly. The port state control process is undertaken largely by states, but it is the fact that they are imposing collectively accepted international standards that makes the process feasible. In addition, though not necessary to the process, the cooperative regional efforts are more effective because states can coordinate inspections and target ships that have fared badly in previous inspections by other states or that have not been inspected by anyone in the system in awhile. This is the club aspect of the process. The fact that they are inspecting based on a collective set of standards is what makes this club effort possible.

The role of industry actors—primarily shipowners and those who make use of ships to transport their goods—is the central feature underlying most of the processes examined in this book. It was Liberian shipowners who, afraid of losing the advantages of flagging in a low-tax, low-fee location, persuaded their flag state to take on higher standards and their registry to create an inspection system, in order to protect the underlying option of "flagging out" from the problems of out-of-control oil spills. It was the fishers who fish legally (with international restrictions) for tuna and toothfish who advocated for trade restrictions on fish caught outside of the system. Even the registration system itself is a business, with decisions about what standards to adopt made based on what the effect will be on running the business of a registry. Clubs are created in these contexts as a way to gain economic rent: by excluding others, those inside the club obtain economic advantages.

Despite efforts by shipowners to avoid costly regulation through flag-of-convenience registration, there has been, as Braithwaite and Drahos note, "a decisive triumph of global harmonization of standards" in ocean shipping.[56] Not only are these standards created, most frequently through international organizations, but nongovernmental actors and states then work to increase the extent to which they are actually adopted and followed, despite the relative ease of opting out of such regulations or avoiding detection when not following them. Even industry organizations join the effort, attempting to ensure that ships owned or used by their members are not excluded from access to markets or ports. Most frequently international pressure has led to increased standards when actors have been able to create some way to deny access to a benefit to those that do not accept the standards in question.

The extent to which these standards have been successfully enforced hinges primarily on the ability of actors to create mechanisms for excluding ships from the benefits they would otherwise gain by avoiding an international regulatory system. This fits the argument that standards internationally are coming to rely on what Sassen characterizes as private regulatory systems.[57]

Because there may still be advantages to continuing to fly a flag of convenience, ships that do so may want to reform their behavior sufficiently that they will not have to abandon those flags. Open registry states, similarly, may be willing to undertake such reforms as are necessary to protect their ability to continue to gain revenue from running a registry where ships will want to flag. A combination of international pressure and individual incentives may therefore be what is needed to hold ships to international standards.

Most of the mechanisms outlined in this book function to give open registry flag states the incentive to increase their standards by providing

56. Braithwaite and Drahos, 431.

57. Sassen, 14–16.

information about the quality of their ships (individually or in aggregate) to others. Other actors involved in the shipping industry can use this information to decide whether to hire the ships to transport their goods, whether to inspect ships in port state control, whether to invoke strikes against low labor standards, whether to accept imports of the fish they catch, and whether to insure or register them, or hire them to transport cargo. Ships registered in flag states with good records have far more options than do those registered in less reputable flags. That alone often can be a sufficient incentive for open registries to increase the standards to which ships are held or to take on additional international agreements.

But in addition some open registry states hope to create systems that will increase the competitive advantage they experience by making their records, compared to their competitors, even clearer. Additional actions proposed by high-quality open registries, discussed in chapter 5, have characteristics of the creation or augmentation by these flag states of clubs. The efforts by the Marshall Islands registry to create a "network of quality registers" certainly fits this model, as does the support of the highest-quality open registries for the creation of a mandatory IMO audit scheme, neither of which has yet come into being.

The broader question represented by the shift of ship registrations to open registries and the resulting collective action to influence ship standards is what impact it has on how states and other actors conduct themselves in the global marketplace. Does this form of globalization change the overall international regulatory structure? One of the important pieces of evidence that the flag-of-convenience phenomenon is not a fundamental challenge to the structure of the global political economy is its constant and predictable evolution: new states enter the market to provide ship registrations, and do so at the low end of the regulatory spectrum. Over time, the processes outlined in this book work to persuade them to increase their standards and to specialize at a certain type and level of middle-range regulation. As that happens, the previous low-standard ship registries are replaced by new entrants to the market, again offering lower standards than existing states.

From an activist perspective this evolution could appear depressing: there will always be a bottom end in regulatory stringency. But rather than suggesting that those who want to raise standards should simply give up because they will never fix the problem, it suggests that it is precisely the actions—self-interested though they may be—of these various actors that consistently raise standards in this process. Each time an open registry takes on new standards, some of its registered ships leave, to register in a registry that demands less. But some stay, willing to accept the higher standards in exchange for the increased access they provide to the benefits of the globalized trading system.

In some ways the evidence confirms the existence of regulatory havens, but with a twist: the havens never remain the same. At any given point there is an option to "locate" a ship in a low-standard haven. But there are costs to doing so, especially over time, and any registry that wants to remain competitive will end up increasing its standards at least to a minimally acceptable level. Those industries or shipowners who want to keep their standards at the lowest possible level will thus have to keep switching ship registrations (a cost in and of itself) to the new registries that arise. One scholar drew optimism from the fact that "eventually we'll run out of states"[58]—in other words, when there are no states that have not yet entered the market for providing ship registrations, there will be no more states to enter at the low end of standards. Shipowners who are not pleased when their flag state gives in to pressure to increase standards will have nowhere else to go. While this view might be overly optimistic, the advantages to flag states that offer registration to truly substandard ships are decreased by the mechanisms of exclusion outlined in this book. As these processes continue and expand it will become less profitable to enter the low-standard ship-registry market.

Accidents like the one experienced by *The Prestige* will always be possible. And there will always be disreputable shipowners, willing to operate at the margins of the international system, causing problems for others. But instead of creating a race to the regulatory bottom, the system of open ship registration, in combination with the self-interest of nongovernmental actors and states, creates a regulatory middle ground, where profit is still possible and a moderate level of protection achievable.

58. Interview with Jaime Veiga, Seafarers International Research Centre, Cardiff, May 17, 2004.

Appendixes

APPENDIX A
Gross Tonnage in Selected Registries 1953–2004

State	1953	1954	1955	1956
Antigua and Barbuda				
Australia	573,965	588,758	612,430	609,965
Bahamas				
Barbados				
Belgium	482,779	497,270	497,536	539,829
Belize				
Bolivia				
Cambodia				
Canada	1,651,914	1,610,342	1,521,015	1,503,573
China	659,006	660,428	567,283	552,552
China, Republic of (Taiwan)				
Comoros				
Cyprus	10,036	4,797	6,005	5,191
Denmark	1,529,169	1,613,903	1,651,686	1,695,221
DIS				
Equatorial Guinea				
France	3,825,783	3,840,888	3,922,478	3,943,201
French Antarctic Territory				
Germany, Federal Republic of	1,747,473	2,224,337	2,644,130	3,197,773
Greece	1,222,209	1,176,373	1,245,388	1,307,336
Honduras				
India	487,707	512,706	569,718	580,456
Indonesia				
Italy	3,455,785	3,798,385	3,910,658	4,196,762
Japan	3,250,412	3,577,826	3,735,318	4,075,781
Korea, South	44,895	67,601	70,808	79,032
Latvia				
Liberia	1,434,085	2,381,066	3,996,904	5,584,378
Luxembourg				
Malta				
Marshall Islands				

1957	1958	1959	1960	1961
		0		
599,280	631,240	663,885	619,996	593,080
			98,179	192,323
579,432	601,441	728,316	728,981	713,197
1,521,241	1,515,887	151,025	1,578,077	1,668,955
541,690	539,830	623,435	402,417	472,677
			281,662	372,898
		0		
1,450	1,846	905	991	138
1,857,478	2,034,687	2,204,283	2,269,847	2,306,746
4,009,783	4,337,935	4,538,370	4,808,728	5,117,303
3,597,079	4,055,853	4,439,690	4,536,591	4,771,080
1,471,545	1,611,119	2,150,938	4,529,234	5,439,204
	338,170	201,836	153,625	119,772
625,641	673,678	749,711	858,916	955,441
	119,128	155,710	172,355	273,885
4,551,956	4,899,640	5,118,764	5,122,240	5,319,334
4,415,070	5,465,442	6,276,689	6,931,436	7,953,984
106,239	112,381	103,317	100,936	108,825
7,466,429	10,078,778	11,936,250	11,282,420	10,929,551

APPENDIX A
(continued)

State	1953	1954	1955	1956
Mongolia				
Namibia				
Netherlands	3,371,836	3,442,537	3,695,610	4,006,077
Netherlands Antilles				
New Zealand				
Cook Islands				
Norway	6,262,700	6,805,157	7,249,087	8,035,340
Norway (NIS)				
Panama	3,906,901	4,091,013	3,922,529	3,925,751
Philippines	153,707	153,957	149,305	133,621
Portugal				
Portugal (MAR)				
Singapore				
Spain	1,270,817	1,309,244	1,383,239	1,437,805
CSR				
St. Vincent and Grenadines				
Sweden	2,575,397	2,701,110	2,807,166	2,922,092
Tonga				
Turkey	478,269	487,336	532,123	601,485
Ukraine				
United Kingdom	18,583,808	19,014,220	19,356,660	19,545,875
Bermuda				
Cayman Islands				
Gibraltar				
Isle of Man				
United States	27,236,876	27,344,018	26,422,683	26,145,642
USSR/Russia	2,292,330	2,370,669	2,505,850	2,635,961
Vanuatu				
World	93,351,800	97,421,526	100,568,779	105,200,361

1957	1958	1959	1960	1961
4,335,356	4,599,788	47,431,223	4,884,049	4,909,687
	255,989	258,783	247,100	233,760
8,488,164	9,384,830	10,444,268	11,203,246	12,024,641
4,129,029	4,357,800	4,582,539	4,235,983	4,049,377
115,487	123,020	135,085	170,770	317,299
	551,926	579,911	602,867	677,159
1,505,224	1,607,212	1,711,818	1,800,721	1,958,065
3,047,535	3,303,078	3,623,423	3,746,866	3,996,335
593,505	595,625	588,176	651,109	668,085
19,857,491	20,285,776	20,756,535	21,130,874	21,464,522
25,910,855	25,589,596	25,287,972	24,837,069	24,238,022
2,708,607	2,965,819	3,155,054	3,429,472	4,066,157
110,246,081	118,033,731	124,935,479	129,769,500	135,915,958

APPENDIX A
(continued)

State	1962	1963	1964	1965
Antigua and Barbuda				
Australia	574,491	557,052	593,700	726,999
Bahamas	172,097	213,214	218,163	254,412
Barbados				
Belgium	745,344	718,813	796,133	831,976
Belize				
Bolivia				
Cambodia				
Canada	1,703,549	1,796,440	1,823,387	1,829,741
China	522,481	502,038	535,427	511,143
China, Republic of (Taiwan)	485,601	520,049	588,355	638,274
Comoros				
Cyprus	138	138	17,435	46,454
Denmark	2,339,245	2,418,207	2,431,020	2,561,599
DIS				
Equatorial Guinea				
France	5,162,121	5,216,098	5,116,232	5,198,435
French Antarctic Territory				
Germany, Federal Republic of	4,923,846	5,050,250	5,159,186	5,279,493
Greece	6,537,419	7,093,974	6,887,624	7,137,244
Honduras	112,886	103,104	89,978	81,008
India	1,012,866	1,211,139	1,448,237	1,522,693
Indonesia	335,107	421,821	470,395	505,091
Italy	5,411,652	5,604,558	5,707,817	5,701,342
Japan	8,870,155	9,976,668	10,813,228	11,971,157
Korea, South	103,870	108,206	122,254	128,999
Latvia				
Liberia	10,573,158	11,391,210	14,549,645	17,539,482
Luxembourg				
Malta				54,740
Marshall Islands				

	1966	1967	1968	1969	1970
	744,356	803,027	818,247	893,613	1,074,112
	255,930	281,584	303,407	376,132	276,097
			484	484	1,183
	875,582	940,426	932,900	1,051,882	1,062,152
			358	620	620
			4,230	4,230	4,230
	2,125,424	2,305,502	2,402,983	2,450,944	2,399,949
	669,299	772,125	765,545	791,893	867,994
	770,028	775,397	762,515	961,807	1,166,230
	181,806	360,615	652,588	770,463	1,138,229
	2,839,367	3,014,094	3,204,040	3,490,334	3,314,320
	5,260,248	5,576,500	5,796,360	5,961,963	6,457,900
	5,766,534	5,990,395	6,527,946	7,027,384	7,881,000
	7,163,209	7,432,793	7,415,984	8,580,753	10,951,993
	69,816	74,586	68,958	65,659	60,216
	1,794,554	1,886,513	1,945,037	2,238,344	2,401,656
	582,417	624,202	711,500	598,155	642,530
	5,850,921	6,219,041	6,623,643	7,037,846	7,447,610
	14,722,805	16,883,353	19,586,902	23,987,079	27,003,704
	193,185	305,905	473,991	767,315	849,457
	20,603,301	22,597,808	25,719,642	29,215,151	33,296,644
?		52,483	67,742	58,112	35,393

APPENDIX A
(continued)

State	1962	1963	1964	1965
Mongolia				
Namibia				
Netherlands	5,166,172	5,226,815	5,110,022	4,891,041
Netherlands Antilles				
New Zealand	241,037	244,272	239,087	227,632
Cook Islands				
Norway	12,511,082	13,668,815	14,477,112	15,641,498
Norway (NIS)				
Panama	3,851,159	3,893,701	4,269,462	4,465,407
Philippines	365,878	406,311	454,201	500,541
Portugal	666,974	673,757	701,676	597,627
Portugal (MAR)				
Singapore				
Spain	1,995,088	2,007,340	2,047,715	2,132,002
CSR				
St. Vincent and Grenadines				
Sweden	4,166,728	4,176,326	4,308,042	4,290,103
Tonga				
Turkey	728,853	723,595	680,239	571,681
Ukraine				
United Kingdom	21,658,142	21,565,150	21,489,948	21,530,264
Bermuda			167,551	200,063
Cayman Islands				
Gibraltar				
Isle of Man				
United States	23,272,856	23,132,781	22,430,249	21,527,349
USSR/Russia	4,684,077	5,433,765	6,957,512	8,237,874
Vanuatu				
World	139,979,813	145,863,463	152,999,621	160,391,504

1966	1967	1968	1969	1970
4,979,950	5,123,237	5,267,681	5,254,883	5,206,663
244,354	216,740	191,618	180,561	185,836
16,421,123	18,381,867	19,667,441	19,679,094	19,346,911
4,543,071	4,756,154	5,096,956	5,373,722	5,645,877
604,492	720,286	854,256	929,317	946,400
748,808	755,000	771,643	825,355	870,008
18,134	41,592	133,855	233,271	424,417
2,241,490	2,570,890	2,820,784	3,199,035	3,440,952
		4,361	665	1,142
4,399,641	4,634,648	4,865,365	5,029,407	4,920,704
		1,987	1,987	1,987
640,334	611,078	494,625	651,325	696,824
21,541,740	21,716,148	21,920,989	23,843,799	25,824,820
221,575	346,332	380,053	354,923	683,529
		16,749	18,818	22,371
		59,394	44,474	54,075
20,797,435	20,332,626	19,668,421	19,550,394	18,463,207
9,492,031	10,617,418	12,061,833	13,704,640	14,831,775
171,129,833	182,099,644	194,152,378	211,660,893	227,489,864

APPENDIX A
(continued)

State	1971	1972	1973	1974
Antigua and Barbuda				
Australia	1,105,236	1,184,010	1,160,205	1,168,367
Bahamas	357,845	205,862	179,494	153,202
Barbados	?	1,676	2,958	3,897
Belgium	1,131,081	1,191,555	1,161,609	1,214,707
Belize		620	620	620
Bolivia				
Cambodia	?	1,880	2,090	2,090
Canada	2,366,175	2,380,635	2,422,802	2,459,998
China	1,022,256	1,181,179	1,478,992	1,870,567
China, Republic of (Taiwan)	1,321,758	1,494,903	1,467,311	1,416,833
Comoros				
Cyprus	1,498,114	2,014,675	2,935,775	3,394,880
Denmark	3,520,021	4,091,927	4,106,525	4,460,219
DIS				
Equatorial Guinea				
France	7,011,476	7,419,596	8,288,773	8,834,519
French Antarctic Territory				
Germany, Federal Republic of	8,678,584	8,515,669	7,914,679	7,980,453
Greece	13,065,930	15,328,860	19,295,143	21,759,449
Honduras	?	74,030	67,274	69,561
India	2,478,031	2,649,677	2,886,595	3,484,751
Indonesia	?	618,589	668,964	762,278
Italy	8,138,521	8,187,323	8,867,205	9,322,015
Japan	30,509,280	34,929,214	36,785,094	38,707,659
Korea, South	940,009	1,057,408	1,103,925	1,225,679
Latvia				
Liberia	38,522,240	44,443,652	49,904,744	55,321,641
Luxembourg				
Malta	?	14,641	11,022	38,011
Marshall Islands				

1975	1976	1977	1978	1979
		149	410	410
1,205,248	1,247,172	1,374,197	1,531,739	1,651,747
189,890	147,814	106,317	84,269	120,581
3,897	3,897	4,448	4,448	5,107
1,358,425	1,499,431	1,595,486	1,684,692	1,788,538
620	620	620	620	620
				15,130
1,208	1,208	3,558	3,558	3,558
2,565,501	2,638,692	2,822,948	2,954,499	3,015,752
2,828,290	3,558,726	4,245,446	5,168,898	6,336,747
1,449,957	1,483,981	1,558,713	1,619,595	2,011,311
		765	765	467
3,221,070	3,114,263	2,787,908	2,599,529	2,355,543
4,478,112	5,143,022	5,331,165	5,530,408	5,524,416
		3,070	3,070	6,412
10,745,999	11,278,016	11,613,859	12,197,354	11,945,837
8,516,567	9,264,671	9,592,374	9,736,667	8,562,780
22,527,156	25,034,585	29,517,059	33,956,093	37,352,597
67,923	71,042	104,903	130,831	193,256
3,869,187	5,093,984	5,482,176	5,759,224	5,854,285
859,378	1,046,198	1,163,173	1,272,387	1,309,911
10,136,989	11,077,549	11,111,182	11,491,873	11,694,872
39,739,598	41,663,188	40,035,853	39,182,079	39,992,925
1,623,532	1,796,106	2,494,724	2,975,389	3,952,946
65,820,414	73,477,326	79,982,968	80,191,329	81,528,175
45,950	39,140	100,420	101,541	116,299

APPENDIX A
(continued)

State	1971	1972	1973	1974
Mongolia				
Namibia				
Netherlands	5,269,145	4,972,244	5,029,443	5,500,932
Netherlands Antilles				
New Zealand	?	181,901	156,503	163,399
Cook Islands				
Norway	21,720,202	23,507,108	23,621,096	24,852,917
Norway (NIS)				
Panama	6,262,264	7,793,598	9,568,954	11,003,227
Philippines	945,508	924,564	947,210	7,664,778
Portugal	?	1,027,070	1,271,815	1,243,128
Portugal (MAR)				
Singapore	581,777	870,513	2,004,269	2,878,327
Spain	3,934,129	4,300,055	4,833,048	4,949,146
CSR				
St. Vincent and Grenadines	?	1,477	2,247	4,808
Sweden	4,978,278	5,632,336	5,669,340	6,226,659
Tonga	?	2,502	2,502	9,081
Turkey	713,767	743,071	756,807	971,682
Ukraine				
United Kingdom	27,334,695	28,624,875	30,159,543	31,566,298
Bermuda	?	813,586	860,953	1,153,280
Cayman Islands	?	26,172	44,419	39,717
Gibraltar	?	21,375	20,855	28,293
Isle of Man				
United States	16,265,669	15,024,148	14,912,432	14,429,076
USSR/Russia	16,194,326	16,733,674	17,396,900	18,175,918
Vanuatu				
World	274,202,634	268,340,145	289,926,686	311,322,626

1975	1976	1977	1978	1979
5,679,413	5,919,892	5,290,360	5,180,392	5,403,350
162,520	164,192	199,462	211,112	258,476
26,153,682	27,943,834	27,801,471	26,128,428	22,349,377
13,667,123	15,631,180	19,458,419	20,748,679	22,323,931
879,043	1,018,065	1,146,529	1,264,995	1,606,019
1,209,701	1,173,710	1,281,439	1,239,963	1,205,478
3,891,902	5,481,720	6,791,398	7,489,205	7,869,152
5,433,354	6,027,763	7,186,081	8,056,080	8,313,658
5,507	5,663	8,428	11,523	12,718
7,486,196	7,971,246	7,429,394	6,508,255	4,636,662
9,644	13,720	14,180	20,663	23,549
994,668	1,079,347	1,288,282	1,358,779	1,421,715
33,157,422	32,923,308	31,646,351	30,896,606	27,951,342
1,450,387	1,562,483	1,751,515	1,814,455	1,726,672
49,320	78,251	123,787	169,100	229,973
28,850	21,526	10,549	832	2,291
14,586,616	14,908,445	14,599,681	16,187,636	17,542,220
19,235,973	20,667,892	21,438,291	22,261,927	22,900,201
342,162,363	371,999,926	393,678,369	406,001,979	413,021,426

APPENDIX A
(continued)

State	1980	1981	1982	1983
Antigua and Barbuda	410	559	559	559
Australia	1,642,594	1,767,930	1,875,316	2,022,481
Bahamas	87,320	196,682	432,502	860,952
Barbados	5,257	5,124	44,967	84,386
Belgium	1,809,829	1,916,765	2,271,096	2,273,503
Belize	620	620	620	620
Bolivia	15,130	15,129	15,129	14,913
Cambodia	3,558	3,558	3,558	3,558
Canada	3,180,126	3,158,864	3,212,562	3,384,677
China	6,837,608	7,653,195	8,056,849	8,674,599
China, Republic of (Taiwan)	2,039,123	1,887,836	2,225,977	2,879,200
Comoros	1,116	328	977	977
Cyprus	2,091,089	1,818,997	2,149,869	3,450,241
Denmark	5,390,365	5,047,734	5,214,063	5,115,097
DIS				
Equatorial Guinea	6,412	6,412	6,412	6,412
France	11,924,557	11,455,033	10,770,880	9,868,075
French Antarctic Territory				
Germany, Federal Republic of	8,355,638	7,708,227	7,706,661	6,896,961
Greece	39,471,744	42,004,990	40,035,204	37,477,642
Honduras	213,421	201,280	234,148	221,665
India	5,911,367	6,019,902	6,213,489	6,226,646
Indonesia	1,411,688	1,744,958	1,846,824	1,949,699
Italy	11,095,694	10,641,242	10,374,966	10,015,211
Japan	40,959,683	40,835,681	41,593,612	40,751,915
Korea, South	4,334,114	5,141,505	5,529,398	6,386,002
Latvia				
Liberia	80,285,176	74,906,390	70,718,439	67,564,201
Luxembourg				
Malta	132,861	231,353	425,563	906,736
Marshall Islands				

1984	1985	1986	1987	1988
559	559	1,048	51,875	323,469
2,172,850	2,088,349	2,368,462	2,404,559	2,365,923
3,191,971	3,907,267	5,985,011	9,105,182	8,962,892
8,414	8,408	7,572	8,348	8,470
2,406,714	2,400,292	2,419,661	2,268,383	2,118,422
620	620	620	620	620
14,913	14,913	14,913	13,824	9,610
3,558	3,558	3,558	3,558	3,558
3,449,496	3,343,823	3,160,043	2,971,155	2,902,394
9,300,358	10,568,236	11,566,974	12,314,477	12,919,876
3,958,418	4,327,487	4,272,795	4,512,749	4,631,474
977	1,302	1,261	1,795	1,187
6,727,887	8,196,056	10,616,809	15,650,207	18,390,642
5,211,262	4,942,175	4,651,224	4,714,495	4,321,851
6,412	6,412	6,412	6,412	6,412
8,945,046	8,237,418	5,936,268	5,141,304	4,104,270
			123,439	291,359
6,242,467	6,177,032	5,565,214	4,317,616	3,917,257
35,058,593	31,031,544	28,390,800	23,559,852	21,978,820
276,736	356,610	555,202	506,974	582,170
6,414,741	6,604,548	6,540,121	6,725,776	6,160,773
1,856,967	1,936,420	2,085,635	2,120,531	2,126,016
9,157,867	8,843,181	7,896,569	7,817,353	7,794,247
40,358,749	39,940,135	38,487,773	35,932,117	32,074,417
6,771,402	7,168,940	7,183,617	7,214,070	7,333,704
62,024,700	58,179,717	52,649,444	51,412,029	49,733,615
				1,731
1,366,149	1,855,807	2,014,947	1,725,984	2,685,888

APPENDIX A
(continued)

State	1980	1981	1982	1983
Mongolia				
Namibia				
Netherlands	5,723,845	5,467,486	5,393,104	4,939,806
Netherlands Antilles				
New Zealand	263,543	243,518	250,208	251,194
Cook Islands				
Norway	22,007,490	21,674,886	21,861,635	19,229,966
Norway (NIS)				
Panama	24,190,680	27,656,573	32,600,278	34,665,508
Philippines	1,927,869	2,539,817	2,773,855	2,964,472
Portugal	1,355,989	1,376,529	1,401,589	1,357,681
Portugal (MAR)				
Singapore	7,664,229	6,888,452	7,183,326	7,009,106
Spain	8,112,245	8,133,658	8,130,693	7,504,690
CSR				
St. Vincent and Grenadines	19,679	25,442	25,966	80,331
Sweden	4,233,977	4,033,893	3,787,567	3,437,683
Tonga	14,886	18,363	17,405	15,680
Turkey	1,454,838	1,663,679	2,127,921	2,524,374
Ukraine				
United Kingdom	27,135,155	25,419,427	22,505,265	19,121,457
Bermuda	1,723,682	499,029	474,402	819,450
Cayman Islands	256,715	279,771	311,396	329,893
Gibraltar	2,291	40,136	15,708	231,122
Isle of Man				
United States	18,464,271	18,908,281	19,111,092	19,358,496
USSR/Russia	23,443,534	23,492,898	23,788,668	24,549,350
Vanuatu		5,837	3,035	26,726
World	419,910,651	420,834,813	424,741,682	422,590,317

1984	1985	1986	1987	1988
4,585,991	4,301,234	4,324,135	3,513,574	3,293,976
			394,657	432,488
284,850	295,899	314,206	334,193	332,491
				4,314
17,662,916	15,338,557	9,294,630	6,359,349	9,350,303
37,244,233	40,674,201	41,305,009	43,254,716	44,604,071
3,441,076	4,593,979	6,922,499	8,681,227	9,311,555
1,571,007	1,436,892	1,114,444	1,028,090	961,645
6,512,344	6,504,582	6,267,627	7,098,116	7,208,974
7,004,852	6,256,188	5,422,002	4,845,310	4,320,452
101,176	235,183	509,878	699,947	900,477
3,520,352	3,161,939	2,516,614	2,269,511	2,116,079
16,038	17,252	16,349	18,295	13,585
3,124,784	3,684,357	3,423,745	3,336,093	3,281,153
15,874,062	14,343,512	11,567,117	6,567,595	6,108,406
822,123	980,707	1,208,276	1,925,297	3,774,298
347,825	413,752	1,389,903	706,160	476,505
247,458	583,270	1,612,948	2,827,098	3,041,811
			1,914,209	2,137,224
19,291,868	19,517,571	19,900,843	20,178,236	20,832,137
24,492,469	24,745,435	24,960,888	25,232,091	25,783,969
89,591	138,025	164,953	540,088	789,506
418,682,442	416,268,534	404,910,267	403,498,122	403,406,079

APPENDIX A
(continued)

State	1989	1990	1991	1992
Antigua and Barbuda	391,519	358,844	485,344	80,1645
Australia	2,494,021	2,511,785	2,571,867	2,688,503
Bahamas	11,578,891	13,626,335	17,541,196	20,616,451
Barbados	8,322	7,745	7,745	50,516
Belgium	2,043,594	1,954,478	314,198	240,922
Belize	620	620		37,459
Bolivia	9,610	9,610	9,610	9,610
Cambodia	3,558	3,558	3,558	3,558
Canada	2,824,852	2,744,221	2,684,614	2,610,035
China	13,513,578	13,899,448	14,298,912	13,899,468
China, Republic of (Taiwan)	5,169,337	5,766,283	5,888,100	6,192,796
Comoros	2,253	2,253	2,621	1,897
Cyprus	18,134,011	18,335,929	20,297,661	20,487,370
Denmark	772,321	547,164	572,491	533,549
DIS	4,013,098	4,460,349	5,125,762	4,735,837
Equatorial Guinea	6,412	6,412	6,412	6,527
France	3,950,653	3,382,591	3,432,383	3,409,587
French Antarctic Territory	335,384	337,577	446,988	458,013
Germany, Federal Republic of	3,966,571	4,300,786	5,971,254	5,360,064
Greece	21,324,340	20,521,561	22,752,919	25,738,640
Honduras	691,465	711,956	815,916	1,044,798
India	6,315,135	6,475,615	6,516,780	6,545,970
Indonesia	2,035,060	2,178,646	2,336,880	2,367,193
Italy	7,602,032	7,991,404	8,121,595	7,512,891
Japan	28,030,425	27,077,943	26,406,930	25,101,697
Korea, South	7,832,453	7,783,075	7,820,532	7,407,194
Latvia				1,206,565
Liberia	47,892,529	54,699,564	52,426,516	55,917,675
Luxembourg	3,542	3,338	1,703,482	1,655,551
Malta	3,329,120	4,518,682	6,916,325	11,004,869
Marshall Islands				1,675,899

1993	1994	1995	1996	1997
1,063,444	1,506,698	1,841,984	2,176,204	2,214,334
2,861,786	3,012,177	2,853,061	2,717,870	2,606,573
21,224,164	22,915,349	23,602,812	24,408,787	25,523,201
49,224	76,332	291,940	496,959	887,587
217,967	233,390	239,779	277,869	168,565
147,649	279,549	516,523	1,015,838	1,760,619
				2,426
5,772	5,772	59,958	206,225	438,651
2,540,984	2,489,520	2,401,047	2,406,161	2,526,567
14,944,999	15,826,688	16,943,220	16,992,863	16,338,610
6,071,191	5,996,103	6,104,294	6,174,535	5,931,264
1,897	1,897	1,897	2,138	1,530
22,842,009	23,292,954	24,652,547	23,798,904	23,652,626
677,190	572,695	627,356	684,182	678,372
4,615,542	5,125,947	5,119,877	5,200,332	5,075,438
3,457	3,457	3,457	20,618	35,817
2,701,333	2,132,299	1,820,403	1,756,663	2,107,636
1,550,960	2,116,011	2,266,040	2,534,242	2,462,746
4,978,566	5,696,088	5,626,178	5,842,091	6,949,555
29,134,435	30,161,758	29,434,695	27,507,109	25,288,452
1,116,137	1,206,252	1,205,989	1,197,837	1,052,971
6,574,733	6,485,374	7,126,850	7,127,246	6,934,329
2,440,471	2,678,333	2,770,513	2,972,579	3,195,007
7,033,237	6,818,178	6,699,484	6,594,302	6,193,692
24,247,525	22,101,606	19,913,211	19,200,927	18,516,363
7,047,183	7,004,199	6,972,148	7,557,931	7,429,510
1,154,993	1,033,778	798,144	723,362	318,784
53,918,534	57,647,708	59,800,742	59,988,908	60,058,368
1,326,526	1,143,185	880,819	878,477	820,441
14,163,357	15,455,370	17,678,303	19,479,431	22,984,206
2,197,961	2,149,430	3,098,574	4,897,062	6,314,364

APPENDIX A
(continued)

State	1989	1990	1991	1992
Mongolia				
Namibia				16,948
Netherlands	3,233,764	3,329,682	3,304,876	3,345,531
Netherlands Antilles	421,209	455,085	567,425	841,436
New Zealand	251,506	253,912	268,126	237,608
Cook Islands	5,090	6,311	6,723	47,736
Norway	2,231,107	1,983,884	1,862,787	2,018,482
Norway (NIS)	13,365,793	21,445,116	21,722,874	20,211,536
Panama	47,365,362	39,298,123	44,949,330	52,485,614
Philippines	9,384,757	8,514,876	8,625,561	8,470,441
Portugal	696,027	821,918	783,845	299,193
Portugal (MAR)		918	71,762	640,983
Singapore	7,272,506	77,927,866	8,488,172	9,905,142
Spain	3,863,483	3,712,860	3,533,839	2,420,272
CSR				
St. Vincent and Grenadines	1,486,102	1,936,814	2,709,794	4,698,481
Sweden	2,166,918	2,774,808	3,174,274	2,884,056
Tonga	34,800	39,584	39,596	10,666
Turkey	3,239,825	3,718,641	4,107,075	4,135,924
Ukraine				5,221,961
United Kingdom	5,524,809	4,883,753	4,668,817	4,081,240
Bermuda	4,076,093	4,258,282	3,036,987	3,338,357
Cayman Islands	410,981	415,018	395,099	363,492
Gibraltar	2,611,304	2,008,456	1,410,271	492,337
Isle of Man	2,111,324	1,824,532	1,937,529	1,627,509
United States	20,587,812	21,328,131	18,564,858	14,435,413
USSR/Russia	25,853,712	26,737,418	26,405,044	16,301,753
Vanuatu	920,333	2,163,618	2,172,621	2,064,392
World	410,480,693	423,627,198	436,026,858	445,168,553

1993	1994	1995	1996	1997
35,837	44,271	51,791	58,591	55,263
3,085,644	3,349,292	3,409,241	3,994,632	3,879,532
1,038,835	1,046,954	1,196,772	1,168,031	1,067,396
217,854	246,429	307,262	385,733	366,574
4,776	4,776	4,168	4,912	6,383
2,152,258	2,411,447	2,648,030	2,856,943	3,058,844
19,383,417	19,976,489	18,902,880	18,948,844	19,780,346
57,618,623	64,170,219	71,921,698	82,130,668	91,127,912
8,466,171	9,413,228	8,743,769	9,033,949	8,849,248
285,596	264,302	266,181	264,626	264,292
715,955	617,800	630,768	411,522	687,799
11,034,831	11,894,846	13,610,818	16,448,536	18,874,767
1,745,793	1,559,755	1,294,634	1,185,453	1,141,457
6,562	346	324,005	489,263	546,258
5,287,171	5,420,484	6,164,878	7,134,236	83,744,971
2,438,789	2,796,519	2,955,425	3,001,719	2,754,113
10,666	9,533	11,810	11,411	12,366
5,043,840	5,452,798	6,267,629	6,425,682	6,567,295
5,264,478	5,279,112	4,613,003	3,825,390	2,689,977
4,116,868	4,430,158	4,412,683	3,871,768	3,485,692
3,139,736	2,904,490	3,047,535	3,462,210	4,610,468
383,355	382,992	368,251	826,527	843,584
384,273	330,598	307,128	305,593	297,348
1,563,113	2,093,278	2,300,402	3,140,113	4,759,132
14,086,825	13,655,438	12,760,810	12,024,644	11,788,820
16,813,761	16,503,871	15,202,349	13,755,374	12,282,373
1,945,731	1,998,017	1,874,211	1,711,294	1,577,538
457,914,808	475,859,036	490,662,091	507,873,011	522,197,193

APPENDIX A
(continued)

State	1998	1999	2000	2001
Antigua and Barbuda	2,782,829	3,621,890	4,224,380	4,688,330
Australia	2,188,146	2,084,180	1,912,063	1,887,808
Bahamas	27,715,783	29,482,531	31,445,118	33,385,713
Barbados	687,586	724,797	733,319	687,331
Belgium	126,926	132,084	143,901	150,976
Belize	2,382,478	2,368,152	2,251,422	1,828,190
Bolivia	15,583	178,937	177,736	174,042
Cambodia	616,405	998,716	1,447,491	1,996,738
Canada	2,501,274	2,495,904	2,657,570	2,726,976
China	16,503,355	16,314,512	16,498,790	16,646,097
China, Republic of (Taiwan)	5,491,718	5,371,388	5,086,185	4,617,926
Comoros	1,202	744	19,866	53,801
Cyprus	23,301,517	23,641,000	23,206,439	22,761,778
Denmark	595,344	455,559	465,254	310,060
DIS	5,091,330	5,353,607	6,357,827	6,603,437
Equatorial Guinea	58,506	43,916	45,838	37,225
France	2,054,411	1,813,460	1,502,535	1,406,815
French Antarctic Territory	2,683,295	2,952,915	3,178,664	3,087,799
Germany, Federal Republic of	8,083,620	6,513,775	6,552,202	6,300,177
Greece	25,224,543	24,833,280	26,401,716	28,678,240
Honduras	1,083,193	1,219,554	1,110,987	966,511
India	6,777,102	6,914,780	6,662,093	6,688,153
Indonesia	3,252,093	3,241,462	3,384,240	3,613,139
Italy	6,818,632	8,048,464	9,048,652	9,654,983
Japan	17,780,396	17,062,556	15,256,624	14,564,840
Korea, South	5,694,216	5,734,806	6,199,801	6,394,994
Latvia	117,951	118,118	97,914	68,253
Liberia	60,492,104	54,107,214	51,450,917	51,784,010
Luxembourg	931,824	1,343,002	1,078,550	1,469,208
Malta	24,074,712	28,205,481	28,170,010	27,052,529
Marshall Islands	6,441,843	6,761,811	9,745,233	11,718,971

2002	2003	2004
5,066,005	6,004,650	6,914,568
1,861,321	1,905,778	1,971,876
35,798,075	34,751,748	35,388,244
327,593	467,653	580,262
186,748	1,392,901	3,973,267
1,473,200	1,533,673	1,687,460
358,070	420,356	302,971
2,425,828	2,048,296	1,821,464
2,797,619	2,723,001	2,663,566
17,315,517	18,427,955	20,369,157
4,289,028	3,477,144	3,556,310
407,206	416,739	388,519
22,997,023	22,054,166	21,283,373
307,626	320,356	297,125
7,095,429	7,246,602	7,284,769
28,546	31,299	27,933
1,541,221	1,459,752	1,375,270
3,032,279	3,285,721	3,524,865
6,545,767	6,111,779	8,246,428
28,782,843	32,203,117	32,040,682
933,244	812,524	784,125
6,142,073	6,960,567	7,517,583
3,723,052	3,840,408	4,072,144
9,595,897	10,245,809	10,955,957
13,917,948	13,561,521	13,180,189
7,049,734	6,757,400	7,826,141
88,741	90,927	294,295
50,400,182	52,434,624	53,898,761
1,493,785	1,005,966	689,658
26,331,381	25,134,314	22,352,570
14,672,878	17,628,157	22,494,505

APPENDIX A
(continued)

State	1998	1999	2000	2001
Mongolia				
Namibia	54,794	55,265	63,142	65,822
Netherlands	4,263,326	4,813,849	5,167,722	5,605,047
Netherlands Antilles	970,587	1,109,577	1,235,471	1,249,762
New Zealand	336,278	264,988	180,049	174,942
Cook Islands	6,652	6,652	5,925	5,202
Norway	3,218,007	3,650,755	3,912,084	3,585,968
Norway (NIS)	19,918,331	19,795,504	18,692,052	19,004,803
Panama	98,222,372	105,248,069	114,382,270	122,352,071
Philippines	8,508,313	7,650,058	7,002,097	6,029,876
Portugal	289,738	295,129	281,757	276,036
Portugal (MAR)	839,763	869,638	909,735	923,208
Singapore	20,370,399	21,780,112	21,491,085	21,022,604
Spain	1,206,765	1,269,002	1,552,626	517,192
CSR	631,496	634,079	477,462	1,630,353
St. Vincent and Grenadines	7,875,497	7,105,479	7,026,358	7,072,895
Sweden	2,552,365	2,946,851	2,886,973	2,957,871
Tonga	22,205	25,071	25,319	337,622
Turkey	6,251,395	6,324,631	5,832,717	5,896,708
Ukraine	2,033,160	1,775,161	1,546,281	1,407,736
United Kingdom	4,084,970	4,331,016	5,531,986	6,029,066
Bermuda	4,810,939	6,186,973	5,751,816	5,312,780
Cayman Islands	1,281,638	1,164,588	1,796,353	2,053,934
Gibraltar	313,681	450,576	604,008	816,323
Isle of Man	4,202,970	4,728,579	5,430,510	6,057,118
United States	11,851,660	12,025,775	11,110,901	10,907,179
USSR/Russia	11,089,922	10,648,965	10,485,916	10,247,803
Vanuatu	1,602,226	1,444,160	1,378,832	1,496,422
World	531,893,296	543,609,561	558,053,957	574,551,264

Source: Lloyd's Register Fairplay, *World Fleet Statistics 1953–2004* (London: Lloyd's Register Fairplay, 1954–2005).

2002	2003	2004
	336,836	359,901
69,488	74,524	92,299
5,664,268	5,702,641	5,622,902
1,391,130	1,510,656	1,661,631
180,435	205,188	206,415
7,971	17,615	26,108
3,779,968	3,512,740	3,519,717
18,414,575	16,996,583	15,416,521
124,729,059	125,721,658	131,451,672
5,319,573	5,115,708	5,137,022
267,876	263,868	193,174
831,807	892,466	1,143,306
21,148,090	23,240,945	26,282,777
560,911	676,163	1,045,804
1,810,290	1,974,844	1,823,323
6,583,995	6,318,042	6,324,289
3,177,541	3,579,269	3,666,905
290,529	169,975	109,074
5,658,754	4,950,588	4,678,885
1,349,867	1,378,806	1,144,777
8,045,095	10,843,724	11,122,871
4,798,336	4,844,432	6,166,162
2,376,980	2,801,797	2,608,796
960,898	993,022	1,142,448
5,671,930	6,416,425	7,168,533
10,371,488	10,408,896	10,744,126
10,379,992	10,430,783	8,638,887
1,381,351	1,618,179	1,756,498
585,583,396	605,218,368	633,321,120

APPENDIX B
International Agreements Pertaining to Standards on Ships

Environment

International Convention for the Prevention of Pollution of the Sea by Oil (OILPOL) (1954)
International Convention Relating to Intervention on the High Seas in Cases of Oil Pollution Casualties (1969)
International Convention on Civil Liability for Oil Pollution Damage (CLC) (1969)
Convention Relating to Civil Liability in the Field of Maritime Carriage of Nuclear Material (1971)
International Convention on the Establishment of an International Fund for Compensation for Oil Pollution Damage (FUND) (1971)
Convention on the Prevention of Marine Pollution by Dumping of Wastes and Other Matter (1972)
Protocol to the International Convention Relating to Intervention on the High Seas in Cases of Pollution Other Than Oil (1973)
International Convention for the Prevention of Pollution from Ships (MARPOL) (1973/1978)
MARPOL Annex I/II
MARPOL Annex III
MARPOL Annex IV
MARPOL Annex V
Convention on Limitation of Liability for Maritime Claims (LLMC) (1976)
Protocol to the International Convention on Civil Liability for Oil Pollution Damage (1976)
Protocol to the International Convention on the Establishment of an International Fund for Compensation for Oil Pollution Damage (FUND Protocol) (1976)
International Convention on Oil Pollution Preparedness, Response and Cooperation (OPRC) (1990)
Protocol to the International Convention on Civil Liability for Oil Pollution Damage (1992)
Protocol to the International Convention on the Establishment of an International Fund for Compensation for Oil Pollution Damage (FUND Protocol) (1992)

Protocol to the Convention on Prevention of Marine Pollution by Dumping of Wastes and Other Matter (1996)

Protocol to MARPOL (Annex VI) (1996)

Protocol to the Convention on Limitation of Liability for Maritime Claims (LLMC Protocol) (1996)

Protocol on Preparedness, Response and Cooperation to Pollution Incidents by Hazardous and Noxious Substances (OPRC/HNS Protocol) (2000)

International Convention on the Control of Harmful Anti-Fouling Systems on Ships (AFS) (2001)

International Convention on Civil Liability for Bunker Oil Pollution Damage (2001)

Safety

Prevention of Accidents (Seafarers) Convention (1970) [ILO C134]

International Convention on Load Lines (1966)

Special Trade Passenger Ships Agreement (STP) (1971)

Convention on International Regulations for Preventing Collisions at Sea (COLREG) (1972)

International Convention for Safe Containers (CSC) (1972)

Protocol on Space Requirements for Special Trade Passenger Ships (1973)

SOLAS Convention (1974)

Convention on the International Maritime Satellite Organisation (INMARSAT) (1976)

Operating Agreement for the International Maritime Satellite Organisation (1976)

Torremolinos International Convention for the Safety of Fishing Vessels (SFV) (1977)

Convention on Standards of Training, Certification and Watchkeeping (STCW) (1978)

SOLAS Protocol (1978)

International Convention on Maritime Search and Rescue (SAR) (1979)

SOLAS Protocol (1988)

Protocol to the International Convention on Load Lines (1988)

Convention for the Suppression of Unlawful Acts against the Safety of Maritime Navigation (SUA) (1988)

SFV Protocol (1993)
Convention on Standards of Training, Certification and Watchkeeping for Fishing Vessel Personnel (STCW-F) (1995)
IMO: Stockholm Agreement (Ferry Safety) (1996)

Labor

Conventions all under the auspices of the International Labour Organisation

C7: Minimum Age (Sea) Convention (1920)
C8: Unemployment Indemnity (Shipwreck) Convention (1920)
C9: Placing of Seamen Convention (1920)
C16: Medical Examination of Young Persons (Sea) Convention (1921)
C22: Seamen's Articles of Government Convention (1926)
C23: Repatriation of Seamen Convention (1926)
C53: Officers' Competency Certificates Convention (1936)
C54: Holidays with Pay (Sea) Convention (1936)
C55: Shipowners' Liability (Sick and Injured Seamen) Convention (1936)
C56: Sickness Insurance (Sea) Convention (1936)
C57: Hours of Work and Manning (Sea) Convention (1936)
C58: Minimum Age (Sea) Convention (1936)
C68: Food and Catering (Ships' Crew) Convention (1946)
C69: Certification of Ships' Cooks Convention (1946)
C70: Social Security (Seafarers) Convention (1946)
C71: Seafarers' Pensions Convention (1946)
C72: Paid Vacations (Seafarers) Convention (1946)
C73: Medical Examination (Seafarers) Convention (1946)
C74: Certification of Able Seamen Convention (1946)
C75: Accommodations of Crew Convention (1946)
C76: Wages, Hours of Work, and Manning (Sea) Convention (1946)
C87: Freedom of Association and Protection of the Right to Organize Convention (1948)
C91: Paid Vacations (Seafarers) Convention (Revised) (1949)
C92: Accommodation of Crews Convention (Revised) (1949)

C93: Wages, Hours of Work, and Manning (Sea) Convention (Revised) (1949)

C98: Rights to Organize and Collective Bargaining Convention (1949)

C108: Seafarers' Identity Documents Convention (1958)

C109: Wages, Hours of Work, and Manning (Sea) Convention (Revised) (1958)

C112: Minimum Age (Fishermen) Convention (1959)

C113: Medical Examination (Fishermen) Convention (1959)

C114: Fishermen's Articles of Agreement Convention (1959)

C125: Fishermen's Competency Certificates Convention (1966)

C126: Accommodation of Crews (Fishermen) Convention (1966)

C133: Accommodation of Crews (Supplementary Provisions) Convention (1970)

C134: Prevention of Accidents (Seafarers) Convention (1970)

C138: Minimum Age Convention (1973)

C145: Continuity of Employment (Seafarers) Convention (1976)

C146: Seafarers' Annual Leave with Pay Convention (1976)

C147: Merchant Shipping (Minimum Standards) Convention (1976)

P147: Labor Protocol to Merchant Shipping (Minimum Standards) Convention (1996)

C163: Seafarers' Welfare Convention (1987)

C164: Health Protection and Medical Care (Seafarers) Convention (1987)

C165: Social Security (Seafarers) Convention (Revised) (1987) [revision of C70]

C166: Social Security (Seafarers) Convention (Revised) (1987) [revision of C23]

C178: Labour Inspection (Seafarers) Convention (1996)

C179: Recruitment and Placement of Seafarers Convention (1996)

C180: Seafarers' Hours of Work and the Manning of Ships Convention (1996)

APPENDIX C
Percentage of International Agreements Adopted by Selected Registries

State	GT2004	Total environ-ment (out of 24)	Environ-mental (percent-age)	Total labor (out of 47)	Labor (percentage)	Total safety (out of 19)	Safety (percentage)
Panama	131,451,672	13	54.17	24	51.06	8	42.11
Liberia	53,898,761	17	70.83	14	29.79	11	57.89
Bahamas	35,388,244	16	66.67	6	12.77	10	52.63
Greece	32,040,682	16	66.67	22	46.81	15	78.95
Singapore	26,282,777	13	54.17	5	10.64	11	57.89
Hong Kong	26,085,134	15	62.50	13	27.66	13	68.42
Marshall Islands	22,494,505	16	66.67	0	0.00	11	57.89
Malta	22,352,570	15	62.50	14	29.79	11	57.89
Cyprus	21,283,373	14	58.33	9	19.15	14	73.68
China	20,369,157	13	54.17	5	10.64	12	63.16
NIS (Norway)	15,416,521	22	91.67	32	68.09	18	94.74
Japan	13,180,189	18	75.00	13	27.66	13	68.42
United Kingdom	11,122,871	19	79.17	22	46.81	16	84.21
Italy	10,955,957	17	70.83	29	61.70	15	78.95
United States	10,744,126	9	37.50	7	14.89	12	63.16
Russian Federation	8,638,887	16	66.67	17	36.17	14	73.68

GIS (Germany)	8,246,428	21	87.50	22	46.81	16	84.21
Korea, Republic of	7,826,141	14	58.33	2	4.26	12	63.16
India	7,517,583	15	62.50	3	6.38	14	73.68
DIS (Denmark)	7,284,769	22	91.67	20	42.55	16	84.21
Isle of Man (UK)	7,168,533	17	70.83	21	44.68	15	78.95
Antigua and Barbuda	6,914,568	13	54.17	4	8.51	7	36.84
St. Vincent and Grenadines	6,324,289	12	50.00	7	14.89	10	52.63
Bermuda (UK)	6,166,162	17	70.83	22	46.81	15	78.95
Netherlands	5,622,902	18	75.00	28	59.57	15	78.95
Phillippines	5,137,022	9	37.50	7	14.89	7	36.84
Turkey	4,678,885	7	29.17	14	29.79	9	47.37
Indonesia	4,072,144	6	25.00	3	6.38	10	52.63
Belgium	3,973,267	17	70.83	29	61.70	11	57.89
Sweden	3,666,905	23	95.83	22	46.81	17	89.47
Taiwan	3,556,310	0	0.00	0	0.00	0	0.00
French Antarctic Territory	3,524,865	18	75.00	30	63.83	16	84.21
Norway	3,519,717	22	91.67	32	68.09	18	94.74
Canada	2,663,566	13	54.17	12	25.53	9	47.37
Brazil	2,628,338	8	33.33	23	48.94	10	52.63
Cayman Islands (UK)	2,608,796	18	75.00	22	46.81	13	68.42
Australia	1,971,876	20	83.33	18	38.30	12	63.16
CSR (Spain)	1,823,323	24	100.00	36	76.60	15	78.95
Cambodia	1,821,464	9	37.50	3	6.38	7	36.84
Vanuatu	1,756,498	20	83.33	0	0.00	10	52.63

APPENDIX C
(continued)

State	GT2004	Total environment (out of 24)	Environmental (percentage)	Total labor (out of 47)	Labor (percentage)	Total safety (out of 19)	Safety (percentage)
Belize	1,687,460	9	37.50	21	44.68	6	31.58
Saudi Arabia	1,678,474	10	41.67	0	0.00	10	52.63
Netherlands Antilles	1,661,631	18	75.00	28	59.57	15	78.95
Finland	1,428,880	21	87.50	26	55.32	14	73.68
France	1,375,270	20	83.33	42	89.36	16	84.21
Ukraine	1,144,777	7	29.17	15	31.91	11	57.89
MAR (Portugal)	1,143,306	15	62.50	18	38.30	12	63.16
Gibraltar (UK)	1,142,448	13	54.17	20	42.55	13	68.42
Spain	1,045,804	24	100.00	36	76.60	15	78.95
Venezuela	1,010,860	13	54.17	5	10.64	8	42.11
Honduras	784,125	5	20.83	4	8.51	7	36.84
Luxembourg	689,658	8	33.33	20	42.55	9	47.37
Barbados	580,262	15	62.50	8	17.02	10	52.63
Myanmar	444,330	2	8.33	3	6.38	6	31.58
Argentina	436,738	12	50.00	14	29.79	13	68.42
Comoros	388,519	8	33.33	3	6.38	6	31.58
Estonia	334,920	11	45.83	12	25.53	9	47.37
Bolivia	302,971	6	25.00	3	6.38	7	36.84

Denmark	297,125	22	91.67	20	42.55	16	84.21
Latvia	294,295	15	62.50	8	17.02	13	68.42
New Zealand	206,415	14	58.33	15	31.91	13	68.42
Portugal	193,174	15	62.50	18	38.30	12	63.16
Lebanon	184,055	8	33.33	11	23.40	8	42.11
Poland	162,736	20	83.33	24	51.06	11	57.89
Sri Lanka	156,608	12	50.00	8	17.02	9	47.37
Jamaica	131,215	14	58.33	7	14.89	7	36.84
Tonga	109,074	18	75.00	0	0.00	13	68.42
Mauritius	79,000	15	62.50	8	17.02	9	47.37
São Tomé and Príncipe	57,809	6	25.00	3	6.38	7	36.84
Equatorial Guinea	27,933	9	37.50	5	10.64	8	42.11
Cook Islands (NZ)	26,108	14	58.33	15	31.91	13	68.42

APPENDIX D
Port-State Control Detention Ratios: Paris, Tokyo, and the U.S. Coast Guard

	Paris MOU Detention Ratio (annual detention rate divided by annual								
State	1985	1986	1987	1988	1989	1990	1991	1992	1993
Antigua and Barbuda			1.09	0.78	1.05	0.41	1.00	0.92	0.91
Argentina						0.99	2.03	1.40	0.00
Australia						0.00	0.00	0.00	0.00
Bahamas	0.763			0.919		0.716	1.178	1.005	0.482
Barbados						0	13.7	0	0
Belgium			1.892			0.597		2.094	0.00
Belize									9.35
Bolivia								0	0.00
Brazil				1.353	3.175	0	1.37	0.474	1.59
Cambodia									
Canada						0	0	0	6.23
China			0.9		0.895	1.449	0.354	1.069	0.739
China, Rep. (Taiwan)							0	0	0.35
Comoros						0			
Cyprus	1.626	1.742	1.336	0.884	1.412	1.494	1.387	1.395	1.69
Denmark						0.36	0.168	0.253	0.316
Faeroes						1.758	0	1.005	0.98
Equatorial Guinea									9.35
Estonia							0	0.359	1.03
France						0.688	0.498	0.231	0.561
Germany						0.387	0.381	0.161	0.401
Greece	0.94					0.706	0.973	0.921	1.008
Honduras	2.952	5.11	1.077	4.252	4.076	3.262	2.138	2.981	3.14
India					4.301	2.26	2.019	4.799	1.30
Indonesia						7.032	3.914	0	4.15
Jamaica									
Japan						0	0.668	0.318	0.389
Korea, South	1.493					1.758	0.637	0	1.206
Latvia								0.331	1.159
Lebanon	3.072	1.42	1.318		1.839	2.693	2.834	1.092	2.526
Liberia						1.117	1.482	0.961	0.54
Luxembourg						0	0	0.644	0.34
Malta	4.768	3.157	2.855	1.926	1.847	3.047	2.705	1.089	1.408
Marshall Islands						4.521	3.425	2.284	0

regional average)										
1994	1995	1996	1997	1998	1999	2000	2001	2002	2003	2004
0.64	0.587	0.624	0.621	0.594	0.519	0.565	0.641	0.714	0.692	0.664
3.04	1.115	1.558	0	0			5.501			
0.00	0	4.673	0	0		0				
0.535	0.481	0.587	0.56	0.751	0.586	0.705	0.598	0.539	0.565	0.509
0	0.731	1.113	0.697	0.511	0.127	0.619	0.579	0.288	0.967	0.459
1.42	0	0	0	0	0	0	0	1.253	1.418	0.438
2.66	2.379	2.259	3.594	3.345	3.255	2.612	1.473	2.55	1.389	1.611
				8.278	7.65	5.263	5.177	7.628	3.733	3.805
1.36	1.784	2.67	0	0.818	1.15	0	1.834	0.895	1.891	4.281
		1.335	2.123	1.86	3.32	3.433	2.58	2.769	3.193	2.209
0.00	1.487	0.935	2.07	1.84	3.123	0	0	0	0	0
0.943	1.526	1.326	0.625	0.686	0.248	0.409	0.393	0.133	0.478	0.199
0.76	0.515	0.164	0.23	0.394	0.729	0.752	11	1.474	1.289	4.567
		0					7.334	5.013	4.342	3.154
1.31	1.04	1.151	1.205	1.199	1.089	1.022	0.974	0.931	1.05	0.978
0.4	0.268	0.253	0.267	0.649	0.214	0.363	0.354	0.569	0.494	0.252
0.00	0.991	1.649	0.739	1.84	1.987	1.17	0.734	0.783	1.668	1.142
			0	3.311	1.561	2.871	6.286		0	
1.16	1.107	1.226	0.767	0.957	0.643	0.697	0.871	0.845	1.793	0.248
0.438	0.238	0.195	0.668	0.225	4.586	0.332	0.268	0.653	0	0.219
0.361	0.269	0.231	0.22	0.238	0.287	0.328	0.369	0.138	0.287	0.291
1.277	1.043	0.983	0.712	0.771	0.639	0.594	0.538	0.615	0.651	0.897
2.44	2.914	3.132	3.341	3.832	4.495	3.74	3.048	3.367	4.933	3.425
1.55	0.679	0.117	0.851	0.184	1.317	1.094	1.811	0.709	1.455	1.557
4.25	0	0	3.451	0	0	7.018	11			17.12
								6.266	0	2.447
0.177	0.372	0	0	0	0	0.421	0	0	0	0
0	0.622	0.534	0.478	0.409	0	0.376	1.065	0	1.576	0.428
1.099	0.966	0.637	1.01	1.623	1.599	0.81	0.55	0.783	0	0.611
2.48	1.784	3.197	3.583	3.566	3.264	3.551	3.868	3.381	3.767	3.877
0.533	0.373	0.503	0.5	0.627	0.445	0.536	0.327	0.46	0.47	0.469
0.708	0.223	0.623	0.531	0.368	0.248	0.185	0.361	0.182	0.216	0
1.816	1.543	1.312	1.264	1.159	1.162	1.244	1.043	0.926	0.887	1.214
1.012	0.388	0.33	0.285	0.321	0.293	0.505	0.562	0.482	0.528	0.368

APPENDIX D
(continued)

State	Paris MOU Detention Ratio (annual detention rate divided by annual							
	1985	1986	1987	1988	1989	1990	1991	1992	1993
Mauritius						0		0	7.477
Myanmar						0	1.522	1.142	1.206
Netherlands						0.246	0.398	0.54	0.428
Netherlands Antilles						0.428	0.814	1.216	0.452
New Zealand							0		
Cook Islands									
Norway						0.809	0.722	0.568	0.475
Panama	1.408	0.992	1.337	1.147	0.858	1.393	1.791	1.666	1.279
Phillippines	1.054	0.842	1.272			0.952	0.618	1.523	0.681
Poland						0.101	0.157	0.238	0.399
Portugal					1.616	0	0	1.753	1.466
Russian Federation						0.134	0.257	0.484	1.017
São Tomé and Príncipe									
Saudi Arabia		0.888				0	0	0	
Singapore						0.226	0.23	0.445	0.603
Spain	0.964		0.9	1.222	0.784	0.525	1.279	0.661	0.74
Sri Lanka						1.319	1.712	0	1.335
St. Vincent			3.14	3.634	3.831	3.058	3.032	2.747	2.013
Sweden			1.288			0.446	0.362	0.394	0.757
Tonga									
Turkey	0.831	2.357	2.952	0.984	0.86	1.905	1.116	1.59	2.146
Ukraine								0	0.637
United Kingdom				0.814	0.768	0.438	0.604	0.613	0.3
Bermuda						0	0	0.866	0
Cayman Islands		3.839				3.165	3.914	4.711	1.1
Gibraltar	2.987	2.185	4.1	2.418		4.747		0	0
Isle of Man				1.536	0.92	0.609	1.274	1.047	0
United States						0.891	0.87	0.364	0
Vanuatu						1.073	0	0.474	1.068
Venezuela						4.219	1.957	0	4.673
Regional average	5.58	3.52	2.71	3.52	3.75	3.16	3.65	3.98	5.35

Source: Paris MOU, *Annual Reports 1985–2004* (The Hague: Paris MOU, 1986–2005).

regional average)

1994	1995	1996	1997	1998	1999	2000	2001	2002	2003	2004
0	1.274	2.077	3.451	2.759	1.093	1.504	0	0		
1.518	0	0.467	0.545	0	0	1.17	0	0	0	0
0.458	0.413	0.35	0.332	0.326	0.319	0.452	0.267	0.474	0.309	0.449
0.775	0.804	0.876	0.913	0.69	0.874	0.585	0.417	0.387	0.633	0.998
	0			0					0	17.12
			0					12.53	7.092	6.849
0.481	0.496	0.552	0.299	0.432	0.349	0.408	0.428	0.472	0.495	0.428
1.296	1.131	1.209	1.193	1.11	1.055	1.215	1.136	1.182	0.991	1.205
1.028	0.543	0.954	0.789	0.984	0.729	0.513	0.175	1.099	0.519	0
0.656	0.721	0.804	0.391	0.764	0.556	0.506	0.175	0.855	0.721	0.952
1.308	1.338	0.482	0.357	0.88	0.979	1.003	0.757	0.718	0.155	0.555
0.968	1.004	1.067	1.024	1.143	0.991	0.754	0.826	0.885	0.797	1.259
					4.372	5.263	5.077	6.266	0	
0	0.686		0.45	0	1.093	0.421	0	0	0	0
0.169	0.295	0.435	0.473	0.386	0.439	0.269	0.684	4.843	0.472	0.546
0.886	0.478	0.187	0.586	0.245	0.533	0.596	0.197	0.634	1.081	0.325
0	0	0	0.863	0	0	3.509		0	7.092	0
1.694	1.709	1.759	1.812	1.854	1.962	1.695	1.903	2.214	2.201	2.277
0.429	0.161	0.153	0.378	0.175	0.278	0.146	0.213	0.246	0.22	0.51
							3.667	5.322	5.911	3.805
1.94	2.912	3.169	2.515	1.944	2.679	2.508	2.705	2.353	2.481	1.478
0.713	1.282	1.6	1.181	1.286	1.681	1.443	1.633	1.439	1.887	1.274
0.392	0.302	0.214	0.426	0.133	0.354	0	0	0.288	0.323	0.173
0.304	0	0.334	0.207	0.34	0.317	0	0.603	0.209	0.194	0.202
0	0	1.121	0.37	0.92	0.926	1.008	0.898	0.822	0.308	0.611
2.657	1.487	2.336	0	0	1.821	1.108	0.289	1.104	0.391	1.197
0.599	0.432	0.374	0.796	0.442	0.546	0.258	0.272	0.113	0.282	0.211
0.599	0.313	0.203	0	0.35	0.377	0.413	0.344	0	0	0.276
1.226	0.731	1.1	0.69	0.662	0.28	0.658	0.449	0.348	0	1.351
3.188	0	3.115		3.679				6.266		
9.41	11.21	10.7	9.66	9.06	9.15	9.5	9.09	7.98	7.05	5.84

APPENDIX D
(continued)

State	Tokyo MOU Detention Ratio (annual detention rate divided by annual regional average)										
	1994	1995	1996	1997	1998	1999	2000	2001	2002	2003	2004
Antigua and Barbuda	0.97	0.28	0.00	1.10	0.99	1.31	0.54	0.76	0.55	0.53	0.73
Argentina									7.50	0.00	0.00
Australia	0.00	0.00	0.00	0.78	0.00	0.00	0.00	0.00	0.00	0.00	0.00
Bahamas	0.18	0.41	0.44	0.44	0.40	0.59	0.36	0.41	0.39	0.43	0.50
Barbados	0.00		0.00	0.00	1.05	0.00	2.08	0.00	1.87	0.00	0.00
Belgium	0.00	0.00			0.00		0.00		0.00	0.00	1.10
Belize	3.95	1.94	2.23	2.79	3.87	3.70	2.74	3.54	2.94	2.24	2.41
Bolivia							7.28	5.37	6.43	5.30	4.27
Brazil	1.88	5.62	1.78	0.00	4.57	3.48	7.28	4.30	3.00	1.31	2.05
Cambodia				2.75	3.28	5.01	3.09	3.80	3.80	3.13	2.81
Canada			0.00						0.00	0.00	0.00
China	2.62	2.07	2.29	1.67	0.94	0.89	0.43	0.33	0.26	0.20	0.26
China, Rep. (Taiwan)	1.25	1.08	1.22	1.03	1.13	0.99	1.60	1.21	0.86	1.87	1.50
Comoros				0.00	0.00	0.00		0.00	0.00	0.00	3.41
Cyprus	1.62	1.57	1.56	1.35	0.78	0.75	0.73	0.84	0.95	0.83	0.81
Denmark	0.00	0.48	0.00	0.30	0.43	0.48	0.39	0.65	0.00	0.00	0.38
Equatorial Guinea				0.00	4.57	0.00					
France	0.00	0.73	1.27	1.08	1.19	0.00	0.00	0.39	0.00	0.00	0.31
Germany	0.00	0.37	0.00	0.00	0.49	0.36	0.10	0.75	0.25	0.56	0.29
Greece	1.18	0.92	1.21	0.64	0.53	0.86	0.67	0.38	0.48	0.60	0.36
Honduras	0.48	2.63	1.47	2.16	1.76	1.24	2.39	2.11	2.39	6.60	5.66
India	1.42	1.44	1.53	0.87	0.91	0.95	1.31	0.64	1.42	0.86	0.69
Indonesia	2.06	2.91	2.43	3.20	1.99	2.25	5.56	4.09	3.23	3.08	4.30
Japan	0.17	0.42	0.53	0.42	0.42	0.23	0.17	0.36	0.35	0.89	0.60
Korea (South)	1.29	0.83	1.18	0.60	1.37	1.27	1.30	0.80	0.35	0.24	0.04
Latvia	0.00	16.86	8.88	0.00	0.00	0.00	0.00	0.00		0.00	0.00
Lebanon	8.77	2.81	0.00	0.00	0.00		0.00	0.00	0.00	0.00	7.68
Liberia	1.09	0.80	0.79	0.42	0.67	0.40	0.45	0.39	0.48	0.37	0.56
Luxembourg	0.00	0.00	0.00	0.00	0.00	0.00	0.00	0.00	0.00	0.00	0.00
Malta	0.93	1.26	1.71	1.18	2.04	1.17	1.03	0.88	1.02	0.79	1.22
Marshall Islands	2.39	1.69	1.11	0.00	0.27	0.57	0.48	0.33	0.32	0.30	0.58
Mauritius	8.77	0.00		15.60			0.00	0.00	0.00	0.00	0.00
Myanmar	0.00	0.64	0.61	0.92	0.72	1.18	0.77	1.50	0.00	2.23	1.57
Netherlands	0.00	0.00	0.15	0.23	0.08	0.28	0.37	0.11	0.71	0.56	0.48
N. Antilles	0.00	1.20	0.81	0.00	0.00	0.00	0.00	0.00	1.67	0.57	0.39

APPENDIX D
(continued)

State	Tokyo MOU Detention Ratio (annual detention rate divided by annual regional average)										
	1994	1995	1996	1997	1998	1999	2000	2001	2002	2003	2004
New Zealand	0.00	0.00	0.00	0.00	0.91	1.27	0.00	0.00	0.00	0.00	0.00
Cook Islands			0.00	0.00	0.00	13.93	0.00	0.00	0.00	0.00	0.00
Norway	1.01	0.75	0.41	0.42	0.25	0.41	0.52	0.22	0.34	0.43	0.30
Panama	0.79	0.89	0.65	0.79	0.70	0.69	0.67	0.71	0.65	0.68	0.69
Phillippines	1.13	1.02	0.72	0.37	0.51	0.72	0.77	0.37	0.60	0.57	0.50
Poland	0.00	0.00	0.63	1.30	3.43	0.00	7.28	0.00		11.78	0.00
Portugal	0.00	0.00	0.00	0.00	4.57	0.00	0.00	0.00	0.00	2.36	3.07
Russian Federation	0.65	0.99	0.75	0.89	1.08	1.89	1.78	1.50	1.24	0.82	1.15
São Tomé and Príncipe								2.97	3.00	0.00	0.00
Saudi Arabia	2.63	1.12	1.61	2.40	2.74	0.00	0.00	0.99	0.00	0.00	0.00
Singapore	0.49	0.84	0.51	0.90	0.75	0.60	0.71	0.32	0.56	0.57	0.63
Spain				0.00		0.00	0.00	0.00	0.00	2.94	0.00
Sri Lanka	0.00	0.00	0.00	0.00	1.96	0.00	0.00	0.00	0.00	0.00	6.144
St. Vincent	1.49	1.15	1.66	2.75	2.17	1.56	1.41	0.88	1.50	1.05	1.06
Sweden	0.00	0.00	0.00	0.00	0.00	0.00	0.00	0.00	0.79	0.00	0.00
Tonga	0.00	0.00	0.57	2.60	0.91	1.64	0.86	0.54	1.87	3.05	1.10
Turkey	2.45	1.72	2.05	1.91	2.19	2.37	1.17	1.17	1.85	0.91	1.35
Ukraine	0.00	1.81	3.23	2.34	0.00	0.00	4.16	0.00	1.36	2.94	0.00
United Kingdom	0.00	0.00	0.00	0.21	0.53	0.24	0.00	0.17	0.25	0.22	0.26
Bermuda	0.00	0.00	0.00	0.00	0.00	0.44	0.00	0.60	0.00	0.47	0.31
Cayman Islands	0.00		0.00	0.00	0.86	2.23	0.00	0.34	1.96	0.75	0.53
Gibraltar	8.77					0.00	0.00	0.00	0.00	0.00	1.62
Isle of Man	0.00	0.00	0.00	0.54	0.00	0.57	0.00	0.00	0.30	0.55	0.46
United States	0.00	0.50	0.63	0.62	0.00	0.93	0.00	0.74	0.46	0.00	0.29
Vanuatu	0.00	0.37	0.59	0.00	0.28	0.17	0.38	0.37	0.18	0.34	0.85
Venezuela	8.77		0.00				2.08				
Regional average	3.80	5.93	5.63	6.41	7.29	7.18	6.87	7.76	6.67	8.49	6.51

Source: Tokyo MOU, *Annual Reports on Port State Control in the Asia-Pacific Region 1994–2004* (Tokyo: Tokyo MOU, 1995–2005).

APPENDIX D
(continued)

State	U.S. Coast Guard Detention Ratio (detentions by "distinct vessel arrivals" divided by regional average)						
	1998	1999	2000	2001	2002	2003	2004
Antigua and Barbuda	0.90	0.75	0.88	1.11	0.76	1.07	1.16
Argentina	16.67	0.00	0.00	0.00	0.00	0.00	
Australia	0.00	0.00	0.00	0.00	0.00	0.00	0.00
Bahamas	0.74	0.73	0.44	1.36	0.66	0.76	0.41
Barbados	0.00	1.25	0.00	0.00	0.00	0.00	0.00
Belgium	0.00	0.00	0.00	0.00	0.00	0.00	0.00
Belize	5.11	8.97	7.09	2.06	6.09	0.00	0.00
Bolivia			30.49	12.35	0.00	19.53	0.00
Brazil	0.00	0.00	0.00	16.46	5.35	0.00	10.48
Cambodia		0.00	20.33	8.82	9.05	14.20	6.99
Canada	0.00	0.00	0.00	0.00	1.28	2.79	0.00
China	0.56	1.11	0.00	0.75	0.00	0.95	0.56
China, Rep. (Taiwan)	0.93	0.00	1.00	1.26	0.00	0.00	0.00
Cyprus	1.70	1.22	0.89	1.02	1.33	1.09	1.44
Denmark	0.14	0.00	0.30	0.46	0.49	0.00	1.44
Equatorial Guinea	0.00	0.00	0.00	0.00	0.00	0.00	
Estonia	0.00	2.99	0.00	0.00	0.00	0.00	0.00
France	0.65	0.00	0.00	0.00	0.00	0.00	4.19
Germany	0.72	0.18	0.55	0.32	0.00	0.63	0.92
Greece	0.46	0.48	0.66	0.60	0.60	0.49	1.01
Honduras	2.90	6.62	6.00	1.58	2.10	3.00	1.31
Hong Kong	0.59	0.37	0.88	0.92	0.44	0.00	0.70
India	0.46	3.09	3.34	1.82	0.95	0.00	2.62
Indonesia	0.00	4.48	0.00	0.00	0.00	0.00	
Jamaica	0.00	0.00	0.00	0.00	0.00	26.04	0.00
Japan	1.57	0.61	1.17	0.00	0.00	0.00	0.00
Korea (South)	0.32	1.06	0.00	2.81	0.64	0.00	0.00
Latvia	0.00	7.47	5.54	0.00	0.00	0.00	7.86
Lebanon		0.00	0.00	0.00	0.00	0.00	
Liberia	0.56	0.80	0.36	0.61	0.76	0.38	0.77
Luxembourg	0.00	0.00	0.00	0.00	0.00	0.00	0.00
Malta	1.33	1.08	1.60	1.25	1.65	1.64	1.86
Marshall Islands	0.00	0.00	0.33	1.93	0.79	0.20	0.00
Mauritius	0.00	0.00	0.00	0.00	0.00	0.00	
Myanmar	0.00	0.00	0.00	0.00	0.00	0.00	

APPENDIX D
(continued)

State	U.S. Coast Guard Detention Ratio (detentions by "distinct vessel arrivals" divided by regional average)						
	1998	1999	2000	2001	2002	2003	2004
Netherlands	0.50	0.00	0.00	0.27	0.27	0.33	1.04
Netherlands Antilles	1.17	0.00	0.94	2.17	2.45	1.09	2.52
New Zealand	0.00	0.00				0.00	0.00
Norway	0.27	0.08	0.52	0.25	0.32	0.24	1.05
Panama	1.31	1.38	1.42	0.90	1.15	1.54	1.15
Phillippines	1.12	1.47	0.58	0.36	0.50	1.78	0.73
Poland	0.00	0.00	0.00	0.00	0.00	0.00	0.00
Portugal	2.22	3.20	0.00	5.61	0.00	0.00	0.00
Russian Federation	1.22	1.31	0.96	0.00	0.00	0.00	1.52
Saudi Arabia		1.72	0.00	0.00	5.35	0.00	0.00
Singapore	0.50	0.82	1.87	0.40	0.62	0.41	0.93
Spain	0.00	0.00	0.00	0.00	0.00	0.00	1.28
St. Vincent and Grenadines	2.07	1.49	2.18	2.25	4.63	6.37	3.16
Sweden	0.00	0.00	0.00	1.99	0.00	0.00	2.29
Tonga	8.33	0.00	0.00	0.00	19.61	0.00	0.00
Turkey	1.67	1.50	2.26	2.92	2.54	0.64	0.00
Ukraine	1.96	0.00	0.00	0.00	0.00	17.36	0.00
United Kingdom	0.00	0.00	0.00	0.00	0.00	0.75	0.46
Bermuda	0.00	0.00	0.00	0.00	1.78	0.00	0.00
British Virgin Islands			0.00	0.00	0.00	0.00	
Cayman Islands	0.56	0.69	1.49	1.18	2.08	0.63	0.00
Gibraltar	0.00	0.00	0.00	0.00	0.00	0.00	3.31
Isle of Man	0.00	0.00	0.00	0.00	0.00	0.00	1.08
Vanuatu	1.14	1.28	0.00	2.81	0.00	0.00	0.00
Venezuela	2.02	3.59	3.59	10.29	3.68	9.77	0.00
Regional average	3.00	2.23	1.64	1.62	1.70	1.28	1.59

Source: U.S. Coast Guard, *Port State Control Report 1998, 1999, 2000, 2001, 2002, 2003* (Washington, D.C.: U.S. Coast Guard, 1999, 2000, 2001, 2002, 2003, 2004). Note that "detention ratio" as used here is different from the U.S. Coast Guard usage, and that calculations are done—using distinct vessel arrivals rather than number of ships inspected—to make this rate comparable to the Paris and Tokyo MOU statistics.

APPENDIX E
ITF-Designated Flags of Convenience 2005

Antigua and Barbuda
Bahamas
Barbados
Belize
Bermuda (UK)
Bolivia
Burma
Cambodia
Cayman Islands
Comoros
Cyprus
Equatorial Guinea
French International Ship Register (FIS)
Georgia
German International Ship Register (GIS)
Gibraltar (UK)
Honduras
Jamaica
Lebanon
Liberia
Malta
Marshall Islands
Mauritius
Mongolia
Netherlands Antilles
North Korea
Panama
São Tomé and Príncipe
Sri Lanka
St. Vincent
Tonga
Vanuatu

Source: ITF, "FOC Countries," http://www.itfglobal.org/flags-convenience/flags-convenien-183.cfm

APPENDIX F
Percentage of Ships in Registries with ITF Collective Agreements 1995–2001

State	1995	1996	1997	1998	1999	2000	2001
Antigua and Barbuda	31.00	28.00	35.00	38.00	38.00	42.00	41.80
Bahamas	36.00	39.00	49.00	53.00	43.00	46.00	38.00
Barbados			19.00	15.00	21.00	30.00	32.30
Belize			2.00	2.00	1.00	0.70	0.47
Bermuda (UK)			57.00	52.00		54.00	32.60
Cambodia				9.00	5.00	7.00	5.20
Cayman Islands (UK)				61.00	41.00	26.00	42.00
Cook Islands					0.00	0.00	0.00
CSR (Spain)				0.00	0.00	0.00	0.53
Cyprus	16.00	16.00	18.00	20.00	22.00	22.00	32.30
French Antarctic Territory				8.00	8.00	7.00	11.50
Gibraltar (UK)				6.00	29.00	40.00	46.00
GIS	43.00	47.00	59.00	51.00	42.00	19.00	92.60
Honduras				2.00	1.00	0.70	0.53
Hong Kong				3.00	1.00	4.00	3.60
Isle of Man (UK)				27.00	24.00	33.00	27.80
Lebanon				6.00	5.00	7.00	0.99
Liberia	46.00	48.00	50.00	57.00	53.00	54.00	40.70
Luxembourg				5.00	5.00	14.00	14.20
Malta	26.00	29.00	31.00	34.00	32.00	35.00	24.30
MAR (Portugal)				13.00	20.00	28.00	29.60
Marshall Islands			84.00	77.00	37.00	38.00	35.90
Mauritius				11.00	10.00	5.00	0.00
Myanmar			5.00	5.00	2.00	6.00	6.90
Netherlands Antilles				20.00	24.00	21.00	23.70
NIS (Norway)				3.00	2.00	6.00	2.74
Panama	23.00	23.00	35.00	40.00	33.00	34.00	27.60
Philippines				0.20	0.00	0.80	0.87
Singapore				7.00	4.00	4.00	3.30
Sri Lanka				27.00	9.00	1.60	1.58
St. Vincent and Grenadines	8.00	11.00	17.00	16.00	12.00	13.00	8.29
Vanuatu				51.00	14.00	15.00	10.50

Source: ITF, *Flags of Convenience Campaign Reports 1995–2001/2002* (London: ITF, 1996–2003).

References

Abrams, Alan. 1994. "Tanker Association Seeks to Require Pollution Insurance." *Journal of Commerce* (12 May): 7B.

Acuerdo, Latino. n.d. "Concentrated Inspection Campaigns." http://200.45.69.62/Campanas_concentradas_i_htm.

Agnew, D. J. 2000. "The Illegal and Unregulated Fishery for Toothfish in the Southern Ocean, and the CCAMLR Catch Documentation Scheme." *Marine Policy* 24(5): 316–374.

Agnew, David J., and Colin T. Barnes. 2004. "Economic Aspects and Drivers of IUU Fishing: Building a Framework." OECD, Fisheries Committee, Directorate for Food, Agriculture and Fisheries," AGR/FI/IUU(2004)(2) (March).

Agreement to Promote Compliance with International Conservation and Management Measures by Fishing Vessels on the High Seas. 1993.

"All Is Not Well on the Island of Vanuatu." 2001. *Lloyd's List* (30 June): 4.

Anderson, Arthur, and Company. 1979. *Cost of Regulation, Study for the Business Roundtable*. New York: Arthur Anderson and Company (March).

Anderson, H. Edwin III. 1996. "The Nationality of Ships and Flags of Convenience: Economics, Politics, and Alternatives." *The Maritime Lawyer* 12 (Fall): 139–170.

Australian Delegation. 2002. "Report in his Capacity as Representative of the Depository Government for the Convention on the Conservation of Antarctic Marine Living Resources to the Twenty-Fifth Antarctic Treaty Consultative Meeting." ATCM XXV. Information Paper IP-111.

Bahamas Investment Authority. n.d. "The Bahamas' Shipping Registry." http://www.interknowledge.com/bahamas/investment/shipng01.htm.

"Bahamas—Questions over Need for Voluntary Auditing." 2002. *Lloyd's List* (3 September): 15.

Baldwin, Tom. 1999. "Who's in Charge Here?" *Journal of Commerce*. (15 January): 1B.

Balton, David A. 2004. "IUU Fishing and State Control over Nationals." OECD, Fisheries Committee, Directorate for Food, Agriculture and Fisheries. AGR/FI/IUU(2004)2 (6 April).

Barbera, Anthony J., and Virginia D. McConnell. 1990. "The Impact of Environmental Regulations on Industry Productivity: Direct and Indirect Effects." *Journal of Environmental Economics and Management* 18: 56–65.

Barkin, J. Samuel. 1998. "The Evolution of the Constitution of Sovereignty and the Emergence of Human Rights Norms." *Millennium* 27 (Summer): 229–252.

Barkin, J. Samuel. 2003. "The Counterintuitive Relationship between Globalization and Climate Change." *Global Environmental Politics* 3(3) (August): 8–13.

Barkin, J. Samuel. 2004. "Time-Horizons and Multilateral Enforcement in International Cooperation," *International Studies Quarterly* 48(2) (June): 63–382.

Barkin, J. Samuel, and Elizabeth R. DeSombre. 2000. "Unilateralism and Multilateralism in International Fisheries Management." *Global Governance* 6: 339–360.

Barkin, J. Samuel, and Kashif Mansori. 2001. "Backward Boycotts: Demand Management and Fishery Conservation." *Global Environmental Politics* 1(2): 30–41.

Barkin, J. Samuel, and George E. Shambaugh, eds. 1999. *Anarchy and the Environment: The International Relations of Common Pool Resources*. Albany: SUNY Press.

Basinger, Scott J. and and Mark Hallerberg. 2004. "Remodeling the Competition for Capital: How Domestic Politics Erases the Race to the Bottom." *American Political Science Review* 98(2): 261–276.

Bate, Allison. 1998. "INTERTANKO: Most Tankers Will Meet Standards by Deadline." *Journal of Commerce* (23 February): 3B.

Baulmol, William J., and Wallace E. Oates. 1988. *The Theory of Environmental Policy* 2nd ed. Cambridge: Cambridge University Press.

"Being Small Is More Beautiful by Belize Flag's Reckoning." 2005. *Lloyd's List* (7 September): 14.

Bennett, Paul. 2000. "Mutuality at a Distance: Risk and Regulation in Marine Insurance Clubs." *Environment and Planning A* 32: 147–163.

Bennett, Paul. 2001. "Mutual Risk: P&I Insurance Clubs and Maritime Safety and Environmental Performance." *Marine Policy* 25: 13–21.

Bernfeld, Jessica S. 2004. *Changing Tides: The Effects of Globalization on the Shipping Industries of Traditional Maritime States*. Wellesley College Honors Thesis, Wellesley, Mass.

"Better Control." 1992. *Lloyd's List* (3 March): 8.

Binnendijk, Hans, and Richard L. Kugler. 2001. "Managing Change: Capability, Adaptability, and Transformation." *Defense Horizons* (June). http://www.ndu.edu/inss/DefHor/DH1/DH1.html.

Birdsall, Nancy, and David Wheeler. 1992. "Trade Policy and Industrial Pollution in Latin America: Where Are the Pollution Havens?" In Patrick Low, ed. *International Trade and the Environment*, 159–167. World Bank Discussion Papers. Washington, D.C.: World Bank.

Bloor, Michael, Michelle Thomas, and Tony Lane. 2000. "Health Risks in the Global Shipping Industry: An Overview." *Health, Risk & Society* 2(3): 329–340.

Boczek, Boleslaw Adam. 1962. *Flags of Convenience: An International Legal Study*. Cambridge: Harvard University Press.

Boisson, Philippe. 1994. "Classification Societies and Safety at Sea." *Marine Policy* 18(5): 363–377.

Bonanno, Alessandro, and Douglas Constance. 1996. *Caught in the Net: The Global Tuna Industry, Environmentalism, and the State*. Lawrence: University Press of Kansas.

Bonior, David. 1999. "Defending Democracy in the New Global Economy." Statement to an AFL-CIO Conference on Workers' Rights, Trade Development, and the WTO, Seattle, Wash. (December); quoted in David Wheeler. 2002. "Beyond Pollution Havens," *Global Environmental Politics* 2(2): 1–10.

"Box Hopes Are Pinned on Keeping Up with the Jones Act." 2004. *Lloyd's List* (23 January): 13.

Braithwaite, John, and Peter Drahos. 2000. *Global Business Regulation*. Cambridge: Cambridge University Press.

Bray, Julian. 1997. "Intercargo Poised to Set Up Safety Scheme." *Lloyd's List* (11 June): 1.

Bray, Julian. 2005. "IACS Clinches 'Peace in Our Time.'" *Lloyd's List* (14 June): 1.

Brewer, James. 2002. "OECD—Shipping Nations Under Fire in Tax Haven Probe." *Lloyd's List* (22 April): 1.

Brewer, James. 2005. "P&I Clubs Look High and Low on Renewals." *Lloyd's List* (20 October): 1.

Briggs, Herbert Whittaker. 1952. *The Law of Nations*. 2nd ed. New York: Appleton-Century-Crofts.

Broeze, Frank. 1998. "Containerization and the Globalization of Liner Shipping." In D. Starkey and G. Harlaftis, eds., *Global Markets: The Internationalization of the Sea Transport Industries since 1850*, 867–876. St. Johns: International Maritime History Association.

Brown, Drusilla K., Alan V. Deardorff, and Robert M. Stern. 1996. "International Labor Standards and Trade: A Theoretical Analysis." In Jagdish Bhagwati and Robert E. Hudec, eds., *Fair Trade and Harmonization*, vol. 1, 227–272. Cambridge: MIT Press.

Brunnermeier, Smita B., and Arik Levinson. 2004. "Examining the Evidence on Environmental Regulations and Industry Location." *Journal of Environment and Development* 13(4) (March): 6–41.

Buchanan, J. M. 1965. "An Economic Theory of Clubs." *Economica* 32: 1–14.

Cafruny, Alan W. 1985. "The Political Economy of International Shipping: Europe versus America." *International Organization* 39(1): 79–119.

"Cambodia—Tribulations Continue for a Poor Performer." 2003. *Lloyd's List* (10 February): 16.

Camilleri, Joseph, and Jim Falk. 1992. *The End of Sovereignty?* Cheltenham: Edward Elgar.

Carlisle, Rodney P. 1981. *Sovereignty for Sale: The Origins and Evolution of the Panamanian and Liberian Flags of Convenience.* Annapolis: Naval Institute Press.

Carraro, C., and D. Sinisalco. 1992. "Environmental Innovation Policy and International Competition." *Environmental and Resource Economics* 1(2): 183–200.

Castleman, Barry I. 1985. "The Double Standard in Industrial Hazards." In Jane Ives, ed., *The Export of Hazard*, 60–89. London: Routledge.

Castleman, Barry I. 1987. "Workplace Health Standards and Multinational Corporations in Developing Countries." In Charles S. Pearson, ed., *Multinational Corporations, Environment, and the Third World*, 149–278. Durham: Duke University Press.

CCAMLR. 2000. Resolution 19/XXI.

CCAMLR. 2002. "Scheme to Promote Compliance by Contracting Party Vessels with CCAMLR Conservation Measures." CCAMLR Conservation Measure 10-06. http://www.ccamlr.org/pu/E/pubs/cm/03-04/10-06.pdf.

CCAMLR. 2003. "Scheme to Promote Compliance by Non-Contracting Party Vessels with CCAMLR Conservation Measures." CCAMLR Conservation Measure 10-07. http://www.ccamlr.org/pu/E/pubs/cm/03-04/10-07.pdf.

CCAMLR. 2003. Resolution 15(XXII), "Use of Ports Not Implementing the Catch Documentation Scheme for Dissostichus spp."

CCAMLR. 2004. "List of Parties Implementing the CDS." http://www.ccamlr.org/pu/E/cds/list-of-parties.htm.

CCAMLR. 2004. Conservation Measure 10-05.

CCAMLR. n.d. "Catch Documentation Scheme." http://www.ccamlr.org/pu/E/cds/intro.htm.

CCAMLR. n.d. "Explanatory Memorandum on the Introduction of the Catch Documentation Scheme (CDS) for Toothfish." http://www.ccamlr.org/pu/E/cds/p2.htm.

CCAMLR. n.d. "Policy to Enhance Cooperation between CCAMLR and Non-Contracting Parties." http://www.ccamlr.org/pu/E/cds/p4.htm.

CCSBT. 2005. "Management of SBT." http://www.ccsbt.org/docs/management.html.

Chambers, Sam. 2005. "Flag Failure Costs Tokyo a Yen Fortune." *Lloyd's List* (12 July): 10.

Chapman, Paul K. 1992. *Trouble on Board: The Plight of International Seafarers*. Ithaca: ILR Press.

Charnovitz, Steve. 1992. "Environmental and Labour Standards in Trade." *The World Economy* 15: 335–356.

Chemical Distribution Institute. 2002. "Ship Audit Report, Marine Pack Cargo, Ship Questionnaire." 1st ed. (1 June). http://www.cdi.org.uk.

Clapp, Jennifer. 2002. "What the Pollution Havens Debate Overlooks." *Global Environmental Politics* 2(2) (May): 11–19.

Clark, Gordon. 1993. "Global Competition and the Environmental Performance of Australian Mineral Companies: Is the 'Race to the Bottom' Inevitable?" *International Environmental Affairs* 5(3): 147–172.

"Class Societies Get Tough on Flag States as IACS Pair Drop Cambodia." 2002. *Lloyd's List* (30 September): 1.

Coles, Richard M. F., ed. 2002. *Ship Registration*. London: LLP.

Colombis, C. John. 1967. *The International Law of the Sea*. 6th rev. ed. New York: David McKay.

COLTO. 2003. "Rogues Gallery: The New Face of IUU Fishing for Toothfish." *COLTO Brochure* (October): 2.

COLTO. n.d. "The Wanted Campaign." http://www.colto.org/Wanted_Campaign.htm.

Commission of the European Communities. 1999. *Report Updating the Commission Opinion on Malta's Application for Membership*. COM(1999)69. Brussels: EU.

"Cooperation Is Linchpin of Registry's Drive to Maintain High Standards." 2005. *Lloyd's List* (6 October): 13.

Cornes, R., and T. Sander. 1996. *The Theory of Externalities, Public Goods and Club Goods*. Cambridge: Cambridge University Press.

Corporate and Maritime Administrator for the Republic of the Marshall Islands. n.d. "Vessel Registration and Mortgage Procedures—Register IRI." http://www.register-iri.com/content.cfm?catid=28.

Couper, A. D. 1999. *Voyages of Abuse: Seafarers, Human Rights, and International Shipping*. London: Pluto Press.

Cunard Steamship Co. Ltd. et al. v. Mellon, Secretary of the Treasury, et al. 1923. Supreme Court of the United States. 262 U.S. 100; 43 S. Ct. 504, Decided 30 April.

Davies, Rachel. 1991. "Fishing Boat Registration Rules Contravene EC Law." *Financial Times* (14 August): 21.

Dearsley, D. A. 1997. "ISF Wages Survey 1997." IF(97)47(IF.9). London: International Shipping Federation.

Dearsley, D. A. 2001. "ISF Shipping Wages Survey 2000." ISF (01) 11. London: International Shipping Federation.

Dehejia, Vivek H., and Yiagadeesen Samy. 2004. "Trade and Labour Standards: Theory and New Empirical Evidence." *Journal of International Trade & Economic Development* 13(2): 179–198.

Delegation of Japan. 2003. *Report on the Progress in the Measures to Eliminate IUU Large Scale Tuna Longline Fishing Vessels*. Preparatory Conference for the Commission for the Conservation and Management of Highly Migratory Fish Stocks in the Western and Central Pacific. 4th session. WCPF/PrepCon/DP.11 (9 May).

Dempsey, Paul Stephen, and Lisa L. Helling. 1980. "Oil Pollution by Ocean Vessels—An Environmental Tragedy: The Legal Regime of Flags of Convenience, Multilateral Conventions, and Coastal States." *Journal of International Law and Policy* 10: 37–87.

Denison, Edward P. 1979. *Accounting for Slower Economic Growth: The United States in the 1970s*. Washington, D.C.: Brookings Institution.

DeSombre, Elizabeth R. 1995. "Baptists and Bootleggers for the Environment: The Origins of United States Unilateral Sanctions." *Journal of Environment and Development* 4 (Winter): 53–75.

DeSombre, Elizabeth R. 2000. *Domestic Sources of International Environmental Policy: Industry, Environmentalists, and U.S. Power*. Cambridge: MIT Press.

DeSombre, Elizabeth R., and J. Samuel Barkin. 2002. "Turtles and Trade: The WTO's Acceptance of Environmental Trade Restrictions." *Global Environmental Politics* 2(1) (February): 12–18.

Dickey, Alan. 1994. "Flag Tightens up on Inspections." *Lloyd's List* (10 November): 7.

Drezner, Daniel W. 2001. "Sovereignty for Sale." *Foreign Policy* 125 (September/October): 76–77.

Drezner, Daniel W. 2007. *All Politics Is Global: Explaining International Regulatory Regimes*. Princeton: Princeton University Press.

Economist Intelligence Unit, Ltd. 1979. *Open Registry Shipping*. London: Economist Intelligence Unit (27 September).

Ehrenberg, Ronald G. 1994. *Labor Markets and Integrating National Economies*. Washington, D.C.: Brookings Institution.

Elmslie, Bruce, and William Milberg. 1996. "Free Trade and Social Dumping: Lessons from the Regulation of U.S. Interstate Commerce." *Challenge* (May/June): 46–52.

European Council. 1986. Resolution 4055/86.

European Council. 1992. European Council Resolution 3577/92 (7 December).

European Parliament and European Council. 2001. Directive 95/21/EC (19 December).

European Union. 2003. "Regulation (EC) No 1726/2003 of the European Parliament and of the Council amending Regulation (EC) No 417/2002 on the accelerated phasing-in of double-hull or equivalent design requirements for single-hull oil tankers." (22 July).

Fallon, Liza D., and Lorne Kriwoken. 2004. "International Influence of an Australian Nongovernmental Organization in the Protection of Patagonian Toothfish." *Ocean Development & International Law* 33: 221–266.

FAO. 2002. *Report of the Expert Consultation of Regional Fisheries Management Bodies on Harmonization of Catch Certification*. FAO Fisheries Report 697, FIIT/R697. La Jolla: FAO.

"Flags of Convenience Hit Back over UAE Port Ban." 2001. *Lloyd's List* (28 June): 22.

Franz, Douglas. 1999. "Gaps in Sea Laws Shield Pollution by Cruise Lines." *New York Times*. (January 3): 1, 20.

Freudmann, Aviva. 1998. "Liberia Taps DC Lawyers to Handle Registry." *Journal of Commerce*. (21 December): 2B.

Freudmann, Aviva. 2000. "U.S. Resists Deal in Maritime Services." *Lloyd's List* (13 January): 1.

Frommer, Arthur. 2004. "A Hawaiian Cruise, Detour Not Required." *Los Angeles Times* (4 April): L6.

Fulton, Thomas Wemyss. 1911. *The Sovereignty of the Sea*. Edinburgh: W. Blackwood.

Furger, Franco. 1997. "Accountability and Systems of Self-Governance: The Case of the Maritime Industry." *Law and Policy* 19(4): 445–476.

Garcia-Johnson, Ronie. 2000. *Exporting Environmentalism: U.S. Multinational Chemical Corporations in Brazil and Mexico*. Cambridge: MIT Press.

Garner, Clare. 1999. "Diesel Oil Tanker Snaps in Two Off the French Coast." *The Independent (London)* (13 December): 9.

Garrett, Geoffrey. 1998. *Partisan Politics in the Global Economy*. Cambridge: Cambridge University Press.

Gavin, Alan G. 2003. Speech before the 12th International Command Seminar. (21–22 May).

Gianni, Matthew, and Walt Simpson. 2004. *Flags of Convenience, Transshipment, Re-Supply and at-Sea Infrastructure in Relation to IUU Fishing*. AGR/FI/IUU(2004)22. Paris: OECD, Fisheries Committee, Directorate for Food, Agriculture and Fisheries. (April).

Gilotte, Tony. 2004. "Cambodia Claims Its Register Has Turned Corner." *Lloyd's List* (13 February): 3.

Gilpin, Robert. 1975. *U.S. Power and the Multinational Corporation*. New York: Basic Books.

Gilpin, Robert. 1982. *War and Change in World Politics*. Cambridge: Cambridge University Press.

Glass, Joel. 1996. "Eleven Registers Added to 1996 USCG Blacklist." *Lloyd's List* (16 April): 12.

Gray, Tony. 1993. "Leading Registry Status Is within Reach." *Lloyd's List* (7 September): 8.

Gray, Wayne B. 1987. "The Cost of Regulation: OSHA, EPA, and the Productivity Slowdown." *American Economic Review* 77: 998–1006.

Green, Julie, and David Agnes. 2002. "Catch Documentation Schemes to Combat Illegal, Unreported, and Unregulated Fishing: CCAMLR's Experience with Southern Ocean Toothfish." *Ocean Yearbook* 16: 171–194.

Grey, Michael. 2000. "Belize Flag Dismisses Substandard Inspectors." *Lloyd's List* (23 May): 1.

Grey, Michael. 2003. "Inspectors Target Cruiseships." *Lloyd's List* (11 April): 14.

Grey, Michael. 2001. "Mouzouropoulos: More Than Three Decades' Experience in Commercial Shipowning and Management." *Lloyd's List* (25 July): 2.

Grey, Michael. 2001. "U.S. Guard Identifies 400-Plus for Qualship 21." *Lloyd's List* (28 August): 3.

Grey, Michael. 2001. "Honduras Purges Substandard Ships." *Lloyd's List* (23 November): 6.

Grey, Michael. 2003. "Shipowners Launch Their Own Guide for Assessing Flag 'Respectability.'" *Lloyd's List* (25 November): 1.

Grey, Michael. 2004. "Belize Flag Seeks Removal from USCG Blacklist." *Lloyd's List* (7 December): 12.

Grey, Michael. 2003. "Blacklisted Flag States Gain Help from IACS." *Lloyd's List* (19 December): 1.

Grossman, Gene M., and Alan B. Krueger. 1993. "Environmental Impacts of the North American Free Trade Agreement." In P. Garber, ed., *The Mexico-U.S. Free Trade Agreement*, 13–56. Cambridge: MIT Press.

Grossman, Gene M., and Alan B. Krueger. 1995. "Economic Growth and the Environment." *Quarterly Journal of Economics* 110(2) (May): 353–377.

Guest, Andrew. 1992. "Liberia Calls for IACS Backing." *Lloyd's List* (6 July): 1.

Guest, Andrew. 1993. "Belize Flag Popularity Grows." *Lloyd's List* (31 March): 12.

Guest, Andrew. 1993. "Vanuatu Agrees to New Contract." *Lloyd's List* (31 March): 12.

Guest, Andrew. 1993. "Ship Management: IMEC Steps into a Global Market." *Lloyd's List* (6 July): 5.

Hailey, Roger. 2003. "Cyprus and Malta in Safety Pledge." *Lloyd's List* (2 October): 3.

Hall, Derek. 2002. "Environmental Change, Protest, and Havens of Environmental Degradation: Evidence from Asia." *Global Environmental Politics* 2(2) (May): 20–28.

Hamon, Jean-Yves, and Jean-Claude Dubois. 1999. "L'Avenire de la Flotte de Commerce Française." Affaire No. 1999-0217-01. Paris: Conseil Général des Ponts et Chaussées et Inspection Général des Services des Affaires Maritimes.

Hand, Marcus. 2003. "The Great Divide on Minimum Pay Issue." *Lloyd's List* (19 September): 7.

Hardin, Garrett. 1968. "The Tragedy of the Commons." *Science* 162 (December 13): 1243–1248.

Hare, John. 1997. "Port State Control: Strong Medicine to Cure a Sick Industry." *Georgia Journal of International and Comparative Law* 26 (Summer): 571–594.

Harrington-Shelton, Kevin. 1995. "Panama Recognized as a Reliable Long-Term Player." Letter to the editor. *Lloyd's List* (6 November): 5.

Hassans. n.d. "The Registration of Ships and Yachts in Gibraltar." http://www.gibraltarlaw.com/registration_ships_yachts_gibraltar.htm.

Hill, Christopher, Bill Robertson, and Steven J. Hazelwood. 1988. *An Introduction to P&I*. London: Lloyd's of London Press, Ltd.

Hindell, Keith. 1995. "Hong Kong Owners are Biggest Users of Vanuatu." *Lloyd's List* (29 March): 9.

Hindell, Keith. 1994. "Cyprus Makes Rapid Progress." *Lloyd's List* (30 March): 9.

Hindell, Keith. 1994. "Panama Faces Clean-Up Campaign." *Lloyd's List* (30 March): 9.

Hindell, Keith. 1994. "Special Report on World Ship Registers: Malta Becomes One of Major Players." *Lloyd's List* (30 March): 9.

Hoekman, Bernard M., and Michael M. Kostecki. 1995. *The Political Economy of the World Trading System: From GATT to WTO*. Oxford: Oxford University Press.

Holzinger, Katharina, and Christoph Knill. 2004. "Competition and Cooperation in Environmental Policy: Individual and Interaction Effects." *Journal of Public Policy* 24(1): 25–47.

"Honduras Lowers Flag on 1500 Problem Ships." 2001. *Lloyd's List* (26 March): 1.

Honka, Hannu. 1994. "The Classification System and Its Problems with Special Reference to the Liability of Classification Societies." *The Maritime Lawyer* (Winter): 1–36.

Honka, Hannu. 1996. "European Shipping Policies." In William A. Lovett, ed., *United States Shipping Policies and the World Market*. Westport: Quorum Books.

H. P. Dewry (Shipping Consultants), Ltd. 1980. *The Performance of "Open Registry" Bulk Fleets* 81. London: H. P. Dewry (Shipping Consultants), Ltd. (March).

Hugill, Peter J. 1993. *World Trade Since 1431: Geography, Technology, and Capitalism*. Baltimore: Johns Hopkins University Press.

IACS. 2004. "What Are Classification Societies?" (January). http://www.iacs.org.uk/.

ICCAT. 1992. "Recommendation by ICCAT Concerning the ICCAT Bluefin Tuna Statistical Document Program." Recommendation 92-1.

ICCAT. 1999. "Ecuatorial Guinea Pursuant to 1996 Compliance Recommendation—BFT and N SWO Fisheries." Recommendation 99-10.

ICCAT. 1999. "Panama: Lift BFT Import Prohibition." Recommendation 99-9.

ICCAT. 2000. "Belize, Cambodia, Honduras, St. Vincent and the Grenadines Pursuant to 1998 IUU Resolution." Recommendation 00-15.

ICCAT. 2000. "Equatorial Guinea Pursuant to 1998 IIU Resolution." Recommendation 00-16.

ICCAT. 2001. "Lifting of BFT and SWO on Honduras." Recommendation 01-15.

ICCAT. 2001. "Recommendation Establishing BET Statistic Program." Recommendation 01-21.

ICCAT. 2001. "Recommendation Establishing a SWO Statistical Documentation Program." Recommendation 01-22.

ICCAT. 2001. "Recommendation by ICCAT Concerning the Importation of Bigeye Tuna and Bigeye Tuna Products from St. Vincent and the Grenadines." Recommendation 01-14.

ICCAT. 2002. "Recommendation by ICCAT Concerning the Establishment of an ICCAT Record of Vessels over 24 Meters Authorized to Operate in the Convention Area." Recommendation 02-22.

ICCAT. 2002. "Recommendation by ICCAT Concerning the Importation of Atlantic Bluefin Tuna, Atlantic Swordfish, and Atlantic Bigeye Tuna and Their Products from Belize." Recommendation 02-16.

ICCAT. 2002. "Recommendation by ICCAT Concerning the Importation of Bigeye Tuna and Its Products from Honduras." Recommendation 02-18.

ICCAT. 2002. "Recommendation by ICCAT Concerning the Trade Sanction against St. Vincent and the Grenadines." Recommendation 02-20.

ICCAT. 2002. "Recommendation by ICCAT to Establish a List of Vessels Presumed to Have Carried Out Illegal, Unreported and Unregulated Fishing Activities in the ICCAT Convention Area." Recommendation 02-23.

ICCAT. 2002. "Recommendation by ICCAT Regarding Bolivia Pursuant to the 1998 Resolution Converning the Unreported and Unregulated Catches of Tuna by Large-Scale Longline Vessels in the Convention Area." Recommendation 02-17.

ICCAT. 2002. "Recommendation by ICCAT for Trade Restrictive Measures on Sierra Leone." Recommendation 02-19.

ICCAT. 2003. "Recommendation by ICCAT for Bigeye Tuna Trade Restrictive Measures on Georgia." Recommendation 03-18.

ICCAT. 2003. "Recommendation by ICCAT Concerning the Continuance of Trade Measures against Equatorial Guinea." Recommendation 03-17.

ICCAT. 2003. "Recommendation by ICCAT Concerning Minimum Standards for the Establishment of a Vessel Monitoring System in the ICCAT Convention Area." Recommendation 03-14.

ICCAT. 2004. "Recommendation by ICCAT Concerning the Lifting of Bigeye Tuna, Bluefin Tuna, and Swordfish Trade Restrictive Measures against Sierra Leone." Recommendation 04-14.

ICCAT. 2004. "Recommendation by ICCAT Concerning the Lifting of Bigeye Tuna Trade Restrictive Measures against Cambodia." Recommendation 04-15.

ICCAT. 2004. "Recommendation by ICCAT Concerning the Lifting of Trade Sanctions against Equatorial Guinea." Recommendation 04-13.

ICFTU, Trade Union Advisory Committee to the OECD, ITC, and Greenpeace International. 2002. "More Troubled Waters: Fishing, Pollution and FOCs."

Major Group Submission for the 2002 World Summit on Sustainable Development, Johannesburg (August).

IFCS. n.d. "IFCS Member Societies." http://www.classification-society.org/memsocs.html.

ILO. 2005. "ILOlex: Database of International Standards." http://www.ilo.org/ilolex/english/convdisp2.htm.

IMEC. 2001. "Agreement with ITF." Press release. http://www.marisec.org/IMEC/press%20dec%202001.htm.

IMO. 1948. "Convention on the International Maritime Organization." http://www.imo.org/Conventions/mainframe.asp?topic_id=771.

IMO. 2002. "IMO Adopts Comprehensive Security Measures." Press briefing.

IMO. 2004. "Secretary-General Mitropoulos Pays Tribute to the Efforts Made to Implement the ISPS Code." http://www.imo.org/Newsroom/mainframe.asp?topic_id=848&doc_id=3698.

IMO. 2004. "Status of Conventions: Complete List." (31 July). http://www.imo.org.

"IMO to Develop a Model Audit Scheme." 2002. *Lloyd's List* (3 September): 17.

Institute of London Underwriters. 1999. *Casualty Statistics 1998*. London: Institute of London Underwriters.

Institute of Shipping Economics and Logistics. 2003. *ISL Shipping Statistics Yearbook 2003*. Bremen: ISL.

Institute of Shipping Economics and Logistics. 2004. *ISL Shipping Statistics Yearbook 2004*. Bremen: ISL.

INTERCARGO. 2005. *2004–2005 Review*. http://www.intercargo.org/

INTERCARGO. n.d. "Members Charter." http://www.intercargo.org/

International Court of Justice. 1960. "Case Summaries: Constitution of the Maritime Safety Committee of the Inter-Governmental Maritime Consultative Organization." Advisory Opinion (8 June). http://www.icj-cij.org/icjwww/idecisions/isummaries/imscsummary600608.htm.

International Labour Office in Collaboration with the Seafarers International Research Centre. 2004. *The Global Seafarer: Living and Working Conditions in a Global Industry*. Geneva: International Labour Organisation.

International Labour Organisation. 1995. *World Employment 1995*. Geneva: ILO.

International Maritime Organization. http://www.imo.org.

International Registries. n.d. "Welcome: Maritime and Corporate Administrator for the Republic of the Marshall Islands." http://www.register-iri.com/index.cfm.

International Shipping Federation. 2001. *The ISF Year 2001*. London: ISF.

International Transport Workers Federation. n.d. *The ITF Handbook*. London: ITF.

International Union for the Conservation of Nature (IUCN), United Nations Environment Program (UNEP), Tufts University's Fletcher School of Law and Diplomacy, British Columbia Ministry of Environment, Lands, & Parks, Antarctic Research Center, American Society of International Law (ASIL), and Center for International Earth Science Information Network (CIESIN). n.d. *Environmental Treaties and Resource Indicators (ENTRI) Query Service*. Palisades, N.Y.: CIESIN, Columbia University. http://sedac.ciesin.columbia.edu/entri.

INTERTANKO. n.d. "General Information." http://www.intertanko.com/about/.

INTERTANKO. n.d. "Mission Statement." http://www.intertanko.com/about/mission/.

Intertrust. n.d. "Ship Registration in Panama." http://www.intertrustpanama.com/panama/ship.html.

IOTC. 2001. "Resolution 01/03 Establishing a Scheme to Promote Compliance by Non-Contracting Party Vessels with Resolutions Established by IOTC." http://www.iotc.org/English/resolutions/reso_detail.php?reso=14.

IOTC. 2001. "Resolution 01/06 Concerning the IOTC Bigeye Tuna Statistical Document Programme." http://www.iotc.org/English/resolutions/reso_detail.php?reso=22.

IOTC. 2002. "Resolution 02/04 on Establishing a List of Vessels Presumed to Have Carried Out Illegal, Unregulated, and Unreported Fishing in the IOTC Area." http://www.iotc.org/English/resolutions/reso_detail.php?reso=17&apndx=1.

IOTC. 2002. "Resolution 02/05 Concerning the Establishment of an IOTC Record of Vessels Over 24 Metres Authorised to Operate in the IOTC Area." http://www.iotc.org/English/resolutions/reso_detail.php?reso=23.

IOTC. 2003. "Recommendation 03/05 Concerning Trade Measures." http://www.iotc/English/resolutions/reso_detail.php?reso=32.

ITF. 1998. *Flags of Convenience Campaign Report 1997*. London: ITF.

ITF. 1998. *The ITF Seafarers' Trust Annual Report 1997/1998*. London: ITF.

ITF. 1999. *Flags of Convenience Campaign Report 1998*. London: ITF.

ITF. 2000. *Flags of Convenience Campaign Report 1999*. London: ITF.

ITF. 2001. *Flags of Convenience Campaign Report 2000*. London: ITF.

ITF. 2001. *ITF Standard Collective Agreement for Crews on Flag of Convenience Ships*. (1 January).

ITF. 2002. *Flags of Convenience Campaign Report 2001/2002*. London: ITF.

ITF. 2003. *Flags of Convenience Campaign Report 2002/2003*. London: ITF.

ITF. 2003. "Steering the Right Course." London: ITF.

ITF. 2003. "Total FOC Live Agreements." ITF database (May).

ITF. n.d. *Oslo to Delhi: A Comprehensive Review of the ITF FOC Campaign*. London: ITF.

ITF. n.d. "What Are FOCs?" http://www.itfglobal.org/flags-convenience/sub-page.cfm.

ITF. n.d. "What Is the Trust?" http://itf.org.uk/seafarers_trust/information/what_is_the_trust.htm.

"ITF Set to Open Talks in New Bargaining Forum." 2003. *Transport International* (13 October). http://www.itf.org.uk/TI/13/english/bargainingforum.htm.

Jaffe, Adam B., et al. 1993. "Environmental Regulations and International Competitiveness: What Does the Evidence Tell Us?" Unpublished draft (21 December).

Jänicke, Martin, Manfred Binder, and Harald Mönch. 1997. "Dirty Industries: Patterns of Change in Industrial Countries." *Environmental and Resource Economics* 9: 467–491.

"Japan to Ban Tuna Imports from Panama, Honduras, Belize." 1996. *AP Worldstream*. (December 3) (Lexis/Nexis.)

Jinks, Beth. 2001. "ITF Starts Major Drive in Europe." *Business Times Singapore* (24 September): SHIP1.

Jorgenson, Dale W., and Peter J. Wilcoxen. 1992. "Impact of Environmental Legislation on U.S. Economic Growth, Investment, and Capital Costs." In Donna L. Bodsky, ed., *U.S. Environmental Policy and Economic Growth: How Do We Fare?*, 1–39. Washington, D.C.: American Council for Capital Formation.

Kahler, Miles. 1998. "Modeling Races to the Bottom." Paper presented at the Annual Meeting of the American Political Science Association, Boston (September). http://www-irps.ucsd.edu/academics/f-kahler-rs.php.

Kahveci, Erol. 2000. "Fast Turnaround Ships: Impact on Seafarers' Lives." *Seaways* (March): 8–12.

Kalt, Joseph. 1988. "The Impact of Domestic Environmental Regulatory Policies on U.S. International Competitiveness." In A. Michael Spence and Heather A. Hazard, eds., *International Competitiveness*, 221–262. Cambridge: Ballinger.

Kapstein, Ethan. 1997. "Racing to the Bottom? Regulating International Labor Standards." *Politik und Gesellschaft* 2: 155–160.

Kasoulides, George C. 1993. *Port State Control and Jurisdiction: Evolution of the Port State Regime*. Dordrecht: Martinus Nijhoff.

Keohane, Robert O. 1984. *After Hegemony: Cooperation and Discord in the World Political Economy*. Princeton: Princeton University Press.

Knögden, Gabriele. 1979. "Environment and Industrial Siting: Preliminary Results of an Empirical Survey of Investment by West German Industry in Developing Countries." *Zeitschrift für Umweltpolitik*, 407–434.

Knudsen, Olav. 1973. *The Politics of International Shipping*. Lexington: Lexington Books.

Krasner, Stephen. 1976. "State Power and the Structure of International Trade." *World Politics* 28(3): 317–347.

Krasner, Stephen. 1999. *Sovereignty: Organized Hypocrisy*. Princeton: Princeton University Press.

Krasner, Stephen. 2002. "Sovereignty." *Foreign Policy* (122)(January–February): 20–29.

Lack, M., and G. Sant. 2001. "Patagonian Toothfish: Are Conservation and Trade Measures Working?" *TRAFFIC Bulletin* 19(1): 1–18.

Langewiesche, William. 2004. *The Outlaw Sea: A World of Freedom, Chaos, and Crime*. New York: North Point Press.

Langille, Brian A. 1994. "International Labour Standards and Economic Interdependence." In Werner Sengenberger and Duncan Campbell, eds., *International Labour Standards and Economic Interdependence*, 329–338. Geneva: International Institute for Labour Studies.

Leamer, Edward E. 1993. "Wage Effects of a U.S.-Mexican Free Trade Agreement." In Peter M. Garber, ed., *The Mexico-U.S. Free Trade Agreement*, 57–125. Cambridge: MIT Press.

Leonard, H. Jeffrey. 1988. *Pollution and the Struggle for World Product: Multinational Corporations, Environment, and International Comparative Advantage*. Cambridge: Cambridge University Press.

Leonard, H. Jeffrey, and Christopher Duerksen. 1980. "Environmental Regulations and the Location of Industry: An International Perspective." *Columbia Journal of World Business* (Summer): 52–68.

Levinson, Arik. 1996. "Environmental Regulations and Industry Location: International and Domestic Evidence." In Jagdish Bhagwati and Robert E. Hudec, eds., *Fair Trade and Harmonization: Prerequisites for Free Trade? Vol. 1: Economic Analysis*, 429–457. Cambridge: MIT Press.

Levinson, Arik. 1996. "Environmental Regulations and Manufacturers' Location Choices." *Journal of Public Economics* 62(1): 5–29.

Lillie, Nathan. 2003. *A Global Union for Global Workers: The International Transport Worker's Federation and the Representation of Seafarers on Flag of Convenience Shipping*. Doctoral dissertation, Cornell University.

Lillie, Nathan. 2004. "Global Collective Bargaining on Flag of Convenience Shipping." *British Journal of Industrial Relations* 42(1) (March): 47–67.

Lillie, Nathan. 2004. "Industrial Regulation by International Regime: Negotiating a Consolidated Maritime Labor Convention in the ILO." Unpublished draft manuscript, 1 December, cited with permission.

Lillie, Nathan. 2005. "Union Networks and Global Unionism in Maritime Shipping." *Relations Industrielles* 60(1) (Winter): 88–111.

Litan, Robert E., and Wiliam D. Nordhaus. 1983. *Reforming Federal Regulation*. New Haven: Yale University Press.

Lizza, Ryan. 2001. "Double Take: Can Charles Taylor's Apologists Explain his Ties to Al Qaeda?" *New Republic* (19 November): 21–23.

Ljunggren, David. 2002. "Ban Ships with Flags of Convenience—Canada." *Reuters News Service*. (21 November).

Lloyd's Register Fairplay. 1949–2005. *World Fleet Statistics 1948–2004*. London: Lloyd's Register.

Lobach, Terje. 2003. *Port State Control of Foreign Fishing Vessels*. FAO Fisheries Circular 987. FIP/C987(Eng).

Lobach, Terje. 2004. "Port State Measures." OECD, Fisheries Committee, Directorate for Food, Agriculture and Fisheries. AGR/FI/IUU(2004)9 (8 April).

Lowry, Nigel. 1997. "Cyprus Set to Tighten Up Register: Clampdown on Substandard Ships." *Lloyd's List* (21 July): 1.

Lowry, Nigel. 2000. "Posidonia: Safety Worries Prompt Cyprus to Launch Bulker Strength Study." *Lloyd's List* (6 June): 1.

Lowry, Nigel. 2002. "Mare Forum—Belize Protests over Three-Year Black-List Rule." *Lloyd's List* (20 September): 5.

Lucas, Robert E. B., David Wheeler, and Hemamala Hettige. 1992. "Economic Development, Environmental Regulation, and the International Migration of Toxic Pollution: 1960–1988." In Patrick Low, ed., *International Trade and the Environment*, 89–103. Washington, D.C.: World Bank.

Luxner, Larry. 2000. "Cyprus Tightens the Screws on Its Ship Registry." *Journal of Commerce—JoC Online* (3 August) (Lexis/Nexis.)

Mah, J. S. 1997. "Core Labour Standards and Export Performance in Developing Countries." *The World Economy* 20(6): 773–785.

Mani, Muthukumara, and David Wheeler. 1998. "In Search of Pollution Havens? Dirty Industry in the World Economy, 1960 to 1995." *Journal of Environment and Development* 7(3) (September): 215–247.

"Marshall Islands Wins Stamp of Approval from US Programme." 2002. *Lloyd's List* (6 February): 19.

"Marshall Islands—It's the Applications They Turn Down. . . ." 2003. *Lloyd's List* (10 February): 16.

Mayer, Christopher. 2002. "Belize Flag Weeds Out 668 Ships to Polish Tarnished Image." *Lloyd's List* (16 January): 3.

McGuire, M. 1982. "Regulation, Factor Rewards, and International Trade." *Journal of Public Economics* 17: 335–354.

McLaughlin, John. 1996. "Gonzalez to Head Belize Ship Register." *Lloyd's List* (2 February): 12.

Mayer, Christopher. 2003. "LR Warns Registers to Seek IACS Role." *Lloyd's List* (17 March): 1.

Miller, Denzil G. M. 2004. "Patagonian Toothfish—the Storm Gathers." OECD, Fisheries Committee, Directorate for Food, Agriculture and Fisheries." AGR/FI/IUU(2004)7 (1 April).

Mitchell, Ronald B. 1992. "Membership, Compliance, and Non-Compliance in the International Convention for the Regulation of Whaling." Unpublished paper.

Mitchell, Ronald B. 1994. *Intentional Oil Pollution at Sea*. Cambridge: MIT Press.

Mody, Ashoka, and David R. Wheeler. 1990. *Automation and World Competition: New Technologies, Industrial Location, and Trade*. New York: St. Martin's.

Moloney, Sean. 1992. "Norway to Meet on Panama Flag Safety." *Lloyd's List* (5 February): 3.

Moloney, Sean. 1994. "Euros Flag Drive Stepped Up." *Lloyd's List* (3 February): 12.

Moloney, Sean. 1994. "Panama Rejects Eight Classification Societies." *Lloyd's List* (19 May): 16.

Moloney, Sean. 1997. "Societies Force Ship Fault Move." *Lloyd's List* (7 February): 3.

Morris, Jim. 1996. "Lost at Sea: 'Flags of Convenience' Give Owners a Paper Refuge." *Houston Chronicle*. (22 August): 15.

Mulrenan, Jim. 1994. "Vanuatu off USGC Hit List." *Lloyd's List* 1(12 August): 10.

Mulrenan, Jim. 1995. "Cyprus Shipping Reforms Urged." *Lloyd's List* (11 November): 10.

Murphy, Dale D. 2004. *The Structure of Regulatory Competition: Corporations and Public Politics in a Global Economy*. Oxford: Oxford University Press.

NEAFC. 2005. "Non-Contracting Party Scheme." (January).

NEAFC Secretariat. 2004. "IUU Fishing in NEAFC: How Big Is the Problem and What Have We Done?" OECD, Fisheries Committee, Directorate for Food, Agriculture and Fisheries. AGR/FI/IUU(2004)5 (15 April).

Nelson, Rainbow. 2003. "Panama Flag Detentions Fall." *Lloyd's List* (23 May): 3.

Norsworthy, J. R., Michael J. Harper, and Kent Kunze. 1979. "The Slowdown in Productivity Growth: Analysis of Some Contributing Factors." *Brookings Papers on Economic Activity* 2: 387–421.

Northrup, Herbert R., and Richard L. Rowan. 1983. *The International Transport Workers Federation and Flag of Convenience Shipping*. Philadelphia: Industrial Relations Research Unit, Wharton School, University of Pennsylvania.

Northrup, Herbert R., and Peter B. Scrase. 1996. "The International Transport Workers' Federation Flag of Convenience Shipping Campaign 1983–1995." *Transportation Law Journal* 23(3): 369–423.

OCIMF. "Oil Companies International Marine Forum." http://www.ocimf.com/index.cfm?pageid=10.

OCIMF. n.d. "SIRE Introduction." http://www.ocimf.com/index.cfm?pageid=8.

Open Registry Shipping: Some Economic Considerations. 1979. London: The Economist Intelligence Unit.

Operating Agreement for the International Maritime Satellite Organisation. 1976.

OECD. 1995. *Trade and Labor Standards*. Paris: OECD.

OECD. 1996. *Competitive Advantages Obtained by Some Shipowners as a Result of Non-Observance of Applicable International Rules and Standards*. OECD/GD(96)(4). Paris: OECD.

OECD. 2002. *Cost Savings Stemming from Non-Compliance with International Environmental Regulations in the Maritime Sector*. DSTI/DOT/MTC(2002)8/FINAL. Paris: OECD.

OECD. 2004. "Draft Chapter 1—Economics of IUU Fishing Activities." OECD, Fisheries Committee, Directorate for Food, Agriculture and Fisheries. AGR/FI/IUU(2004)3/PROV, (12 March).

OECD. 2004. "Draft Chapter 2—Framework for Measures Against IUU Fisheries Activities." OECD, Fisheries Committee, Directorate for Food, Agriculture and Fisheries. AGR/FI/IUU(2004)5/PROV (23 March).

OECD. 2004. "National Measures against IUU Fishing Activities." OECD, Fisheries Committee, Directorate for Food, Agriculture and Fisheries. AGR/FI/IUU(2004)6/PROV, (12 April).

OECD, by SSY Consultancy and Research, Ltd. 2001. *The Cost to Users of Substandard Shipping*. Paris: OECD Directorate for Science, Technology, and Industry (January).

Ohmae, Kenichi. 1995. *The End of the Nation State: The Rise of Regional Economies*. New York: Free Press.

Olson, Mancur. 1965. *The Logic of Collective Action: Public Goods and the Theory of Groups*. Cambridge: Harvard University Press.

O'Mahony, Hugh. 2003. "Late Bid to Amend IMO Meets Opposition." *Lloyd's List* (26 November): 1.

O'Mahoney, Hugh. 2005. "Mitropolous Praises State Audit Scheme." *Lloyd's List* (30 March): 5.

Organisation for Economic Cooperation and Development. 1985. *Environmental Policy and Technical Change*. Paris: OECD.

Osler, David. 1996. "Registers 'Bring Benefits.'" *Lloyd's List* (22 November): 3.

Osler, David. 1998. "British Tory Party Has a Stake in Belize Flag." *Lloyd's List* (21 November): 1.

Osler, David. 1999. "IRS Tops List for Worst Detention Record in US." *Lloyd's List* (6 September): 16.

Osler, David. 2000. "Europe: Red Ensign Group Sets Agenda." *Lloyd's List* (2 June): 3.

Osler, David. 2001. "Registers Targeted in ITF Campaign." *Lloyd's List* (25 September): 2.

Osler, David. 2002. "Vanuatu Registry Chief Bohn Arrested over $100 M Scam." *Lloyd's List* (10 December): 1.

Osler, David. 2003. "Slovenia Signs Up to Paris MOU." *Lloyd's List* (21 May): 5.

Osler, David. 2004. "Marshall Islands/US in Flag Security Pact." *Lloyd's List* (18 August): 3.

Osler, David, and Jennie Harris. 1998. "Intercargo Opts for Shake-Up to Lift Membership." *Lloyd's List* (30 March): 3.

Osler, David, and Nigel Lowry. 1998. "Flags Offered for 'Appalling' Ships." *Lloyd's List* 1(10 September): 1.

Ostrom, Elinor, Roy Gardner, and James Walker. 1994. *Rules, Games, and Common-Pool Resources*. Ann Arbor: University of Michigan Press.

Özçcayir, Z. Oya. 2001. *Port State Control*. London: LLP.

Paci, Giovanni. 2001. "Malta Steps Up Policing of Its Euro-Friendly Register." *Lloyd's List* (21 May): 3.

Palen, Ronen. 2003. *The Offshore World: Sovereign Markets, Virtual Places, and Nomad Millionaires*. Ithaca: Cornell University Press.

"Panama to Allow US to Search Its Ships." 2004. *Lloyd's List* 1(12 May): 12.

"Panama Increases Lead as Merchant Fleet Reaches Record Tonnage." n.d. *Lloyd's Register News Release*. http://www.lr.org.news/pr/4wfs.html.

Paris MOU. 1986–2005. *Annual Report 1985–2004*. The Hague: Paris MOU.

Paris MOU. n.d. "Target Factor Calculator." http://www.parismou.org/.

Paris MOU Press Release. 2003. "New Requirements from 22 July 2003." (13 May), http://www.parismou.org/.

Parliament of the Commonwealth of Australia. 1992. *Ships of Shame: Inquiry into Ship Safety*. Report from the House of Representatives Standing Committee on Transport, Communications, and Infrastructure. Canberra: Australian Government Publishing Service (December).

Pasurka, Carl A., Jr., and Deborah Vaughn Nestor. 1992. "Environmental Protection Agency, Trade Effects of the 1990 Clean Air Act Amendments." Unpublished study.

Peel, Michael, and Toby Shelley. 2004. "Liberia Under Pressure to Become More Shipshape." *Lloyd's List* 6 September: 16.

Perkins, Julie A. 1997. "Ship Registers: An International Update." *The Maritime Lawyer* 22 (Winter): 197–199.

Permanent Court of Arbitration. 1916. "Muscat Dhows Case, Award of the Tribunal." *Hague Court Reports*, The Hague. (Originally arbitrated August 8, 1905.)

Pethig, R. 1976. "Pollution, Welfare, and Environmental Policy in the Theory of Comparative Advantage." *Journal of Environmental Economics and Management* 2 (February): 160–169.

Pierson, Paul, and Stephan Leibfried. 1995. "Multitiered Institutions and the Making of Social Policy." In Stephan Leibfried and Paul Pierson, eds., *European Social Policy: Between Fragmentation and Integration*, 1–40. Washington, D.C.: Brookings Institution.

"Placing a Value on Crew Experience." 1996. *Lloyd's Shipping Economist* 18 (3) (March): 9.

Pohl, Otto. 2004. "European Environmental Rules Propel Change in U.S." *New York Times* (6 July): F4.

"The Politics of an Oil Spill." 2002. *The Economist* (21 November): 46–47.

Poole, Anthony. 1997. "Intercargo Gives Pledge on ISM Code." *Lloyd's List* (19 November): 3.

Porter, Gareth. 1999. "Trade Competition and Pollution Standards: 'Race to the Bottom' or 'Stuck at the Bottom'?" *Journal of Environment and Development* 8(2) (June): 133–151.

Porter, Janet. 1994. "INTERTANKO to Discuss Stricter Guidelines." *Journal of Commerce* (5 May): 8B.

Porter, Janet. 1995. "INTERTANKO Expels Greek Tanker Owner." *Journal of Commerce* (24 May): 8B.

Porter, Janet. 1995. "Bulker Group to Tighten Membership Conditions." *Journal of Commerce* (22 June): 13B.

Porter, Janet. 1997. "The Sorry State of Cyprus Ships." *Journal of Commerce* (June 11): 7A.

Porter, Michael E. 1990. *The Competitive Advantage of Nations*. London: Macmillan.

Porter, Michael E. 1991. "America's Green Strategy." *Scientific American* (April): 168.

Portnoy, Paul R. 1981. "The Macroeconomic Impacts of Federal Environmental Regulation." In Henry M. Peskin, Paul R. Portnoy, and Allan V. Kneese, eds., *Environmental Regulation and the U.S. Economy*, 25–54. Baltimore: Johns Hopkins University Press.

Prescott, John. 1990. "Maltese Flag to Register Ten Chinese Vessels." *Lloyd's List* (27 December): 3.

Pronin, Lyuba. 2005. "Moscow Gives Green Light to Ship Register Reforms to Boost Maritime Industry." *Lloyd's List* (16 June): 3.

"PRS Must Shake Off Taint Left by IACS Explusion." 2005. *Lloyd's List* (7 January): 12.

"Registers—Belize Flag Weeds Out 668 Ships to Polish Tarnished Image." 2002. *Lloyd's List* (16 January): 3.

"Regulation—OECD Cracks Down on Alleged Tax Havens." 2000. *Lloyd's List* (27 June 2000): 2.

Revesz, Richard L. 1992. "Rehabilitating Interstate Competition: Rethinking the 'Race-to-the-Bottom' Rationale for Federal Environmental Regulation." *New York University Law Review* 67 (December): 1210–1254.

Reyes, Brian. 2004. "Paris MoU Plans Radical Overhaul of Inspections." *Lloyd's List* (18 May): 1.

Reyes, Brian. 2004. "IACS Members Rate Well in Paris MOU List." *Lloyd's List* (9 July): 3.

Rienow, Robert. 1937. *The Test of the Nationality of a Merchant Vessel*. New York: Columbia University Press.

Roca, Jordi. 2003. "Do Individual Preferences Explain the Environmental Kuznets Curve?" *Ecological Economics* 45(1) (April): 3–10.

Rodriguez, Gabriel, and Yiagadeesen Samy. 2003. "Analysing the Effects of Labour Standards on US Export Performance: A Time Series Approach with Structural Change." *Applied Economics* 35(9) (15 June): 1043–1051.

Rodrik, Dani. 1996. "Labour Standards in International Trade: Do They Matter and What Do We Do About Them?" In Robert Z. Lawrence, Dani Rodrik, and

John Whalley, eds., *Emerging Agenda for Global Trade: High Stakes for Developing Countries*. Washington, D.C.: Overseas Development Council.

Rossi, Melissa, and Christian Caryl. 2002. "Just Missing the Boat." *Newsweek* (2 December): 7.

Ruggie, John Gerard. 1993. "Territoriality and Beyond: Problematizing Modernity in International Relations." *International Organization* 47(1) (Winter): 139–174.

Sabourenkov, Eugene N., and Denzil G. M. Miller. 2004. "The Management of Transboundary Stocks of Toothfish, *Dissostichus spp*., under the Convention on the Conservation of Antarctic Marine Living Resources." In A. I. L. Payne, C. M. O'Brien, and S. I. Rogers, eds., *Management of Shared Fish Stocks*, 68–94. Oxford: Blackwell.

Sano, Hiroya. 2004. "Are Private Initiatives a Possible Way Forward? Actions Taken by Private Stakeholders to Eliminate IUU Fishing Activities." OECD, Fisheries Committee, Directorate for Food, Agriculture and Fisheries. AGR/FI/IUU(2004)13 (8 April).

Sassen, Saskia. 1996. *Losing Control? Sovereignty in an Age of Globalization*. New York: Columbia University Press.

Schubert, William G. 2002. Maritime Administrator, Department of Transportation, Statement before the Special Oversight Panel on the Merchant Marine, U.S. Congress, House Armed Services Committee. (13 June) (Lexis/Nexis).

"Shipping: Follow the Flag of Convenience." 1997. *The Economist* (22 February): 75.

"Snag in Toothfish War." 2003. *The Mercury (Australia)* (8 November) (Lexis/Nexis).

Snidal, Duncan. 1985. "The Limits of Hegemonic Stability Theory." *International Organization* 39(4): 579–614.

Sohmen, Helmut. 1983. *Profitability in Shipping*. Tübingen: J. C. B. Mohr.

"Special Report on Ship Registries: Liberian Registry All Set to Change Hands After Parties Settle 'Restongate' Dispute." 1999. *Lloyd's List* (6 September): 8.

Special Trade Passenger Ships Agreement (STP). 1971.

"Spotlight on Belize." 1999. *Lloyd's List* (6 September): 9.

Spruyt, John. 1994. *Ship Management*. London: Lloyd's of London Press.

Spurrier, Andrew. 1996. "Register Growing as Inspections Improve." *Lloyd's List* (28 November): 6.

Spurrier, Andrew. 2005. "How New French Register Became an FOC." *Lloyd's List* 22 April: 7.

Stares, Justin. 2005. "IACS Alarmed Over Barrot Threat." *Lloyd's List* (7 February): 1.

Stares, Justin. 2005. "Brussels in Regulatory Clampdown on Classification Industry." *Lloyd's List* (22 February): 1.

Steinberg, Philip E. 2001. *The Social Construction of the Ocean.* Cambridge: Cambridge University Press.

Stockholm Agreement (Ferry Safety). 1996.

Stokke, Olav Schram, and Davor Vidas. 2004. "Regulating IUU Fishing or Combating IUU Operations?" OECD, Fisheries Committee, Directorate for Food, Agriculture and Fisheries. AGR/FI/IUU(2004)8 (30 March).

Stopford, Martin. 1997. *Maritime Economics.* 2nd ed. London: Routledge.

Sumaila, U. R. 2004. "The Cost of Being Apprehended Fishing Illegally: Empirical Evidences and Policy Implications." OECD, Fisheries Committee, Directorate for Food, Agriculture and Fisheries. AGR/FI/IUU(2004)11 (6 April).

"Support Vessels Underpin Vanuatu Growth." 2005. *Lloyd's List* (7 February): 11.

Swan, Judith. 2002. *Fishing Vessels Operating under Open Registers and the Exercise of Flag State Responsibilities—Information and Options.* FAO Fisheries Circular 980. FITT/C980. Rome: FAO.

Swire, Peter P. 1996. "The Race to Laxity and the Race to Undesirability: Explaining Failures in Competition Among Jurisdictions in Environmental Law." *Yale Law and Policy Review, Symposium Issue: Constructing a New Federalism* 14(2): 67–110.

Thompson, Peter, and Laura A. Strohm. 1996. "Trade and Environmental Quality: A Review of the Evidence." *Journal of Environment and Development* 5(4): 363–388.

Thorpe, Alan. 1995. "Special Report on Quality Assurance and Management." *Lloyd's List* (17 July): 7.

Tiebout, Charles. 1956. "A Pure Theory of Local Expenditures." *Journal of Political Economy* 64: 416–424.

Tobey, James. 1990. "The Effects of Domestic Environmental Policies on Patterns of World Trade: An Empirical Test." *Kyklos* 43: 191–209.

Tobey, James. 1993. "The Impact of Domestic Environmental Policies on International Trade." In OECD, *Environmental Policies and Industrial Competitiveness*, 48–54. Paris: OECD.

Tokyo MOU. 1995–2005. *Annual Report on Port State Control in the Asia-Pacific Region 1994–2004.* Tokyo: Tokyo MOU.

Tokyo MOU. 2003. "Press Release: The Twelfth Meeting of the Port State Control Committee in the Asia-Pacific Region Held in Chile." (8 April) http://www.tokyo-mou.org/psc12prs.pdf.

"Tonga Pulls the Plug on Tarnished Register." 2002. *Lloyd's List* (16 April): 1.

Tønnessen, J. N., and A. O. Johnsen. 1982. *The History of Modern Whaling.* Berkeley: University of California Press.

Torremolinos International Convention for the Safety of Fishing Vessel (SFV). 1977.

Treaty of Versailles. 1919.

"Two Strikes and You're Out." 2003. *Lloyd's List* (14 May): 1.

"UK P&I Club Mandates Security Certification for Annual Policy Renewal." 2005. *Lloyds List* (31 January): 19.

UNIDO. 1980. *Mineral Processing in Developing Countries*. New York: United Nations.

United Nations Conference on Trade and Development, Trade and Development Board. 1977. "Economic Consequences of the Existence of Lack of a Genuine Link between Vessel and Flag of Registry." TD/B/c.4/168 (10 March 1977).

United Nations Convention on Conditions for Registration of Ships. 1986.

United Nations Convention on the Law of the Sea. 1982.

United States, *Merchant Marine Act*. 1936. 49 Stat. 2015 (29 June).

United States, *National Prohibition Act*. 1919. 41 Stat. 305 (repealed 1935).

"An Uphill Task to Meet Tough Demands of EU Entry." 2003. *Lloyd's List* (29 December): 10.

U.S. Coast Guard. n.d. "Boarding Priority Matrix." http://www.uscg.mil/hq/g-m/pscweb/matrix.htm.

U.S. Coast Guard. 1994. "Port State Control Targeted Flag List 1991–1993." Unpublished document supplied by CDR Lonnie P. Harrison Jr., Commandant, U.S. Coast Guard Headquarters, Washington, D.C.

U.S. Coast Guard. 1996. "Port State Control 1995 Flag List." Unpublished document supplied by CDR Lonnie P. Harrison Jr., Commandant, U.S. Coast Guard Headquarters, Washington, D.C.

U.S. Coast Guard. 1997. "Port State Control 1996 Flag List." Unpublished document supplied by CDR Lonnie P. Harrison Jr., Commandant, U.S. Coast Guard Headquarters, Washington, D.C.

U.S. Coast Guard. 1998. "Coast Guard Publishes Port State Control Flag State and Classification Society Targeting Lists." Unpublished document supplied by CDR Lonnie P. Harrison Jr., Commandant, U.S. Coast Guard Headquarters, Washington, D.C.

U.S. Coast Guard. 1999–2005. *Port State Control in the United States*. Annual Reports 1998–2004. Washington, D.C.: U.S. Coast Guard.

U.S. Congress, 101st Session. "Oil Pollution Act of 1990." 101 P.L. 380; 104 Stat. 484.

U.S. General Accounting Office. 1991. "U.S.-Mexico Trade: Some U.S. Wood Furniture Firms Relocated from Los Angeles Area to Mexico." *Report to the Chairman, Committee on Energy and Commerce, House of Representatives* GAO/NSIAD-91-191. (April).

U.S. General Accounting Office. 2000. "Marine Pollution: Progress Made to Reduce Marine Pollution by Cruise Ships, but Important Issues Remain." GAO/RCED-00-48 (February).

van Beers, Cees. 1998. "Labour Standards and Trade flows of OECD Countries." *The World Economy* 21(1): 57–73.

van Beers, Cees, and J. C. J. M. van der Bergh. 1999. "An Empirical Multi-Country Analysis of the Impact of Environmental Regulations on Foreign Trade Flows." *Kyklos* 50(1): 29–46.

"Vanuatu: Active Year Sees Further Reduction in Detentions." 2002. *Lloyd's List* (6 February): 19.

"Vanuatu Emphasizes Safety in Bid to Be the 'First Alternative.'" 1999. *Lloyd's List* (6 September): 9.

Vida, Miguel. 2002. "Stricken Tanker Towed Away From Spanish Coast." *Reuters News Service*, 18 November.

Vogel, David. 1993. "Representing Diffuse Interests in Environmental Policymaking." In R. Kent Weaver and Bert A. Rockman, eds., *Do Institutions Matter? Government Capabilities in the United States and Abroad*, 237–271. Washington, D.C.: Brookings Institution.

Vogel, David. 1995. *Trading Up: Consumer and Environmental Regulation in a Global Economy*. Cambridge: Harvard University Press.

Vogel, David, and Robert A. Kagan, eds. 2004. *Dynamics of Regulatory Change: How Globalization Affects National Regulatory Policies*. Berkeley: University of California Press.

Walter, Ingo. 1982. "Environmentally Induced Industrial Relocation to Developing Countries." In Seymour J. Rubin and Thomas R. Graham, eds., *Environment and Trade*, 67–101. Montclair, NJ: Allanheld, Osmun Publishers.

Ward, Robert. 1996. "Cyprus Sets Out to Lose 'Bad Boy' Name." *Lloyd's List* (27 March): 14.

Ward, Robert. 1996. "Vanuatu Puts Focus on Safety." *Lloyd's List* (27 March): 14.

Ward, Robert. 1997. "Detentions Show First Decline in 10 Years." *Lloyd's List* (19 September): 8.

Ward, Robert. 1997. "ITF Gets Set for Action." *Lloyd's List* (19 September): 9.

Welham, Marion. 1993. "Tanker Owners Quit ABS After Rules Tighten." *Lloyd's List* (3 June): 16.

"We Must Take a Hardline on Substandard Vessels, Says Coughlin." 2005. *Lloyd's List* (31 January): 16.

Wheeler, David. 2002. "Beyond Pollution Havens," *Global Environmental Politics* 2(2): 1–10.

Wilson, John Douglas. 1996. "Capital Mobility and Environmental Standards: Is There a Theoretical Basis for a Race to the Bottom?" In Jagdish Bhagwati and Robert E. Hudec, eds., *Fair Trade and Harmonization*, vol. 1, 393–427. Cambridge: MIT Press.

Winchester, Nik, and Tony Alderton. 2003. *Flag State Audit 2003*. Cardiff: Seafarers International Research Centre.

Wiswall, Frank L. Jr. 1996. "Flags of Convenience." In William A. Lovett, ed., *United States Shipping Policies and the World Market*. Westport: Quorum Books.

Woodbridge, Clive. 1993. "Inspectorate Adds to Island's Appeal." *Lloyd's List* (23 November): 7.

Woodyard, Doug. 1994. "IRI Advances on Strength of Safety Inspections." *Lloyd's List* (12 October): 11.

World Bank. 1992. *World Development Report 1992: Development and the Environment*. New York: Oxford University Press.

WTO. 2000. *The Environmental Benefits of Removing Trade Restrictions and Distortions: The Fisheries Sector*. Note by the Secretariat. WT/CTE/W/167. Geneva: WTO (6 October).

Xing, Yuqing, and Charles D. Kolstad. 2000. "Do Lax Environmental Regulations Attract Foreign Investment?" *University of California Santa Barbara Department of Economics Working Papers* 28: 5–95.

Yohe, Gary W. 1979. "The Backward Incidence of Pollution Control—Some Comparative Statics in General Equilibrium." *Journal of Environmental Economics and Management* 6: 187–198.

Young, Emma, and James Randerson. 2005. "Mauraders of the High Seas." *New Scientist*, 5 November: 12.

Zarsky, Lyuba. 2002. "Stuck in the Mid? Nation States, Globalization, and the Environment." In Kevin Gallagher and Jacob Werksman, eds., *The Earthscan Reader of International Trade and Sustainable Development*, 19–44. London: Earthscan.

Zhao, Minghua, and Maragtas S. V. Amante. 2005. "Chinese and Filipino Seafarers: A Race to the Top or the Bottom?" *Modern Asian Studies* 39(3): 535–557.

Interviews

Alan G. Gavin, Marine Director, Lloyd's Register, London, June 2003.

Nigel Hartley, A. Bilbrough and Co., London, June 2003.

Jaime Veiga, Seafarers International Research Centre, Cardiff, May 2004.

Graham Young, Assistant Secretary, Special Seafarers Division, International Transport Workers Federation, London, May 2004.

Index

Adriatic Tankers Shipping Company, 195
Agreement for the Implementation of the Provisions of UNCLOS Relating to the Conservation and Management of Straddling Fish Stocks and Highly Migratory Fish Stocks. *See* United Nations Convention on the Law of the Sea
Alcohol, 75, 76
American Bureau of Shipping (ABS), 2, 182, 187
Amoco Cadiz, 91
Antigua and Barbuda, 42, 44, 48
Arab American Oil Company (Aramco), 89
Australia, 11, 90n12, 133, 175

Back pay, 144, 145
Bahamas, 1, 39, 42, 48, 71, 72, 100, 130, 133, 136, 137, 214
Ballast. *See* Segregated ballast tanks
Bangladesh, 34
Banks, 78, 80, 81, 199, 214. *See also* Offshore, banks
Barbados, 42, 44, 48
Barcelona Conference on Communications and Transit, 70
Basques, 77
Belen Quezada, 76
Belgium, 45, 47, 91n16
Belize, 42, 44, 94, 98, 110–115, 129, 132, 161, 164, 166, 169, 179, 216
Beneficial ownership, 45, 47, 85, 139, 213
Bermuda, 82, 101
Blacklist
  fisheries, 59, 163, 165, 172
  ITF, 116, 145
Black list (Port State Control), 94, 95, 96, 101, 102, 108–109, 114, 115, 117, 118, 120, 121, 122, 123, 126, 131, 145. *See also* MOUs; Port State Control
Blue certificate, 141–142, 144, 146, 147. *See also* Collective agreement
Bluefin Tuna Statistical Document (BTSD), 160
Bolivia, 14n13, 42, 44, 51, 56n2, 85n66, 132, 152, 164
Boilers, 72, 75
Boycott, 7, 139–140, 144, 145, 146, 149, 224
Break-bulk liners, 79
Britain, 2, 71, 77, 79, 80, 82, 101, 138, 141, 153, 154, 184, 207, 209, 213. *See also* United Kingdom
British Navigation Acts, 207, 210
Bulk carriers, 3, 79, 93, 95, 97, 118, 187, 189, 190, 191, 196
Bureau Veritas, 182, 183, 185–186

Cabotage, 208–209
California effect, 12, 26
Cambodia, 42, 44, 48, 78, 132, 152, 162–163, 164, 166, 179, 186, 224

Canada, 29, 76, 114, 174, 209
Captain, 1, 70
Cargo ship, 64, 77, 79, 110, 138, 193, 194–196, 208, 212, 228
Catch documentation, 159, 160, 161, 166. *See also* CCAMLR
Catch limits, 155, 169
Cayman Islands, 82, 146
CCAMLR, 159–160, 169–176, 178, 180
Catch Documentation Scheme (CDS), 170–175
CCSBT, 159, 166–167
Certificates, 88, 92, 96, 129, 193. *See also* Blue certificate; Collective agreement; Green certificate; International Ship and Port Facility Security Code
Chemical Distribution Institute (CDI), 194
Chemical tankers, 93, 194
China, 26, 118, 130, 137, 169, 174, 190, 222
China Shipowners Mutual Assurance Association, 190
Chilean seabass. *See* Toothfish
Civil society, 68, 197, 224. *See also* Nongovernmental organizations; Nonstate actors
Classification society, 2, 8, 65, 93, 95, 96, 105, 113, 126, 127, 133, 181, 182–189, 191, 193, 194, 195, 196, 197, 218, 223, 224
Clean Air Act, United States, 19–20, 36
Club good, 6, 55, 57, 60, 61, 62, 63, 64, 67, 68, 217, 218, 219
Coalition of Legal Toothfish Operators (COLTO), 175
Cold War, 75, 143
Collective action, 6, 53, 55, 56, 181, 218, 219, 222, 228
Collective Agreement (ITF), 140 –144, 146–148, 225
Commission on the Conservation of Southern Bluefin Tuna. *See* CCSBT
Comoros, 42, 44
Common-pool resource, 14, 55, 57–59, 60, 61, 63, 67, 219–220, 223
Comparative advantage, 16, 21, 143. *See also* Competitive advantage
Competition in laxity. *See* Laxity
Competitiveness, 16–22, 23, 32, 52, 81, 218
Competitive advantage, 22, 35, 228
Competitive disadvantage, 12, 20, 21, 75, 221
Compliance, 15, 17, 20, 66, 96, 105, 108, 109, 113, 114, 121, 156, 161, 162, 170, 178, 189, 191, 195, 218
Consolidated Maritime Labor Convention, 128, 148–149
Container ships, 3, 79
Convention on the Conservation of Antarctic Marine Living Resources. *See* CCAMLR
Convention on Limitation of Liability for Maritime Claims, 105
Cook Islands, 43, 47. *See also* New Zealand
Croatia, 137
Credit, 80, 189
Crew, 1, 14, 45, 65, 70, 74, 76, 81, 82, 84, 85, 90, 135, 136, 137, 138, 142, 144, 152, 153, 189, 218, 220
Cruise ships, 48, 75–76, 96, 208
CSR, 42, 45, 47, 50, 82. *See also* Spain
Cyprus, 42, 48, 49, 66, 71, 78, 100, 115–118, 121, 130, 137, 191

Deficiencies, 93, 95, 109, 113, 188, 221. *See also* Port state control; MOUs
Denmark, 45, 47, 82, 91n16, 133. *See also* DIS
Deregister, 164, 174
Detention, 7, 8, 93, 94, 95, 96, 97, 101–104, 106, 108–110, 112–119, 122–126, 129, 130, 131, 132, 186, 188, 223
ratio, 101, 102, 104, 108, 112, 116, 119, 122, 125, 129

Det Norsk Veritas (DNV), 182, 184, 186
Developing countries, 22, 24, 30, 31, 32, 53, 65, 137, 139, 143, 203
DIS, 42, 45, 47, 82. *See also* Denmark
Discharge standards, 62, 87
Discrimination, 8, 21, 65, 93, 173, 177, 181, 187, 209, 225
Dockworkers, 7, 9, 64, 139, 140. *See also* Ship workers
Dolphins, 62, 154, 158, 177, 222
Dolphin-safe tuna, 62, 222
Domestic politics, 13, 23, 28, 36, 38, 51, 68, 110, 203, 214
Domestic regulation, 4, 12, 19, 20, 26, 27, 35, 39, 40, 53, 64, 71, 75, 83, 90, 118, 140, 151, 204, 208, 226

Eastern Europe, 65
Effective U.S. Controlled Fleet (EUSC), 214–215
Electronic tracking. *See* Tracking
Enforcement, 3, 27, 53, 55, 58, 62, 63, 65, 66, 123, 127, 128, 135, 139, 140, 148, 157, 193, 221, 222, 223, 224, 227
Environmental Protection Agency (United States), 18, 19
Equatorial Guinea, 43, 132, 162, 164, 179
Equipment standards, 2, 56, 62–63, 64, 128, 129, 135, 155, 185
Erika, 120, 183, 188, 205
ESSO. *See* Standard Oil of New Jersey
EU. *See* European Union
European Commission, 66, 120
European Court of Justice, 154
European Parliament, 120
European Union, 2, 66, 83, 95, 117, 120, 154, 187, 205, 208
  membership, 66, 117, 120
Excludable, 6, 56, 57, 60, 219
Exclusion, 8, 55, 60, 62, 63, 64, 65, 66, 178, 197, 206
  mechanisms of, 61, 62, 68, 181, 197, 205, 219, 222, 224, 229
  strategies of, 7, 8
Export Processing Zones, 16
Externalities, 21, 24–25, 51
Externalize, 15
Exxon Valdez, 195

Factory fishing, 153
FAO, 159
  Code of Conduct for Responsible Fisheries, 156
  Compliance Agreement, 156
  International Plan of Action on IUU Fishing, 156
Fees, 2, 3, 11, 14, 16, 39, 45, 72, 74, 78, 81, 83, 132, 211, 226
Fishing seasons, 155, 173
Fish stocks, 58, 156, 175, 219
Fisheries, 8, 56, 57, 58, 61, 151–180, 204–205, 219, 221
Fishers, 9, 58, 68, 151, 154, 160, 168, 178, 206, 219, 221, 222, 226
Fishery agreement. *See* Regional fisheries management agreements
Fishery regulation. *See* Regional fisheries management agreements
Fishing vessels, 8, 9, 64, 151–180
Flagging out, 46, 52, 82, 86, 154, 226
Flag hopping, 154, 156
Flag State Performance. *See* Shipping Industry Guidelines on Flag State Performance
Foreign capital, 78
Foreign direct investment (FDI), 30–31
France, 45, 47, 82, 183, 205. *See also* French Antarctic Territory
Freight, 11, 81
Free riders, 59, 220, 223
Free riding, 6, 56, 58, 60, 217, 223
Free trade. *See* Trade, free
Free trade agreements, 27, 60, 61. *See also* General Agreement on Tariffs and Trade; Trade; World Trade Organization
French Antarctic Territory, 42, 82
French International Registry (RIF), 82

G7, 213
Garment industry, 38, 90
Gas carriers, 93
GATT. *See* General Agreement on Tariffs and Trade
General Accounting Office, United States (GAO), 29
General Agreement on Tariffs and Trade (GATT), 37, 177
Geneva Convention on the High Seas, 70, 84, 85
Genuine link, 67, 70, 84–86
Georgia, 152, 163, 164, 166
Germany, 33, 34, 45, 47, 71, 82, 92n16
Gibraltar, 82, 146, 209
GIS, 32, 45, 47, 82
Globalization, 2–6, 9, 10, 11–15, 25, 35, 38, 50–54, 55, 57, 63, 81, 136, 155, 199–203, 204, 210, 217–219, 228–229
Greece, 1, 77, 130, 133, 137, 209, 222
Green Certificate, 142, 144. *See also* Collective agreement
Grey list, 110, 118, 121. *See also* MOUs; Port State Control

Havens (regulatory) 5, 13–16, 28–33, 35–37, 52, 54, 63, 229
Harmonization, 13, 16, 35, 41, 221, 227
  upward, 3, 5, 13, 15, 16, 38, 51, 53–54, 204, 221
  downward, 15, 35, 37 (*see also* Race to the bottom)
High seas, 15, 70, 152, 155, 159, 211, 212
Honduras, 42, 47, 48, 71, 72, 77, 111, 121–124, 129, 132, 139, 152, 153, 156, 161, 164, 166, 179, 214
Hours (working), 21, 26, 34, 65, 75, 136, 140
Hulls, 1, 72, 75
  double, 1, 2, 41, 185, 205
  single, 1, 2, 120, 121, 205

IATTC, 160
ICCAT, 159, 160–166, 168, 178, 179
ILO, 20, 21, 41, 90, 91, 138, 146, 226
  conventions, 40, 41, 48, 66, 90, 91, 92, 96, 116, 121, 127, 128, 140, 148, 226
India, 34, 136, 141, 222
Indian Ocean Tuna Commission. *See* IOTC
Indonesia, 29, 85n66, 137, 169, 222
Inspection, 2, 3, 7, 8, 9, 65, 72, 75, 87–134, 140, 143, 144, 145, 148, 153, 167, 176, 179, 181–184, 189–191, 193–194, 196, 205, 212, 215, 218, 221, 224, 225, 226, 228
Institute of London Underwriters, 105, 111, 129
Insurance, 29, 79. 109, 182, 184, 189, 195, 197, 223, 224
  protection and indemnity, 2, 8, 105, 135, 140, 181, 189–192, 195, 196, 197, 218, 223, 224
Inter-American Tropical Tuna Commission. *See* IATTC
INTERCARGO, 194, 195–196
International Association of Classification Societies (IACS), 105, 113, 121, 126, 183–188, 195, 196
International Association of Dry Cargo Ship Owners. *See* INTERCARGO
International Association of Independent Tanker Owners. *See* INTERTANKO
International Bargaining Forum (IBF), 142–144, 146, 148
International Commission for the Conservation of Atlantic Tunas. *See* ICCAT
International Convention for Safe Containers, 105
International Convention for the Establishment of an International Fund for Compensation for Oil Pollution Damage, 105

International Convention for the Prevention of Pollution from Ships. *See* MARPOL
International Convention for the Regulation of Whaling, 77
International Convention for the Safety of Life at Sea. *See* SOLAS
International Convention on Civil Liability for Oil Pollution Damage, 105
International Convention on Load Lines, 88, 91
International Convention on Standards of Training, Certification, and Watchkeeping for Seafarers. *See* STCW
International Convention on Tonnage Measurement of Ships, 88, 92
International Convention Relating to Intervention on the High Seas in Case of Oil Casualties, 105
International Court of Justice (ICJ), 89, 212–213
International Federation of Classification Societies (IFCS), 184
International Group of P&I Clubs, 190, 196
International Labour Organisation. *See* ILO
International Law Commission, 84
International Mariners' Management Association of Japan (IMMAJ), 141–142
International Maritime Employers' Committee (IMEC), 141–142
International Maritime Organization (IMO), 41, 43, 64, 87, 91, 96, 99, 107, 113, 119, 121, 126, 133, 140, 141, 183, 189, 194, 205, 212, 213, 216, 226, 228
  Maritime Safety Commission (MSC), 212–213
International organizations. *See names of specific organizations*
International Organization for Standardization. *See* ISO
International Register of Shipping (classification society), 113
International Registries (ship registration company), 79, 104–105, 184n11, 216
International registry, 16, 45, 46, 52, 82, 83, 140, 218. *See also names of specific international registries*
International Regulations for Preventing Collisions at Sea, 91–92
International Safety Management (ISM) Code, 96–97, 113, 114, 189, 195, 196
International Ship and Port Facility Security Code, 114, 191–192
International Shipowners Federation (ISF), 136–138, 146–147
International Transport Workers Federation. *See* ITF
International Whaling Commission, 153. *See also* International Convention for the Regulation of Whaling
Internet, 39, 63, 199
INTERTANKO, 194–195, 196, 197
IOTC, 159, 167–169, 178
  Bigeye Tuna Statistical Document, 168
Ireland, 24
Isle of Man, 82, 213
ISO, 105, 110
  9002 (Quality Management System), 105
  14001 (Environmental Management System), 113
ISOFISH, 175
ITF, 7, 64, 65, 67, 97, 116, 135–149, 223, 225. *See also* Blacklist, ITF; Blue Certificate; Collective Agreement; Green Certificate; International Bargaining Forum
  Fair Practices Committee, 140, 141
  Seafarer's Section, 139, 144
  Welfare Fund, 144, 146, 148, 223

Jamaica, 22, 43, 48n17
Japan, 20, 28, 29, 64, 76, 83, 114, 120, 130, 141–142, 154, 157, 165, 167, 168–169, 178, 206

Kerguelen Islands. *See* French Antarctic Territory
Kuwait, 82

Labor unions. *See* Unions
La Follette Seaman's Act (1915), 75
Landlocked states, 14n13, 51, 56n2, 70, 152
Laxity, 5, 25, 26, 27, 63. *See also* Harmonization downward
Lebanon, 42
Liability, 113, 181, 188, 189, 190, 192
Liberia, 1, 42, 43, 48–49, 71, 72, 73, 74, 77, 78, 79, 98–99, 100, 104, 105, 107, 109, 127, 130, 132, 133, 137, 146, 182, 184n11, 212, 214, 215, 216, 226
Liberia Corporation, 74
Lloyd's Register, 182, 184, 186, 224
London Steamship Owners Mutual Insurance (London Club), 2, 190
Longline tuna vessels, 163, 168, 175
Luxembourg, 42, 45n107, 47

Malta, 42, 66, 71, 118–121, 100, 130, 132, 137, 179
MAR, 42, 45, 47, 82. *See also* Portugal
Marine Mammal Protection Act (U.S.), 154
Maritime States, 6, 45, 46, 50, 52, 72, 81–82, 84, 85, 133, 143, 145, 149, 170, 199, 202, 203, 204, 206, 207, 208, 210, 212, 213, 214, 218, 222
MARPOL, 2, 87, 88, 91, 99, 119, 183, 185
Marshall Islands, 42, 44, 48, 71, 73, 79, 100, 103–107, 110, 130, 132, 134, 146, 184n11, 212, 214, 215, 216, 228
Mauritius, 43, 44, 174, 179
Memorandum of Understanding. *See* MOU
Merchant marine, 75, 77, 84, 120, 123, 215
Mexico, 24, 29, 85n66, 209
Ministry of International Trade and Industry, Japan (MITI), 28–29
Mongolia, 42, 43, 44, 56, 132, 186, 224
Monitoring, 63, 135, 142, 151, 159, 163, 164 165, 170, 176, 185, 204. *See also* Vessel monitoring system
Moral hazard, 61
Moray Firth, 153
MOUs, 64, 91–131, 145, 193
  Black Sea, 91
  Caribbean, 91
  Mediterranean, 91
  Paris, 91–97, 100, 101, 102, 104, 106, 108, 110, 112, 114, 116–123, 125, 129, 130 131, 186, 188
  Riyadh (Persian Gulf), 91
  Tokyo, 91, 92, 94, 96, 97, 100, 101, 102, 104, 106, 108, 112, 113, 116, 117, 118, 119, 122, 123, 125, 127, 130, 131
  Viña del Mar (Latin American), 91, 97
  for the West and Central Africa Region, 91
Multinational corporations, 12, 17, 78
Myanmar, 42, 48, 222

NAFO, 156, 160, 176
Namibia, 173–174
Nationality (of ships), 4, 39, 69–70, 83, 136
National waters, 14, 87, 211
Negotiations, 59, 65, 91, 113, 128, 141, 142, 145, 148, 155, 209, 211
Netherlands, 45, 47, 91n16, 101–102, 133
Netherlands Antilles, 42, 45, 47, 101–102
New Zealand, 29, 47, 133, 137, 154, 176. *See also* Cook Islands
NGOs. *See* Nongovernmental organizations
Nicaragua, 89
Niches (regulatory), 6, 46–50, 54, 99, 132–133

high environment, 48–49, 99
high end, 47
high safety, 49
low end, 47
low labor, 48
middle, 49
NIS. *See* Norwegian International Registry
Nonexcludable, 57, 58, 59, 219
Nongovernmental organizations (NGOs), 6, 39, 53, 68, 181, 221, 227
Nonrival, 6
Nonstate actors, 3, 5, 9, 10, 62, 65, 67, 175, 221, 225. *See also* Nongovernmental organizations
Nontariff barriers, 12, 57, 61, 177
North American Free Trade Agreement (NAFTA), 27
North East Atlantic Fisheries Commission (NEAFC), 176
Northwest Atlantic Fisheries Organization. *See* NAFO
Norway, 45, 47, 72, 77, 82, 91n16, 126, 130, 136, 153, 176
Norwegian International Registry (NIS), 41, 42, 45, 47, 50, 82

Ocean resources, 32, 37, 56, 57, 151, 158, 219
OECD, 15, 33, 152, 213, 214
Offshore (generally), 9, 45, 79, 98, 199–201, 213
banks, 63, 79, 109, 213, 213
insurance, 79, 109
Oil Companies International Maritime Forum (OCIMF), 193
Oil spill, 1–2, 91, 99, 120, 182, 183, 185, 188, 193, 195, 204, 205, 220, 226
Oil tanker. *See* Tanker (oil)
Olympic Challenger, 153, 157
Olympic Whaling Company, 153
Onassis, Aristotle, 77, 153, 157
Organization for the Promotion of Responsible Tuna Fisheries (OPRT), 169
Pacific freighters, 72n15, 75
Pakistan, 34
Panama, 39, 42, 49, 53, 71, 72, 73–78, 98, 99, 100, 102, 112, 124–127, 130, 132, 133, 137, 139, 152, 153, 156, 157, 161, 164, 165, 166, 169, 174, 179, 191, 202, 221, 222, 224
Paris MOU. *See* MOUs
Passenger ships, 48, 92, 93, 95, 97, 185, 189, 190
Patagonian toothfish. *See* Toothfish
Peru, 157
Philippines, 26, 29, 137, 166, 169, 222
P&I clubs. *See* Insurance, Protection and Indemnity
Poland, 85n66, 222
Pollutants, 14
Pollution, 25, 27, 28, 29, 30, 31, 32, 35, 51, 89, 91, 207, 220
oil, 1–2, 56, 62–63, 99, 185, 195, 207, 220 (*see also* Oil spill)
Polski Rejestr Statkow, 186
Ports, 1, 2, 7, 8, 9, 14, 51, 64, 70, 73, 87–124, 136, 138, 144, 145, 147, 149, 151, 153, 167, 170, 172, 175, 176, 179, 193, 205, 208, 222, 223, 227, 228
Port state control (PSC), 2–3, 6–8, 9, 64, 67, 87–134, 135, 136, 140, 148, 149, 168, 176, 179, 181, 182, 183, 186, 193, 194, 196, 197, 215, 220, 221, 223, 224, 225, 226. *See also* MOUs
officers (PSCOs), 88, 92–93, 128
Port state inspection. *See* Port state control; MOUs
Port states, 70, 89–93, 103, 126, 170, 184, 197. *See also* Port state control
Portugal, 1, 42, 45, 47, 82. *See also* MAR
Prestige, 1–3, 188, 190, 205, 229
Private goods, 56, 57, 63, 223
Prohibition (U.S., alcohol), 75, 96, 211
Protection and Indemnity. *See* Insurance

Protocol Relating to Intervention on the High Seas in Cases of Pollution by Substances Other than Oil, 105
Public goods, 55, 57, 59, 60, 62, 63, 67, 219–220

Qualships 21, 106
Quotas (fishing), 154

Race to the bottom, 3, 5, 13–15, 16, 23, 24, 25, 33, 35–38, 52, 54, 63, 218, 29. *See also* Harmonization
Race to the middle, 5, 10, 16, 46, 49, 127, 229
Race to the regulatory bottom. *See* Race to the bottom
Red ensign, 82
Regional average (port state control), 100, 101, 108, 114, 122, 131
Regional fisheries management agreements, 8, 9, 58, 59, 61, 64, 66, 68, 114, 151–180, 182, 218, 221, 226. *See also specific organizations by name*
Registro Italiano Navala, 183
Regulatory havens. *See* Havens, regulatory
RIF. *See* French International Registry
Rival, 6, 56, 57, 58, 59, 61, 219, 220, 223
Rolling average, 94, 101, 114
Romania, 1, 24
Russia, 1, 83, 85, 137, 222

St. Vincent and the Grenadines, 42, 44, 48, 129, 152, 162, 166, 179
Sanctions, 64, 66, 162, 165, 168, 177, 178, 179, 213
São Tomé and Principé, 43, 44
Satellite tracking. *See* Tracking
Seafarers, 26, 41, 74, 75, 81, 88, 128, 136–144, 146, 147, 149, 207, 223
Seafarers' International Assistance, Welfare, and Protection Fund. *See* ITF, Welfare Fund
Seafarers International Research Centre (SIRC), 41, 46, 47, 48, 49, 50
Seafarers' Trust, 144, 147
Second registry, 6, 16, 42, 45, 46, 47, 49, 52, 81–83, 84, 101, 136, 214, 218. *See also specific second registries by name*
Second World War. *See* World War II
Segregated ballast tanks, 41–42, 62–63, 185
Seychelles, 168, 174
Shipbreaking, 34
Ship Inspection Report (SIRE) Program, 193
Ships. *See by type of ship*
Ship management companies, 81, 145. *See also* International Mariners' Management Association of Japan
Ship manufacturing, 80
Shipowners, 2, 3, 4, 5, 6, 7, 8, 14, 15, 39, 45, 47, 50, 52, 55, 64, 65, 70, 71, 72, 73, 74, 77, 80, 81, 82, 83, 84, 96, 98, 99, 103, 109, 111, 117, 118, 120, 128, 132, 134, 138, 140, 141, 142, 143, 144, 145, 147, 148, 149, 151, 152, 153, 154, 155, 181, 182, 184, 187, 189, 190, 191, 192, 193, 194, 195, 196, 197, 198, 199, 202, 206, 201, 211, 213, 215, 216, 217, 218, 225, 226, 227, 229
Shipping capacity, 80–81
Shipping Industry Guidelines on Flag State Performance, 197–198
Ship workers, 4, 7, 39, 48, 56, 67, 76, 136, 137, 138, 141, 142, 143, 144, 145, 218, 222, 224. *See also* Dockworkers, Seafarers
Side payments, 61
Sierra Leone, 132, 163, 164, 166, 179
Singapore, 1, 130, 163, 174
Size (of ships), 79–80
Slave trade, 71
SOLAS, 88, 91, 98, 99, 117, 183
Sovereign territory, 56, 89, 199, 200, 201

Sovereignty, 3, 9, 63, 87, 89, 199–229
Spain, 1, 24, 45, 47, 77, 82, 154, 170, 204, 209
  international registry (*see* CSR)
Sri Lanka, 42, 48n117
Standard Oil of New Jersey, 76–77
Stateless vessels, 180
STCW, 88, 91, 183
Stettinius, Edward, 73, 74
Straddling Stocks Agreement. *See* United Nations Convention on the Law of the Sea
"Stuck in the Mud," 12, 52, 53
Subsidy, 22, 80
Subtractable. *See* Rival
Suez Canal, 80
Switzerland, 1, 70
Swordfish, 159, 160–163, 164

Taiwan, 40, 169
Tanker (oil), 74, 79, 93, 95, 98, 99, 120, 133, 183, 185, 189, 194, 205, 220
  double-hulled, 1–2, 51, 185, 205
  single-hulled, 1–2, 121, 122, 205
Tanker Advisory Center, 185–186
Target-factor calculator, 93–94
Tax, 2, 3, 4, 11, 39, 45, 63, 72, 75, 80, 81, 83, 99, 113, 132, 153, 198, 199, 211, 213–214, 226
Tax haven, 153, 213–214
Tokyo MOU. *See* MOUs
Toll, 60, 61. *See also* Club goods
Tonga, 43, 44, 48n117
Tonnage, 3, 39, 41, 47, 48, 49, 71, 72, 80, 82, 99, 100, 103, 107, 111, 114, 115, 120, 123, 124, 127, 183, 213
Toothfish, 159, 170–175, 226
Torrey Canyon, 193
Toxic, 30, 31
Tracking, 165, 171. *See also* Vessel monitoring system
Trade, 3, 4, 9, 12, 19, 22, 28, 30, 32, 66, 67, 75, 79, 178, 199, 202, 204, 206, 207, 208, 209, 217, 218, 225
  agreements, 60, 61, 178 (*see also* General Agreement on Tariffs and Trade; North American Free Trade Agreement; World Trade Organization)
  barriers to, 26, 60
  free, 14, 16, 35
  freer, 4, 12, 13
  restriction, 8, 67, 114, 155, 157–176, 178, 178, 181, 205, 206, 221, 223, 225, 226
Trade Information Scheme (TIS), 166–167
Transparency, 175, 188, 197, 213, 214
Tranship, 158, 159, 163, 167, 168, 170, 173, 176, 225
Treaty of Versailles, 70
TRAFFIC, 173
Transaction costs, 23, 204
Transportation, 3, 4, 7, 9, 33, 64, 65, 67, 72–73, 79, 80, 87, 120, 121, 146, 154, 185, 190, 192, 204, 205, 206, 207, 208, 209, 211, 217, 220, 222, 226, 228
Tuna, 62, 154, 158, 159–169, 171, 177, 180, 222, 226. *See also* Dolphin-safe tuna
  Bigeye, 160–163, 164, 168
  Bluefin (Atlantic), 154, 160–166
  Southern Bluefin, 154, 159, 166–167
Turkey, 66, 222

Ukraine, 137, 222
UNCLOS. *See* United Nations Convention on the Law of the Sea
Unfair competition, 74, 143, 203
UNIDO, 22
Unions, 7, 8, 9, 21, 26, 64, 90, 128, 135, 149, 181, 220, 222, 223, 224. *See also* ITF
United Arab Emirates, 123
United Fruit Company, 72, 77
United Kingdom (UK), 45, 47, 72, 80, 82, 91n16, 101, 130, 154. *See also* Britain Second registries, 42, 45, 47, 82, 101 (*see also by name of specific registries*)

United Nations Conference on Trade and Development (UNCTAD), 84
United Nations Convention on the Conditions for Registration of Ships (UNCCORS), 85
United Nations Convention on the Law of the Sea (UNCLOS), 85, 88–91, 105, 119, 156
  Straddling Stocks Agreement, 155
United States, 2, 17, 18, 19, 20, 21, 24, 28, 29, 37, 40, 53, 68, 71, 72, 73, 74, 75, 76, 77–78, 84, 89, 90, 91, 104, 107, 108, 110, 112, 114, 116, 119, 122, 125, 131, 154, 158, 165, 166, 177, 206, 208, 209, 211, 212, 215, 222
Uruguay, 153, 170, 174–175
U.S. Coast Guard PSC process, 91, 94, 96, 100, 101, 102, 104, 106, 108, 109, 110, 112, 113, 114, 116–117, 118, 119, 122, 123, 125, 126, 127, 129, 130, 131, 211
U.S. Proliferation Security Initiative, 211–212
U.S. Shipping Board, 75–76

Vanuatu, 42, 48–49, 79, 108–111, 132, 133, 137, 152, 168, 174, 214, 215, 216
Vanuatu Maritime Authority, 109
Vanuatu Maritime Services, 79
Venezuela, 29, 77
Vessel monitoring system, 159, 165, 176. *See also* Monitoring; Tracking

Wages, 15, 20, 21, 24, 26, 27, 29, 34, 37, 38, 44, 53, 56, 65, 67, 83, 132, 136, 137, 138, 140, 141, 142, 143, 144, 147, 148, 149, 207, 222, 225
  benchmark, 137, 141, 142
  rates, 21, 22, 24, 25, 26, 28, 34, 37, 38, 52, 67, 76, 135, 136, 137, 139, 141, 142, 144, 146, 148
War of 1812, 71
Whaling, 77, 153–154, 157, 158
White list (port state control), 94, 101, 102, 106, 113, 127. *See also* MOUs; Port state control
Whitelist (fishing agreements), 159, 163
World Bank, 25
World Trade Organization (WTO), 11, 158, 170, 176–178, 209, 226
Word War II, 4, 21, 47, 74, 77, 80, 122, 128, 212